Provocative and persuasive. Its u  he
page. Anyone interested in qualita y
and epistemology, should read thi:
Martin .·

Thought-provoking and thoroughly e. ,-,aole. Qualitative researchers of all methodological stripes will be challenged to think again by this excellent book.

Peter Allmark, *University of Sheffield, UK*

This is a wonderful book! I wish more authors in the qualitative space wrote with such clarity, deliberateness, and honesty.

James Salvo, *Wayne State University, USA*

CONSTRUCTIVISM AND THE METAPHYSICS OF QUALITATIVE RESEARCH

This book challenges the widespread assumption that a necessary preliminary to qualitative research is the formulation of ontological and epistemological beliefs. It argues that the metaphysical claims which supposedly underpin different approaches to social research do not make sense. Literally. Sentences such as 'There is a single objective reality' and 'There are multiple constructed realities' fail to make information-providing statements. They do not refer or describe. Despite appearances, they say nothing about reality (or realities) at a fundamental level, so they cannot be used to justify, ground, or align with, methodological decisions. The 'necessary preliminary' turns out not to be necessary at all; and we can dispense with, not just 'paradigms', but metaphysical underpinnings in general, whether structured as paradigms or not.

Drawing on Wittgenstein's later philosophy, Carnap's metametaphysics, and contemporary linguistics, the book suggests that the metaphysical claims of qualitative texts can be reinterpreted as performative. Ontological and epistemological beliefs are resolutions and proposals, recommendations for the use of language. They form part of a creed by means of which researchers enact the joining of an academic community. Written in Paley's trademark clear, accessible, and conversational style, the book points to a revolution in our understanding of the relation between metaphysics and social research. It will be essential reading for anyone interested in qualitative research and its philosophical foundations.

John Paley was formerly senior lecturer at the University of Stirling and is currently Honorary Fellow at the University of Worcester. He is the author of two previous books for Routledge: *Phenomenology as Qualitative Research: A Critical Analysis of Meaning Attribution* and *Concept Analysis in Nursing: A New Approach*.

CONSTRUCTIVISM AND THE METAPHYSICS OF QUALITATIVE RESEARCH

John Paley

Routledge
Taylor & Francis Group

LONDON AND NEW YORK

Designed cover image: hiro-k / Getty Images

First published 2025
by Routledge
4 Park Square, Milton Park, Abingdon, Oxon OX14 4RN

and by Routledge
605 Third Avenue, New York, NY 10158

Routledge is an imprint of the Taylor & Francis Group, an informa business

© 2025 John Paley

British Library Cataloguing-in-Publication Data
A catalogue record for this book is available from the British Library

ISBN: 978-1-032-30717-6 (hbk)
ISBN: 978-1-032-30718-3 (pbk)
ISBN: 978-1-003-30638-2 (ebk)

DOI: 10.4324/9781003306382

Typeset in Optima
by SPi Technologies India Pvt Ltd (Straive)

CONTENTS

FIGURES

ACKNOWLEDGEMENTS

In October 2021, while I was working on the proposal for this book, I fell and broke my leg. A pretty clichéd thing for an older person to do. It turned out to be a subtrochanteric fracture, and meant several months keeping as much weight off the leg as possible before rehabilitation could begin. I mention this because the people who got me through the two years that followed made a major contribution to this book. My surgeon, Hayat Khan, and his team; the nurses in the trauma and orthopaedic ward; my physiotherapists, Priya Barmi and Rebecca Colledge; and my partner, Lynda Frampton, who cared, cajoled, and badgered pro re nata. I don't think any of them will read it, but without them it wouldn't exist.

Of the people who *have* read it, in draft, I'd like to thank Peter Allmark, who made a lot of very helpful suggestions, and asked some annoyingly good questions; and Martin Lipscomb, who, not content with comments on every chapter, kept up an endless barrage of make-you-think emails. I have also benefited from discussions with Trevor Hussey, Roger Chafe, Sam McQuillin, Teresa Atkinson, Michael Traynor, Sally Thorne, George Mycock, Paul Snelling, and James Salvo. I have made various changes as a result, but none of these people can be held responsible for the finished article, because I pig-headedly ignored some of their criticisms.

Substantial passages in Chapter 2 are taken from my chapter 'Metaphysics and research education in nursing': *Complexity and Values in Nurse Education: Dialogues on Professional Education* (pp. 96–112), edited by Martin Lipscomb, copyright 2022, Routledge. Reproduced by permission of Taylor & Francis Group. And, speaking of Routledge, I'm grateful to Eleanor Taylor, Matt Bickerton, Lucy Kennedy, and Adam Woods for their help and support, and especially to Hannah Shakespeare, who was enthusiastic about the book from the very beginning.

Biggest thanks, once again, to Lynda. She was effectively a full-time carer for six months when I could barely move, and during the rehabilitation process she made sure that I did the stuff I didn't want to do, or was afraid to try. It would be impossible to overstate my debt to her.

PROLOGUE

Here is the take-home message of this book. It consists of two theses.

THESIS 1 It is generally assumed that a necessary preliminary to qualitative research is the formulation of ontological and epistemological beliefs. However, the sentences which supposedly express these beliefs are referentially unsuccessful. They appear to make information-providing statements but fail to do so. The constituent words are meaningful, but the sentences themselves don't *say* anything. So they cannot be used to justify, or ground, or align with, methodological decisions.

THESIS 2 The metaphysical sentences can still be construed as having a function, but it is not to describe reality (or realities) at any 'fundamental' level. Instead, their role is one of resolving and recommending; they are optings and joinings. For the qualitative researcher, they *enact* the joining of a research culture, they do not *justify* it. They are essentially performative.

A few short notes on what to expect and what not to expect:

The 40-year-old orthodoxy

There's no getting away from the fact that the book is an attempt to dismantle what is, for some sectors and some disciplines, a 40-year-old orthodoxy. We can call it the 'underpinnings' orthodoxy, the idea that social research must be 'underpinned by' – or perhaps 'aligned with' – metaphysical beliefs. I'll be suggesting that the metaphysical sentences in qualitative methods texts can't be understood as reality-describing or information-providing. They can't be parsed as saying: 'The world is like *this* (therefore we must study it *this* way).' They don't tell us anything about the world. They have a different function.

Scope

In general, I use 'metaphysics' as a loose classification covering ontology, other metaphysical questions, and epistemology. I use the expression 'qualitative metaphysics' as shorthand for metaphysical claims of the kind typically discussed, however briefly, in qualitative methods texts. Two examples are: 'There exist multiple constructed realities' and 'There exists a single objective reality.' The book is exclusively about such claims. Nothing I say about the sentences of qualitative metaphysics should be generalised to other metaphysical views.

-isms and -ologies

For reasons which will quickly become apparent, I have no interest in arguing for, or against, any of the major '-isms and -ologies' of qualitative metaphysical debate. Those expecting general arguments in support of, or opposed to, positivism, postpositivism, realism, idealism, critical realism, constructivism, social constructionism, phenomenology, hermeneutics, postmodernism, post-structuralism, pragmatism, or a dozen other metaphysically inflected views, will be disappointed. The approach I take in this book doesn't work like that. Instead, I draw on the later Wittgenstein, Carnap, and linguistics.

Wittgenstein

In the *Philosophical Investigations*, Wittgenstein doesn't have theories. So he doesn't need to elaborate arguments to defend his theories. No theories, therefore no arguments. What he does have, in profusion, are examples – thought experiments, analogies, pictures, objects of comparison, simple language-games, conversations, the 'assembling of reminders'. In the end, it's only by studying these that you can begin to catch his drift. Part II presents examples relevant to qualitative metaphysics, including reminders about the ubiquity of causal language, and the use of words such as 'reality', 'know', and 'experience'.

Ordinary language philosophy

In assembling reminders, then, I talk a great deal about the ordinary use of words. So I take myself to be doing something akin to ordinary language philosophy (OLP). This approach has been unfashionable – some would say discredited – since the 1960s, but it has experienced a renaissance in recent years, with a number of philosophers adopting its methods. I sometimes supplement OLP with themes and methods from linguistics. For example, I make use of the Corpus of Contemporary American English (COCA), and refer to the linguistics of causative constructions, and the existential 'there' ('There exists…').

Carnap

Carnap was a logical positivist, and logical positivism is redundant, anachronistic, of no contemporary relevance. Many methods textbooks spend a bit of time reminding us of this, their authors possibly unaware of the resurgence of philosophical interest in Carnap over the last 30 years. But Carnap has had a marked influence on recent metametaphysics, and I'll argue that his expressivism helps us to recognise the performative nature of metaphysical claims. To avoid misunderstanding, I should add that I'm not proposing a reversion to the 'positivist paradigm'. On the contrary, I think all qualitative metaphysical claims – 'positivist', constructivist, whatever-ist – can be dispensed with.

Positivism

However, it might seem, on occasion, that I'm trying to smuggle positivism back. Not guilty. I don't believe in a single objective reality any more than I believe in multiple constructed realities. I don't think that 'the knower' and 'the known' are 'independent, a dualism', any more than I think that they are 'inseparable, interactive'. The fact that I'm relaxed about causation and truth, for example, is due to what I see as the purely linguistic function of 'is true', and the ubiquity of causal language.

Paradigms

The paradigm wars are over, and I won't be trying to refight old battles. I *will* be commenting on the invention of (non-Kuhnian) paradigms by Lincoln and Guba, but only with a view to showing that the concept, as it is understood in qualitative research texts, was less than fully coherent from the start. But even if we dispense with paradigms, we still have the metaphysics. We still have 'underpinnings' and 'alignments'. So the deflationary job is only half done. Part II of the book will provide reasons for scepticism about all qualitative metaphysics, whether embedded in 'paradigms' or not.

Lincoln and Guba

There's a fair amount about Lincoln and Guba in the book. This is because their versions of 'paradigm' and 'positivism' have become canonical. The tropes they devised are still recycled, generally without much in the way of argument, and their original vision is still built into the foundations of how many writers think about qualitative research, even when it isn't acknowledged. Consequently, while I focus on Lincoln and Guba's constructivism, a lot of other stuff gets caught in the crossfire. The book can't do its job properly without dislodging their legacy.

Illusions of thought

If the statements of qualitative metaphysics don't describe 'reality' or 'realities' at a fundamental level, then the writers who think they do, and who accept one or more of them, must be subject to an 'illusion of thought'. I think that's true, and in various ways I attempt to dispel illusions of this kind. One way is to have conversations with a hypothetical *Reader*, whose objections include some I would have voiced myself not all that long ago.

1

INTRODUCTION

Terms and conditions apply

I'll begin by repeating the take-home message of the book.

> **THESIS 1** It is generally assumed that a necessary preliminary to qualitative research is the formulation of ontological and epistemological beliefs. However, the sentences which supposedly express these beliefs are referentially unsuccessful. They appear to make information-providing statements but fail to do so. The constituent words are meaningful, but the sentences themselves don't *say* anything. So they cannot be used to justify, or ground, or align with, methodological decisions.

> **THESIS 2** The metaphysical sentences can still be construed as having a function, but it is not to describe reality (or realities) at a 'fundamental' level.[1] Instead, their role is one of resolving and recommending; they are optings and joinings. For the qualitative researcher, they *enact* the joining of a research culture, they do not *justify* it. They are essentially performative.

1.1 Clarifications

Some brief clarifying footnotes on these two theses.

> **A** The idea that the metaphysical sentences are referentially unsuccessful is shorthand for: 'they do not succeed in describing anything; they provide no information, even if, grammatically speaking, they appear to do just that'. So an alternative to the expression 'referentially unsuccessful' is 'not providing information' or, as I will sometimes say, 'not reality-describing'.[2]

DOI: 10.4324/9781003306382-1

B Thesis 1 refers to all qualitative metaphysics sentences, not just the constructivist ones. If we take 'There are multiple constructed realities' and 'There exists a single objective reality' as examples, it implies that *both* are referentially unsuccessful. They both fail to provide information. They are both failed statements.

C Thesis 2 can be classified, roughly, as a form of philosophical 'expressivism'. Indicative sentences can be used to perform a number of different functions, only one of which is referring/describing. They can instruct, give directions, express opinions, enact rituals (marry, give a verdict), and many more. The example sentences in *B* do not refer/ describe. They resolve, recommend, and enact.

D Thesis 1 and Thesis 2 are both based on a reading of the recent literature on metametaphysics. This is the name given to debates about methods used in metaphysics, and to arguments about the status of metaphysical claims. The book takes a neo-Carnapian perspective on metametaphysics but also draws on the later Wittgenstein and linguistics.

E If the two theses are accepted, 'philosophical underpinnings' are redundant, except as resolutions, recommendations, and enactments. If Thesis 1 is correct, there are various implications. The Epilogue briefly explores these implications, and indicates what qualitative research might look like if no longer subject to (referentially understood) metaphysical premises.

The remainder of this introduction expands on the take-home message. The rest of the book expands on the expansion.

1.2   Referentially unsuccessful sentences

If I say that an indicative metaphysical sentence is referentially unsuccessful, what I mean is that – in spite of grammatical appearances – it does not successfully make a *statement* about anything. It does not describe a state of affairs. Some examples of sentences that don't succeed in making statements:

(1) Colourless green ideas sleep furiously.

(2) There are square circles all over the lawn.

(3) The nothing noths tembraciously.

(4) It is 5 o'clock on the sun.

These are all, for different reasons, failed statements.[3] I'm not implying that metaphysical sentences are failed statements for any of the reasons that might apply here (with one exception). For example, they don't incorporate non-existent words like 'noths' and 'tembraciously', or contradictions like 'square circles' and 'colourless green'. All I'm doing is illustrating the kind of thing I mean by 'referentially unsuccessful'. A sentence which, syntactically, seems to make a statement about something, does not, in fact, do so.[4]

I am also not implying that referentially unsuccessful sentences are completely without value. They can be useful for other reasons. For example, 'Colourless green ideas sleep furiously' has proved extremely useful to many different people. Chomsky used it to make the point that even a nonsensical sentence can be perfectly grammatical, but it has since been a 'source of poems, arguments, music and so on' (Jahn 2002: 47).[5] Again, this is not to suggest that the only value of metaphysical sentences is that they can be used as examples of grammatically correct nonsense. Though it has sometimes been said, in the history of philosophy, that metaphysical claims are meaningless, it's not currently a popular view, even among those who are sceptical about metaphysics. My point is only that some indicative sentences, while not referentially successful, can nevertheless have a function.

1.3 'It's 5 o'clock on the sun'

I want to say a little more about sentence (4). This is the exception I referred to a couple of paragraphs back. It is taken from Wittgenstein (2009: §350):

> It is as if I were to say: "You surely know what 'It's 5 o'clock here' means; so you also know what 'It's 5 o'clock on the sun' means. It means simply that it is just the same time there as it is here when it is 5 o'clock."

Individually, the words in sentence (4) are all familiar and intelligible, so the sentence just seems to be an example of an everyday expression – unusual, perhaps, given the reference to the sun, but otherwise unexceptionable. I have a clear impression of 'knowing what it means'.

But what statement does it make? How can it be 5 o'clock on the sun? I know what it means to say 'It's 5 o'clock in London', or 'It's 5 o'clock in Washington.' But on the sun? 'It's 5 o'clock in Washington' indexes the sun's position *relative to a specific place on the earth* (using conventions about the division of time into hours). So how can it be 5 o'clock on the sun? Suppose someone says: 'It's 12 o'clock, mid-day, in London.' Mid-day in London is when the sun is at its highest point, relative to London.[6] Okay, so now imagine someone saying: 'It's 12 o'clock, mid-day, on the sun.' What can this possibly mean? How can the sun be at its highest point relative to the sun? If you are *on* the sun, the sun *can't* be overhead. So 'It's 12 o'clock mid-day on the sun' makes no sense. For the same reason, 'It's 5 o'clock on the sun' makes no sense either.

And yet there is, at least initially, an illusion that it does make sense. Perhaps this is because we picture a clock on the sun pointing to 5:00. But that's all it is: a picture. A snippet of visual imagination. It does not tell us what substantive statement 'It's 5 o'clock on the sun' is making. What the picture *could* be taken to represent is the statement: 'There is a clock on the sun pointing to 5:00.' This *is* referentially successful: it makes a reality-describing statement, though (presumably) a false one.

So how can something which initially seems to be an information-providing statement turn out not to be? There are several ways of coming at this. One is to suggest that an expression which makes sense in one context can cease to make sense in another. But this depends on what counts as a 'context'. 'It's 5 o'clock in London' makes sense, but it also makes sense when transferred from the 'London context' to Auckland, or Dar es Salaam. So we have to be careful about the difference between 'making sense' contexts and 'not making sense' contexts. The Auckland and Dar es Salaam 'transfers' work, but the 'sun transfer' doesn't; and it is possible to explain *why* it doesn't work by identifying the conditions in which 'It's 5 o'clock in …' sentences can be legitimately applied. I will refer to these conditions as the expression's *application conditions*, or more jocularly its 'terms and conditions'.[7]

So 'It's 5 o'clock on the sun' illustrates how a sentence can 'have meaning' – in the sense that the words are familiar, the sentence is grammatically correct, and the O'CLOCK construction is a well-known one – and yet not make an information-providing statement. It's possible to have a sentence which conforms to all these requirements, but which is nevertheless referentially unsuccessful. This is crucial, because I'll be arguing throughout Part II that the metaphysical sentences intended to serve as research 'underpinnings' are *not unlike*: 'It's 5 o'clock on the sun.' They seem to say something, but don't.

1.4 Familiar expressions, unfamiliar contexts

'It's 5 o'clock on the sun' is an example of a familiar expression being used in an unfamiliar context, in which its application conditions aren't fulfilled. An expression which, *prima facie*, is tied to locations on earth, is instead, applied to the sun. The speaker/writer of this sentence *may* have been trying to convey an unfamiliar – but still intelligible – idea, but in the absence of further explanation it is not clear what that idea is.

This is an important observation: we don't *necessarily* have to rule out the possibility that the sentence is conveying an intelligible idea; but, in order to be convinced that it is, we need a clear explanation of how the expression is being used, and an indication of what the speaker/writer was trying to say. The author may be able to produce both, but unless and until she does we have no alternative but to assume that the sentence is not actually saying anything.[8]

This leads to an interesting question. Is it *possible* to use a familiar expression in an unfamiliar context – one in which its established terms and conditions are not met – to convey an intelligible but unfamiliar idea? Let's assume it is. The question then becomes: how? In what circumstances, and on what basis, can we parachute a familiar expression into a context in which its terms and conditions are inapplicable, and still make sense? This is a question to which I will return frequently.

It's also important to remember that the sceptical reaction to 'It's 5 o'clock on the sun' is *not* tantamount to saying: 'No, that's not true.' It is instead a matter of suggesting that it is *neither true nor false*. It does not make sense, it fails to make a statement, it is not referentially successful. That must be the verdict till an explanation of some kind is forthcoming. This is discussed further in Chapters 3 and 4.

1.5   Reality: Do terms and conditions apply?

Back to metaphysics. The sentences intended to express the metaphysical views 'underpinning' research are (I've suggested) not unlike: 'It's 5 o'clock on the sun.' For example, consider this sentence from a methods textbook. It is an 'ontological' belief attributed, by the authors, to positivists:

> **(5)** Reality exists 'out there' and… it is observable, stable, and measurable.
> *(Merriam & Tisdell 2016: 9)*

I will take it that this is an example of a sentence that is intended to be referentially successful, both by the positivists (who allegedly think it's true) and by the authors (who think it's false).[9] It is intended to be ultimate-reality-describing. Why do I say that sentences of this kind are not unlike 'It's 5 o'clock on the sun'? This is a question I will consider in detail in Part II. Here, I'll just say that, as with Wittgenstein's example, these are familiar words being used in a context in which their application conditions aren't met. In expanding on this, I will focus (for now) on just one phrase: 'out there'. This is an expression that is frequently included among the ontological 'beliefs' attributed to positivists (by non-positivists). It's almost always placed in inverted commas, which perhaps signals the authors' awareness that there is something slightly strained, or perhaps 'metaphorical', about it.

In Section 1.4, I emphasised that to point out that (on a particular occasion) an ordinary expression's 'application conditions' have not been fulfilled, is not necessarily to rule out the possibility that a non-ordinary idea *is* being conveyed. However, until we have been given an explanation as to how this is accomplished, it is not unreasonable to suspend judgement. To provide an example of the dialogue that 'explanation seeking' might involve, I'll switch to conversation mode.

1.6 'Out there'

One reaction to what I said in the previous section:

Reader: Hang on a minute. 'Reality exists "out there", and it is observable, stable, and measurable.' Why are the words in that sentence being used in a context that doesn't meet their application conditions? I can't see anything peculiar about the context. Aren't *all* these words being used in their ordinary senses, including 'out there'?'

Me: Well, if the words *are* being used in their ordinary sense, this sentence states a truism. My wheelbarrow, which is definitely part of reality, exists 'out there'. I can see it through the window. It's observable, stable and measurable.[10] The point is: the application conditions of 'out there' require a region of space differentiated from, and relative to, another point in space (aka 'here').

Reader: I'm talking – as you well know – about the *whole* of reality, not just a small bit of it. Not just your wheelbarrow.

Me: Yes, but that's the problem. Normally, 'out there' refers to something that is *not here*. Its use is relative to a particular place. My wheelbarrow is out there relative to my house. The stars are 'out there' relative to the Earth. How can *reality-as-a-whole* be 'out there'? 'Out there' relative to what? Outside what?

Reader: Out there, relative to the mind. Outside the mind.

Me: See, that doesn't really help. The mind isn't a physical place,[11] and if it were – let's say it's in your head – it would be inside *reality-as-a-whole*. So then *reality-as-a-whole*, which includes your mind, would be 'out there' relative to your mind. Which means that your mind would be 'out there' relative to your mind.

Reader: If the mind *isn't* a physical place, then reality is out there – relative to the mind – almost by definition.

Me: But 'out there' is a spatial idea. So how can reality be 'out there' relative to something non-spatial?

Reader: Separate from the mind, then. If reality is spatial and the mind is non-spatial, then clearly they are different kinds of thing. So they are intrinsically *separate*.

Me: The fact that 'the mind' is a non-spatial concept doesn't entail that it's a kind of *thing*. 'Taste' is a non-spatial concept, but taste isn't a type of object. And it isn't separate from reality. We apply 'mind' predicates to people, and people are part of reality. So reality and the mind can't be *that* separate.

Reader: Okay, 'separate from the mind' in the sense of unaffected by it. Unshaped by our concepts and categories. Not socially constructed.

Me: But that's either another truism, or a falsism.[12] If it's *reality-as-a-whole* we're referring to – the entire universe, with its radius of 46.5 billion light years, and its 2 trillion galaxies, each with 100 billion stars – then it's fairly clear that 'our concepts and categories' have done nothing to 'shape' *that*. If you have something more local in mind, setting aside *reality-as-a-whole*, then equally clearly my house, my garden, my wheelbarrow *have* been affected by concepts and categories. They're all designed and 'shaped'. But that isn't a metaphysical statement, it's an empirical claim.

Reader: Galaxies and stars *are* shaped by our concepts and categories. The fact that we call them 'stars' and 'galaxies', that we think about them in the way we do, that we identify them *as* galaxies and stars – none of that would be possible without concepts and categories, would it?

Me: No, you're right. What we *call* galaxies and stars, how we think and theorise about them, is obviously dependent on our concepts. But the *existence* of stars and galaxies doesn't depend on our concepts.[13] If it did, nothing at all could have existed before humans started using language. Two distinct questions: 'How do we refer to stars?' and 'How can stars exist?'

Reader: Oh, come on. This is getting ridiculous. You're just playing with words. You know what I'm talking about. You know perfectly well what I mean by 'out there', 'separate', 'shaped', and 'socially constructed'.

Me: The trouble is, I don't. I acknowledge that we use concepts to conceptualise, and categories to categorise. But if that's what 'shaped' and 'socially constructed' mean, then they're truisms dressed up as profundities. But notice the *'if'*. The problem is to find a way of using ordinary words to convey non-ordinary ideas when their 'terms and conditions' are inapplicable. This is *far* harder than (often glib) ontological sentences make it seem

This is not the kind of conversation that can ever be resolved.[14] There will be further qualifications and attempts at greater precision on the part of the would-be metaphysician, and there will be endless 'yes-butting' on the part of the sceptic (i.e. me). People always want to say 'You *know* what I mean. You're just pretending not to. You're just playing games with words.' No, actually. I'm not pretending. I really don't understand what you're saying.

1.7 'Constructed' reality

The example used in Section 1.5 is what a qualitative methods text attributes to 'positivism'. But a version of non-positivism would have served just as well. Here is Merriam and Tisdell's account of the 'interpretivist' ontology (2016: 9):

(6) Reality is socially constructed; that is, there is no single, observable reality. Rather, there are multiples realities, or interpretations of a single event.

I could have similar conversations – and will have in Chapters 5–7 – with someone wishing to explain this belief, since the 'interpretivist' ontology has to solve the same basic problem: how to use familiar words in contexts where their 'application conditions' are not met. These dialogues will have similar features to the one in Section 1.6. There will be the same struggle to force ordinary words into saying something *metaphysical*. We will sometimes find inverted commas ('out there'), implying that a term is being used in a non-ordinary way. There will be parallel attempts to avoid truisms and falsisms. There will be a comparable procession of ordinary expressions, each trying to justify the 'ordinariness' of the previous one: 'out there', 'separate from the mind', 'not shaped by it', 'not socially constructed'. And there will be numerous pairs of statements where it looks as if both cannot be true, but there is no way of adjudicating between them.[15] Not if ordinary words are being used in ordinary senses. But again: notice the 'if'. The problem remains: how to get ordinary words to mean something non-ordinary, and how to identify the conditions under which that can be achieved. It's difficult, but perhaps not impossible.

One complication is that there are various formulations of the 'positivist' ontology – not all of them include the expression 'out there', for example – and various formulations of the constructivist ontology. If I persuade you that one version doesn't make sense, there are plenty of alternative versions you could adopt instead. I can't deal with every one of them, and some bright spark is bound to insist that I missed *the* crucial one, the one that gets it right. Can't be helped.

Ultimately, however, I will be arguing that the challenge of explaining how ordinary words can convey non-ordinary metaphysical truths cannot be met. To that extent, I'm adopting a form of deflationism. To be deflationist about metaphysics is to believe that all metaphysical sentences are failed statements. The type of deflationism I have in mind, in common with several recent writers on metametaphysics (Blatti & Lapointe 2016), is associated with Rudolf Carnap, a card-carrying logical positivist, but one whose reputation has been re-evaluated in recent years.[16]

1.8 Expressivism and enactment

If the metaphysical 'beliefs' referred to in research methods texts cannot be parsed as reality-describing; if, to that extent, they are referentially unsuccessful; if, in short, I am adopting deflationism with respect to metaphysical sentences, the question arises as to what value, if any, these sentences have. One way to answer this question is to adopt *expressivism* as an alternative to *representationalism*.[17] The idea is that we should drop the assumption that metaphysical sentences provide information about reality/realities, and focus on the *use* to which they are put.

This is where Carnap comes in. Writers vary on the views they attribute to Carnap, even though they agree about his deflationism. The view I incline towards is that 'Carnap's theory of ontology parallels noncognitivist theories of morality' (Kraut 2016: 31). Comparable ideas can be found in Price (2007) and Thomasson (2015). Noncognitivist views in ethics reject the assumption that moral claims describe an aspect of reality: there are no moral *facts* or *properties* to be described. Instead, to make a moral claim is to express an attitude, usually approval or disapproval, and/or to urge, recommend, or caution against, certain types of behaviour. Carnap takes a similar line with metaphysical sentences. They do not describe facts or properties; rather, they enable the 'explicit articulation of pragmatically motivated commitments to the adoption of certain linguistic forms' (Kraut, *ibid*). Carnap's ontology 'is, in the current parlance, an *expressivist* theory'.[18]

Two alternative ontological sentences: 'There is a single reality' and 'There are multiple realities.'[19] On an expressivist view, neither of these provides information, despite their syntax. What they do instead is *resolve* to use (or *recommend* the use of) a certain linguistic framework: a 'one reality' language, or a 'many realities' language. In each case, the sentence expresses a commitment to the corresponding framework, and to a set of application conditions/rules governing the use of the relevant expressions. However, as Kraut (2016) suggests, these commitments are pragmatically motivated. In one case, it is claimed that 'single reality' talk will be useful; in the other, it is claimed that 'multiple realities' talk will be. One thing we might do, in such circumstances – something Carnap suggests – is to monitor both, and see which is *more* useful. This is a pragmatic question,[20] not a dispute about what (in a fundamental-reality-describing sense) is the case.

However, I'd like to take an additional step. I agree with Kraut's account, but I think there is a further function which metaphysical pronouncements have in the case of qualitative research. It is not just the commitment to a *language* that is at stake here, but the commitment to a *culture* – to a certain tribe. Goertz and Mahoney (2012) argue that the qualitative and quantitative traditions 'exhibit all the traits of separate cultures', each with its own norms and practices. 'Quantitative-qualitative disputation in the social sciences is really a clash of cultures'.[21] In line with this, I take metaphysical sentences to be a cultural ritual. It is generally assumed that they make different claims about metaphysical reality and that these claims justify the methodological preferences concerned. In my view, however, they are not claims but enactments. They *enact* the commitment to a tribe; they don't *justify* it.

This account needs to be qualified. Consider two antithetical ontological statements: [ER] 'An external reality exists independent of our beliefs or understandings.' [NR] 'No external reality exists independent of our beliefs and understandings' (Ormston *et al.* 2013: 5). I have implied that ER enacts the joining of the quantitative tribe, while NR enacts the joining of the qualitative tribe. It is more nuanced than that. In fact, NR enacts the joining of the qualitative tribe, but ER is the enactment which the qualitative tribe *attributes* to the quantitative tribe.[22] Quantitative researchers, for the most part, don't bother much with metaphysics.

1.9 Metaphysically ungrounded research

Reader: But surely research has to be based on *something*. It can't have no foundations at all.

Me: What kind of 'foundations' do you have in mind? Carnap's point is that, if it's metaphysical sentences you want, you've still got them. It's just that they don't do the job you thought they did. They don't describe reality. But they do have a function. They're the language you want to speak; they're the colours you nail to the mast.

Reader: By 'foundations' I don't mean this 'resolving and enacting' stuff. I mean something on which research is *grounded*. Something that tells you what reality is *like*. How can you do research without something like that to draw on?

Me: Where did I say that you can't draw on something that tells you what reality is like?

Reader: Well, most of this chapter, for a start.

Me: No, this chapter suggests that *metaphysical sentences* don't tell you what reality is like. It has not said anything about empirical statements that *do* tell you what reality is like (or provide evidence of what it might be like).

A researcher draws on 'what is already known' or, more precisely, what she has empirical grounds for thinking. The 'what is known' will include previous research, the theoretical and practical context, the methodological options available, the relevant meta-research – research on research method – and the cognitive- and social-psychological processes involved in responding to different types of interview question. These are empirical findings, not metaphysical axioms, so they are subject to revision. They are not 'foundational' in the sense that they are without 'foundation' themselves; they are empirically evidenced 'groundings'. If research is to be based on something descriptive of 'reality', examples like these are the only plausible candidates.

Reader: But you have to know what reality is like, ontologically speaking, before you can do *any* research. You have to know what you're dealing with.

Me: Well, you could argue the opposite. You have to do research before you can have any idea what reality is like. How do you know what you're dealing with until you've researched it?

Reader: But that's what ontology is *for*. Telling you about reality *prior* to empirical inquiry.

Me: Telling you about reality on what basis? 'Underpinnings' metaphysicians say you have to know something metaphysical about the world before you can find things out about it. But they are not very forthcoming about how they know what they claim to know. How do they *know* that 'there are multiple realities' (or not)? Intuition? Armchair reflection? Revelation? They won it in a raffle?

Reader: People see things differently, interpret things differently. They create their own realities.

Me: Well, okay, if you like. But those are empirical claims. So are you claiming that we need empirical findings… to justify metaphysical 'basic beliefs'… to justify empirical research? Doesn't that strike you as, well, a bit circular?

Alternatively, it might be said that the metaphysical beliefs underpinning qualitative research are just arbitrary. That's what Lincoln and Guba say (as we'll see in the next chapter). But if the metaphysical foundations are not grounded in anything – and according to Lincoln and Guba, they can't be – you're saddled with the view that research needs groundings, but the groundings don't. But if it's okay to have ungrounded metaphysical groundings, why is it not okay to have metaphysically ungrounded research? Why not just cut out the middle man?

1.10   Five observations

1   Let me confirm what I implied in Section 1.1. Throughout the book, I'll be doing equal opportunities metaphysical scepticism. I am not trying to shore up a version of positivism (or postpositivism). I think that all metaphysical sentences – whether they turn up in the 'positivist' or the 'constructivist' column of the paradigm contrast table – are referentially unsuccessful. None of them make sense.

2   One problem in promoting this view is the fact that the concept of metaphysical 'underpinnings' represents a 40-year orthodoxy. It is rarely if ever challenged, and the sentences used to express the ontological and epistemological 'beliefs' which supposedly do the underpinning have become familiar tropes: 'There is a single objective reality'; 'The knower and the

known are interactive, inseparable'; and numerous variations on the theme. These are constantly repeated, creating the impression that they are understood, transparent, taken for granted. People assume they make sense, and think they believe one or more of them. I'll argue that this is an illusion of thought. In a philosophical context, 'illusions of thought' are discussed by Cappelen (2013): 'a subject can take herself to have a thought even though she does not have one' (29).[23] If that's right, it's possible that a qualitative researcher might think she believes that 'There are multiple constructed realities', even though it doesn't make sense. Ditto for 'There is a single objective reality.' This might explain why *Reader* says: 'you know what I mean', 'you're just pretending not to understand'. Clearly, everyone in the research community 'understands' these frequently recycled expressions, because they are so familiar. 'If everybody else understands them, I must understand them as well. So must you.' Only I don't.

3 What I've said about ordinary words and non-ordinary senses presupposes a view of meaning which will emerge in Part I. Here, I will just say this. Meaning is not a 'property' of words. If it is anything at all, it is the pattern of usage associated with particular words and phrases. That's not a property; it's a distribution. Baz (2017: 133) suggests that 'what makes a word suitable for certain uses but not others – call it "its meaning" – is its history, or in other words "former acts of expression"'. So, from my point of view, the jobs that a word has done in the past are the starting point for the jobs it can be asked to do in the future. This does not imply that it can *only* perform tasks it has performed before. That would prevent any kind of novelty or creativity in language. But any departure from past usage must either be explained (as in scientific appropriations of words like 'force' or 'work'), or be intelligible given the context in which the word appears. It must be possible to specify *how* the expression is used in those circumstances. This view of 'meaning' implies, among other things, the 'assembling of reminders' (in Wittgenstein's terms) about the ordinary use of words; so, as I noted in the Prologue, I take myself to be doing something akin to ordinary language philosophy. For a thorough account of the renewed interest in ordinary language philosophy in recent years, see Crary & de Lara (2019).

4 I have not, so far, been very precise about the concept of 'application conditions'. This will get further discussion in Chapter 3. Intuitively, however, the idea is that metaphysical sentences use expressions in ways which tear them away from the contexts in which they make sense. Just as 'It's 5 o'clock on the sun' strips the o'clock construction away from its 'on earth' application conditions, so 'Reality exists "out there"…' strips a locative phrase away from its spatial application conditions. Still, we have not yet ruled out the possibility that this stripping away can result in a non-ordinary idea being conveyed. But then there are three key questions to answer. First, how do we articulate this non-ordinary idea? Second, given the relevant

expression's history of use, how does the reader know what the non-ordinary idea is? Third, how do the words concerned acquire non-ordinary senses, and under what conditions is that possible? Indifference to these questions contributes significantly to the illusion of thought mentioned in [2].

5 For some readers, the fact that Carnap is one of the main points of reference in this book will be problematic. After all, a majority of philosophers who write about metaphysics regard his influence as pernicious. Meanwhile, among those who write about qualitative research methods, it is almost always assumed that positivism, Carnap included, is discredited. But here are just some of the philosophers who have contributed to Carnap's rehabilitation in recent years: Yablo (2010), Hirsch (2011), Price (2011), Thomasson (2015), Creath (2016), Hofweber (2016), Kraut (2016), Sidelle (2016), Sambrotta & Jorge (2018), Bradley (2018), Jaksland (2020), Broughton (2021), Cohen & Marschall (2023), Flocke (2024). All published in the past 15 years. There's even a case for saying that Carnap's influence is growing.

1.11 A quick outline

The book suggests that qualitative metaphysical sentences, which are assumed to have an information-providing function, have a different function altogether, an expressivist or performative one.

1.11.1 Part I The key players

Chapter 2 examines Lincoln and Guba's canonical concept of a 'paradigm'. I argue that their concept is not the same as Kuhn's, and that it is less than fully coherent. The other two chapters discuss the relation between metametaphysics, Wittgenstein's understanding of philosophy, and Carnap's expressivism. The aim is to indicate where the methods adopted in Part II have come from.

1.11.2 Part II The key concepts

Each chapter examines a key expression used in sentences which supposedly represent the metaphysical foundations of research. The aim is to show how the use of these expressions exceeds their application conditions, and why this fact creates a problem for methodological writers seeking to depict ontological and epistemological 'beliefs'.

1.11.3 Epilogue

Since metaphysical claims seek to impose restrictions on both methods and language use, the effect of quietly binning them is to remove these restrictions. The Epilogue is a brief sketch of what that implies.

Notes

1 As noted in the Prologue, I'll be using 'metaphysical' as a generic term covering both epistemology and ontology, as well as other metaphysical topics. Any use of 'metaphysics' on its own should be taken as a reference to the metaphysical claims found in qualitative methods writing *unless* it's clear that I'm referring to the wider metaphysics literature.

2 An alternative to the expression 'not reality-describing' might be 'describing nothing'.

3 More colloquially, they 'don't make sense'. I'll be using this handy expression again, but it must be qualified. First, sentences (1) to (4) are grammatically correct and, apart from (3), they use familiar, meaningful words. So they are not 'meaningless'. Second, some referentially unsuccessful sentences, including those used in qualitative metaphysics, have a significant function; so they cannot just be dismissed as 'nonsense'.

4 'Referentially unsuccessful' does not imply 'false'. 'There are unicorns on the lawn' is a claim I can test by looking out at the lawn. I know, roughly, what I would see if it were true. So it is *not* referentially unsuccessful. It makes an empirically confirmable statement. As it happens, though, it's not true. I've looked, and there aren't any.

5 The chapter by Jahn has an appendix of 'Colourless Green Ideas Poems'.

6 Inevitably, it's not quite that simple. Solar midday is when the sun crosses the local meridian. This is not necessarily at exactly 12:00 local time because of time zones. For example, if it's 12 o'clock in London, it will also be 12 o'clock in Lisbon, because London and Lisbon are in the same time zone. But if, at 12 o'clock, the sun is crossing the local meridian in London, it won't also be crossing the meridian in Lisbon, given that London is 0.12° W, while Lisbon is 9.14° W.

7 Another way of saying approximately the same thing is to suggest that there are 'rules' for the use of the o'clock construction (although the word 'rule' can have misleading connotations). I borrow the expression 'application conditions' from Thomasson (2015). However, my use of it is not exactly the same as hers.

8 I will be saying 'unless and until' quite a bit. The idea is that the sentences of qualitative metaphysics don't make sense – *unless and until* the author explains how her 'ordinary' words convey a non-ordinary idea. See further Sections 3.6 and 4.4.

9 Many non-positivists are suspicious of the word 'true', but I'm not sure what other word to use. Some qualitative writers argue that truth is a positivist idea. What are their reasons, then, for preferring a non-positivist ontological sentence to a positivist one?

10 I don't blame anybody for being impatient with this. But the question is: how are ordinary words used to convey something less obvious – something less of a truism – than this? No one digs their heels in over 'out there'. Compared to 'single', or 'objective', or 'reality', it's dispensable. That's what makes it a good introductory illustration. The heavy stuff comes later.

11 'Isn't that a metaphysical statement?' Well yes, if you want. However, it's not reality-describing. It is what Wittgenstein might call a 'grammatical remark'. It makes a point about how the word 'mind', and expressions referring to 'mental states', are used. Your foot may be in your shoe, but your mind isn't in your balaclava. Your head may be in the MRI scanner, but your thoughts aren't.

12 Strangely, I hadn't come across this word before I started writing this. The opposite of 'truism'.

13 See Hilpinen (1996) for a discussion of this kind of argument, and Thomasson (2015: 59–61) for a helpful summary.

14 Appeals to metaphor are popular. 'Out there' is said to be used metaphorically. Here's a response. Suppose I say: 'There is a single objective reality hanging about

outside'. Are you going to question 'outside' and 'hanging about'? 'Outside what?' 'How can reality hang about?' If you are, I'll reply that I'm using both expressions metaphorically. Is that an intelligible answer? Without further explanation? And I could ask: why do you (implicitly) appeal to the ordinary sense of these words, when you were reluctant to do that with 'out there'? *Reader*: 'You know perfectly well what I mean by "out there".' *Me*: 'Well, okay, in that case, *you* know perfectly well what *I* mean by "hanging about outside".' Goose, meet gander.

15 For comparable accounts, see Sidelle (2002) and Balaguer (2021). Sidelle suggests that 'there is no fact of the matter' about which of the competing ontological claims is true. They 'don't really make different claims about the world, but just provide different ways of describing the material contents of space-time' (118). Balaguer argues that 'there are no right answers to the relevant metaphysical questions', and that the reason for this is that 'the language in which these questions are formulated is catastrophically imprecise' (7).

16 According to Sidelle (2016: 79), Carnap issues a challenge to metaphysicians of the kind I have just described. Carnap's analysis, he says, 'gives rise to a *challenge* to find *another* meaning for the relevant questions and claims, a challenge Carnap thought could not be met' (italics in original). My challenge is of the same kind: can you explain how you get ordinary words to mean something non-ordinary, and can you identify the conditions under which that can be achieved? Like Carnap, I don't think the challenge can be met.

17 Alternatively 'cognitivism', 'descriptivism', or 'referentialism'. Technically, these four terms are not identical, but in practice they refer to closely related sets of assumptions: that the function of language is to refer, describe, represent, and be 'declarative'.

18 Whenever italics appear in a quotation, they are found in the original, unless otherwise stated.

19 Obviously, I'm using the shortest versions for the purposes of exposition. As I've already noted, there are a number of variations, given that the relevant beliefs have been expressed in different ways over the years, even by Lincoln and Guba.

20 Here, I'm using 'pragmatic' colloquially. I'm not adopting a form of pragmatism.

21 Ironically, Goertz and Mahoney exclude 'interpretive approaches' from their analysis. I suspect that the inclusion of interpretive approaches in the 'qualitative tradition' would not make the clash they describe any less intense.

22 The point about the impossibility of parsing either 'There is a single reality' or 'There are multiple realities' as information-providing still stands. Non-positivists have invented two equal-and-opposite impossible 'beliefs', one of which is attributed to positivism. See Section 4.7.

23 I say more in Section 3.6.

References

Balaguer, M. (2021). *Metaphysics, Sophistry, and Illusion: Toward a Widespread Non-Factualism*. Oxford: Oxford University Press.

Baz, A. (2017). *The Crisis of Method in Contemporary Analytic Philosophy*. Oxford: Oxford University Press.

Blatti, S., & Lapointe, S. (Eds.). (2016). *Ontology After Carnap*. New York: Oxford University Press.

Bradley, D. (2018). Carnap's epistemological critique of metaphysics. *Synthese, 195*, 2247–2265.

Broughton, G. L. (2021). Carnapian frameworks. *Synthese, 199*, 4097–4126.

Cappelen, H. (2013). Nonsense and illusions of thought. *Philosophical Perspectives,* *27,* 22–50.

Cohen, W. A., & Marschall, B. (2023). Would Carnap have tolerated modern metaphysics? *The Monist, 106,* 326–341.

Crary, A., & de Lara, J. (2019). Who's afraid of ordinary language philosophy? A plea for reviving a wrongly reviled philosophical tradition. *Graduate Faculty Philosophy Journal, 39*(2), 317–339.

Creath, R. (2016). Carnap and ontology: foreign travel and domestic understanding. In S. Blatti & S. Lapointe (Eds.), *Ontology After Carnap* (pp. 31–58). Oxford: Oxford University Press.

Flocke, V. (2024). Carnap is not against metaphysics. In A. Richardson & A. T. Tuboly (Eds.), *Interpreting Carnap: Critical Essays* (pp. 32–49). Cambridge, UK: Cambridge University Press.

Goertz, G., & Mahoney, J. (2012). *A Tale of Two Cultures: Qualitative and Quantitative Research in the Social Sciences.* Princeton, NJ: Princeton University Press.

Hilpinen, R. (1996). On some formulations of realism, or how many objects are there in the world? In R. S. Cohen, R. Hilpinen, & Q. Renzong (Eds.), *Realism and Anti-realism in the Philosophy of Science: Beijing International Conference, 1992* (pp. 1–10). Dordrecht: Springer.

Hirsch, E. (2011). *Quantifier Variance and Realism.* New York: Oxford University Press.

Hofweber, T. (2016). *Ontology and the Ambitions of Metaphysics.* Oxford: Oxford University Press.

Jahn, M. (2002). "Colourless green ideas sleep furiously": A linguistic test case and its appropriations. In M. Gymnich, A. Nünning, & V. Nünning (Eds.), *Literature and Linguistics: Approaches, Models, and Applications: Studies In Honour of Jon Erickson* (pp. 47–60). Trier, Germany: Wissenschafter Verlag.

Jaksland, R. (2020). Old problems for neo-positivist naturalized metaphysics. *European Journal for Philosophy of Science, 10,* Article 16. https://doi.org/10.1007/s13194-13020-00282-13190

Kraut, R. (2016). Three Carnaps on ontology. In S. Blatti & S. Lapointe (Eds.), *Ontology After Carnap* (pp. 31–58). Oxford: Oxford University Press.

Merriam, S. B., & Tisdell, E. J. (2016). *Qualitative Research: A Guide to Design and Implementation.* Fourth Edition. San Francisco: Jossey-Bass.

Ormston, R., Spencer, L., Barnard, M., & Snape, D. (2013). The foundations of qualitative research. In J. Ritchie, J. Lewis, C. M. Nicholls, & R. Ormston (Eds.), *Qualitative Research Practice: A Guide for Social Science Students and Researchers* (pp. 1–26). London: Sage.

Price, H. (2007). Metaphysics after Carnap: the ghost who walks? In D. J. Chalmers, D. Manley, & R. Wasserman (Eds.), *Metametaphysics* (pp. 320–346). New York: Oxford University Press.

Price, H. (2011). *Naturalism Without Mirrors.* New York: Oxford University Press.

Sambrotta, M., & Jorge, A. G. (2018). Expressivism without mentalism in meta-ontology. *International Journal of Philosophical Studies, 26*(5), 781–800.

Sidelle, A. (2002). Is there a true metaphysics of material objects? *Nous, 36*(S1), 118–145.

Sidelle, A. (2016). Frameworks and deflation in "Empiricism, Semantics, and Ontology" and recent metametaphysics. In S. Blatti & S. Lapointe (Eds.), *Ontology After Carnap* (pp. 59–80). Oxford: Oxford University Press.

Thomasson, A. L. (2015). *Ontology Made Easy*. New York: Oxford University Press.

Wittgenstein, L. (2009). *Philosophical Investigations*. Revised 4th edition by P. M. S. Hacker and Schulte Joachim. Malden, MA: Wiley-Blackwell.

Yablo, S. (2010). *Things: Papers on Objects, Events, and Properties*. Oxford: Oxford University Press.

PART I

The key players

2

LINCOLN AND GUBA'S PARADIGMS

There are such things as metaphysical truths, metaphysical beliefs, metaphysical assumptions. Some of these truths represent the foundations of enquiry. All research methods are underpinned by, grounded in, or aligned with, them. It is impossible to justify, or challenge, metaphysical truths by reference to deeper truths. Metaphysical truths *are* 'deeper' truths, and they are not answerable to any other truths, beliefs, or assumptions. A particular set of metaphysical truths/beliefs can be organised into a system, known as a 'paradigm'. This sense of the term 'paradigm' is the same as the one introduced by Kuhn.

I will be questioning all these claims. I don't think metaphysical truths are the foundations of all enquiry. I don't think metaphysics – at least the kind of metaphysics found in qualitative textbooks – is necessary. I don't think qualitative researchers must decide what their metaphysical beliefs are. I don't think the sense of 'paradigm' found in qualitative texts even resembles the sense introduced by Kuhn. I *do* think that the metaphysical sentences found in qualitative texts don't make sense.[1] To be clear, I'm referring to *all* the metaphysical sentences found in these texts: positivist, interpretivist, constructivist, whatever. I am not trying to smuggle positivism, postpositivism, empiricism, or realism back in.[2]

The claims in the first paragraph were made by Lincoln and Guba. Why focus on them? Good question.

2.1 Why Lincoln and Guba

Lincoln and Guba (1985) did not originate any of the ideas outlined above, but they were instrumental in giving them a canonical form. Let me explain, in a preliminary way, what I mean by this.

DOI: 10.4324/9781003306382-3

One way of establishing the importance of *Naturalistic Inquiry* is to look at citations. A quick and dirty way of doing this is to consult Google Scholar. As I write, the book's count is 145,081, a figure which represents total citations since original publication.[3] I've found only four comparable books with higher numbers:

Robert Yin	*Case Study Research: Design and Methods*	218,412
Creswell and Poth	*Qualitative Inquiry and Research Design*	190,754
Glaser and Strauss	*The Discovery of Grounded Theory*	167,931
Miles and Huberman	*Qualitative Data Analysis: An Expanded Sourcebook*	155,046
Lincoln and Guba	*Naturalistic Inquiry*	145,081

In terms of the numbers, then, *Naturalistic Inquiry* is a highly significant book; and if a Google Scholar citation rate is any guide to influence, it counts as one of the most influential qualitative methods texts (and the only one of these five whose primary focus is philosophy).

Certainly, many recent textbooks echo key passages of the book, even when it is not directly cited. For example, Merriam and Tisdell (2016) assert that a 'positivist orientation assumes that reality exists "out there" and that it is observable, stable, and measurable'. According to interpretive research, by contrast, 'there is no single, observable reality. Rather there are multiple realities, or interpretations, of a single event' (9). The echoes are unmistakable. Lincoln and Guba's (1985: 37) positivist version of *Axiom 1* is: 'There is a single tangible reality "out there" fragmentable into independent variables.' The naturalist version is: 'There are multiple constructed realities that can be studied only holistically.' These tropes, referring to the 'single objective reality "out there"', and 'multiple constructed realities', are extremely common in qualitative methods textbooks.

Merriam and Tisdell only refer to *Naturalistic Inquiry* once, but they classify Guba's (1978) monograph alongside Glaser and Strauss (1967) in terms of its importance for 'defining' qualitative research.[4] Even so, it was the 1985 book that brought 'naturalistic inquiry' to the masses and popularised the idea that a necessary preliminary to all types of enquiry is the formulation of metaphysical beliefs.

This assumption, that metaphysical beliefs are fundamental to enquiry, is now taken for granted by many authors, and this in itself is one of the twin achievements of *Naturalistic Inquiry*. There have been shifts in emphasis and terminology over the past 40 years, but the idea that there must be some 'alignment' between your metaphysical beliefs and your methods is still with us. So is the critical divide between positivism (plus postpositivism) and all alternative paradigms,[5] despite the advent of mixed methods, the inception of 'post-humanist' approaches, and an armistice in the 'paradigm wars'. This is the second of the twin achievements. Lincoln and Guba's version of 'paradigm' became canonical; so did their version of 'positivism'. In that sense, 'paradigm' and 'positivism', as they are understood in the contemporary qualitative literature, are conceptual twins, born at the same moment.[6]

Lincoln and Guba begin *Naturalistic Inquiry* by introducing the concept of a 'metaphysical truth', which 'cannot be tested for truthfulness against some external norm such as correspondence with nature' (14). Metaphysical beliefs, they say, 'must be accepted at face value' and 'represent the ultimate benchmark against which *everything else* is tested'. A particular set of metaphysical beliefs may be constituted as a system of ideas: 'we shall call this systematic set of beliefs, together with their accompanying methods, a *paradigm*' (15). Paradigms 'represent a distillation of what we *think* about the world (but cannot prove)'. In a footnote, they add that this 'definition of *paradigm* is consistent with the use of that term by Kuhn' (45: italics original).

Let's start with that footnote.

2.2   k-paradigms *versus* m-paradigms

Whatever Lincoln and Guba's view, their sense of 'paradigm' – a sense inherited by qualitative methods textbooks – bears no resemblance to Kuhn's original. So from here on, I'll distinguish between Kuhn's sense (*k-paradigm*),[7] and the methodological sense (*m-paradigm*), which originates with Lincoln and Guba.[8] In this section, I will outline four major differences.

2.2.1   *Substantive/metaphysical*

For Kuhn, the main constituents of a *k-paradigm* – or 'disciplinary matrix', to use the term he preferred subsequently – are symbolic generalisations, models, and exemplars (Kuhn 1974). These are substantive theoretical commitments shared by the members of a community of scientists. Symbolic generalisations are expressions, such as $f=ma$, which can be cast in mathematical/logical form. Models are metaphorical representations; for example, electrons and nuclei represented by 'tiny bits of charged matter interacting under the laws of mechanics and electromagnetic theory' (Kuhn 1993: 538).[9] Exemplars are 'concrete problem solutions': historical, specific points of reference which constitute theoretical or experimental landmarks in the discipline.

Contrast *m-paradigms*. The constituents of an m-paradigm are ontological and epistemological beliefs, which refer to abstract, ahistorical concepts such as the nature of 'reality', the meaning of 'knowledge', and the significance of values. An m-paradigm has no equivalent of symbolic generalisations, models, or exemplars. This shift from substantive to metaphysical discourse is the most obvious difference between k-paradigms and m-paradigms. Whereas the former are organised round real-world, concrete, how-does-this-work questions, along with techniques which have proved successful in answering questions of that type, the latter are defined by philosophical abstractions.

2.2.2 *Problem-solving resources/statements of belief*

The k-paradigm has already, by definition, been successful 'in solving a few problems that the group of practitioners has come to recognise as acute' (Kuhn 1962: 23). Its exemplars are historical scenarios in which one of these problems was solved using particular techniques. For this reason, an exemplar is also a resource: future problems and anomalies may be resolved by adopting the same approach, or perhaps a modification of it. 'Normal science', in fact, is the business of solving further puzzles by the use of these resources. A crucial part of science education is learning to solve textbook problems by employing the exemplars imaginatively. In this way, the student comes to understand, in a hands-on way, what sorts of problems they can be used to solve. This is how the student 'acquires' the k-paradigm.

In contrast, *m-paradigms* are comprised of second-order beliefs, not historical first-order puzzles and resources. They consist of abstract statements such as: 'There is a single tangible reality "out there", fragmentable into independent variables and processes' (Lincoln & Guba 1985: 37). Adopting an m-paradigm is a matter of accepting a particular metaphysical belief. M-paradigm beliefs are not resources and can't be used to solve practical problems. Instead, they point you towards methods. If you believe in a single reality, you'll be inclined to a quantitative approach. If you believe in multiple realities, you'll be inclined to a qualitative approach.

2.2.3 *Community/individual*

A k-paradigm is, again by definition, something which members of a scientific community share (Kuhn 1974). Scientific investigation is organised around the symbolic generalisations, models and exemplars accepted by a determinate group of people, each of whom recognises the same disciplinary landmarks. A k-paradigm intrinsically belongs, as it were, to the community concerned. However, the community has independent existence and has its own networks, culture, social structure, and strategies for education.

This is not true of m-paradigms, which are ascribed to individuals. Indeed, m-paradigms are frequently equated with an individual's 'worldview' (Hackley 2020), and the choice of a method is said to depend on the researcher's own 'philosophical assumptions' (Hesse-Biber 2017). Underlying this claim is the assumption that the individual researcher has an 'antecedent' belief system, on the basis of which she adopts the corresponding m-paradigm. The picture is not one of learning a k-paradigm through practice with models and exemplars but one of individual preferences and perspectives.

2.2.4 Historical process/static abstractions

A k-paradigm can sometimes be superseded by another, and this occurs when certain problems – Kuhn calls them anomalies – addressed by the established k-paradigm prove resistant to the technical puzzle-solving resources which that k-paradigm provides. At this point, a scientific revolution takes place and, when the dust finally settles, the old k-paradigm will have been replaced by a new one.

This is different from m-paradigms, which are never replaced (though new ones may be added). They are presented in parallel, simultaneously available and unvarying, even if one of them has been 'discredited'. Nothing in m-paradigm discourse has the function that Kuhn attributes to anomalies. Empirical evidence can never threaten, let alone disconfirm, your m-paradigm; nor can evidence ever identify problems the m-paradigm cannot deal with.

In summary, a k-paradigm is the disciplinary matrix of symbolic generalisations, substantive models, and exemplars which – at any one time, for a particular scientific community – define a field of enquiry and provide resources for solving puzzles. Learning a k-paradigm requires the study of these resources, and results in the acquisition of cognitive habits which facilitate puzzle solving, but which can make it difficult, subsequently, to recognise the merits of a new k-paradigm.[10] In contrast, an m-paradigm is a set of metaphysical beliefs – ontological, epistemological, axiological – which is selected from the currently available range by an individual on the basis of its affinity with her prior opinions. The m-paradigm embodies neither historical landmarks nor puzzle-solving resources. It requires only the acceptance of a series of unevidenced claims.

2.3 Axioms or basic beliefs?

In the previous section, I described the constituents of m-paradigms as 'beliefs'. This is true, as far as it goes, but it skirts round an important ambiguity. In any m-paradigm, there are some elements which are more fundamental than others. The ambiguity is this: Lincoln and Guba sometimes refer to these elements as 'basic beliefs', sometimes as 'axioms' (and sometimes as 'assumptions'). Take axioms first.

Axiomatic systems are introduced in Chapter 1 of *Naturalistic Inquiry*, with geometrical systems being used as an example. Lincoln and Guba provide an explanation of Euclidean and Lobachevskian geometry and point out that they are applied at different scales. Euclidean geometry works at the 'local', terrestrial level, where distances are measured in miles, but it doesn't work at intergalactic level, where distances can run to billions of light years. Lobachevskian geometry is the other way round: 'astronomers find that Lobachevskian geometry provides a better "fit" to the phenomena they investigate than does Euclidean'.

At this point in the discussion, it seems as if axiomatic systems are the model for m-paradigms; and the implication is that positivism and the naturalistic paradigm are a "fit" for different scales, disciplines, or contexts. Indeed, Lincoln and Guba define naturalism by a set of five axioms, from which characteristics of the naturalistic paradigm are derived. There is an ontological axiom, an epistemological axiom, a 'possibility of generalisation' axiom, a 'possibility of causal linkages' axiom, and an axiological axiom. The 14 'characteristics of inquiry' which follow are claimed to be 'logically dependent' on these axioms. This appears to be more than an analogy. The axioms define the m-paradigm, and the methodological 'characteristics' are inferred from them in approximately the same way that, in Euclid, theorems are inferred from the initial five axioms.[11]

If that's right, different m-paradigms will 'have different utilities depending on the phenomena to which they are applied' (36). We could expect naturalism to be useful in certain circumstances, and positivism in others. But this is not, in fact, the line Lincoln and Guba take. Instead, they do a complete about-face. Positivist and naturalist m-paradigms are incompatible, they say, because their 'axioms are contradictory and mutually exclusive' (267). True enough. But if the comparison with geometry holds, these axioms are the primary constituents of two different formal systems. *Neither* provides a 'description of reality', and should not be construed as doing so. Rather, the m-paradigms should be conceived as separate tools, like Euclid and Lobachevsky, each useful in different contexts. The fact that their respective axioms are mutually exclusive is precisely the point.

But suddenly, at the beginning of Chapter 2, positivism and naturalism cease to be axiom systems. The naturalistic paradigm is instead referred to as 'a logical successor to the positivist point of view', and it is suggested that 'accepting naturalism … is a *revolutionary* move' (47). The grounds for this assertion are presented in the rest of the chapter but are summarised like this (50):

> The paradigm is resonant with vanguard thinking in almost every formal discipline that exists; if one is interested in inquiry that is ongoing at the forefront of disciplines, the naturalistic paradigm is *the* paradigm of choice, the paradigm that provides the best fit to virtually all phenomena.

The rhetoric now shifts from 'different axiom systems have different utilities' to 'naturalism is preferable to positivism across the board'. The language of axiomatic systems, fit-for-purpose in different contexts, is replaced by the language of revolution, and a move from the old, discredited positivist paradigm to its new, vanguard-thinking successor. Rather than a discussion of the criteria for determining when one or the other can legitimately be applied, we are offered reasons for preferring naturalism *tout court*.

This reverts, then, to the vigorous critique of positivism that opens Chapter 1, a critique which lays bare its inadequacies, and which argues that it has '*at least two consequences that are both repugnant and unfounded*', not to mention '*five assumptions that are increasingly difficult to maintain*' (27–8; italics original). The language of this section riffs constantly on the theme of 'what it is no longer possible to believe', and the ways in which the positivist m-paradigm falls short. Positivism is inconsistent with 'emergent conceptual/empirical formulations', and its shortcomings are now so obvious that 'a significant number of vanguard scientists have abandoned the paradigm and moved into the postpositivist era'.[12] We are here no longer talking about axiomatic systems. No mathematician, for example, would claim that Euclidean geometry was 'discredited' by Lobachevsky and Riemann, let alone describe it as 'repugnant and unfounded'. This is rather the kind of argument we would expect from an author intent on substituting one m-paradigm for another. Instead of arguing that positivism works in certain contexts but not in others, the main thrust of the chapter is: positivism has failed.

This ambiguity – two completely different ways of talking about paradigms – is the result of a conflation of 'axiom' and 'basic belief'. The conflation is announced explicitly (33):

> Axioms may be defined as the set of undemonstrated (and undemonstrable) 'basic beliefs' accepted by convention or established by practice as the building blocks of some conceptual or theoretical system.

But an axiom system is not 'theoretical'. Axioms are not 'emergent conceptual/empirical formulations'. They do not describe 'phenomena'. They are abstract postulates – stipulations – adopted, not because they reflect the latest scientific theories, but because they can be used to generate a purely formal system. And a formal system is *not* a description of 'reality', even if it proves useful in some domain of enquiry.

Lincoln and Guba appear not to recognise the ambiguity they have created. On the one hand, they say that 'basic beliefs are arbitrary and may be assumed for any reason', and that metaphysical truths 'cannot be tested for truthfulness against some external norm such as correspondence with nature' (14). On the other hand, they say positivism is 'unfounded', and that its assumptions 'are increasingly difficult to maintain' (28). So, first, 'basic beliefs' *cannot* be tested. Second, they *can* be. And, in the case of positivism, they *have* been tested … and were found to be inadequate.[13]

The point is: beliefs can be tested, axioms can't. Axioms in formal systems are stipulations. They can't be 'justified' by evidence. Beliefs *can* be justified by evidence, and often have to be. Axioms have no descriptive content but, for that very reason, do not require warrant. Beliefs do have descriptive content and normally require justification if they are to be accepted. If the positivist paradigm consists of beliefs, it might turn out to be 'unfounded'. If it consists of axioms, it's not the kind of thing to which the term 'unfounded' can be applied. 'There are multiple constructed realities' has one kind of sense understood as a stipulation in a formal axiomatic system. It has a completely different kind of sense understood as a substantive claim about the world. You can't have it both ways.[14]

2.4   How to pick a paradigm

Step back from your familiarity with m-paradigm discourse for a moment, and consider a question that might occur to someone who is genuinely a novice: 'How do I select/adopt a paradigm?' I have already noted that some qualitative textbooks say that this is done on the basis of the student's 'worldview', the ontological and epistemological beliefs she had before she started thinking about research. So that's one answer to the selection question. You've got to wonder, though. How many pre-research students have thought a great deal about the 'nature of reality', and in particular whether it is singular or multiple?

What is Lincoln and Guba's answer to the selection question? The discussion in Section 2.3 suggests that they have two answers, both different from the 'worldview' answer but also incompatible with each other. One answer trades on the 'axiom system' understanding of 'paradigm'. The other trades on the 'basic belief' understanding. The first implies that axioms are *stipulated*. They aren't inferred from anything else. The second implies that 'basic beliefs' are justified by 'vanguard' science.

The first answer is to this effect: the m-paradigm's 'basic beliefs are arbitrary and may be assumed for any reason' (36).[15] They 'must be accepted at face value' and 'cannot be tested for truthfulness against some external norm'. They 'represent the ultimate benchmark against which *everything else* is tested' (14–15; italics in original). Unlike a k-paradigm, the basic beliefs of an m-paradigm are arbitrary, not accountable to anything. So 'everything else' is tested against something *arbitrary*. In which case, the choice of a research method is also arbitrary. On this view, the novice researcher could adopt a paradigm as the result of a coin toss, and *that* would be the benchmark against which her methodological decisions, along with everything else, are tested/evaluated.

The second answer is implicit in Chapter 1's attacks on positivism, which is said to be 'unfounded'; and it's confirmed in Chapter 2, which argues that the basic beliefs of the naturalistic paradigm are justified by cutting-edge 1970s science. So we're no longer talking about arbitrary postulates; we're talking about two sets of basic beliefs. One of them has failed the 'cutting-edge science' test, the other has passed.

Lincoln and Guba cite only one source for the 'vanguard thinking'. This is a monograph by Schwartz and Ogilvy (1979), commercially produced by SRI International.[16] It is a distillation of concepts 'currently emerging' in a wide variety of disciplines, including physics, linguistics, psychology, neuroscience, politics, and the arts. They argue that these concepts herald a 'new paradigm', and they abstract seven 'major characteristics' of this paradigm, each illustrated by 'vanguard thinking' in all these disciplines.

Example: *It is no longer sufficient to abstract out for intense study one or a few elements while holding everything else 'constant'.* This generalisation now looks horribly off target, but it wasn't plausible even at the time. It's true that 'decomposition' – studying the behaviour of a system's components separately – doesn't always work. But there are systems for which it does, though establishing exactly *which* systems can require trial and error (Bechtel & Richardson 2010). Science also makes extensive use of models and idealisations (Potochnik 2017, Khalifa *et al.* 2022); and, for these, 'abstracting out' is precisely the point. The claim that abstracting out is 'no longer sufficient' seriously misrepresents current scientific practice, scientific inference, and recent philosophy of science.[17]

But I'm not really bothered about whether Schwartz and Ogilvy were right or wrong. The interesting point is that Lincoln and Guba try to *justify* the naturalistic paradigm by referring to 'contemporary science'. This clearly doesn't reflect the claim that 'basic beliefs' are not accountable to anything else. If that were true, the fact that naturalism is implied by 'vanguard thinking' across the disciplines would be irrelevant. Equally, the fact that an alternative paradigm – positivism, say – is contradicted by 'vanguard thinking' would be beside the point.

So the second answer is very different from the first. On the 'axiom' view, basic beliefs are arbitrary. On the 'basic belief' view, naturalism can be defended by reference to modern science (and positivism can be attacked on the same grounds). It's not clear how this tension is resolved.

On the face of it, then, the novice researcher has three options. First, she can decide which paradigm is more in tune with her own antecedent beliefs (if any) about the nature of reality. Second, she can pick a paradigm at random, or because she likes the sound of it. Third, she can invest a lot of time in studying contemporary (2024, not 1979) science, the 'vanguard thinking' of *now*, and try to work out which ontological/epistemological beliefs best fit her evaluation. So her choice is determined *either* by what she already thinks, *or* by an arbitrary selection, *or* by a study of up-to-the-minute science. In the first two cases, her paradigm choice will not be anchored in anything capable of justifying it. In the third, it will require a detailed and massively time-consuming analysis of an extremely wide range of disciplines. It's not hard to see which of these three options is likely to prove the least attractive.

2.5 Fake positivism

Naturalistic Inquiry was instrumental in m-paradigms becoming canonical in the qualitative methods literature. However, it was also pivotal in the development of the qualitative literature's understanding of 'positivism'. In this respect, it is part of an historical arc that stretches back to the 1930s, an arc which involves the warping of positivism into what I will call *f-positivism*. This is a series of repeating tropes which purport to describe positivism. Many of them are untrue, or at best misleading. In effect, a false positivism has been devised, which bears little resemblance to the original, and it is the fictional version that is attacked. From here on, then, I'll distinguish between *positivism* and *f-positivism*. 'F' for 'fake'. I apologise for yet another prefix, but it will help to avoid ambiguity.

The warping of positivism into f-positivism began early with Ayer (1936), as a result of which positivism 'became identified with a rather simple-minded version of radical empiricism' (Friedman 1999: xiv). It continued with Kuhn (1962), who appears to have believed that his views on science contradicted those of the positivists. However, more recent scholarship has shown that he was not familiar with some of the most important logical positivist writers, and he attributed to them views they did not hold. Nevertheless, by 1976, and largely as a result of Kuhn's work, positivism was regarded as defunct.

The critical shift in the later stages of this historical arc was from the anti-metaphysical sensibility of the positivists to a metaphysical belief system. The positivists' approach to philosophy was self-consciously scientific, and averse to metaphysics. Carnap's project was to contribute to scientific progress 'while, at the same time, avoiding all the traditional metaphysical disputes and obscurities' (Friedman 2007: 12). Yet Lincoln and Guba helped to turn 'positivism' into the name of a set of dogmatic metaphysical beliefs. They helped to transform it into a *metaphysical creed*. In doing so, they set the seal on fake positivism, and rendered it canonical, at least for many qualitative researchers.

So the question of metaphysics represents the watershed difference between positivism and f-positivism. What started as an *anti*-metaphysical philosophical movement ends up being defined as a metaphysical ideology, consisting of ontological and epistemological 'basic beliefs'. So it is not merely that Lincoln and Guba (along with Ayer, Kuhn, and others) warped the history of early 20th-century philosophy. They also reintroduced the 'metaphysical disputes and obscurities' which, Carnap suggested, create 'serious obstacles to progress in both philosophy and the sciences', and which (as he anticipated) continue to do so.

A spot of *un*warping might be useful.

2.6   History rewritten

According to Lincoln and Guba, the positivists could not accommodate several developments in science and mathematics: relativity, quantum mechanics, and Gődel's incompleteness theorem. They say that 'much of Einstein's work, for example, would be considered nonscientific by positivists, who would hardly be persuaded by or interested in Einstein's thought (*gedanken*) experiments' (1985: 25). Similarly, determinism – allegedly a positivist assumption – was inconsistent with Heisenberg's Uncertainty Principle, and the indeterminism that followed from it (53–4). Finally, Gődel showed that 'no theory of mathematics asserted to be complete can also be internally consistent' (27), and this 'flies in the face of traditional positivist … postures so violently as to demand rejection' (118).

All this is mistaken. First, Lincoln and Guba clearly did not appreciate the pivotal importance positivists attached to Einstein, whose theory of relativity – with Hilbert's work on the foundations of geometry – created the main impetus for the development of logical positivism. 'Logical empiricism was conceived under the guiding star of Einstein's two theories of relativity' (Ryckman 2007: 194);[18] and Schlick's monograph, *Space and Time in Contemporary Physics*, published in 1917, was the 'first notable attempt at a philosophical elucidation of the general theory of relativity'. It 'received Einstein's enthusiastic praise for its philosophical conclusions' (*ibid*: 195).

Second, the logical positivists welcomed the advent of quantum mechanics (QM), and some of the quantum physicists themselves had positivist sympathies (Ryckman 2007: 217). One of its founders, Pascual Jordan, declared himself to be a 'radical positivist', and contributed to *Erkenntnis* (the journal of the Vienna Circle), embracing the end of materialism, mechanism, and causal determinism. As an anti-realist, and an enthusiastic opponent of metaphysics, he was fully attuned to the Circle's outlook (Beyler 2007). Meanwhile, Schlick (1932/1979) argued that the QM 'overthrow of causality' was not merely consistent with positivism but also 'evidence for the logical empiricist tenet that there are no necessary principles of empirical knowledge' (Ryckman 2007: 217). Reichenbach wrote extensively on quantum mechanics, as did Frank. Neither doubted that it was 'fully compatible with logical empiricism' (Frank 1936/1949).

Third, 'Gödel was himself a part-time participant in the Vienna Circle' (Friedman 1999), contributing to many of its discussions. Moreover, Carnap's work on meta-mathematics 'provided a crucial part of the background, in particular, for Gődel's own work in the early 1930s' (Friedman 2007: 8); while Gődel's results figure centrally in *The Logical Syntax of Language* (Carnap 1934/2002). Asked in 1975 whether there were any influences he would single out as important, Gődel referred explicitly to Carnap as one of them (Gődel 2003: 447).

Lincoln and Guba are oblivious to all this. Of course, the scholarship I have just drawn on was published several years after *Naturalistic Inquiry*. But what is interesting is that Lincoln and Guba do not hesitate to read off the historical 'facts' from their own definition of 'positivism' (f-positivism). This is what our paradigm-contrast tables say about 'positivism'. Therefore, this is what the logical positivists must have believed. Therefore, they must have been unable to accommodate Einstein, Heisenberg, and Gődel.

2.7   Positivism versus f-positivism

The previous section includes several claims which are at odds with f-positivism. The logical positivists, I've implied, were anti-realists, rejected causality, and embraced indeterminism. Rather surprising for a group of philosophers who, notoriously, are supposed to be 'objective realists' and 'causal determinists'. In this section, I will say a bit more about causality, and then review other claims, made routinely about f-positivism, which don't apply to the logical positivists.

2.7.1   Causality

One of the 'positivist' axioms, according to Lincoln and Guba (1985: 27) is the following: 'There are real causes, temporally precedent to or simultaneous with their effects.' They expand this by saying: 'Every action can be explained as the result (effect) of a real cause that precedes the effect temporally (or is at least simultaneous with it).' Similar claims about the 'positivist' view of causation appear regularly in the qualitative literature (recent examples: Bevir & Blakely 2018, Park *et al.* 2020). However, all of this is disconfirmed by the positivists' response to quantum physics. Schlick, for example, argued that the causal principle is 'neither true nor false, but good or bad, useful or idle'; and that the lesson of quantum mechanics is that 'this principle is bad, useless or idle, and incapable of fulfilment' (Schlick 1931/1979: 196). Reichenbach's early (1915) account of causation was Kantian: the principle of causality was a necessary condition of scientific knowledge, not an empirical claim. Later, however, he argued that the principle *is* an empirical claim – but one that has been falsified by quantum mechanics (Ryckman 2007: 214).

2.7.2   Realism and truth

For the f-positivists, there is a 'single, objective reality', and they have a correspondence theory of truth. In contrast, many logical positivists were anti-realists and had a coherentist view of truth (Young 1991). There are, of course, some exceptions. Schlick was a realist (Turner 1996) but of a fallibilist type;

he would probably be classified as a 'postpositivist' now. Feigl 'was the logical empiricist most eager to reconcile logical empiricism with some sort of realism' (Mormann 2007: 159). Most of the others, Carnap and Neurath in particular, were anti-realists of some kind, with pragmatic and instrumentalist leanings (Rowbottom 2011).

There is a prominent thread in logical positivism which sees the clash between realism and anti-realism as an example of outmoded metaphysics. Einstein was inclined to this sort of view: 'It appears to me that the "real" is an intrinsically empty, meaningless category' (quoted in Howard 1996: 131). In a similar way, Carnap thinks there is no well-defined question concerning realism versus idealism (Ricketts 2007). In this sense, Carnap is an 'ontological anti-realist' (Chalmers 2009): 'ontology' is not the name of a truth-seeking, reality-describing form of enquiry.

2.7.3   Verification

Methodologists following in Lincoln and Guba's wake have frequently complained about the positivists' verificationism, but have rarely explained what's supposed to be wrong with it. In its least demanding form, it is the claim that if an indicative sentence is to be considered information-providing, there must be actual or possible observations which have a bearing on its truth. In Carnap's (1928/1967) terms, 'experiential support' for the sentence must at least be conceivable. We know what experiential support would have a bearing on the truth of the sentence 'There is water on Mars.' But it's not clear what experiential support would have a bearing on the truth of the sentence 'The only things that truly exist are minds and their ideas.'

There are several more demanding versions of verificationism (an example is the claim that the *meaning* of a sentence is its *method* of verification). But they were not necessarily espoused by every positivist, or for significant lengths of time (Stadler 2007), and many positivists were critical of them (Neurath 1935/1983). In the recent methodological literature, verificationism is often assumed to be the idea that empirical truths can be established 'with certainty'. Carnap deals with this misconception explicitly: 'If by verification is meant a definitive and final establishment of truth, then no (synthetic) sentence is ever verifiable' (Carnap 1936: 420).

2.8   Recent methods writing

Fast forward. In this section, I'll do a quick review of how Lincoln and Guba's key concepts have fared in the past few years. They're still going strong.

First, 'paradigm' talk and metaphysics remain prominent in debates about qualitative methods, and the term 'paradigm' usually refers to what I've called m-paradigms, even when it is attributed to Kuhn. This is especially true of 'qualitative start-up' disciplines, those which initially lagged behind social science, education, nursing, and others.[19] Subjects such as marketing, management, accounting, leisure, sport and exercise, counselling, and several health-related disciplines, including medicine. For example, in an introduction to qualitative research in the *Journal of Graduate Medical Education*, Teherani *et al.* (2015: 669) say:

> Qualitative research starts from a fundamentally different set of beliefs—or paradigms—than those that underpin quantitative research. Quantitative research is based on positivist beliefs that there is a singular reality that can be discovered with the appropriate experimental methods … Constructivist researchers believe that there is no single reality, but that the researcher elicits participants' views of reality. Qualitative research generally draws on post-positivist or constructivist beliefs.

Note the identification of 'paradigms' with beliefs, and the 'underpinning' relation. 'Positivists' believe that there is a 'singular reality', constructivists don't. There is admittedly no direct reference to ontology or epistemology; but perhaps the authors, in a short introduction, don't want to frighten the horses. For the rest, this is clearly descended from *Naturalistic Inquiry*.

Another example, from media studies, is Brennen (2022), who asks an important question (12–13):

> You may wonder how you might go about selecting an appropriate theoretical framework, worldview or research paradigm to guide your work. I often tell my students that while researchers may try out a variety of perspectives, a theoretical framework usually picks you. What I mean by this is that each of you will develop a specific view of the world that makes sense to you. After some trial and error, each of you will discover a paradigm and/or conceptual perspective that fits with the specific way that you see the world.

This is close to the 'worldview' assumption but, potentially, it makes huge demands on students. Look, for example, at some of the questions Brennen suggests that her students ask themselves:

- What does objectivity mean to you?
- What is your view of the role of science in contemporary society?
- Do you believe that truth is relative?
- Are there cause-and-effect relationships that can be determined in people's behaviour?
- Do you think that reality is socially constructed?

Pernecky (2016) goes even further. He, too, thinks that the novice researcher must work out what her ontological and epistemological views are, and ask herself whether she agrees with statements like: 'Quantum mechanics undermines the notion of the thing-in-itself and also the possibility of absolute and universal truths.' Pernecky and Brennen both suggest that students should answer questions so difficult that the philosophical literature dealing with them is enormous. Inevitably, the student's response will be haphazard, or based on an extremely superficial understanding; or else it will require an intensive study of philosophy, social science, physics, and other scientific disciplines. This is part of Lincoln and Guba's legacy, the long-term consequence of the ambiguity between 'axioms' and 'beliefs' based on 'vanguard thinking'.

Even when we get the more innovative stuff, whether it's mixed methods, 'merging paradigms', or post-qualitative inquiry, the same basic framework remains in place. For example, since its inception, 'mixed methods' has been in search of its 'paradigm'. Is it pragmatism (Teddlie & Tashakkori 2009)? Is it the transformative paradigm (Mertens 2024)? Is it realism (Maxwell & Mittapalli 2010)? Is it the dialectical stance, dialectical pluralism, the performative approach, or decolonising paradigms (see various chapters in Shan 2024)? Does it combine different paradigms? For example, Bogna et al. (2020) attempt to merge critical realism and constructivism (though, on my reading, they tie themselves into impressively tangled knots). But it's still paradigms they're trying to merge, and ontology and epistemology are still the warp and weft.[20] Even with post-qualitative inquiry, we're still tracking paradigms. As an illustration, Østern et al. (2023) build on their 'friction-led research processes at the edges of qualitative research' to argue for an 'onto-epistemological shift' to a 'performative paradigm'. Kuhn is long since left behind, and we are surrounded by ever more complex ontologies, epistemologies and onto-epistemologies. However, the shades of Lincoln and Guba are still with us. It's still an m-paradigm we're after.[21]

As for positivism, there are plenty of writers who recognise that f-positivism is an invention (examples include Capaldi & Proctor 2005, Persson 2010, Maxwell 2012); and some discern positivist threads in constructivism and/or constructionism. A good example is Hibberd (2001), who points out that logical positivism and social constructionism are both conventionalist, and that 'certain features of Gergen's theory are clearly evident in the theories of Schlick, Reichenbach and Carnap' (297). Far more common, though, are paragraphs like this one (Ou et al. 2017: 2), which observes that:

> Positivism could be described as a belief system rooted in realism in which there is an undisputed physical reality governed by natural laws. It employs empirical and objective methods to uncover knowledge and relies on an optimistic view that the truth about reality can be discovered … Positivism presupposes that we live in a deterministic and mechanistic reality that can be improved through knowledge and technology.

This is not positivism but f-positivism. If applied to logical positivism, the passage contains a few half-truths and some routine misconceptions. It is just a reciting of the standard anti-f-positivist tropes.[22]

2.9   Where do we go from here?

In summary, *Naturalistic Inquiry* still provides the skeleton, the fundamental anatomy, that underlies all the 'moments', the innovations, the mixings, the mergings, the morphings, the accretions, the posts-, the onto-epistemological shifts. In the first instance, it represents constructivism, or at least one very popular form of constructivism, but some of its key ideas have also soaked into the qualitative methods writing of other -isms. The inescapable importance of ontology and epistemology. The pathologies of positivism. Transferability and trustworthiness. An aversion to generalisation and causation. In this book, I target Lincoln and Guba's constructivism, but there's a lot of other stuff in the same vicinity. Anything, in fact, which takes it as a truth universally acknowledged that someone in possession of a research idea must be in want of a paradigm.

But it's not just m-paradigms. I'm suggesting that qualitative methods can dispense with metaphysics altogether. Qualitative researchers shouldn't feel obliged to decide what their 'metaphysical beliefs' are. Truth is, they *can't*, given that (on my view) qualitative metaphysical sentences don't make sense. What the book sets out to do is not *demonstrate* this – there are no demonstrations to be had – but something closer to *provide sufficient examples, sufficient lines of sight, to make it possible for you to see it*. If I'm to persuade you that the qualitative metaphysical sentences cannot be parsed as referentially successful, reality-describing claims, you have to get a glimpse of it yourself; or at least get a glimmer of how it *might* be true. We have to discuss some of those sentences, and try to get them to mean something. And fail.

In doing so, we are disadvantaged by the fact that most people's starting assumption is that *of course* they mean something. How can they not? The words used are transparent in meaning, and they are arranged grammatically. What's the problem?

So here's the plan. The remaining two chapters in Part I introduce the main philosophical resources used in Part II. One is devoted to Wittgenstein, the other to Carnap. I explain what I'm taking from each of them and sketch the ways in which their ideas are used later in the book. Then, in Part II, I undertake a detailed examination of the words, phrases and sentences used in familiar constructivist tropes. Examples include 'There is a single objective reality' and 'There exist multiple constructed realities'. Most of us, at some time or another, have assumed that we understand what sentences like these are saying. I think that most of us have been wrong, and the primary purpose of Part II is to convey my own reasons for arriving at this conclusion. But those reasons do not consist of arguments, or clashes between -isms. They reflect my progressively frustrated attempts to pin down exactly what I meant when I told myself I believed that (for example) 'There is a single objective reality.'

I failed. In the nicest possible way, I hope you do too.

2.10   Concluding remark

I no longer believe that there is a single objective reality, but not because I believe that there are multiple constructed realities. I can't get either of these claims to make sense. The same goes for claims about the relation between 'knower' and 'known'. I can't get them to make sense either. Qualitative metaphysics, I now think, is an echo-chamber of non-sense.

Notes

1 This is subject to the 'unless and until' proviso mentioned in Section 1.4.
2 A quick reminder. The book is *exclusively* about the metaphysics of qualitative methods writing. Nothing I say should be generalised to any other metaphysical claims or genres.
3 According to Anne Wil-Harzing's website, Google Scholar has an average of 833 citations per book and 81 citations per book per year. See also Harzing (2011).
4 There is surprisingly little in Guba (1978) that anticipates *Naturalistic Inquiry*. He shows almost no interest in philosophy, he uses 'paradigm' to refer to procedures of inquiry rather than to a set of metaphysical beliefs, there is not a single reference to 'ontology', and he does not discuss Kuhn.
5 There is still an uncrossable boundary between (post-) positivism and the anti-positivist paradigms. 'Just as in the past, one must choose sides; one still cannot embrace both positivism and non-positivist perspectives' (Donmoyer 2006: 16).
6 This might seem like a glaringly unhistorical claim. However, Section 2.2 shows that Lincoln and Guba's version of 'paradigm' has almost nothing to do with Kuhn's; while Sections 2.5–2.7 suggest that their canonical version of 'positivism' bears very little resemblance to the real positivism.
7 Several different senses of the word were identified in *The Structure of Scientific Revolutions* (Masterman 1970), but later work (Kuhn 1970, 1974) does a great deal to clarify what he had in mind.
8 'Contemporary qualitative inquiry is firmly set in the grooves of paradigms' (Pernecky 2016: 16). Pernecky is, of course, referring to Lincoln and Guba-style paradigms. Not every form of qualitative inquiry is set in the these grooves, but quite a lot of it is.
9 This is Bohr's model, which replaced the 'solar system' model. 'Without its aid, one cannot even today write down the Schrodinger equation for a complex atom or molecule, for it is to the model, not directly to nature, that the various terms in that equation refer' (Kuhn 1993: 538).
10 I think Margolis (1993) is right to suggest that the difficulties involved in a transition from paradigm *A* to paradigm *B* are caused primarily by the cognitive habits induced by paradigm *A*. These habits enable the solving of puzzles while paradigm *A* is in force but create barriers to understanding why paradigm *B* might be better at explaining the 'crisis' anomalies of paradigm *A*. This is a different mechanism from 'incommensurability', which was arguably responsible for the idea that Kuhn's view implies relativism.

11 A k-paradigm is not an axiomatic system. There are no axioms, no theorems, no logical derivations. Kuhn (1974) is quite explicit about this, identifying shared examples as the core concept and rejecting the idea of 'rules'.

12 It's important to note that, in *Naturalistic Inquiry*, 'postpositivism' refers to the naturalistic paradigm. This is obviously at odds with its accepted meaning now. By the time of Guba (1990), the terminology has changed: 'postpositivism is best characterised as a modified version of positivism' (20).

13 This ambiguity can lead to double standards. For example, there's the claim that it's illegitimate for a positivist to criticise interpretivism, because she will be doing so from a positivist perspective. However, interpretivists are surprisingly relaxed about criticising positivists from their own perspective. Similarly, Lincoln and Guba argue that a paradigm's 'basic beliefs' cannot be tested against an 'external norm'; but their attacks on positivism 'test' it against several 'norms', and find it wanting.

14 Kuhn's concept of a paradigm does not have any problems of this kind. It does not confuse axioms with 'basic beliefs'.

15 Recall that Lincoln and Guba don't recognise the difference between axioms and 'basic beliefs'.

16 Lincoln and Guba (1985: 68) report that the monograph is 'a summary of a much larger collection of documents'. For many years, the monograph was very difficult to get hold of, and references to it tended to be 'cited in Lincoln and Guba'. However, it is now available on the internet. There can't be many texts as influential as *Naturalistic Inquiry* whose main source was so inaccessible for so long. There is still a bizarre sense of the book resting on a contribution that few people, other than Lincoln and Guba, have ever seen.

17 For more on this theme, see Section 11.6.

18 'Logical positivism' was associated with the Vienna Circle, and 'logical empiricism' with the Berlin Group. However, the current trend is to use 'logical empiricism' as a way of referring, broadly, to the family of views represented by both groups. See Limbeck-Lilienau and Uebel (2022), for example.

19 It's also true for volumes published with emerging scholars in mind, for example Pabel *et al.* (2021).

20 Shan (2022) distinguishes 'ontology-oriented' and 'axiology-oriented' philosophical foundations. The postpositivist position 'privileges' ontological assumptions, which drive its epistemology and axiology. In the transformative position, by contrast, axiological axioms take precedence, 'leading to' its ontology and epistemology. In both cases, however, the ontological and epistemological 'assumptions' are clearly inherited from Lincoln and Guba. 'There is a single, mind-independent reality…' (postpositivist); 'There are multiple realities that are socially constructed…' (transformative).

21 Of course, there are authors who have not succumbed to the paradigm/metaphysics orthodoxy. For example, Tsilipakos (2016) adopts a form of ordinary language philosophy derived from Austin and Wittgenstein. He is sceptical about 'ontological' claims, and is one of several writers classified as 'de-ontologizers' (Lohse 2021). His reasons are akin to mine. Ordinary words are 'conscripted' into 'doing ontology', as though their meanings were transparent and uniform across all circumstances. He shows that this conscripting looks plausible only because the ordinary uses of the expressions concerned are ignored. I think this is spot on.

A second example is Chafe (2023), who argues that the Guba tradition is dispensable. People currently practising qualitative research have learned to talk about it in the language of paradigms, but restricting qualitative studies 'only to what accords with the current qualitative paradigm greatly reduces the impact it could have'. And he concludes: 'we should seriously consider whether the discussion of paradigms still makes sense for most qualitative research projects' (9).

A third is Kelle and Reith (2023), who argue against 'paradigm-bound methodology', the idea that it is necessary to select a single paradigm as a preliminary to social research. They suggest that researchers can instead employ epistemological concepts, not as 'immutable givens' but as 'heuristic devices which are used to identify and solve methodological problems'. It's a less radical view than the one I adopt in this book, but there are some distinct echoes: 'Paradigms of the kind discussed here, which are meant as a faith basis of social research, represent creeds or confessions.'

Other authors in social theory said to be 'de-ontologizers' include Kivinen and Piiroinen (2006), van Bouwel and Weber (2008), and Lauer (2021). The latter adopts a neo-Carnapian position comparable to the one I elaborate in Chapter 4.

22 Constant repetition of 'f-positivism' might get annoying. In the rest of the book, I'll put 'positivism' in inverted commas when referring to what other writers mistakenly (in my view) describe as positivism.

References

Ayer, A. J. (1936). *Language, Truth and Logic*. London: Gollancz.

Bechtel, W., & Richardson, R. C. (2010). *Discovering Complexity: Decomposition and Localization as Strategies in Scientific Research*. Reissue Edition. Cambridge, MA: MIT Press.

Bevir, M., & Blakely, J. (2018). *Interpretive Social Science: An Anti-Naturalist Approach*. Oxford: Oxford University Press.

Beyler, R. H. (2007). Exporting the quantum revolution: Pascual Jordan's biophysical initiatives. In C. I. Zintzen, J. Ehlers, & J. Renn (Eds.), *Pascual Jordan (1902–1980): Mainzer Symposium zum 100. Geburtstag* (pp. 69–81). Berlin: Max Planck Institute for the History of Science.

Bogna, F., Raineri, A., & Dell, G. (2020). Critical realism and constructivism: Merging research paradigms for a deeper qualitative study. *Qualitative Research in Organizations and Management, 15*(4), 461–484.

Brennen, B. S. (2022). *Qualitative Research Methods for Media Studies*. Third Edition. New York: Routledge.

Capaldi, E. J., & Proctor, R. W. (2005). Is the worldview of qualitative inquiry a proper guide for psychological research? *American Journal of Psychology, 118*(2), 251–269.

Carnap, R. (1928/1967). *The Logical Structure of the World and Pseudoproblems in Philosophy*. Berkeley, CA: University of California Press.

Carnap, R. (1934/2002). *The Logical Syntax of Language*. Peru, IL: Open Court Publishing.

Carnap, R. (1936). Testability and meaning. *Philosophy of Science, 3*(4), 419–470.

Chafe, R. (2023). Rejecting choices: The problematic origins of researcher-defined paradigms within qualitative research. *International Journal of Qualitative Methods, 22*, https://doi.org/10.1177/16094069231165951

Chalmers, D. J. (2009). Ontological anti-realism. In D. J. Chalmers, D. Manley, & R. Wasserman (Eds.), *Metametaphysics: New Essays on the Foundations of Ontology* (pp. 77–129). Oxford: Oxford University Press.

Donmoyer, R. (2006). Take my paradigm… please! The legacy of Kuhn's construct in educational research. *International Journal of Qualitative Studies in Education, 19*(1), 11–34.

Frank, P. (1936/1949). Philosophical misinterpretations of quantum theory. In P. Frank (Ed.), *Modern Science and its Philosophy* (pp. 158–171). Cambridge, MA: Harvard University Press.

Friedman, M. (1999). *Reconsidering Logical Positivism*. Cambridge, UK: Cambridge University Press.

Friedman, M. (2007). Introduction: Carnap's revolution in philosophy. In M. Friedman & R. Creath (Eds.), *The Cambridge Companion to Carnap* (pp. 1–18). Cambridge, UK: Cambridge University Press.

Glaser, B. G., & Strauss, A. L. (1967). *The Discovery of Grounded Theory: Strategies for Qualitative Research*. Chicago: Aldine

Gödel, K. (2003). *Collected Works: Volume 4: Correspondence A-G*. New York: Oxford University Press.

Guba, E. G. (1990). The alternative paradigm dialog. In E. Guba (Ed.), *The Paradigm Dialog* (pp. 17–27). Newbury Park, CA: Sage.

Guba, E. G. (1978). *Toward a Methodology of Naturalistic Inquiry in Educational Evaluation*. Los Angeles: UCLA Graduate School of Education, University of California.

Hackley, C. (2020). *Qualitative Research in Marketing and Management: Doing Interpretive Research Projects*. Second Edition. Abingdon, UK: Routledge.

Harzing, A.-W. (2011). *The Publish or Perish Book: Your Guide to Effective and Responsible Citation Analysis*. Melbourne: Tarma Software Research.

Hesse-Biber, S. N. (2017). *The Practice of Qualitative Research: Engaging Students in the Research Process*. Third Edition. Los Angeles: Sage.

Hibberd, F. J. (2001). Gergen's social constructionism, logical positivism and the continuity error. Part 1: Conventionalism. *Theory and Psychology*, *11*(3), 297–321.

Howard, D. (1996). Relativity, Eindeutigkeit, and monomorphism: Rudolf Carnap and the development of the categoricity concept in formal semantics. In R. N. Giere & A. W. Richardson (Eds.), *Origins of Logical Empiricism* (pp. 115–164). Minneapolis, MN: University of Minnesota Press.

Kelle, U., & Reith, F. (2023). Strangers in paradigms!? Alternatives to paradigm-bound methodology and methodological confessionalism. *Forum: Qualitative Social Research*, *24*(1). https://doi.org/10.17169/fqs-17124.17161.14015

Khalifa, K., Millson, J., & Risjord, M. (2022). Scientific representation: An inferentialist-expressivist manifesto. *Philosophical Topics*, *50*(1), 263–291.

Kivinen, O., & Piiroinen, T. (2006). Toward pragmatist methodological relationism: From philosophizing sociology to sociologizing philosophy. *Philosophy of the Social Sciences*, *36*(3), 303–329.

Kuhn, T. S. (1962). *The Structure of Scientific Revolutions*. Chicago: University of Chicago Press.

Kuhn, T. S. (1970). Reflections on my critics. In I. Lakatos & A. Musgrove (Eds.), *Criticism and the Growth of Knowledge* (pp. 231–278). Cambridge, UK: Cambridge University Press.

Kuhn, T. S. (1974). Second thoughts on paradigms. In F. Suppe (Ed.), *The Structure of Scientific Theories* (pp. 459–482). Champaign, IL: University of Illinois Press.

Kuhn, T. S. (1993). Metaphor in science. In A. Ortony (Ed.), *Metaphor and Thought*. Second Edition (pp. 533–542). New York: Cambridge University Press.

Lauer, R. (2021). Instrumentalizing and naturalizing social ontology: Replies to Lohse and Little. *Philosophy of the Social Sciences*, *51*(1), 24–39.

Limbeck-Lilienau, C., & Uebel, T. (2022). Introduction. In T. Uebel & C. Limbeck-Lilienau (Eds.), *The Routledge Handbook of Logical Empiricism* (pp. 1–11). Abingdon, UK: Routledge.

Lincoln, Y. S., & Guba, E. G. (1985). *Naturalistic Inquiry*. Beverly Hills, CA: Sage.

Lohse, S. (2021). Ontological investigations of a pragmatic kind? A reply to Lauer. *Philosophy of the Social Sciences, 51*(1). https://doi.org/10.1177/0048393120916134

Margolis, H. (1993). *Paradigms and Barriers: How Habits of Mind Govern Scientific Beliefs*. Chicago: University of Chicago Press.

Masterman, M. (1970). The nature of a paradigm. In I. Lakatos & A. Musgrove (Eds.), *Criticism and the Growth of Knowledge* (pp. 59–89). Cambridge, UK: Cambridge University Press.

Maxwell, J. A. (2012). *A Realist Approach for Qualitative Research*. Thousand Oaks, CA: Sage.

Maxwell, J. A., & Mittapalli, K. (2010). Realism as a stance for mixed methods research. In A. Tashakkori & C. Teddlie (Eds.), *Sage Handbook of Mixed Methods in Social and Behavioral Research*: Second Edition. Thousand Oaks, CA: Sage.

Merriam, S. B., & Tisdell, E. J. (2016). *Qualitative Research: A Guide to Design and Implementation*. Fourth Edition. San Francisco: Jossey-Bass.

Mertens, D. (2024). The philosophical foundations of a transformative approach to mixed methods. In Y. Shan (Ed.), *Philosophical Foundations of Mixed Methods Research: Dialogues between Researchers and Philosophers* (pp. 30–53). Abingdon, UK: Routledge.

Mormann, T. (2007). The structure of scientific theories in logical empiricism. In A. Richardson & T. Uebel (Eds.), *The Cambridge Companion to Logical Empiricism* (pp. 136–162). Cambridge, UK: Cambridge University Press.

Neurath, O. (1935/1983). Pseudorationalism of falsification. In R. S. Cohen & M. Neurath (Eds.), *Otto Neurath: Philosophical Papers* 1913–1946. Dordrecht: D. Reidel.

Østern, T. P., Jusslin, S., Knudsen, K. N., Maapalo, P., & Bjorkøu, I. (2023). A performative paradigm for post-qualitative inquiry. *Qualitative Research, 23*(2), 272–289.

Ou, C. H. K., Hall, W. A., & Thorne, S. (2017). Can nursing epistemology embrace p-values? *Nursing Philosophy, 18*(4), e12173.

Pabel, A., Pryce, J., & Anderson, A. (Eds.). (2021). *Research Paradigm Considerations for Emerging Scholars*. Bristol, UK: Channel View Publications.

Park, Y. S., Konge, L., & Artino, A. R. (2020). The positivism paradigm of research. *Academic Medicine, 95*(5), 690–695.

Pernecky, T. (2016). *Epistemology and Metaphysics for Qualitative Research*. London: Sage.

Persson, J. (2010). Misconceptions of positivism and five unnecessary scientific theoretic mistakes they bring in their train. *International Journal of Nursing Studies, 47*(5), 651–661.

Potochnik, A. (2017). *Idealization and the Aims of Science*. Chicago: University of Chicago Press.

Ricketts, T. (2007). Tolerance and logicism: logical syntax and the philosophy of mathematics. In M. Friedman & R. Creath (Eds.), *The Cambridge Companion to Carnap* (pp. 200–225). Cambridge, UK: Cambridge University Press.

Rowbottom, D. P. (2011). The instrumentalist's new clothes. *Philosophy of Science, 78*(5), 1200–1211.

Ryckman, T. (2007). Logical empiricism and the philosophy of physics. In A. Richardson & T. Uebel (Eds.), *The Cambridge Companion to Logical Empiricism* (pp. 193–227). Cambridge, UK: Cambridge University Press.

Schlick, M. (1931/1979). Causality in contemporary physics. In H. Mulder & B. F. B. van de Velde (Eds.), *Moritz Schlick: Philosophical Papers Volume 2* (pp. 176–209). Dordrecht: D Reidel.

Schlick, M. (1932/1979). Positivism and realism. In H. Mulder & B. F. B. van de Velde (Eds.), *Moritz Schlick: Philosophical Papers Volume 2* (pp. 259–284). Dordrecht: D Reidel.

Schwartz, P., & Ogilvy, J. (1979). *The Emergent Paradigm: Changing Patterns of Thought and Belief. Analytical Report 7, Values and Lifestyle Program*. Menlo Park, CA: SRI International.

Shan, Y. (2022). Philosophical foundations of mixed methods research. *Philosophy Compass, 17*, e12804.

Shan, Y. (Ed.) (2024). *Philosophical Foundations of Mixed Methods Research: Dialogues between Researchers and Philosophers*. Abingdon, UK: Routledge.

Stadler, F. (2007). The Vienna Circle: context, profile, and development. In A. Richardson & T. Uebel (Eds.), *The Cambridge Companion to Logical Empiricism* (pp. 13–40). Cambridge, UK: Cambridge University Press.

Teddlie, C., & Tashakkori, A. (2009). *Foundations of Mixed Methods Research: Integrating Quantitative and Qualitative Approaches in the Social and Behavioral Sciences*. Thousand Oaks, CA: Sage.

Teherani, A., Martimianakis, T., Stenfors-Hayes, T., Wadhwa, A., & Varpio, L. (2015). Choosing a qualitative research approach. *Journal of Graduate Medical Education, 7*(4), 669–670.

Tsilipakos, L. (2016). *Clarity and Confusion in Social Theory: Taking Concepts Seriously*. Abingdon, UK: Routledge.

Turner, J. L. (1996). Conceptual knowledge and intuitive experience: Schlick's dilemma. In R. N. Giere & A. W. Richardson (Eds.), *Origins of Logical Empiricism* (pp. 292–308). Minneapolis, MN: University of Minnesota Press.

van Bouwel, J., & Weber, E. (2008). De-ontologizing the debate on social explanations: A pragmatic approach based on epistemic interests. *Human Studies, 31*(4), 423–442.

Young, J. O. (1991). Anti-realism and the Vienna Circle. *Synthese, 86*(3), 467–482.

3
WITTGENSTEIN'S METAPHILOSOPHY

The main aim of philosophy is to propose, and justify, theories. Not scientific theories, but metaphysical theories. Philosophy describes the most basic aspects of the world. It analyses fundamental concepts. It sets out to explain what causality is, what space and time are; what consciousness is, what knowledge is. Its goal is to work out whether such things as numbers, concepts, and properties really exist. What truth is. What *being* is. Whether there are essences. How many realities there are. Stuff like that.

Probably the first and most important thing to say about Wittgenstein's approach to philosophy is that he rejects everything in that first paragraph.[1] Philosophy can't do any of these things and shouldn't try. All it can do is assemble reminders about our use of language and show why 'metaphysical' questions can't be answered, at least not in the way philosophers have traditionally tried to answer them. '[W]e may not advance any kind of theory' (Wittgenstein 2009: §109). That includes metaphysical theories, which lead the philosopher into 'complete darkness' (Wittgenstein 1964: 18).

3.1   The second most important thing

Those who think that ontological and epistemological theories make sense vastly outnumber those who, like Wittgenstein, think they don't. Surely, that many people can't be wrong? In which case, it wouldn't be unreasonable to say: 'So much the worse for Wittgenstein, then'. However, if we put the assumption that 'a substantial majority is more likely to be right than wrong' into abeyance for the time being, and explore the discrepancy a bit further, it's clear that there are four questions that need to be answered. In Wittgenstein's view:

DOI: 10.4324/9781003306382-4

i   Why do metaphysical theories not make sense?
ii   Why do metaphysicians believe they do?
iii Why do philosophers regard metaphysics as a legitimate project?
iv   Why are they unable to see (what he thinks is) the problem?

Surprisingly, all four questions can be answered in exactly the same way. According to Wittgenstein:

We don't understand our use of language.

… where 'we' refers to most philosophers, most qualitative methodologists, and almost everybody else. I think, in fact, that this is the second most important thing we can say about Wittgenstein's approach to philosophy. We don't understand our use of language.[2] So brief a statement, of course, hides the nuance, the detail, the numerous variations on the theme. But we'll get to those.

It's essential, though, not to get hold of the wrong end of the stick. Wittgenstein does *not* mean that we don't understand *how to use* language. We understand that perfectly well, and on a minute-by-minute basis it rarely gives us any trouble. What he means is that when we *reflect* on our use of language, when we stop and think about it, we get things wrong. As long as we're not analysing it, we know how to use language in all its complexity. But if asked to explain it, we over-simplify, over-generalise, overlook.

Wittgenstein constantly calls attention to this. 'A main source of our failure to understand is that we don't have an overview of the use of our words' (Wittgenstein 2009: §122). 'Language is a labyrinth of paths. You approach from *one* side and you know your way about; you approach the same place from another side and no longer know your way about' (Wittgenstein 2009: §203). 'Philosophy is a struggle against the bewitchment of our understanding by the resources of our language' (Wittgenstein 2009: §109). He points out that, although we learn how to use words, we don't learn how to *describe* that use. When discussing thought and thinking, for example, he says: 'We are not at all *prepared* for the task of describing the use of the word "to think". (And why should we be? What is such a description useful for?)' (Wittgenstein 1981: §111). The point: when we're learning to use language, no-one says: 'Now I'm going to teach you how to describe language use, because you're going to find that *really* handy.'

So that's the two important things. If you put them together, you get a glimpse of how revolutionary Wittgenstein is:

[A] Philosophy cannot ask or answer metaphysical questions.

[B] We don't recognise this because we don't understand our use of language.

Everything hangs on not understanding our use of language. I mean, yes, it is a ridiculous claim. No-one likes it. Hardly anyone believes it. But, actually, I think it's true.

3.2   The o'clock construction

'It's 5 o'clock on the sun', from Wittgenstein (2009: §350), was used in Section 1.3 to illustrate what I meant by a 'referentially unsuccessful sentence'. It *seems* to say something intelligible, it *seems* to make a statement, but it doesn't. Examined more closely, it makes no sense.[3] The o'clock construction is contingent on certain technicalities. It indexes the apparent position of the sun, as seen from a specific location on the earth's surface, using a system which divides the day into two 12-hour segments. It can be used at any point on earth, except the poles.[4] But, by the same token, it can't be applied to the sun – given that, *on the surface of the sun*, you can't look up and see 'where the sun is'. In other words, 'It's 5 o'clock on the sun' doesn't make sense because an application condition, limiting the expression's use to locations on the earth, doesn't hold.

The point of the illustration was this. I'll be arguing, throughout Part II, that the metaphysical sentences supposedly serving as research 'underpinnings' are *not unlike*: 'It's 5 o'clock on the sun.' They seem to say something … but don't. Subject to certain qualifications, the reason for their referential failure is the same as in the case of 'It's 5 o'clock on the sun'. They employ familiar expressions and constructions in circumstances where a crucial application condition doesn't apply. And this, I'll suggest, is one of the principal ways – though not the only way – in which 'we don't understand our use of language'. There's a sense in which we 'forget' the application conditions of the expressions we employ.

However, it's not quite as simple as that (it never is). The claim that '"It's 5 o'clock on the sun" doesn't make sense' is only a provisional conclusion. It is, we might say, the default conclusion, pending further developments and conversations.[5] Such as:

Reader: Suppose there was a clock on the sun that said '5 o'clock'. I mean, if that were physically possible. Wouldn't that be '5 o'clock on the sun'?

Me: No, that would just be 'a clock on the sun pointing to 5 o'clock'. It wouldn't be *5 o'clock on the sun*. Comparison: I can imagine a clock pointing to 5 o'clock on M51-ULS-1b.[6] But I've no idea what it would mean to say 'It's 5 o'clock on M51-ULS-1b.'

Reader: But suppose we could actually live on the sun. There would have to be some way of telling the time, so then it *could* be 5 o' clock on the sun. As a practical project, it's bonkers. But it's not inconceivable.

Me: Fine, it's conceivable. But you can't just leave it at that. It tells us nothing. The question is whether you can explain how 'telling the time on the sun' would work. What criteria would justify saying 'It's 5 o'clock now'? Just saying 'it's conceivable' is like sprinkling fairy dust, and saying 'it'll be fine, don't worry'.

Reader: Look, I understand the game you're playing here. You want to argue that we can't extend the use of words and expressions beyond the limits of so-called 'ordinary' language. So that you can then say: 'Metaphysics does precisely that kind of extending; therefore it's wrong.'

Me: Not in the least. Wittgenstein has no objection to novel uses. Neither do I. But if you're going to introduce a novel use, we need to understand what its application conditions are.

Reader: You can't expect me to know that for '5 o'clock on the sun'. It's far too technical. I'm not an astronomer.

Me: It doesn't need to be astronomical. Suppose we decide that 'sun time' will, by stipulation, be tied to London time. There's a British space station on the sun, say, and it keeps London time. So 'It's 5 o'clock on the sun' is equivalent to 'It's 5 o'clock in London.'

Reader: Well, there you are, then. It *is* conceivable, just like I said.

Me: I didn't deny that. The point is, we now have an application condition. I now know what 'It's 5 o'clock on the sun' *means*. I can finally understand what's being said when somebody tells me: 'It's 5 o'clock on the sun.' It's been given a sense it didn't have before.

So the key idea is: there are application conditions (Thomasson 2015) for the use of any expression. It is perfectly legitimate to propose exceeding them, *provided* you explain what the application conditions will be for the new use. Saying 'It's a metaphor', or 'it's conceivable…', and leaving it at that doesn't help.[7] It's a form of wishful thinking: 'In-one-bound-she-was-free.' If you can back it up with a clear explanation of the new application condition(s), that's absolutely fine. If you can't, or you don't think it's necessary, you're part of the problem not the solution.[8]

Put another way: if you don't tell me how you're proposing to use an expression, how do you expect me to understand what you're saying? In §350, Wittgenstein's interlocutor says:

> 'You surely know what "It's 5 o'clock here" means; so you also know what "It's 5 o'clock on the sun" means. It means simply that it is just the same time there as it is here when it's 5 o'clock.'

We will find this kind of line cropping up at various times in Part II. 'You surely know what "reality" means; so you also know what "multiple realities" means. It means simply that there is more than one of what you're referring to when you talk about "reality".' Basically, the new use is portrayed as the *same as the old one*. But it can't be, because the expression's terms and conditions have been exceeded. So we need to know what the new terms and conditions are.

3.3   Language and forgetting

In thinking that 'It's 5 o'clock on the sun' makes a statement – one that can be true or false – we 'forget' the o'CLOCK construction's application conditions: that it can only be used in reference to a location on Earth. I place 'forget' in inverted commas because this is an unusual kind of forgetting. If you forget the name of a film star, for example, you can't tell a friend who was in the film you saw yesterday. 'It was what's-her-name, the one who was in *Thingummy* and *X-Men*.' 'Ah,' says the friend, 'you mean Halle Berry.' The forgetting in cases like this is, temporarily, a disabling one. You can't use the name in your description of the film, because that is precisely what it is you've forgotten. Usually, however, this is a temporary problem. Yesterday you remembered the name, tomorrow you'll remember it. Just not today.

The kind of forgetting in question with language use is different. It's not disabling. This is the point that Wittgenstein is making when he says: 'You approach from *one* side and you know your way about; you approach the same place from another side and no longer know your way about.' The side from which you *do* know your way about is the side of everyday speaking, listening, writing, reading: when you're using language without really thinking about it, and certainly without theorising. The side from which you *don't* know your way about is the side of reflection; the side of taking a step back, and theorising, generalising, or philosophising.

Here's an example. Health professionals often talk about 'fostering hope' in their patients. Underlying this project is a certain picture of hope. It implies that it is a psychological something-or-other which resides, or manifests itself, in the individual. This something-or-other has been described in various ways: an emotion, a cognitive process, a state of mind, a disposition, an instinct, a basic need, an inner power, a theological virtue, a multidimensional life force, and transitional dynamic possibilities within uncertainty. Although these conceptions of hope are diverse, they do have things in common. In every case, the implication is that hope is just one kind of thing; it's something that can be characterised universally; it's an 'inner' state of the person; it's a mental phenomenon, or perhaps a spiritual one. 'Hope' is the name of this internal something. The various theories of hope, in both health care and psychology, all presuppose this 'picture' of a determinate inner state, and several 'hope scales' have been devised on that basis.[9]

The picture does fit many 'hope' uses. For example, the following can be construed in this way:

(1) I hope to climb Ben Nevis.

(2) Hope springs eternal.

(3) As darkness fell, hope faded.

(4) New Orleans is a city without hope.

However, it doesn't fit examples like this:

(5) Mike hasn't a hope of getting the job.

(6) There's not a hope in hell that Aya will keep her mouth shut.

(7) It's a system that scientists say has no hope of working.

(8) The position paper cannot hope to answer all the specifics.

(9) The Bears can't hope to win anything playing like this.

In all these examples, there is no reference to anyone's state of mind, or to any mental process or power. In (5), it is *not* being claimed that Mike does not want to get the job, or that he doesn't think he can. In fact, (5) might be true even if Mike 'hopes' to get the job. Similarly, (6) could be true even if some of those being addressed 'hope' that Aya *will* keep her mouth shut. In both cases, it is possible to substitute 'chance' for 'hope' without changing the meaning. The same applies to (7). We can't substitute 'chance' in (8) or (9), given that 'hope' is being used as a verb. However, the same sense is involved: there is no chance that the position paper will include every last detail, and there is no chance of the Bears winning. The message is the same in each case. 'This is not going to happen.' No states of mind are referred to. In any case, systems and position papers don't *have* states of mind.

The theories of hope miss this aspect of use altogether. Nor is this a footling matter, easily dismissed as marginal. When patients with potentially fatal conditions ask 'Is there any hope?', they are not asking whether they have a certain state of mind – presumably they would know – or whether the health care professional has that state of mind. They are asking whether there is any *chance* of them being cured, or any chance of them surviving for longer than the prognosis suggests.

It turns out that the word 'hope' has different functions in different grammatical constructions: positive or negative statements; indicatives or interrogatives; as a count noun, as a mass noun; singular or plural uses; first person and third person uses of the verb; with or without ellipsis.[10] If we 'forget' this complex pattern of use, the result is that our theories of hope are lop-sided. We imagine that we have provided an analysis of *hope* when, in fact, our accounts are based on a narrowly selective range of the word's uses.

There is a kind of forgetfulness here. When theorising about hope, we forget most of the ways in which the word is used. Wittgenstein (1963: §127) says: the 'work of the philosopher consists of assembling reminders for a particular purpose'.[11] 'Assembling reminders' can sound trivial; but tracing the pattern of usage, even for an apparently simple word like 'hope', requires a lot of work, and a refusal to cut corners. How many people, when asked about 'hope', mention its use as a synonym for 'chance'? Yet this sense is perfectly familiar. It's just that when we start theorising, we overlook it. So 'assembling reminders' is coming at things from the 'knowing your way about' side. It is retrieving what you can't fail to *know*, even if you find it hard to *see* (Baz 2020). It's remembering what you forgot.[12]

3.4 The craving for generality

Each of the last two sections has sketched an example of 'not understanding our use of language'. In Section 3.2 it was a case of not understanding – that is, forgetting – the application conditions of a linguistic construction, the o'clock construction. In Section 3.3, it was a matter of overlooking a large chunk of the pattern of usage associated with the word 'hope'. In both these examples, and in lots more (as we'll see), the forgetting-overlooking-not-understanding theme is sustained, and indeed propelled, by what Wittgenstein (1964: 17) calls 'the craving for generality'.

This is an ingrained preference for explanations that cover every aspect, every instance, of a particular phenomenon. So, for example, the interlocutor in Wittgenstein (2009: §350) argues:

> 'You surely know what "It's 5 o'clock here" means; so you also know what "It's 5 o'clock on the sun" means. It means simply that it is just the same time there as it is here when it's 5 o'clock.'

Or, to put it differently, the o'clock construction must always mean the same – whatever location is inserted into it. The craving for generality requires this. Similarly, the word 'hope' must always have the same function – whatever its morphological form, whatever construction it appears in. Hope itself must always be the same type of 'inner something'.

In brief: a word always means the same, whatever construction it occurs in; and a construction always means the same, whatever words are inserted into it. The craving for generality.

Wittgenstein attributes the craving to four philosophical confusions. I'll mention just two of them. First, there is 'the tendency to look for something in common to all the entities which we commonly assume under a general term' (Wittgenstein 1964: 17). This clearly applies to the word 'hope' and reinforces the assumption that its job is always to designate a mental state. But sentences (5) to (9), the reminders assembled in Section 3.3, show that this assumption is well wide of the mark. Second:

> Philosophers 'constantly see the method of science before their eyes, and are irresistibly tempted to ask and answer questions in the way science does. This tendency is the real source of metaphysics, and leads the philosopher into complete darkness'.
>
> *(Wittgenstein 1964: 18)*

The 'method of science' to which Wittgenstein is referring is the search for 'underlying explanations', theories which apply generally to all instances of the phenomenon. Physicists formulate the 'laws' of motion; chemists discover the basic structure of substances such as water (H_2O) and elements such as gold (atomic number 79). This method works brilliantly well with anything in the physical world. Metaphysics, however, is the project of using the same method for mental and abstract 'objects'.[13] It involves treating *hope* and *truth* by analogy with physical things, like water or gold. It assumes that 'underlying explanations' of *hope* and *truth* can be found – in the form of definitions, structures, natures, essences. It is this craving for general theories of *hope*, *truth*, and other non-physical concepts, that leads to 'complete darkness'.

The 'complete darkness' passage brings us back to the opening paragraphs of this chapter. Wittgenstein doesn't do theory, he doesn't do metaphysics; and metaphysics as a continuation of science is precisely the problem. You can't look for general, law-like theories for *hope* and *truth* in the way you can for gold and water. Words like 'water' and 'gold' designate objects, substances, structures, mechanisms. Words like 'hope' and 'truth' don't. Ignoring this wrinkle, metaphysicians opt to treat *hope* and *truth* as objects anyway – but *objects of a non-physical kind*. This is the picture of philosophy that Wittgenstein rejects.

3.5 Against the grain

Here is one kind of reaction to the discussion so far.

Reader: Why *can't* mental states and abstract objects be studied in the way scientists study physical phenomena? Why can't they have structures, natures, essences? Why can't we treat them as non-physical objects? It's all very well Wittgenstein 'rejecting' this approach to philosophy, and tut-tutting about the 'craving for generality', but what are his arguments against it?

Me: Well, there's a burden-of-proof issue here, isn't there? 'Why can't mental states and abstract whatevers be treated as non-physical objects?' I might ask: What makes you think they can? Why do you assume that 'mental state' terms and abstract nouns designate objects of some kind, comparable to physical objects? What are your arguments for *that?*

Reader: 'Give me a reason why they can't' seems more reasonable than 'Give me a reason why they can.'

Me: Only if your default assumption is that anything and everything we talk about is likely to be an object of some sort, including thought, understanding, memory, knowledge, experience, proposition, truth, property, meaning, cause, and so on.

Reader: But my question is: what's wrong with that? What are Wittgenstein's arguments against it?

Me: Arguments aren't Wittgenstein's thing. If he doesn't do theories, he doesn't need arguments. You only get a sense of his approach by examining his examples. Which are legion.

Reader: So why are we bothering? Surely philosophy is about presenting arguments and evaluating them. Does Wittgenstein really want to give that up as well?

Me: Basically, yes. Metaphysicians use language. The *only* way you can see that there might be a problem with *how* they use it is to work through examples. There is no general argument to the effect that certain uses are 'wrong', or 'nonsense'; or that the application conditions for the use of certain terms have been changed, forgotten, or gone AWOL; or that certain terms have been introduced with no application conditions at all. You have to see it for yourself in each individual case.

The examples in Part II of this book are the see-for-yourself cases most relevant to the metaphysics of qualitative research, and getting down and dirty with them is the only way to see what Wittgenstein has in mind when he remarks: 'What *we* do is to bring words back from their metaphysical to their everyday use' (Wittgenstein 2009: §116).

However, this is not a project that appeals to many people, especially those who are looking for theories, arguments, conclusions. Wittgenstein was very much aware of this. 'I am trying to recommend a certain sort of investigation… [T]his investigation is immensely important and very much *against the grain* of some of you' (Wittgenstein 1989: 103). He even describes this reluctance to engage in 'grammatical' investigation as a 'prejudice', although 'it is not a *stupid* prejudice' (Wittgenstein 2009: §340). Still, as ever, the reader has a choice. If the idea of such an investigation is too much in conflict with your own understanding of what philosophy is, there's a ton of stuff out there you'll find more congenial.

The rest of this chapter provides a general sketch of five different, but related, ways of 'forgetting', or 'going astray', in our understanding of how we use language:

- Disregarding application conditions of familiar grammatical construction (Section 3.6)
- Forgetting application conditions for newly introduced expression (Section 3.7)
- New use of an expression, introduced without application conditions (Section 3.8)
- Misunderstanding pleonastic entities (Section 3.9)
- Narrowly selective attention to a familiar term's pattern of usage (Section 3.10)

My classification is somewhat artificial – there are plenty of overlaps – and there are more 'not knowing your way about' scenarios than just five. But the ones I describe here are those which are most relevant to the qualitative metaphysics examples discussed in Part II.[14]

3.6 Disregarding application conditions of familiar grammatical construction

To explain what I mean by this, I'll refer one more time to 'It's 5 o'clock on the sun', and then move on to other examples. The sentence incorporates a familiar construction, the O'CLOCK construction, which permits the user to specify the time at a particular location. A condition of the use of the construction is that the location in question must be on the surface of the earth (other than at the poles). The reasons for this are technical but boil down to the fact that O'CLOCK indexes the apparent position of the sun at that location. Hence, 'It's 5 o'clock on the sun' makes no sense – it is referentially unsuccessful – unless and until a new rule, an alternative application condition, is explicitly introduced.[15]

I'll now consider the application conditions of the LET ALONE construction, first analysed in a landmark paper by Fillmore et al. (1988). Some examples:

(10) She wouldn't lend me 50p let alone £50.

(11) He couldn't walk 100 yards at the moment, let alone five miles.

(12) I can't remember what I did yesterday, let alone last Saturday.

(13) We haven't got enough material for an article, let alone a whole book.

(14) I doubt he's got GCSEs, let alone a PhD.

Technically, the expression 'let alone' is a kind of conjunction, its function being to co-ordinate a pair of grammatically equivalent constituents (in these examples: sums of money, distances, days, documents, qualifications). The conditions associated with the LET ALONE construction include both the following: (a) it has what Fillmore *et al.* call 'negative polarity': the verb in each case is a negative one; (b) there is an implied scalar relation between the co-ordinated items. £50 is more than 50p, five miles is further than 100 yards, a PhD is a more advanced qualification than GCSEs. Importantly, the item referring to the 'more extreme', or the 'less likely', outcome is the one that *follows* 'let alone'.[16]

These two conditions correspond, roughly, to the 'only on Earth' condition associated with the O'CLOCK construction. Infringing against either of them creates a sentence that 'makes no sense'. It fails to make a statement; it is referentially unsuccessful. For example, (15) and (16) infringe against the 'negative polarity' condition; (17) and (18) infringe against the 'less likely outcome' condition.

(15) She would lend me 50p, let alone £50.

(16) He could walk 100 yards at the moment, let alone five miles.

(17) She wouldn't lend me £50, let alone 50p.

(18) He couldn't walk five miles at the moment, let alone 100 yards.

As with 'It's 5 o'clock on the sun', these sentences prompt an 'it makes no sense' reaction. This has to be the default conclusion, but it's only provisional. It might turn out that there are contexts – possibly we could invent some – in which these sentences *do* make sense. However, unless and until such an explanation is forthcoming, and the relevant scenarios are described, the default conclusion remains in place.

The relevance of these examples lies in the fact that qualitative metaphysicians, in using language, use grammatical constructions. One prominent example is the EXISTENTIAL THERE construction.[17] Sentences starting with 'There is…' or 'There exist…' are often employed to articulate the 'ontological beliefs' associated with Lincoln and Guba-style paradigms, particularly the numerous variations on 'There is a single objective reality' and 'There are multiple socially constructed realities'. In Chapters 5 and 6, I'll examine these 'ontological' sentences and show how they infringe against the construction conditions of EXISTENTIAL THERE. I will argue that, just as inserting 'the sun' into the O'CLOCK construction makes no sense, so inserting 'reality' or 'realities' into the EXISTENTIAL THERE construction makes no sense. As always, this conclusion is provisional. However, until qualitative metaphysicians explain how they are using EXISTENTIAL THERE in this context – explain what new application conditions they have adopted, and why – the 'makes no sense' conclusion is the only one we can draw.

This gives rise to an interesting paradox, because a lot of people believe that there are multiple realities (and some, no doubt, believe that there is only one). At least they *believe* they believe it. However, if the 'ontological' sentences don't make sense, how can that be? What precisely is it they believe? In Section 4.8, I'll suggest that they are subject to what Cappelen (2013) calls an 'illusion of thought': they believe that a sentence which doesn't make sense… *does* make sense, and they assume that it makes a statement which they *do* believe.[18]

A parallel case: compare someone who says about 'Colourless green ideas sleep furiously': 'Yes, that makes sense, and I believe the statement it makes.' Cappelen thinks that this kind of illusion could be common in philosophy: people imagining they believe something which is in fact nonsense. This won't be a popular view, as 'the claim that a certain pattern of speech is nonsense is bound to be resisted by those engaging in that speech' (Cappelen 2013: 34). Including, no doubt, writers of qualitative methods texts.

3.7   Forgetting application conditions for new expression

Years ago, there was a philosophical debate about *sense data*.[19] Ayer (1940), in a classic discussion, and drawing largely on the argument from illusion, suggested that objects such as 'pens and cigarettes' are not 'directly perceived'. Rather, we 'directly perceive sense-data', out of which we 'construct' the world of material things.

At one point in his account, he considers the possibility that the 'sense data' language and the 'material thing' language are just alternative ways of speaking. For example, when we say that a blue object *looks* green in a certain light, or that a circular coin *appears* elliptical when viewed from a certain angle, we can translate these statements into the sense-datum language, and instead say that we '*directly perceive* a green sense datum', or that we '*directly perceive* an elliptical sense datum'. Once we have done that, we can generalise to 'veridical' as well as 'non-veridical' perception. I don't 'directly perceive' a tomato, I 'directly perceive' a round, red sense datum.

But is this, Ayer wonders, no more than a linguistic shift, a change of vocabulary? I might just 'prefer to say' (for reasons based on the argument from illusion) that I 'directly perceive' the sense datum, instead of saying I 'directly perceive' the tomato. In the terminology of this chapter, this shift is justified by an application condition: 'Whenever you see a tomato, it is legitimate to state that you "directly perceive a round, red sense datum"; and you are hereby licensed to do so'.[20]

So far, so good. The problems begin when you *forget the application condition* and begin to think of sense data as somehow 'real'. Instead of 'sense data' talk being a mere *façon de parler*, the sense data themselves become ontologically robust. After all, the claim that you are 'directly perceiving a sense datum' *seems* to refer to an object that you are perceiving. It may not be an object familiar to the layperson, but it does appear to be an object of some kind. At this point, a series of tricky questions arise: What *are* sense data? How are they related to the material world? Are they 'private' to each individual? And if we never 'directly perceive' material things, how can we be sure there is a world of material things at all? Is each of us 'alone' in our own sense-datum 'reality'?

Several philosophers have commented on this slide from linguistic fancy footwork to serious ontological possibilities, accompanied by philosophical bewilderment. Ayer comments on it himself but opts finally for 'real' sense-data and a constructed 'world'. More recently, Sellars (1956) suggested that sense datum language could be construed as a code. It *seems* to refer to a new kind of object which is, let's say, red; but in fact it doesn't. It is just an alternative way of talking about seemings, lookings, and appearings in ordinary English. A 'sense datum' is not a new kind of *thing*, and the expression 'red sense datum' is not a reference to a red-coloured object. It is just a code we apply to any situation in which, as described in ordinary English, an object *looks* red. The slide is from a (perhaps convenient) way of referring to the way things *look*, to the assumption that we have discovered a new kind of object. Sellars thinks this was the source of the confusion about the term 'sense datum', and the empty debates it gave rise to.[21]

The relevance of this section to Part II. In Chapter 3 of *Naturalistic Inquiry*, Lincoln and Guba (1985) introduce (their own use of) the expression 'multiple realities' by defining a clear application condition (obviously, they don't put it like that).[22] Essentially, what they do is this: tie the expression to several examples of 'people not experiencing things in the same way'. It is, of course, a truism that people don't see eye-to-eye all the time, and it's difficult to imagine that anyone, ever, has not realised that it happens a lot. Lincoln and Guba introduce 'multiple realities' as a shorthand way of referring to this phenomenon (much as Ayer introduces 'sense data' as a way of referring to the phenomenon of 'looking', 'seeming' and 'appearing').

There can be no objection to using 'multiple realities' in accordance with this condition, provided your audience understands that this is what you're doing. Halfway through the chapter, however, Lincoln and Guba switch abruptly to 'ontology' mode and start to talk as if 'multiple realities' actually exist. They switch, in other words, from using the expression as a convenient linguistic device, shorthand for 'not always experiencing things in the same way', to assuming that it *refers*. Suddenly, it has ontological significance. They do this without warning, without explanation, and without any attempt to modify the application condition. Inevitably, tricky questions arise, and the chapter concludes with a sifting of the ontological options: 'objective reality', 'constructed reality', 'no reality at all', and so on.

The parallel with the Sellars' discussion should be clear. Just as Ayer switches from 'sense datum' as a way of referring to seemings, lookings, and appearings, to 'sense datum' as the name of an ontologically robust *thing*, so

Lincoln and Guba switch from 'multiple realities' as a way of talking about different views and interpretations, to 'multiple realities' as an ontological description of *how things are*. Chapter 6 provides a less sketchy account.

3.8 New use of an expression, introduced without application conditions

Sellars (1956: 264) notes that it would take 'an almost superhuman effort' to stop oneself sliding into the assumption that 'codes' had the same use as they do in ordinary English – the assumption that 'red sense datum' and 'multiple realities' refer to things that actually exist. Indeed, the fact that they don't might never occur to you, even if you were the one who introduced the code in the first place. But given the contexts in which they are introduced, these words don't refer to anything.

This is a special case of the idea that, if it's the 'same' word, then it must have the same meaning, the same function: 'As if the meaning were an aura the word brings along with it and retains in every kind of use' (Wittgenstein 2009: §117). If you put it to them explicitly, most people deny that they believe this; but, in practice, most of us slip too easily into the *same-word-same-meaning* mindset. In science, the appropriation of ordinary words as technical terms is not uncommon and is generally accompanied by a careful specification of the new use's application conditions. However, when new uses of familiar expressions are introduced in other contexts – philosophy, or qualitative methods – the new application conditions are not always explained.

I think there are two main types of case: (a) when a new use of a familiar term is introduced, without any attempt to specify its application conditions, and often without the author realising that it *is* a new use; (b) when the application conditions of the new use *are* specified but are ignored by readers. There are some interesting examples of (b),[23] but more relevant to this book are examples of (a).

One, related to the discussion in the previous section, is Austin's (1962) take-down of Ayer on 'sense data'. According to Ayer (1940: 7), philosophers 'are not, for the most part, prepared to admit that such objects as pens or cigarettes are ever directly perceived'. As Austin suggests, the general doctrine is: 'we never see or otherwise perceive (or 'sense'), or anyhow we never *directly* perceive or sense, material objects... but only sense data' (2). But the obvious question is: what does 'directly perceive' *mean*? It's not as if it's an expression that is well-known and frequently used. And yet, Austin says, 'We are given no explanation or definition of this new use – on the contrary, it is glibly trotted out as if we were all quite familiar with it already' (19).

Austin spends a few pages sketching circumstances in which we *might* refer to 'direct' or 'indirect' perception. But none of these circumstances gives any support to the claim that the ordinary seeing of pens and cigarettes can never be 'direct'. So whatever the application conditions for Ayer's new use are, he hasn't explained them. In which case, it is simply not clear what *statement* 'Pens and cigarettes are never directly perceived' is making. As I keep saying, there is nothing wrong with introducing a new technical term, one that consists of a familiar word used in an unfamiliar way (in this case, 'directly'). However, 'if we use new vocabulary or give special meaning to existing vocabulary, we're bound to do so clearly and explicitly' (Maddy 2017: 112). And this is what Ayer fails to do.

The relevance. In Chapters 7 and 8, I will discuss further examples of familiar words – 'constructed', 'construction', 'know', 'known' – which are introduced into unfamiliar places without any specification of the new application conditions. In the context of qualitative metaphysics, Austin's comment would still be apt: 'We are given no explanation or definition of this new use – on the contrary, it is glibly trotted out as if we were all quite familiar with it already.' In Chapter 7, I will examine Guba's use of 'constructed' and 'construction' in *The Constructivist Credo* (Lincoln & Guba 2013). Guba himself struggles to make sense of these expressions, and it gradually becomes clear that even he has no idea what he means. In Chapter 8, I turn to 'knower' and 'known', as in the sentences 'Knower and known are independent, a dualism' and 'Knower and known are interactive, inseparable'. I suggest that, given the ordinary uses of 'know', it is impossible to determine what *statement* these sentences succeed in making. And if new application conditions are not specified, we must conclude that they make no statement at all.

3.9   Misunderstanding pleonastic entities

A pleonastic entity is the product of a 'pleonastic transformation'.[24] This is a syntactic operation. It is performed on one sentence in order to create another sentence with the same truth value. For example:

   (19) The rose is red.

Here, 'the rose' is the subject of the sentence; 'is red' is the predicate. However, as with any predicate of the form $< is + ADJECTIVE >$, we have the option of using a different form of words:

   (20) The rose has the property of being red.

This is a paraphrase, a pleonastic transformation. If (19) is true, then so is (20). The two say exactly the same thing; they are alternative ways of speaking. Sentence (20) is just the result of a syntactic switch, with one syntactic structure being substituted for another:

$< is + \textsc{adjective} >$ $\longrightarrow$ $< has\ the\ property\ of\ being + \textsc{adjective} >$.

The verb is changed, and a noun has been introduced that was not there before: 'property'.[25] One might wonder about the 'ontological status' of this noun. Does 'the property of being red' refer to a sort of a *thing*? Is it the name of an abstract object? If so, was this object's existence implied by (19) but made explicit in (20)? Is 'the property of being red' a member of a class of similar objects, namely *properties*?

After all, nouns are naming words, and 'property' is a noun, so it must be the name of *something*. But if it is, then it looks as though this something has been conjured up merely by switching the syntax of the sentence. It is, in Schiffer's (2003) terms, the result of a 'something-from-nothing' inference. Switch the syntax, say the same thing, but discover (or perhaps create) a new sort of entity. How can that be if 'has the property of being red' is just a syntactic variation of 'is red'?

There is a more deflationary line of thought. There is nothing more to being a 'property' than syntax. Or, to mix metaphors, we can say: properties are the 'shadows of predicates' (Armstrong 1989). There is a pleonastic equivalence between (19) and (20), and… that's it. Full stop. There aren't any ontological implications. We can, if we like, assert that 'there are such things as properties'; but this is no more than a pleonastic inference. It follows trivially from the fact that we make regular use of $< is + \textsc{adjective} >$ constructions. 'There are such things as properties' is not an ontological pronouncement, a metaphysical discovery. It's what Wittgenstein (1964) might have called a 'grammatical remark'. It simply says: 'We sometimes describe things by saying that *x is F*, but an alternative way of putting this is to say that *x has the property of being F*.

Here's another example, borrowed from Schiffer (1996).

(21) Fido is a dog.

From this sentence, we can trivially infer:

(22) That Fido is a dog is true.

(23) The proposition that Fido is a dog is true.

With sentence (23), we now have a new noun ('proposition') *and* a new adjective ('true'), even though (23) says no more than (21). Does that mean that we have invented (or discovered) a new kind of object (a proposition), *and* a new kind of property (being true)? On the deflationary line of thought, no. This is another syntactic switch. It's a purely linguistic transformation. We're playing around with syntax.

The assumption that nouns are 'naming' words is one that Wittgenstein comments on specifically: 'We are up against one of the great sources of philosophical bewilderment: a substantive makes us look for a thing that corresponds to it' (Wittgenstein 1964: 1). He has in mind questions like 'What is a property?', 'What is a proposition?'; and his point is that whenever we see a substantive – a noun, a noun phrase – we suppose that it must *denote* something. Nouns are names, it says so in the dictionary, so words such as 'proposition' and 'property' must be the names of (presumably abstract) objects. A 'property' must therefore be an object of *some* kind. Similarly for 'proposition'.[26]

Whereas, in fact – according to the deflationary line of thought – both 'property' and 'proposition' are no more than syntactic devices.[27] But they are not, for that reason, arbitrary. They permit us to do things we couldn't do (or couldn't do as easily) without them. For example, 'property' allows reference to a class of predicates without having to itemise them ('the psychometric properties of the scale', 'physical and chemical properties', 'the electrical and geometric properties of wires'). 'Proposition' has a similar function ('one of these propositions must be false', 'is any of these propositions empirically testable?'). So both terms have useful functions – more than I can illustrate here – which is why we use them. But that doesn't make them anything other than linguistic devices.

The relevance of this discussion is as follows. Qualitative research is frequently defined as the 'study of experience', and research papers have titles which take the form: 'The experience of X: a qualitative study.' These do not appear to be metaphysical expressions, but the qualitative literature uses them in a metaphysical way. Chapter 12 suggests that 'experience' is a pleonastic expression. Like 'property' and 'proposition', it appears to introduce an 'entity' of some kind, whose 'nature' can be disputed. However, like them, it is a linguistic device with a series of useful functions. The chapter shows how 'experience' becomes metaphysical when it is understood as a referential term instead of a deflationary syntactic alternative. In 'the study of experience', it is a term generalising over 'things that happen to people'. In the qualitative literature, however, it is usually construed as referring to something 'subjective'.

To close this section, refer back to sentence (23). The pleonastic transformation in this case introduced not merely a new noun but a new adjective. Many discussions of truth, including those in the methods literature, assume that 'is true' designates a property assigned to propositions, statements, or claims. The main dispute is about the nature of this property: correspondence, coherence, pragmatist. In Chapter 11, however, I'll suggest that the 'is true' predicate is useful for two main reasons, neither of them involving reference to a property. The first is: it permits convenient forms of assent, admission, and concession ('That's true'). The second is: it allows succinct forms of generalisation ('Everything he said was true').

So 'is true' is an extremely useful predicate, but it is a linguistic device. It doesn't ascribe a property to anything.[28] It's in daily use, and even constructivists use it. There's no need to put it in scare quotes.

3.10 Narrowly selective attention to a familiar term's pattern of usage

With this one, finally, I can be brief. I said most of what needs to be said about this kind of forgetfulness in Section 3.3, with 'hope' as the primary example. On a minute-to-minute basis, we are familiar with the wide range of uses a particular word has, and handle them adroitly without having to think about it much. But when we stop and theorise, we ignore most of them. We zero in on a restricted range of uses, ignoring all the others, and build our theories round that.

As for relevance. The idea of 'causal law' attracts some of the most forceful rhetoric in the literature: linear, context-free, fixed, deterministic, mechanistic, immutable, prediction, control. To talk about 'causation', it is implied, is to refer to the exceptionless. A always causes B. You can't deflect, divert, alter, or prevent. This is one reason why many authors argue that causality *cannot* be applied to human affairs.[29]

The *cannot* here is a metaphysical 'cannot'. It allegedly tells us something fundamental about the world. But Chapter 10 shows that, if we assemble reminders, and examine the full range of uses, we find that the language of causation is *routinely* applied to human affairs. Everyday social discourse is dense with causal verbs – almost universally ignored in the literature – most of them indexing singular causation rather than implying anything about 'laws'. There *are* causal laws, and some are deterministic, linear, mechanistic, and so on. But they represent just one type of causal claim. There are indefinitely many types of causal relation; and, by assembling reminders, we can catalogue the wide variety of linguistic devices which permit reference to them.

3.11 Concluding remark

In some respects, the take-home message of this chapter is very simple. Wittgenstein doesn't do theory, he doesn't do metaphysics, and he thinks that we routinely fail to understand our use of language. As far as philosophical method is concerned, the *failing to understand* part is the most important. You can't do philosophy unless you are prepared to invest a lot of time in assembling reminders, and the first person you need to remind is almost certainly yourself.

But for most people, as Wittgenstein was well aware, this goes against the grain. It doesn't have the glamour of metaphysics, and it can seem utterly trivial in comparison. It's also very difficult to accept that so many philosophers and researchers are subject to illusions of thought – as they must be if they 'believe' things that don't actually make sense. So when we get to Part II, we'll need a sort of 'willing suspension of disbelief' while we sift the reminders. There will be some close readings of other people's arguments as well – for example, Lincoln and Guba's (2013) account in *The Constructivist Credo* – but ultimately Part II is the examples-not-arguments zone. In that respect, it's the core of the book.

Notes

1 When I make a claim about what Wittgenstein thinks, I'm saying something about what I personally have taken from reading the *Investigations*, plus a chunk of the secondary literature. I'm not offering an interpretation which I regard as 'correct'. Writers I've found particularly helpful include: Baker (2004), Canfield (2004), Kuusela (2008), Fogelin (2009), McGinn (2013), George (2019), Hacker (2021).

2 Wittgenstein goes further. It's not just a failure to understand, it's an urge to *misunderstand*. He says that philosophical problems 'are solved through an insight into the workings of our language, and that in such a way that these workings are recognized – *despite* an urge to misunderstand them' (Wittgenstein 2009: §109). 'Metaphysics, according to Wittgenstein, finds its source in this urge' (Beale 2020: 131).

3 In the colloquial sense, rather than a technical sense (see Chapter 1, note 3), and with the 'unless and until' rider (Chapter 1, note 8). Here's another way of referring to referentially unsuccessful sentences: 'Some grammatically well-formed sentences… are neither true, nor even false, but fail to be *truth-apt*' (Glock 2015: 112).

4 The astronomical technicalities are more complex, as I observed in Chapter 1, note 6. The expression 'of the clock' originated as a way of distinguishing between the time according to a mechanical clock and the time according to some alternative, such as a sundial, during the 13th and 14th centuries, but it became more popular in its shorter form in the 18th century. The history of timekeeping is, incidentally, fascinating. See, for example, Glennie and Thrift (2009).

5 'Fairly accusing another of speaking nonsense is never a matter of merely noting their departure from accepted modes of speech. It is a last resort, and always provisional' (Read 2014: 66).

6 This is an exoplanet in the Whirlpool Galaxy (M51), 28 million light years away. It orbits around a binary system, so has two 'suns', one of which is either a neutron star or a black hole.

7 Metaphor is not a linguistic magic wand that you can just wave over any byzantine form of words (see Chapter 1, note 14). In any case, many writers romanticise metaphor. It's not distinctive in the way they assume. See the deflationary account of metaphor in Wilson and Sperber (2012: 97–122).

8 '[W]hen Wittgenstein is confronted with an utterance that has no clearly discernible place in a language-game, he does not assume that he can parse the utterance; rather, he invites the speaker to explain how she is using her words, to connect them with other elements of the language-game in a way that displays their meaningfulness. Only if the speaker is unable to do this in a coherent way does Wittgenstein conclude that her utterance is nonsense.' (Witherspoon 2000: 345).

9 See Eliott and Olver (2002) and Paley (2021) for a fuller discussion and references.

10 For more about the uses of 'hope', see Chapters 8–11 in Paley (2021).

11 This is the 1963 Anscombe translation. 'Assembling reminders' is more familiar than the Revised 4th edition's version, 'marshalling recollections'.

12 When Wittgenstein talks about the 'grammar' of an expression, he is referring (very roughly) to the pattern of usage, complete with application conditions, that the assembling of reminders reveals. This is not the same as 'syntax', which refers, in linguistics, to the constraints on sentence construction. I have reserved my own use of 'grammar' for Wittgenstein's sense, except where otherwise specified. A good introduction to Wittgenstein's understanding of grammar and grammatical statements is McGinn (2011).

13 Here, I'm using 'object' in a very loose sense, covering all the supposedly non-physical structures and properties modelled on stuff studied by the sciences. In the physical world we have discrete objects, non-discrete substances, states, mechanisms, properties, structures, and so on. In philosophy, therefore – imitating science – knowledge is a mental 'state'; a number is an abstract 'entity'; thought is a mental 'process'; truth is an abstract 'property'. In my loose sense, 'object' refers to any of these. It implies only that the expressions concerned denote allegedly non-physical analogues of physical things, structures and processes.

14 In effect, I'm adopting a pluralist view of 'what (according to Wittgenstein) nonsense results from' (e.g. Glock 2004). There is an alternative view, according to which Wittgenstein thinks that there's only one source of nonsense (e.g. Whiting 2023).

15 'Wittgenstein's goal, as I understand it, is not to prevent us from adopting new ways of speaking but to encourage us to be *explicit* about it… so that we do not confuse our new way of speaking with our old' (Hymers 2017: 11).

16 The *Longman Dictionary of Contemporary English* provides a definition of 'let alone', together with an example sentence: '**Let alone**: used after a negative statement to say that the next thing you mention is even more unlikely: *The baby can't even sit up yet, let alone walk!*'

17 For a study of the EXISTENTIAL THERE construction, see Szekely (2015). Her work will come up again in Chapter 5.

18 Cappelen is not alone. For example: 'it can be true that people think they have a thought when they don't. They can be deeply attached to a linguistic formulation that upon reflection doesn't say anything' (Appiah & Kosi 2017). For a specifically Wittgensteinian take, see Hacker (2021), especially Chapter 6. And here is a similar view in social theory: 'a spoken or written sentence may sound or read like English, it may give an appearance of sense which, however, will prove illusory on closer inspection' (Tsilipakos 2016: 29). For a parallel idea in linguistics, see Collins (2023).

19 In a sense, there still is, but it takes a very different form. See Pautz (2021) for a good introduction to the modern philosophy of perception.

20 Compare this to: 'Whenever it is 5 o'clock in London, it is legitimate to state that "It is 5 o'clock on the sun"; and you are hereby licensed to do so.' See Section 3.2 for context.

21 George (2019) draws on Sellars' discussion when describing the kind of 'muddle' that Wittgenstein seeks to resolve. Another classic examination of 'sense data' talk, and a detailed unpicking of Ayer, is Austin (1962). See Section 3.8.

22 I emphasise 'their own use' of the expression, because they clearly don't use it in the way that, for example, Schutz (1962) does. For comments on how constructivists and constructionists interpret the expression very differently from Schutz, even when they cite him, see Section 6.2. For a comparable view, see Hammersley (2020).

23 One example is the reading of technical terms from 'complexity theory' in the health care literature. In particular, the assumption that the expression 'self-organizing' – which in complexity theory refers to systems in which intentions and goals play no role – describes people organising themselves without an external authority. See Plsek and Greenhalgh (2001) for a statement of this view, and Paley (2010) for a critical comment on it. The exchange continued with Greenhalgh *et al.* (2010) and Paley (2011).

24 The use of the word 'entity' in 'pleonastic entity' should not be taken to imply that the 'objects' in question 'exist'. Compare note 13. For pleonastic transformation, see Schiffer (1996, 2003).
25 We might see the phrase '… the property of being…' (in the sentence 'The rose has the property of being red') as being akin to what Dennett (2010) calls a 'fused expression'. In other words, it could be treated as if it were a single term. Think of it that way, and there is no separate noun 'property' to worry about. The fusion of expressions amounts to a form of 'grammaticalization' (Hoffmann 2005).
26 In both cases, there are enormous literatures on what the 'nature' of these objects is. For example: can properties be identified with universals, or are they tropes? If the former, are they mind-independent or do they function as the meanings of predicates? If the former, can a property exist even if there is nothing that possess it (Plato), or does it exist only if instantiated (Aristotle)? If the former, how do we come to know about them? For a convenient review, see Orilla and Paoletti (2020).
27 In Paley (2021), my account of 'concept' is comparable to what I've said here about 'property' and 'proposition'. We're dealing with nouns which are indispensable, but which don't name anything.
28 This is a form of deflationism influenced by the debates after Strawson (1949), including Horwich, especially his (2020) account of Wittgenstein on truth, and Grover (1992). However, deflationary lines of thought turn up in many other philosophical debates. A particularly important one, in the context of this book, is introduced in Section 4.2.
29 An example is Bevir and Blakely (2018).

References

Appiah, K. A., & Kosi, D. (2017). Interview with Kwame Anthony Appiah: Part I. *Oxford Review of Books*, 22nd September.
Armstrong, D. M. (1989). *Universals*. Boulder: Westview.
Austin, J. L. (1962). *Sense and Sensibilia*. Oxford: Clarendon Press.
Ayer, A. J. (1940). *The Foundations of Empirical Knowledge*. London: Macmillan and Company.
Baker, G. (2004). *Wittgenstein's Method: Neglected Aspects*. Malden, MA: Blackwell Publishing.
Baz, A. (2020). *The Significance of Aspect Perception: Bringing the Phenomenal World into View*. Cham, Switzerland: Springer Nature.
Beale, J. (2020). Wittgenstein's 'grammatical naturalism'. In S. Wuppuluri & N. Da Costa (Eds.), *Wittgensteinian (adj.)* (pp. 124–162). Cham, Switzerland: Springer Nature.
Bevir, M., & Blakely, J. (2018). *Interpretive Social Science: An Anti-Naturalist Approach*. Oxford: Oxford University Press.
Canfield, J. V. (2004) Pretence and the inner. In D. Moyal-Sharrock (Ed.), *The Third Wittgenstein* (pp. 145–158). London: Routledge.
Cappelen, H. (2013). Nonsense and illusions of thought. *Philosophical Perspectives*, *27*, 22–50.
Collins, J. (2023). Copredication as illusion. *Journal of Semantics*, *40*, https://doi.org/10.1093/jos/ffad1014
Dennett, D. C. (2010). *Content and Consciousness: Routledge Classics*. Abingdon, UK: Routledge.
Eliott, J. A., & Olver, I. (2002). The discursive properties of "hope": A qualitative analysis of cancer patients' speech. *Qualitative Health Research*, *12*(2), 173–193.

Fillmore, C. J., Kay, P., & O'Connor, C. (1988). Regularity and idiomacity in grammatical constructions: The case of let alone. *Language, 64*(3), 501–538.

Fogelin, R. J. (2009). *Taking Wittgenstein at His Word: A Textual Study*. Princeton, NJ: Princeton University Press.

George, A. (2019). Anatomy of a muddle: Wittgenstein and philosophy. In J. Conant & S. Sunday (Eds.), *Wittgenstein on Philosophy, Objectivity, and Meaning* (pp. 1–27). Cambridge, UK: Cambridge University Press.

Glennie, P., & Thrift, N. (2009). *Shaping the Day: A History of Timekeeping in England and Wales 1300-1800*. Oxford: Oxford University Press.

Glock, H.-J. (2004). All kinds of nonsense. In E. Ammerella & E. Fischer (Eds.), *Wittgenstein at Work* (pp. 221–245). London: Routledge.

Glock, H.-J. (2015). Nonsense made intelligible. *Erkenntnis, 80*(S1), 111–136.

Greenhalgh, T., Plsek, P. E., Wilson, T., & Holt, T. (2010). Response to 'The appropriation of complexity theory in health care'. *Journal of Health Services Research and Policy, 15*, 115–117.

Grover, D. L. (1992). *A Prosentential Theory of Truth*. Princeton, NJ: Princeton University Press.

Hacker, P. M. S. (2021). *Insight and Illusion: Themes in the Philosophy of Wittgenstein. 3rd Edition*. London: Anthem Press.

Hammersley, M. (2020). On Schutz's conception of science as one of multiple realities. *Journal of Classical Sociology, 20*(4), 281–297.

Hoffmann, S. (2005). *Grammaticalization and English Complex Prepositions: A Corpus-based Study*. Abingdon, UK: Routledge.

Horwich, P. (2020). Wittgenstein on truth. In S. Wuppuluri & N. Da Costa (Eds.), *Wittgensteinian (adj.)* (pp. 151–162). Cham, Switzerland: Springer Nature.

Hymers, M. (2017). *Wittgenstein on Sensation and Perception*. New York: Routledge.

Kuusela, O. (2008). *The Struggle Against Dogmatism: Wittgenstein and the Concept of Philosophy*. Cambridge, MA: Harvard University Press.

Lincoln, Y. S., & Guba, E. G. (1985). *Naturalistic Inquiry*. Beverly Hills, CA: Sage.

Lincoln, Y. S., & Guba, E. G. (2013). *The Constructivist Credo*. New York: Routledge.

Maddy, P. (2017). *What Do Philosophers Do? Skepticism and the Practice of Philosophy*. New York: Oxford University Press.

McGinn, M. (2011). Grammar in the *Philosophical Investigations*. In O. Kuusela & M. McGinn (Eds.), *The Oxford Handbook of Wittgenstein* (pp. 646–666). Oxford: Oxford University Press.

McGinn, M. (2013). *The Routledge Guide to Wittgenstein's Philosophical Investigations*. Abingdon, UK: Routledge.

Orilla, F., & Paoletti, M. P. (2020). Properties. *Stanford Encyclopedia of Philosophy*, https://plato.stanford.edu/entries/properties/

Paley, J. (2010). The appropriation of complexity theory in health care. *Journal of Health Services Research and Policy, 15*, 59–61.

Paley, J. (2011). Complexity in health care: A rejoinder. *Journal of Health Services Research and Policy, 16*(1), 44–45.

Paley, J. (2021). *Concept Analysis in Nursing: A New Approach*. Abingdon, UK: Routledge.

Pautz, A. (2021). *Perception*. Abingdon, UK: Routledge.

Plsek, P. E., & Greenhalgh, T. (2001). The challenge of complexity in health care. *British Medical Journal, 323*, 625–628.

Read, R. (2014). Ordinary/everyday language. In K. D. Jolley (Ed.), *Wittgenstein: Key Concepts* (pp. 63–80). Abingdon, UK: Routledge.

Schiffer, S. (1996). Language-created language-independent entities. *Philosophical Topics, 24*(1), 149–167.

Schiffer, S. (2003). *The Things We Mean*. New York: Oxford University Press.

Schutz, A. (1962). *Collected Papers: The Problem of Social Reality, vol, 1*. The Hague: Martinus Nijhoff.

Sellars, W. (1956). Empiricism and the philosophy of mind. In H. Feigl & M. Scriven (Eds.), *Minnesota Studies in the Philosophy of Science. Vol. 1* (pp. 253–329). Minneapolis, MN: University of Minnesota Press.

Strawson, P. F. (1949). Truth. *Analysis, 9*(6), 83–97.

Szekely, R. (2015). *Truth Without Predication: The Role of Placing in the Existential There Sentence*. Basingstoke, UK: Palgrave Macmillan.

Thomasson, A. L. (2015). *Ontology Made Easy*. New York: Oxford University Press.

Tsilipakos, L. (2016). *Clarity and Confusion in Social Theory: Taking Concepts Seriously*. Abingdon, UK: Routledge.

Whiting, D. (2023). Wittgenstein's later nonsense. In C. Pfisterer, N. Rathgeb, & E. Schmidt (Eds.), *Wittgenstein and Beyond: Essays in Honour of Hans-Johann Glock* (pp. 47–66). New York: Routledge.

Wilson, D., & Sperber, D. (2012). *Meaning and Relevance*. Cambridge, UK: Cambridge University Press.

Witherspoon, E. (2000). Conceptions of nonsense in Carnap and Wittgenstein. In A. Crary & R. Read (Eds.), *The New Wittgenstein* (pp. 315–350). London: Routledge.

Wittgenstein, L. (1963). *Philosophical Investigations*. Oxford: Basil Blackwell.

Wittgenstein, L. (1964). *Preliminary Studies for the "Philosophical Investigations". Generally known as The Blue And Brown Books*. Oxford: Basil Blackwell.

Wittgenstein, L. (1981). *Zettel. Second Edition* (G. E. M. Anscombe & G. R. von Wright Eds.). Oxford: Basil Blackwell.

Wittgenstein, L. (1989). *Wittgenstein's Lectures on the Foundations of Mathematics: Cambridge 1939. From the Notes of R. G. Bosanquet, Norman Malcolm, Rush Ress, and Yorick Smythies. Edited by Cora Diamond*. Chicago: University of Chicago Press.

Wittgenstein, L. (2009). *Philosophical Investigations: Revised 4th edition by P. M. S. Hacker and Joachim Schulte*. Malden, MA: Wiley-Blackwell.

4

CARNAP'S METAMETAPHYSICS

Logical positivism is dead, to begin with. There is no doubt whatever about that. The register of burial was signed by the clergyman, the clerk, the undertaker, and the chief mourner. Scrooge signed it. And Scrooge's name was good for anything he chose to put his hand to. Logical positivism is as dead as a doornail.

Outside mainstream philosophy, Carnap is a forgotten figure. He was a leading member of the Vienna Circle, a bona fide logical positivist; and logical positivism, as everyone knows, is long gone. It's dead, says Passmore (1967: 57): 'dead, or as dead as a philosophical movement ever becomes'. So positivism has passed on. It is no more. It has ceased to be. It has expired and gone to meet its maker. Bereft of life, it rests in peace. It's kicked the bucket, shuffled off its mortal coil, run down the curtain, and joined the choir invisible. It is an ex-philosophy.

However. Inside mainstream philosophy, unbeknown to Dickens, Passmore, and Monty Python, there has been a resurgence of interest in Carnap during the past 30 years, and in particular a renewed interest in what his ideas imply about metaphysics. This chapter sketches the reasons for that unexpected shift, but its main focus is on the way philosophers have drawn on Carnap in the context of metametaphysics. One claim I find both attractive and plausible is that he is an 'expressivist' (Flocke 2020, Kraut 2021), and I think that metaphysical expressivism à la Carnap helps to make sense of qualitative metaphysics. At any rate, that's the view I will be elaborating.

4.1 The new metaphysics

The positivists were averse to metaphysics. It would not be too far from the truth to describe them as 'anti'. Their primary commitment was to empiricism, the view that all genuine knowledge arises from experience, observation, and

DOI: 10.4324/9781003306382-5

experiment, rather than revelation, intuition, or non-sensory awareness of abstract entities. So they were unenthusiastic about claims for the existence of such 'things' as numbers, propositions, universals, or non-natural properties.[1]

But a landmark paper turned philosophy upside down. According to Quine (1948), metaphysics is continuous with science. It takes account of scientific findings, and it adopts broadly scientific criteria in devising an ontology which provides the best 'total theory'. Quine, in effect, green lighted the return of metaphysics and marked the beginning of logical empiricism's decline. He opened the door to analytic philosophers doing metaphysics again. Instead of 'logical analysis', they could go back to discovering fundamental features of reality, and determining 'what *really* exists'. The idea that their labours were now, officially, an extension of the scientific project was an attractive bonus.[2]

However, post-Quine metaphysics is not universally regarded as a success. There are several reasons for this.

i There are a number of strange disputes and odd-sounding claims, whose significance it can be hard to appreciate. Mereological theories, for example. Here is Albert, and over there is the Eiffel Tower. Question: how many existing things have I just referred to? Answers to this question, proposed by various metaphysicians, include: none (mereological nihilism); one (qualified mereological nihilism); two (mereological restrictivism); and three (mereological universalism, sometimes called mereological maximalism).[3] Some of these claims offend against 'common sense'. This is not necessarily a decisive objection, but the offence is great enough to make a number of contemporary philosophers uneasy about metaphysics (or at least the ontology of mereology) if not actively sceptical.

ii Many metaphysical theories don't appear to be 'continuous' with science, and several are *prima facie* in conflict with it. For example, mereological universalism looks flagrantly at odds with physics and chemistry. It's difficult to accept that such theories (in Quine's words) 'accommodate science in the broadest sense'.

iii The sheer proliferation of competing ontological theories is striking. Ditto for the lack of any consensus. There is no hint of movement towards Quine's 'best total theory'. There is no obvious sign of an equivalent to the 'modern synthesis' in biology, or the 'standard model' in physics. 'We have nothing like convergence on the truth… every conference, every volume, seems to propagate more diverse and competing "ontologies", with little agreement and little progress' (Thomasson 2015: 14).

iv In science, empirical adequacy plays a key role in the evaluation of opposing theories. However, in metaphysics there is rarely any empirical difference between competing ontologies. No observation, no experiment, can discriminate between mereological nihilism, restrictivism, and universalism. Empirical evidence can play no part in adjudicating between them.

v Other science-imitating criteria can't discriminate either. Metaphysicians often invoke theoretical virtues such as simplicity, elegance, parsimony, or conservatism as reasons for preferring one ontology to another. However, these virtues tend to be ill-defined, and it's not obvious how they trade off against each other. In any case, why assume that any of these virtues are 'truth-conducive'? As van Fraassen (1980: 90) says: 'it is surely absurd to think that the world is more likely to be simple than complicated'. It is no less absurd to assume, without argument, that it necessarily exhibits features which are elegant or parsimonious.[4]

Reader: Hang on. What has any of this got to do with qualitative metaphysics? From where I'm sitting, this mereology stuff has no relevance at all to the ontological and epistemological premises of research.

Me: Well, I was using mereology to illustrate the reasons why many philosophers have become sceptical about post-Quine metaphysics. This, in turn, is the reason why some of them have gone back to Carnap, the archetypal metaphysics sceptic.

Reader: Got it. But why use mereology as an example? Why not something closer to home?

Me: I don't think it's *that* far from home. For one thing, there has been discussion, recently, of *social* mereology, the idea that committees, and other groups, are composite objects having their members as parts.[5]

Reader: Okay, but it's still not directly relevant to claims about reality/realities, is it?

Me: Well, there are parallels. Translate mereological theories into 'There exist...' sentences. Restrictivism: 'There exist ordinary objects.' Nihilism: 'There exist no ordinary objects.' Universalism: 'There exist ordinary objects *and* multiple composite objects.' Mereology counts objects, qualitative metaphysics counts realities.

Many readers will be invested in qualitative metaphysics but not so much mereology. So the latter's problems are easier to spot than the former's. My strategy here is to start with the shoulder-shrugging stuff, and suggest a parallel with the more invested stuff. That there *are* parallels can hardly be doubted. And if there is no means of adjudicating between competing ontologies in mereology, either empirically or theoretically, the same could be true of the metaphysical sentences of qualitative metaphysics. It's a possibility I'll discuss, anyway.

4.2   Back to Carnap

The disillusion with post-Quine metaphysics experienced by some philosophers encouraged them to re-examine the Carnap-Quine debate (Quine 1948, Carnap 1950, Quine 1951), which Carnap was generally regarded as having lost. It was one of *the* watershed moments in post-war analytic philosophy. Quine's 'victory' predicted the end of the logical positivism era and issued the invitation to a 'continuous-with-science' metaphysics. For some authors, the sheer oddity, apparent triviality, and undecidability of the new metaphysics prompted a search for something in the Carnap-Quine exchange that had been missed.

The search has been enabled by scholarship on the history of analytic philosophy in general, and logical positivism/logical empiricism in particular,[6] much of it appearing during the last two decades. As a result of these historical enquiries, it has become apparent that Carnap's views do not always match those attributed to him (the same can be said of other logical positivists, as I noted in Chapter 2).[7] It transpires that some of his most interesting and radical ideas had been forgotten in the aftermath of the debate with Quine; and in any case, it is now suggested, Quine's arguments did not do the damage they were generally believed to have done (Creath 2007, Price 2009). Most significantly, Carnap's mature work turns out to be of contemporary relevance. For example, it has been argued that, in the face of the current 'bewildering multiplicity of ontological structures', his Principle of Tolerance might provide a way to 'defuse the conflict and reorient the discussion' (Creath 2016: 198).

One view of Carnap that appears to survive the historical rummaging is the idea that he is vehemently anti-metaphysics. He 'regarded traditional, a priori metaphysical inquiry as ill-conceived nonsense' (Blatti & Lapointe 2016: 1). Writers refer to his 'rejection of ontology, and metaphysics more generally' (Hofweber 2017), his 'dismissive attitude towards ontology' (Eklund 2009: 140), 'his celebrated attack on metaphysics' (Price 2011: 13). There is, of course, plenty of textual evidence for these claims. For example, one of his essays is entitled 'The elimination of metaphysics through the logical analysis of language', and in the course of this essay he describes metaphysicians as 'musicians without musical ability' (Carnap 1959: 79). So the 'anti' reputation appears to be justified.

A less in-your-face assessment is the idea that Carnap's mature views are 'deflationist' (Sidelle 2016, Thomasson 2015). There has been some dispute about what counts as 'deflationism' in this context (see Section 3.9 for a different context), but I will use the expression to refer to any writer who thinks that metaphysical claims cannot be taken at face value. Although the indicative form of a metaphysical sentence implies that it makes a possibly true statement about reality, a deflationist (in my terms) is someone who argues that it doesn't. So I'm using the term fairly widely. It includes views ranging from 'Metaphysical sentences are nonsense, pure and simple', to 'Metaphysical sentences are not descriptive-of-reality, but they have a valuable function none the less'. That leaves several 'deflationary' options open, and it does make Carnap a deflationist. But his view is (from my perspective) towards the 'valuable-function' end of the spectrum rather than the 'nonsense-pure-and-simple' end.

In Sections 4.3 and 4.4, I'll look at Carnap's understanding of existence questions, and in particular the existence of numbers, a class of abstract entities to which Carnap pays special attention. In Section 4.5–4.8, I will turn to his expressivism, the view that metaphysical claims have a function other than describing reality.

4.3   The existence of numbers

So what form does Carnap's deflationism take, and why does he think that metaphysical sentences are not reality-describing, even if they are in the indicative? From this point on, nearly everything becomes a matter of interpretation, but it is generally agreed that Carnap (1950) is the central point of reference. The aim of this paper is to propose a solution to what was, for the logical positivists, a tricky problem: how do you reconcile empiricism with the existence of numbers?[8] On the one hand, you're committed to the view that all knowledge arises from experience; on the other, you recognise the indispensability of mathematics to science. The success of mathematics implies that numbers are real; it implies that 'there exist numbers'. But if you accept that, how do you explain our knowledge of them? It is not empirical knowledge, obviously. Numbers seem to reside in some sort of abstract realm, and we don't encounter 'abstract realms' in sensory experience. But empiricism says that, apart from sensory experience, there's no way of finding out about *anything*. Impasse.

Deflationist philosophers frequently make a distinction between 'ordinary' existence questions and 'ontological' or 'metaphysical' existence questions (Chalmers 2009). Carnap is a case in point; but, for reasons which will soon become clear, he calls the former 'internal' questions, and the latter 'external' questions. One example of an 'internal' question is: 'Do mermaids exist?' This is an empirical question, which can be settled by scientific enquiry. A different kind of 'internal' question is: 'Does a largest prime exist?' This is a question about numbers and can be settled by mathematical proof.

Both questions presuppose what Carnap calls a 'linguistic framework', or sometimes just a 'language'. In this case, one framework incorporates rules for talking about physical things. Carnap calls this the 'thing language', the language of physical, observable objects. The other framework incorporates rules for talking about natural numbers. The rules of the 'observable thing' language include methods for identifying physical objects, and for assigning properties to them (blue, animate, lives in water). The rules for the numbers framework specify how numbers are introduced, how they are manipulated, what properties they have (odd, even, prime). Some basic rules are acquired by rote. Children learn first to count, after which they learn the multiplication tables, chanting 'two twos are four, three twos are six, four twos are eight...'.[9] This is a series of rules, recited until they become automatic, and applied at a later stage when the child starts performing calculations.

Questions like 'Do mermaids exist?' and 'Does a largest prime exist?' are called 'internal' questions (by Carnap) precisely because each presupposes the corresponding linguistic framework. Each can only be asked and answered from 'inside' the language concerned. 'Mermaid' belongs to the 'thing' language; 'prime' belongs to the 'numbers' language. In each case, the answer may be 'yes' or 'no', depending on the outcome of the relevant enquiries.[10] Both ask about the existence of an individual item (largest prime), or a class of items (mermaids) in a 'system of entities' defined by the framework to which they belong. It is only in terms of the 'numbers' framework that a question about a largest prime is intelligible, and only in terms of the 'observable thing' framework that we can ask whether objects with the properties of mermaids exist.

Now consider two different types of question: 'Do numbers *actually* exist?' and 'Do physical objects *really* exist? Not as part of a framework, but independently of it?' These, Carnap says, are 'external' questions. Supposedly, they ask what lies 'beyond' the framework, and concern the relevant system of entities as a whole (numbers in general, physical objects in general) rather than individual examples. According to Carnap, there's no way of answering them. Neither empirical enquiries nor mathematical proofs can do the job, since these procedures can only be adopted, and only make sense, *within* their respective linguistic frameworks. So there's nothing that can be used to support a proposed answer.[11]

Consequently, no answer you might suggest – for example: 'Yes, numbers *really* exist'; or 'No, physical objects don't *really* exist' – will make a reality-describing statement. It would be like claiming that chess pieces really do (or don't) exist, 'out there', 'beyond' the framework provided by the rules of the game. But it is the rules that define what 'chess pieces' *are*; so in their absence, what exactly is it you're referring to? What is it, according to you, that does (or doesn't) really exist? If you detach the claim that chess pieces do (or don't) exist from the framework that governs the use of the expression 'chess piece', how can what you're left with make information-providing sense?[12]

Alternatively, coming at the same idea from a slightly different angle: 'To be real in the scientific sense means to be an element of the system; hence this concept cannot be meaningfully applied to the system itself' (Carnap 1950: 22-3). Metaphysical sentences use terms whose rules of application are defined by a particular linguistic framework. So they cannot be applied to *that very framework*. It would be akin to saying that the wedding service is married, or that language takes the accusative.[13]

However, if we ask 'Do physical objects exist?' or 'Do numbers exist?' *within* the language framework concerned, the answer in both cases is: 'Yes. Of course. Obviously.' But this answer is trivial, because one framework defines numbers, along with rules for describing them, while the other defines objects, along with rules for identifying them. These are internal questions, the answers to which are truisms. In the same way, to ask (in the context of chess) whether chess pieces exist is to pose a question with a trivial answer: of course they do. A bishop is a piece, so is a rook. So, quite obviously, there are chess pieces. Likewise, asking whether 'there exist words' while using language. 'Exist' is a word, and 'word' is a word. Therefore…

The questions in the previous paragraph are all internal questions. However, unlike the questions about mermaids and the largest prime – the answers to which are not trivial – the answers to these questions *are* trivial. It's like the difference between 'Is there a word "huasadoe" in English?'[14] and 'Are there words in English?' You might have to check the dictionary to answer the first one, but the second one answers itself. Neither is like 'Do words *really* exist, independently of language?'

Carnap (1950) sets out to show that using a framework which refers to abstract entities – particularly the framework of mathematics – 'does not imply embracing a Platonic ontology but is perfectly compatible with empiricism' (21). The implication is that *referring* to numbers does not entail having to accept that they *really exist*. So an empiricist can happily sign up to arithmetic, geometry, and quadratic equations, and refer to as many numbers as she likes. They are not ontologically committing.[15] On the other hand, using these expressions does commit to *something*. We will talk about exactly what in Section 4.5.

4.4 Carnap's challenge

Suppose somebody answers the question 'Do numbers really exist?' – the external question – by saying 'Yes, they really do.' This is an ontological claim that goes beyond the trivial concession that numbers exist in the internal sense because we use the language framework of mathematics. It's intended to make a statement about the fundamental nature of things. What does Carnap (1950) say about this statement?

It's important to recognise one thing he does *not* say: that 'Numbers really exist' is nonsense. The word 'nonsense' doesn't appear in Carnap (1950) at all. Metaphysics-as-nonsense is not a view that, at this stage of his career, he endorses. It's true that he describes metaphysics as nonsense in his earlier work (Witherspoon 2000). But by the time we get to *Empiricism, Semantics, and Ontology*, he has adopted a different position, and it's this later phase of his thinking on which the Carnapian sympathisers of recent years draw.

Carnap (1950: 25) draws the following conclusion about philosophers who claim that 'numbers really do exist':

> Therefore our judgement must be that they have not succeeded in giving to the external question and to the possible answers any cognitive content. Unless and until they supply a clear cognitive interpretation, we are justified in our suspicion that their question is a pseudo question, that is, one disguised in the form of a theoretical question while in fact it is non-theoretical.

About parallel claims that 'properties really exist', he says: 'the external state-ment, the philosophical statement of the reality of properties – a special case of the thesis of the reality of universals – is devoid of cognitive content' (1950: 28). The key expression in both extracts seems to be *cognitive content*. This is, Carnap claims, what 'external' statements about the 'real' existence of num-bers and/or properties do not have.

I will say more about being 'devoid of cognitive content' in Section 4.5. In the meantime, we should also notice that Carnap says: '*unless and until* they supply a clear cognitive interpretation, we are justified in our suspicion that…'. The implication is that there is something 'these philosophers' can do to retrieve the situation and challenge the provisional verdict: provide a clear cognitive interpretation. If they can do that, then the 'suspicion' that their question is a pseudo question may have to be revoked. So answers to the 'external' question, whichever one it is (about numbers, properties, proposi-tions, or relations), are not simply dismissed as nonsense. The door – however slightly – is left ajar.

Sidelle (2016) describes this as 'an open-ended challenge: Find me a sen-sible meaning for the question *other than* the internal one'. It is 'then left for the metaphysician to come up with some *other* sensible reading' (77). The challenge is open-ended, then, but it is one which has not yet been met and which, in Carnap's opinion, cannot be met. This is not an argument, *per se*, but it is 'backed up with a supporting diagnosis and reasons for suspicion' (78).

This echoes something I said in Sections 3.2 and 3.6: the judgement that a sentence such as 'It's 5 o'clock on the sun' makes no sense is, according to Wittgenstein, only provisional. It's always possible that the person who claims that it *does* make sense will come up with a context, and new application conditions, which give it what Sidelle calls a 'sensible meaning', or what Carnap calls 'cognitive content'. So there is a parallel here; and, in Part II, the provisional judgement will be tested – the challenge – in a series of conversa-tions in which the qualitative metaphysician is invited to explain what the 'cognitive content' (or the 'sensible meaning') could be.[16]

The provisional conclusion about the lack of cognitive content is predi-cated on the assumption that the sentence concerned is supposed to be information-providing. The sentence is meaningful in the sense that its con-stituent words are all familiar, and they are combined in a syntactically cor-rect manner. But it fails to make a statement. It fails to provide information. Suppose, then, that this provisional judgement remains in place, at least *pro tem*. Given that (on this supposition) the sentence is *not* reality-describing, is there anything that can be said about some other function it might be con-strued as having? A non-information-providing function?

If there is, the alternative function would presumably not involve what Carnaps calls cognitive content. It would be 'non-cognitive'. This is precisely the alternative Carnap describes; and the contemporary debate about metaphysics includes the perspective of 'non-cognitivism', though several other terms are used to refer to related ideas: 'non-representationalism', 'non-descriptivism', 'non-factualism'. All these expressions signal resistance to the idea that the primary, or even exclusive, function of language is to depict, describe, represent, or report on reality.[17] Carnap's version is examined in the next section.

4.5 Carnap's non-factualism

I will use Price's (1994: 132) term, 'non-factualism', for the view that certain forms of language are not in the business of stating facts or describing things. Rather, they have a different function. In one sense, of course, this is obvious. We ask questions, we issue instructions. In neither case are we stating a fact or reporting on anything. Typically, however, questions are asked in the interrogative ('Are you there, Moriarty?'), and instructions are issued in the imperative ('Go away!'). The thing about non-factualism, though, is: it says that *indicative* sentences are sometimes not in the business of describing.

The principle is not, in itself, difficult to accept. What's hard is seeing that it applies in certain cases. 'There is a single objective reality.' 'There are multiple, socially constructed realities.' Both of these are in the indicative. They *seem* to be stating a fact. They seem to be reporting on a fundamental feature of the world. Non-factualism says: 'H'm. Not necessarily. Perhaps they're doing something else.'

So it is with Carnap's take on 'Numbers really do exist.' It's in the indicative. It *appears* to state a fact, to say something about how things are. Carnap's view is: 'Actually, no. If we try to construe it as fact-stating, we will conclude – unless and until – that it doesn't make sense. But it's possible to construe it differently. We can interpret it as performing a different function.' The function in question is a kind of endorsement. It endorses the adoption of the mathematics language framework – including the use of terms like 'five' and 'twenty' as names as well as adjectives – and recommends it as a framework likely to prove its practical value. Instead of making a factual claim about the existence of 'five' and 'twenty' outside the framework, it commits to the framework itself.[18]

For most people, the question of the 'real' existence of numbers doesn't have the same importance as it did for early 20th-century empiricists. Most of us don't care or think it's an absurd angels-on-the-head-of-a-pin dispute. So let's bring it closer to home. Take 'There exist multiple realities' [MR] as an example. Carnap's non-factualism implies that: (a) MR does not provide 'ontological' information, any more than 'numbers really exist' does; (b) the expression 'multiple realities' does not refer to anything, independently of a particular language framework; (c) MR signals a preference for, and a commitment to, that framework.

The MR framework is not merely a *façon de parler*. Its rules and application conditions will need to be fully spelt out. It will need, crucially, to incorporate rules for the use of the MR language. This will be a complex matter, but one (over-simplified) possibility might be: 'If A experiences something as *X-like*, and if B experiences the same thing as *not X-like* but instead *Y-like*, then *X* and *Y* define two different realities, A's and B's.'[19] Once all the necessary rules and application conditions have been introduced, it will be possible to specify the methodological permissions and constraints associated with MR.

The alternative, 'There exists a single reality' [SR], faces the same implications and requirements.[20] It does not provide 'ontological' information, and 'single reality' doesn't refer to anything independently of a language framework. The SR framework will have different rules, one of which might be: 'If A experiences something as *X-like*, and if B experiences the same thing as *not X-like* but instead *Y-like*, then *X* and *Y* refer to two different (not necessarily accurate) accounts of a single reality.'

Given that there are two frameworks, there will also be debate about the relative merits of SR and MR, and what achievements each can claim. What is at stake, Carnap says, is:

> a practical, not a theoretical question; it is the question of whether or not to accept the new linguistic forms. The acceptance cannot be judged as being either true or false because it is not an assertion. It can only be judged as being more or less expedient, fruitful, conducive to the aim for which the language is intended.
>
> *(Carnap 1950: 31–32)*

He suggests that some languages may be better than others for particular purposes. However, this is something that can only be determined empirically. It's not a matter that can be resolved by ontological argument, or by using hard-to-explain 'epistemically metaphysical' methods (Sider 2011, 187). So any participant in an ontological dispute should be prepared 'to make explicit (1) the data they seek to deal with; (2) their sense of what it would be to deal with it adequately; (3) their criteria for treating one way of dealing with it as superior to another' (Kraut 2016: 40).[21]

Subject to these conditions, you're free to adopt any linguistic framework you see fit. But so is everyone else. Carnap had previously referred to this idea as 'the Principle of Tolerance'. Which says: 'everyone is at liberty to build his own logic, i.e. his own form of language, as he wishes. All that is required of him is that, if he wishes to discuss it, he must state his methods clearly, and give syntactical rules instead of philosophical arguments' (Carnap 1937, §17).

The intention is to legitimate, rather than to repudiate, metaphysical questions – but to do so in a way that gets rid of undecidable disputes about the existence of abstract objects, or the nature of 'reality', and in a way that opens them up to empirical enquiry and linguistic analysis.[22]

But the phenomenological dimension still looks like a problem.[23] Ontological pronouncements, whether referring to the number of realities or the existence of abstract entities, don't *look* or *feel* like expressions of commitment to a language framework. They look like truth-claims. They feel like claims about how some fundamental aspect of the world *is*. Given that they're in the indicative, and that they're presented as conclusions or discoveries, Carnap's suggestion that they are doing something completely different – his readiness to 'flout appearances of descriptiveness'[24] – seems quite absurd. It invites immediate, out-of-hand rejection.

I'm going to park that one for now and return to it in Sections 4.7 and 4.8. Meanwhile, I want to develop further the broadly Carnapian position I'm preparing in anticipation of Part II.

4.6 Expressivism

The idea that indicatives can be used to do things other than describe has been around since at least the 1930s, and there have been many warnings about succumbing to the 'descriptivist fallacy' (Macarthur 2010: 81). Wittgenstein and Austin frequently suggest that language is just another set of tools. Austin (1962) wrote a book called *How To Do Things With Words*, and Wittgenstein emphasised on numerous occasions that it is not difficult to be misled by grammatical similarities. 'We don't notice the enormous variety of all the everyday language games, because the clothing of our language makes them all alike' (Wittgenstein 2009: 236).

Many non-factualist functions of indicatives are routine, like those listed below. There are game rules (1), formal procedures (2), definitions (3), conventions (4), etiquette (5), drills (6), and instructions (7). All of these are indicatives, with a subject-predicate structure, but they don't *report* on anything.[25] Each is a variation on the idea of a *rule*. They all prescribe how something is done: how the game starts, how the word 'bachelor' is to be understood, where to put dowel A.

   (1) Black moves first.

   (2) If the vote is tied, the chair has the casting vote.

   (3) A bachelor is an unmarried man.

   (4) Fido is a dog's name.

   (5) The bride and her parents are photographed before the groom and his.

(6) When the big hand points to 12 and the little hand points to 3, it's three o'clock.

(7) Dowel A is inserted into hole B.

These are, of course, mundane examples. In philosophy, the topics in which non-factualist accounts are most often found are the analysis of 'truth', reference to mental states, and metaethics (see, for example, the essays in Gross *et al.* 2016). In particular, one form of non-factualism – metaethical expressivism – is 'the now familiar view that ethical statements are best thought of not as representing or describing the world but as expressing our attitudes towards it' (Simpson 2020: 140).

Given that the mundane examples are variations on the theme of 'rule' or 'instruction', it is perhaps not surprising that non-factualism should have been applied to ethics. Non-cognitivist views in ethics reject the assumption that moral claims describe an aspect of reality: there are no moral *facts* or *properties* to be described. Instead, to make a moral claim is to express an attitude, usually approval or disapproval, and/or to urge, recommend, or caution against, certain types of behaviour. This matches Carnap's line with metaphysics. And given that the preferred modern term for non-cognitivist theories of this kind is 'expressivism', that term can also be used to describe Carnap's metametaphysics. 'To cut to the chase,' Kraut (2016: 31) says, 'Carnap's theory of ontology parallels non-cognitivist theories of morality… It is, in current parlance, an *expressivist* theory'.

So I need to say something more about what 'expressivist' implies. It should not be taken too narrowly. The earliest non-cognitivist theories of ethics were 'emotivists'. They argued that moral statements are 'expressive' in the sense that they express the feelings of the speaker, or voice a certain kind of reaction: approval/approbation or disapproval/censure. The authors associated with this view are Ayer (1936) and Stevenson (1937).[26] The 'rule/instruction' theme of the mundane examples is rather more apparent in the prescriptivism of Hare (1952). Prescriptions, Hare thinks, come in diverse flavours, ranging from orders, to rules of games, to etiquette, to advice and recommendations. The primary function of the word 'good' is, he claims, 'commendation'. Carnap-like, Hare refers to a *language*. In this case, it is the 'language of values', 'admirably suited for the expression of everything that we require to say in the course of either deciding on or instructing in or modifying principles' (136). For Hare, to talk about morality is to adopt a language which has a particular kind of *use*. Just as, for Carnap, to talk about numbers or properties is to do exactly the same.

If the term 'expressivism' means 'nothing more than that the views in question theorise about language in non-representational terms' (Price 2008), then Ayer, Stevenson, Hare, and Carnap are all, in their different ways, expressivists. They think that the dimensions of language they focus on are not in the business of representing and describing, even though the relevant sentences are indicative.

However, there are two obvious differences between Carnap and the other three. First, Carnap (1950) is expressivist about metaphysics. This is in contrast to ethical concerns, but it has the same orientation.[27] He assigns an expressivist significance to metaphysical claims. Consider, for example, a comment on Heidegger: 'The (pseudo) statements of metaphysic do not serve for the description of states of affairs... They serve for the expression of the general attitude of a person towards life' (Carnap 1959: 78).

Second, the early non-cognitivists propose an analysis of what ethical words and sentences *mean*. The same is true of subsequent, more sophisticated expressivists (Gibbard 1990, Blackburn 1993). Carnap, however, is not proposing an *analysis* of ontological claims. He's not suggesting that a statement like 'Numbers really exist' *means* 'Given our goals, it is pragmatically advisable to accept the linguistic framework of mathematics'. Rather, he is interested in the *function* of such statements: 'formulating commitments, expressing attitudes, or carrying out some other non-fact-stating task' (Kraut 2016: 38).

Carnap's claim that 'the (pseudo) statements of metaphysics... serve for the expression of the general attitude of a person towards life' is, on my reading, a significant one. It hints at the relation between expressivism in a moral context and expressivism in a metaphysical one. In the next section, I will take this idea a step further.

4.7 Enactings and joinings

If (external) metaphysical sentences are construed as reality-describing, they make no sense (unless and until). They are pseudo-statements. However, Carnap doesn't think we can just dismiss them. Instead, he construes them as signalling acceptance/rejection of the relevant language framework. In endorsing/opposing this framework, the metaphysician thereby expresses her 'general attitude towards life'. If she accepts the numbers framework, for example, she embraces the use of quantification, mathematics, and statistics in the assessment of empirical hypotheses.

But this is not *just* a question of an individual's acceptance of a framework. Attitudes can be shared, and they can be the basis of a community, at least in part. Consider the Christian attitude towards life. This does involve individual commitment to a framework, but the commitment takes place in the context of a community. Indeed, it involves *joining* that community, and is consummated by an *enactment* or series of enactments. Essential to these enactments is the reciting of metaphysical sentences, as for example in the Apostle's Creed (8) or the ceremony of baptism (9):

(**8**) I believe in God, the Father almighty, creator of heaven and earth. I believe in Jesus Christ, his only Son, our Lord, who was conceived by the Holy Spirit... On the third day he rose again; he ascended into heaven...

(9) Faith is the gift of God to his people… Baptism marks the beginning of a journey with God… In baptism the Lord is adding to our number those whom he is calling… Christ claims you for his own.

As with other metaphysical sentences, these examples are all in the indicative.[28] In some cases, they are prefaced with 'I believe', which in this context can be classified as an 'expositive' speech act.[29] In other cases, the sentence is not so prefaced ('On the third day…'). However, the whole Creed arguably counts as a single speech act. Here, then, as in other examples of metaphysics (on Carnap's understanding), we have indicatives which, construed as reality-describing claims, are undecidable;[30] but which can also be construed as expressing commitment to the Christian language framework, and to the community which embodies it. The framework provides a matrix of criteria – scripture, revelation, theological argument – for answering religious questions, and for solving religious puzzles (the problem of evil, for example).

There is an analogy here, I think, with the pronouncements of qualitative metaphysics. It is not just the commitment to a *language* that is at stake here, but the commitment to a *culture* – to a methodological tribe. Goertz and Mahoney (2012) have argued that the qualitative and quantitative traditions 'exhibit all the traits of separate cultures', each with its distinctive norms and practices. 'Quantitative-qualitative disputation in the social sciences is really a clash of cultures'. In line with this, I take the metaphysical pronouncements to be a cultural ritual. Assenting to constructivist ontology, for example, is like reciting the Apostle's Creed. It is an enacting and, like baptism, a joining. We assume that the pronouncements are claims about the fundamental nature of reality and that they justify the methodological preferences concerned. But on my Carnapian line of thought, that is not what they do. They *enact* the commitment to a methodological tribe; they don't *justify* it.

This account needs to be qualified. There's an asymmetry. Consider two opposed ontological statements (Ormston *et al.* 2013: 5):

[R] An external reality exists independent of our beliefs or understanding.

[N] No external reality exists independent of our beliefs and understandings.

I have implied that R enacts the joining of the quantitative – actually, the 'positivist' – tribe, and that N enacts the joining of the qualitative tribe. It is more nuanced than that. Qualitative methods texts are written by qualitative methodologists. It's probably safe to assume, then, that N enacts the joining of the qualitative tribe. However, we can't just assume that R enacts the joining of the 'positivist' tribe. It may simply be the enactment that the qualitative tribe *attributes* to the 'positivists'. Is there evidence that non-qualitative researchers independently adopt R as an ontological premise, affirmation of which is necessary for doing research? Well, you might find stuff that's interpretable that way. But 'positivists' tend not to regard ontological premises as a sort of research driving-licence. So we have to bear in mind that R is positivist-ontology-according-to-self-confessed-non-positivists.

4.8 Keep off the grass

Imagine that something like this is true. The function of metaphysical sentences is something other than describing, even though they are indicative. Consider two sentences from a popular methods text.[31]

(10) There is no single, observable reality. Rather, there are multiple realities.

These are both indicative sentences, and they appear to make statements about how things are. Suppose they don't. Suppose they are referentially unsuccessful. They don't describe 'reality' or 'realities'. They have a different kind of function: possibly expressing a certain attitude towards research, or articulating a research 'rule', or announcing a commitment to a particular research community. For the time being, the details don't matter. The point is: these are indicative sentences, but they are not in the 'describing' business. They do something else. Saying what this something else is, and explaining why it's expressed in the indicative, is a philosophical job for later. This is still hypothetical, remember.

Anyway, assume that's true. What happens, and how do we respond, if someone tries to construe (10) as reality-describing? Well, *ex hypothesi*, it can't be done. The sentences cannot be parsed that way. So, if you try, you're going to end up with… perhaps not nonsense, exactly, but something that in a significant sense, doesn't *work*. You try to parse it as reality-describing, but that doesn't fit. A description of reality is *not* what you achieve. But, quite conceivably, you still *believe* you have achieved it.

By analogy, think of a notice which issues a warning or an order. 'Keep off the grass.' Try parsing *that* as a description of reality, and you'll either get nowhere or down a dark rabbit hole. 'Who keeps off the grass? Which grass do they keep off? Isn't there a bit missing?' If you ask questions like this, you have missed the point. 'Keep off the grass' isn't in the describing business. It does something else. And the something else, in this case, is an imperative: an instruction issued to anyone in the vicinity who reads it. Of course, this isn't exactly like (10) because it's in the imperative mood, not the indicative. But that's the point of calling it an analogy. I'm attempting to convey a flavour of what it's like trying to parse a non-reality-describing sentence as a reality-describing one. You end up with something that doesn't make sense, and a pile of unanswerable questions.

Just one more bit of imagining. Suppose that a philosophical Martian, call her Mynan, doesn't recognise (or doesn't accept) that 'Keep off the grass' is *not* reality-describing. She is convinced, in fact, that it is, and decides to work out the details of what it means, why what it says is true, the semantics which make it come out true, and why it is a better description of reality than some alternative ('Don't keep off the grass', perhaps). To anyone who doesn't share her conviction, this will look utterly bonkers. In debate, though, Mynan insists that she believes 'Keep off the grass' is true (or better, or preferable), and that – crucially – she believes it. The fact that other people, bewildered, ask '*What* do you believe, exactly?' doesn't impress her. Her reply, if pushed, is: 'Keep off the grass'.

At this point, we would suspect that Mynan is subject to a weird kind of illusion. She thinks she believes something; but, as far as the rest of us are concerned, she doesn't and can't. *There is no statement there to believe.* It's not that 'Keep off the grass' is nonsense in the sense of being meaningless; obviously it isn't. But it is referentially unsuccessful. It doesn't make a statement. So there's nothing that Mynan *can* believe when she utters the sentence, despite her insistence that there is. She is suffering from an illusion of thought.

On my Carnapian view, if you try to construe ontological sentences as referentially successful, you are making a comparable mistake, and the result will be the same: something as good as nonsense, a heap of unanswerable questions, and the illusion of having a reality-describing belief when you haven't. This is a partial response to the phenomenological objection in Section 4.5. Basically, it says you might have to accept that a cognitive illusion is involved.

As noted in Section 3.6, the possibility of philosophical 'illusions of thought' is discussed by Cappelen (2013): 'a subject can take herself to have a thought even though she does not have one' (29). If this is right, then it's possible that a qualitative researcher might believe that she has the thought 'There are multiple, socially constructed realities' when there is no such thought to be had. And this because the sentence is referentially unsuccessful: it does not *say* anything. The researcher's belief that she has the thought, and that she believes the corresponding proposition, is mistaken. She is subject to an illusion.[32]

Reader: You can't be serious. How is it possible to think you have a thought and be wrong?

Me: 'Colourless green ideas sleep furiously.' If someone told you they believed that, what would you say?

Reader: Oh, come on! That's obvious nonsense! You can't compare it to 'There are multiple socially constructed realities'.

Me: I can. I *am* doing. The point is: if Carnap's right about ontological sentences, then they *are* nonsense if construed as reality-describing. So the belief that they're not – the belief that they say something, and that you believe what they say – must be illusory.

Reader: What about 'unless and until'?

Me: Right. Unless and until the metaphysician comes up with a clear explanation of what the ontological sentence means.

Reader: Okay, so that's all I have to do, then.

Me: Yes. But that's been with us since the 'out there' conversation in Section 1.6. That's why we have to have a dialogue, where you give me an explanation, and I tell you what's wrong with it.

Reader: And of course there *will* always be something wrong with it. Obviously. The deck is stacked in your favour. I mean, you're the one writing this, aren't you?

Me: Yes. But I honestly don't think illusions of thought are inevitable. Although Carnap does. It's like Cappelen says: there are no blanket arguments. We have to consider each case separately on its merits.

Cappelen's view is broadly Carnapian, but he doesn't agree with Carnap that *all* metaphysical sentences are nonsensical when construed as reality-describing. He thinks that 'to establish in any serious way that even one particular use of an expression instantiates nonsense requires a lot of evidence', the evidence concerned consisting largely of data on linguistic practices. He does, however, suspect that 'we will find pockets of nonsensical speech in many domains.[33] To conclusively establish this will require a separate paper for each case' (42). I agree with this, and it is the strategy I pursue in Part II.

4.9 Concluding comments

'Keep off the grass' is meaningful, but it doesn't make a statement. It doesn't report on anything. But it does have a function. Mynan's task, if she can be disabused of the notion that it *does* make a statement, is to work out what that function is. The chapters in Part II take a similar form. The first job will be to persuade the reader that there is a case to answer. Does this sentence, construed as a reality-describing statement, make sense or not? Does it, in the sense of Sections 3.6–3.10, 'go astray'? This is the Wittgensteinian contribution. The second task is to answer the question: 'If it can't be construed as reality-describing, what other function might it have?' This is the Carnapian angle. However, both Wittgenstein and Carnap issue the same challenge to the metaphysician: to provide an account that will overturn the provisional judgement that metaphysical sentences are pseudo-statements, referentially unsuccessful.

I've made no secret of the fact that I don't think this challenge can be met. I don't think metaphysical pronouncements describe fundamental features of the world. I think, instead, that they are proposings, recommendings, endorsing a language framework. They 'record our determination to speak in certain ways' (Thomasson 2020: 30). They function as enactings and joinings, committing to one culture, one community, rather than another. Still, I'd like the reader to feel that I have given the pronouncements a reasonably fair crack of the whip; and I'll proceed on that basis. In any case, as Cappelen suggests, each case needs individual consideration. There is no escape from working through examples.

Notes

1 This presented them with a problem. Given their allegiance to science, they could hardly doubt the usefulness of numbers. So there was a marked tension between their empiricism and their adherence to mathematics. Carnap, as we'll see in Section 4.3, had a solution to this problem. The solution can be generalised to other dubious, but apparently indispensable, entities; and this is one reason for the renewed interest in his work.
2 The story of this turning point has been told by several authors and is obviously more complex than I can convey here. The Introduction to Thomasson (2015) provides an especially clear account.
3 Mereological nihilism: the view that the only things that really exist are 'simples', things without *any* parts (presumably physics' fundamental particles). So Albert and the Eiffel Tower don't *really* exist. Qualified mereological nihilism: living organisms are the exception. So Albert exists, but the Eiffel Tower doesn't. Restrictivism is the more-or-less common-sense view that the Eiffel Tower and Albert both exist. Mereological universalism (or mereological maximalism) is the view that, for any group of separate objects, there is an additional object consisting of all the objects in the group. So the Eiffel Tower exists, and Albert exists, and the Eiffel-Tower-Albert composite object exists. *Faites vos jeux*. Mereology can get technical, but Simons (2006), reviewing arguments for and against maximalism, provides a clear introduction to some of the issues.
4 For a good review of the adjudication problems, see Kriegel (2013). Bennett (2009) is another author who argues that metaphysical views are undecidable, but her line of attack is different from Kriegel's. She thinks metaphysical claims are underdetermined by evidence, while Kriegel argues that theoretical virtues of simplicity, elegance, and so on, can't adjudicate between them either.
5 See, for example, Hawley (2018).
6 Examples include Creath (1990), Friedman (1999), Richardson and Uebel (2007), Friedman and Creath (2007), Beaney (2013), Uebel and Limbeck-Lilienau (2022).
7 One popular, if puzzling, view portrays Carnap as if he belongs to the tradition of British empiricism. For example, he is supposed to have believed that some empirical claims are theory-independent, and can be known with certainty. 'Carnap's position, it turns out, has virtually nothing to do with such views' (Friedman 2007: 3). Similar things can be said of logical empiricism generally: 'It turns out that much that is written about it in standard histories of philosophy – and taught in introductory philosophy courses – is at least seriously misleading' (Limbeck-Lilienau and Uebel 2022: 1).
8 Carnap (1950) does talk about other abstract entities as well: 'properties, classes, relations, numbers, propositions, etc.' These all give rise to the same sort of problem. However, the paper's main example is numbers.
9 These are indicative sentences, but they don't describe. Each is a rule or licence. It is an 'instruction' concerning what *can* (licence) or *should* (rule) be inferred when you encounter two pairs, 3 twos, or four couples.
10 In this case, it's a 'no' for both. Euclid proved that there is no largest prime, circa 300 BCE.

11 Unless intuition or revelation count as evidence/argument. The problem is that people have different intuitions and different revelations. It's not like demonstrating that there is a prime between 7 and 13, or that dropped objects accelerate as they fall to the ground.

12 'To be able to speak about a kind of entity at all, or inquire about its existence, we must introduce terms (governed by rules) for the relevant entity in our language or "linguistic framework"' (Thomasson 2015: 31).

13 An example suggested by Section 3.9 is 'property'. If the term is introduced as an alternative way of referring to predicates such as < is + ADJECTIVE >, what does it mean to ask whether properties 'really' exist? The framework of 'properties' is briefly discussed by Carnap (1950: 28).

14 I've cribbed this word from Thomasson (2015: 40).

15 'Existence is not a prerequisite for being talked about' (Bricker 2014). Think mermaids, phlogiston, the average star, Sherlock Holmes.

16 There's also a link with the principle of relevance (Sperber & Wilson 1995), which is a theory of communication. The idea is that you assume that any sentence you see/hear is relevant to the discussion you're involved in. If, in the first instance, you can't make sense of it, you try to think of a context in which it *would* make sense. Sometimes you're successful, sometimes not. But it's always possible that inspiration might strike at a later time. Equally, it's always possible that the qualitative metaphysician will eventually be able to specify application conditions which explain what she is trying to say. To that extent, the door is left open. But in the meantime – unless and until – the suspicion that she's not saying *anything* can be considered justified.

17 To adopt non-representationalism, the idea that language does not 'mirror' reality, is not to assume that language instead 'constructs' reality. The irony of the latter view, in most versions, is that it is still descriptivist. Constructivists don't repudiate 'description'. It's just that they think descriptions *create* reality/realities rather than *portraying* it/them. 'Debt is a prison' attaches a 'meaning', and thereby constructs an individual reality. It doesn't report on something that would be 'true' independently of how it is described. 'Debt is a prison' is still a description; but (so says the constructivist) 'realities' mirror language, not the other way round. Non-representationalism (non-descriptivism, non-factualism) *does* repudiate description. So we're not stuck with a choice between portraying and constructing.

18 Carnap seeks to 'legitimize a region of discourse [ontology] by portraying it as a non-descriptive mechanism for formulating commitments, expressing attitudes, or carrying out some other non-fact-stating task' (Kraut 2016: 38).

19 Lincoln and Guba (1985) do something *vaguely* like this, at least by implication. However, I postpone further discussion of their understanding of 'constructed realities' until Chapter 6.

20 To reject MR is *not* thereby to accept SR. You can reject both. Each of them assumes that 'reality' is the name of something that can be 'single' or 'multiple'. In Chapter 6, I explain why I don't accept this assumption.

21 Given the different possible interpretations of Carnap's view, Kraut attributes this view to 'Carnap*', who may (or may not) be the historical Carnap, circa 1950.

22 Carnap creates space for a form of pluralism. If, instead, you espouse ontology X on what you think are good grounds, then those who espouse ontology Y are wrong. In this respect, ontological debate is about shutting the other side down. This is why, in Paradigm Land, you have to make a *choice*. Pick a paradigm, any paradigm. This is a very different logic from one based on: You have your commitments, I have mine. We can both proceed accordingly. We don't have to try and prove each other wrong.

23 The 'phenomenological dimension' is Kraut's (2016: 51) expression.

24 Kraut again, Kraut (2016: 38). See also Flocke (2020), which takes a comparable, though not identical, view.
25 'But surely these *are* descriptions!' The problem is, it's not the most precise term. Wittgenstein says: 'Remember how many different kinds of thing are called "description"' (Wittgenstein 2009: §24). So there's an ambiguity. I mean 'description' in the sense of *reportage*. 'Black moves first' isn't a report. It's a requirement, a rule.
26 The clearest introduction to non-cognitivism in ethics, and to the emotivists in particular, is Schroeder (2023).
27 In fact, Carnap endorses a version of metaethical non-cognitivism, not that far removed from Hare's. See Carnap (1963), and the helpful introductory notes by A.W. Carus in Carnap (2017).
28 The baptism ceremony also includes several non-indicatives. Imperative: 'Receive the sign of his cross.' Interrogative: 'Do you reject the devil and all rebellion against God?' Optative: 'May almighty God deliver you from the powers of darkness.'
29 See Austin (1962), Lecture XII.
30 Undecidable in the sense that they are underdetermined by evidence, and cannot be evaluated by the theoretical virtues of simplicity, modesty, parsimony, or elegance. See note 4.
31 Merriam and Tisdell (2016: 9).
32 The mechanics of this illusion, if Cappelen is right, are interesting. Consider a nonsensical sentence. 'You can read it, you can say it, you can try to assert it, you can try to think it, and you'll probably even think you believe it', Cappelen says. 'There will be many thoughts in the vicinity,' he says, 'and they will accompany the illusion' (40-1). Thoughts in the vicinity of 'There exist multiple realities' might include: 'I am thinking about reality', 'I'm thinking about what exists.' 'What one person thinks is real, another person might not', 'With some things there's only one, with others there are several', 'There are many worlds in quantum physics', and so on. Some people report vague mental pictures accompanying these thoughts; for example, intersecting circles or light cones for multiple realities, an unchanging slab for the single reality. This recalls Wittgenstein's suggestion about 'It's 5 o'clock on the sun': that one might picture a clock on the sun pointing to 5 (see Sections 1.3 and 3.2).
33 For an example, see Cappelen and Dever (2013).

References

Austin, J. L. (1962). *How To Do Things With Words: The William James Lectures Delivered at Harvard University in 1955*. Oxford: Clarendon Press.
Ayer, A. J. (1936). *Language, Truth, and Logic*. London: Victor Gollancz Ltd.
Beaney, M. (Ed.) (2013). *The Oxford Handbook of the History of Analytic Philosophy*. Oxford: Oxford University Press.
Bennett, K. (2009). Composition, colocation, and metaontology. In D. J. Chalmers, D. Manley, & R. Wasserman (Eds.), *Metametaphysics: New Essays on the Foundations of Ontology* (pp. 38–76). Oxford: Oxford University Press.
Blackburn, S. (1993). *Essays in Quasi-Realism*. Oxford: Oxford University Press.
Blatti, S., & Lapointe, S. (2016). Introduction. In S. Blatti & S. Lapointe (Eds.), *Ontology After Carnap* (pp. 1–11). Oxford: Oxford University Press.
Bricker, P. (2014). Ontological commitment. *The Stanford Encyclopedia of Philosophy*. https://plato.stanford.edu/entries/ontological-commitment/

Cappelen, H. (2013). Nonsense and illusions of thought. *Philosophical Perspectives*, *27*, 22–50.

Cappelen, H., & Dever, J. (2013). *The Inessential Indexical: On the Philosophical Insignificance of Perspective and the First Person*. Oxford: Oxford University Press.

Carnap, R. (1937). *The Logical Syntax of Language*. London: K. Paul, Trench, Trubner & Co.

Carnap, R. (1950). Empiricism, semantics, and ontology. *Revue Internationale de Philosophie*, *4*(11), 20–40.

Carnap, R. (1959). The elimination of metaphysics through logical analysis of language. In A. J. Ayer (Ed.), *Logical Positivism* (pp. 60–81). New York: Free Press.

Carnap, R. (1963). Replies and expositions. In P. A. Schilpp (Ed.), *The Philosophy of Rudolf Carnap* (pp. 859–1013). LaSalle, IL: Open Court.

Carnap, R. (2017). Value concepts (1958). *Synthese*, *194*, 185–194.

Chalmers, D. J. (2009). Ontological anti-realism. In D. J. Chalmers, D. Manley, & R. Wasserman (Eds.), *Metametaphysics: New Essays on the Foundations of Ontology* (pp. 77–129). Oxford: Oxford University Press.

Creath, R. (2007). Quine's challenge to Carnap. In M. Friedman & R. Creath (Eds.), *The Cambridge Companion to Carnap* (pp. 316–335). Cambridge, UK: Cambridge University Press.

Creath, R. (2016). Carnap and ontology: foreign travel and domestic understanding. In S. Blatti & S. Lapointe (Eds.), *Ontology After Carnap* (pp. 31–58). Oxford: Oxford University Press.

Creath, R. (Ed.) (1990). *Dear Carnap, Dear Van: The Quine-Carnap Correspondence and Related Work*. Berkeley, CA: University of California Press.

Eklund, M. (2009). Carnap and ontological pluralism. In D. J. Chalmers, D. Manley, & R. Wasserman (Eds.), *Metametaphysics: New Essays on the Foundations of Ontology* (pp. 130–156). Oxford: Oxford University Press.

Flocke, V. (2020). Carnap's noncognitivism about ontology. *Nous*, *54*(3), 527–548.

Friedman, M. (1999). *Reconsidering Logical Positivism*. Cambridge, UK: Cambridge University Press.

Friedman, M. (2007). Introduction: Carnap's revolution in philosophy. In M. Friedman & R. Creath (Eds.), *The Cambridge Companion to Carnap* (pp. 1–18). Cambridge, UK: Cambridge University Press.

Friedman, M., & Creath, R. (Eds.). (2007). *The Cambridge Companion to Carnap*. Cambridge, UK: Cambridge University Press.

Gibbard, A. (1990). *Wise Choices, Apt Feelings*. Cambridge, MA: Harvard University Press.

Goertz, G., & Mahoney, J. (2012). *A Tale of Two Cultures: Qualitative and Quantitative Research in the Social Sciences*. Princeton, NJ: Princeton University Press.

Gross, S., Tebben, N., & Williams, M. (Eds.). (2016). *Meaning Without Representation: Essays on Truth, Expression, Normativity, and Naturalism*. New York: Oxford University Press.

Hare, R. M. (1952). *The Language of Morals*. Oxford: Oxford University Press.

Hawley, K. (2018). Social mereology. *Journal of the American Philosophical Association*, *3*(4), 395–411.

Hofweber, T. (2017). Logic and ontology. *The Stanford Encyclopedia of Philosophy*. https://plato.stanford.edu/entries/logic-ontology/

Kraut, R. (2016). Three Carnaps on ontology. In S. Blatti & S. Lapointe (Eds.), *Ontology After Carnap* (pp. 31–58). Oxford: Oxford University Press.

Kraut, R. (2021). Rudolf Carnap: Pragmatist and expressivist about ontology. In R. Bliss & J. T. M. Miller (Eds.), *The Routledge Handbook of Metametaphysics* (pp. 32–48). Abingdon, UK: Routledge.

Kriegel, U. (2013). The epistemological challenge of revisionary metaphysics. *Philosophers' Imprint, 13*(12), 1–30.

Limbeck-Lilienau, C., & Uebel, T. (2022). Introduction. In T. Uebel & C. Limbeck-Lilienau (Eds.), *The Routledge Handbook of Logical Empiricism* (pp. 1–11). Abingdon, UK: Routledge.

Lincoln, Y. S., & Guba, E. G. (1985). *Naturalistic Inquiry*. Beverly Hills, CA: Sage.

Macarthur, D. (2010). Wittgenstein and expressivism. In D. Whiting (Ed.), *The Later Wittgenstein on Language* (pp. 81–95). London: Palgrave Macmillan.

Merriam, S. B., & Tisdell, E. J. (2016). *Qualitative Research: A Guide to Design and Implementation*. Fourth Edition. San Francisco: Jossey-Bass.

Ormston, R., Spencer, L., Barnard, M., & Snape, D. (2013). The foundations of qualitative research. In J. Ritchie, J. Lewis, C. M. Nicholls, & R. Ormston (Eds.), *Qualitative Research Practice: A Guide for Social Science Students and Researchers* (pp. 1–26). London: Sage.

Passmore, J. (1967). Logical positivism. In P. Edwards (Ed.), *The Encyclopedia of Philosophy, Vol 5* (pp. 52–57). New York: Macmillan.

Price, H. (1994). Semantic minimalism and the Frege point. In S. L. Tsohatzidis (Ed.), *Foundations of Speech Act Theory: Philosophical and Linguistics Perspectives* (pp. 132–155). Abingdon, UK: Routledge.

Price, H. (2008). The semantic foundations of metaphysics. In I. Ravenscroft (Ed.), *Minds, Ethics, and Conditionals: Themes from the Philosophy of Frank Jackson* (pp. 111–140). Oxford: Oxford University Press.

Price, H. (2009). Metaphysics after Carnap: the ghost who walks? In D. J. Chalmers, D. Manley, & R. Wasserman (Eds.), *Metametaphysics* (pp. 320–346). New York: Oxford University Press.

Price, H. (2011). *Naturalism Without Mirrors*. New York: Oxford University Press.

Quine, W. V. O. (1948). On what there is. *The Review of Metaphysics, 2*(1), 21–38.

Quine, W. V. O. (1951). Two dogmas of empiricism. In W. V. O. Quine (Ed.), *From a Logical Point of View* (pp. 203–211). Cambridge, MA: Harvard University Press.

Richardson, A., & Uebel, T. (Eds.). (2007). *The Cambridge Companion to Logical Empiricism*. New York: Cambridge University Press.

Schroeder, M. (2023). *Noncognitivism in Ethics*. Second Edition. Abingdon, UK: Routledge.

Sidelle, A. (2016). Frameworks and deflation in "Empiricism, Semantics, and Ontology" and recent metametaphysics. In S. Blatti & S. Lapointe (Eds.), *Ontology After Carnap* (pp. 59–80). Oxford: Oxford University Press.

Sider, T. (2011). *Writing the Book of the World*. Oxford: Oxford University Press.

Simons, P. (2006). Real wholes, real parts: Mereology without algebra. *The Journal of Philosophy, 103*(12), 597–613.

Simpson, M. (2020). What is global expressivism? *The Philosophical Quarterly, 70*(278), 140–161.

Sperber, D., & Wilson, D. (1995). *Relevance: Communication and Cognition*. Second Edition. Oxford: Blackwell.

Stevenson, C. L. (1937). The emotive meaning of ethical terms. *Mind, 46*(181), 14–31.

Thomasson, A. L. (2015). *Ontology Made Easy*. New York: Oxford University Press.

Thomasson, A. L. (2020). *Norms and Necessity*. New York: Oxford University Press.

Uebel, T., & Limbeck-Lilienau, C. (Eds.). (2022). *The Routledge Handbook of Logical Empiricism*. Abingdon, UK: Routledge.

van Fraassen, B. C. (1980). *The Scientific Image*. Oxford: Oxford University Press.

Witherspoon, E. (2000). Conceptions of nonsense in Carnap and Wittgenstein. In A. Crary & R. Read (Eds.), *The New Wittgenstein* (pp. 315–350). London: Routledge.

Wittgenstein, L. (2009). *Philosophical Investigations: Revised 4th Edition by P. M. S. Hacker and Joachim Schulte*. Malden, MA: Wiley-Blackwell.

PART II
The key concepts

5

'THERE IS', 'THERE EXIST'

There is no escape from working through examples. So in Part II, I'll examine some of the sentences, clauses, phrases, and individual words that turn up in qualitative metaphysics, and assess the extent to which they make sense.

The hardest part of this project is finding ways to suggest that something readers thought made sense… doesn't. It's even harder if, in addition to thinking it makes sense, they also think they believe it. 'There exist multiple constructed realities' is something a lot of people believe. It never occurs to them – why should it? They've read it often enough – that it might, in colloquial parlance, be nonsense. In my own case, as I mentioned in Section 2.9, it was 'There exists a single, objective reality'. I assumed it made sense and, with a qualification about the 'objective' bit, I would have said I believed it. It took me a while to recognise that it *doesn't* make sense; and that, therefore, the question of whether I believed it or not didn't arise. The real question was: why did I *think* it made sense?

I'll separate the ontological claims into two parts: the 'There exists…' part (known as the EXISTENTIAL THERE construction in linguistics),[1] and the 'single reality/multiple realities' part. Linguistically, as well as philosophically, everything hangs on whether the two parts can sensibly be combined. Can 'multiple realities' or 'single reality' be slotted into the EXISTENTIAL THERE construction? This is similar to: 'Can 'on the sun' be slotted into the O'CLOCK construction?' The answer (in each case) is 'no'. But it will take Chapters 5 and 6 to make the case fully.

Start with the EXISTENTIAL THERE construction. It's a construction which is an essential component of the ontological claims made by qualitative metaphysicians, but it is not one to which they have paid much attention.[2] Linguists, on the other hand, have taken a lot of interest in it, so let's see what they've said.[3]

DOI: 10.4324/9781003306382-7

5.1 Existential there

Contrast two sentences:

(1) The cat is in the garden.

(2) There is a cat in the garden.

Syntactically, these are very different (and what they say is not the same). Sentence (1) has the subject-predicate form. 'The cat' is a noun phrase acting as the grammatical subject of the sentence; '… is in the garden' is the predicate. In this case, the predicate consists of the verb 'is', and a prepositional phrase ('in the garden'). So this type of subject-predicate sentence is comprised of:

NOUN PHRASE + *is* + PREPOSITIONAL PHRASE

Sentence (2) is an example of the EXISTENTIAL THERE construction.

There is + NOUN PHRASE + PREPOSITIONAL PHRASE

The noun phrase from sentence (1) now *follows* the verb (and has the indefinite, rather than the definite, article). 'There' starts the sentence, and the prepositional phrase 'in the garden' – in this construction, it acts as what linguists call the *locative coda* – completes it. I will make some short preliminary notes on each component.

'There': is not a name, noun phrase, or pronoun, which is what the grammatical subject of a subject-predicate sentence would be, as in sentence (1). So the question arises as to whether the existential 'there' is a grammatical subject, given that it's the first word in the sentence and is followed by a verb. Some modern linguists think it is; others think it is a locative adverb; yet others would classify it as an *expletive*, a type of word that has no semantic content.

The verb: is usually the third person of 'exist' or 'be'.[4] These are often interchangeable but not always. Examples (3) and (4) in the list below say more or less the same thing. Examples (5) and (6) don't. The verb can be either singular or plural ('is'/'are', 'exists'/'exist'), but this does not depend on the apparent subject of the sentence ('There'). Rather, the verb agrees with the post-verbal noun phrase. Contrast (7) and (8). This is one of the reasons for thinking that 'There…' is not the grammatical subject.

The post-verbal noun phrase: must be indefinite. So (9) works, but (10), which has the definite article, doesn't.[5] The combination of 'There is', or 'There are', and the definite article does occur in a different construction, DEICTIC THERE. So sentence (8) should not be confused with (11). The latter illustrates the DEICTIC THERE, and in this construction 'there…' *is* a locative adverb, and the post-verbal noun phrase is definite ('the').[6] In EXISTENTIAL THERE, the head of the noun phrase can be concrete ('coffee'), abstract ('prime'), an event ('concert'), or almost any other ontological category.

The locative coda: is not always included; but, if not explicit, a coda can generally be retrieved from the context (5). This is a topic of interest in Section 5.4. A locative coda can be spatial (7, 8), or it can refer to some analogical index or dimension, such as time (12) or natural numbers (13). A coda which refers to a domain of discourse (14) can also be classified as locative, but this variation needs further examination (Sections 5.2 and 5.5). The coda does not always appear at the end of the sentence. In (15), it precedes all the other components.

(3) There is a god.

(4) There exists a god.

(5) There's coffee.

(6) There exists coffee.

(7) There is a boy in the garden.

(8) There are boys in the garden.

(9) There exists a secret society at Yale.

(10) *There exists the secret society at Yale.

(11) There are the boys! In the garden!

(12) There is a concert at 8:00.

(13) There is a prime between 7 and 13.

(14) There are unicorns in mythology.

(15) In mythology there are unicorns.

All of this may seem a bit dry, and of questionable relevance. Dryness? A matter of taste. Questionable relevance? I'll argue not. One reason why sentences such as 'There is a single objective reality' and 'There are multiple constructed realities' are assumed to make sense is that the application conditions for the EXISTENTIAL THERE construction have not been studied by those who refer to them in qualitative research texts. We'll see how this pans out in the rest of the chapter.

5.2 Existence and location

So we have (1) the subject-predicate sentence, and (2) the EXISTENTIAL 'there'. They don't say the same thing, and their syntax is different, but they do have something in common: they both ascribe location to something. In (1), it is '*the* cat', one which (in context) is already known about, or which has previously been mentioned. The sentence refers to this particular cat and describes its whereabouts. In (2), the location is ascribed to just '*a* cat', any old cat, one that is not already known by the speaker. So in (1), the existence of the subject is presupposed; and the sentence is true if the subject has the property it is said to have (being in the garden). In (2), the existence of the relevant item isn't presupposed. Instead, it is *introduced*;[7] and the sentence is true if something with the relevant property (being a cat) is found in the specified location. An alternative way of putting it: in (1), *the cat* is described as being in the garden; in (2), *the garden* is described as containing a cat.

Despite this difference, however, both sentences do ascribe location to something. So McNally (1997) poses an interesting and important question: does the 'existential construction form a class with locative constructions'? And she notes: 'there is a persistent intuition in the linguistics literature that existential sentences have something in common with sentences that ascribe location to an individual' (xi). But if this intuition is right, and existential claims and location ascriptions are closely linked, does it imply an intrinsic connection between location and existence? Is it true that 'to be is to be *somewhere*' (Szekely 2015: 106), a claim going as far back as Aristotle?[8] Are EXISTENTIAL THERE (ET) and locative ascription (LA) somehow bound together?

There are several considerations suggesting that the answer is 'yes'. For example, the *existential* use of 'be' is 'rare in English without a locative or temporal complement' (Lyons 1968: 390). This fact itself suggests that ET sentences and LA sentences might be related. Moreover, since ET sentences generally do have a locative coda, 'there' as the first word in ET sentences could be a device used to 'anticipate' the locative phrase. This idea is supported by the use of comparable terms in comparable constructions in other European languages: for example, French *y* (*il y a*), Italian *ci* (*ci sono*), and German *da* (*ist da*). All of which, Lyons argues, implies a locative origin for existential sentences.

Lyons also points out that there is little difference in meaning between sentences such as (16) and (17), the latter being an indefinite LA, and he suspects they might be linked by a transformation rule. A simple illustration of the kind of thing he has in mind is the so-called *there-insertion* rule, which 'transforms' an ordinary LA sentence, such as (17), into an ET sentence (16).[9]

(16) There is a unicorn in the garden.

(17) A unicorn is in the garden.

The transformation rule is relatively straightforward. For any sentence of the form illustrated by (17), slide the pre-verbal NP to the right, so that it takes up a position immediately after the verb rather than immediately before it. Pre-verbal becomes post-verbal. Then, because English requires something that can function as a grammatical subject, insert 'There' at the beginning of the sentence.

On this analysis, 'There' is a dummy pronoun, whose only role is to act as the grammatical subject. It has no intrinsic meaning of its own. In which case, it's presumably just an accident that the word chosen to fulfil this function is the same as the locative adverb. But if there's no locative link at all between (16) and (17), why doesn't some other word, with no locative connotations, introduce ET? (Like the pronoun 'It' in 'It is raining'.) Why not, for example, 'chop suey'?[10] If the *there-insertion* transformation rule is correct, it does seem a bit of a coincidence that 'There...' is used to begin a construction that regularly features a locative coda (especially as many writers find it difficult to construe 'there' as a pronoun).[11]

However, we can tiptoe past transformational approaches and adopt a cognitive grammar perspective instead. On this view, the link between ET and LA has nothing to do with transformation rules. Instead, it reflects the similarities between the constructions. Lakoff (1987: 541), for example, doesn't think that existential *there* is a semantically empty 'dummy' pronoun, serving a purely syntactic purpose. He sees it rather as designating a 'mental space'. It introduces the idea that there is a space in which an entity is to be located, while the locative coda indicates the nature of the space.

Have a look at some examples:

(18) There was a unicorn in my dream.

(19) There are unicorns in heraldry.

(20) There are unicorns in mythology.

(21) There is a unicorn in the garden.

In these examples, 'There' sets up a space, which is characterised by the locative coda. The entity being situated in the space is, in this case, a unicorn or unicorns. Only in (21) does the space correspond to the real, spatiotemporal world. In the absence of codas like 'in my dream' or 'in mythology', Lakoff notes, 'it is assumed that mental spaces are meant to correspond to reality. In all such cases, the existential constructions are concerned with real-world existence' (543).

My own view is that there *is* a connection between existentials and locatives but that 'there' plays no direct role in this. I'm inclined to agree that it is semantically empty, and merely fills a syntactic gap (but not as a result of *there-insertion*). I find an account developed by Szekely (2015) more plausible. The next section is about that.

5.3   Feature placing

Virtually all the linguists who have written on this topic share a certain assumption. This is the view that, despite their surface characteristics, ET sentences have a subject-predicate form. This assumption follows from the general understanding that the structure of *all* sentences is subject-predicate, an idea that can be traced back to Aristotle. Consequently, one chunk of the literature tries to explain which component of an ET sentence is the subject and which is the predicate. It's certainly not self-evident. 'Virtually every possible combination of the elements of the *there*-sentence has been argued, at one point or another, to instantiate the subject-predicate form' (Szekely 2015: 43). For example, Williams (1996) proposes 'there' as the subject, and the post-verbal NP as predicate. Moro (1997) proposes the reverse: the post-verbal NP as subject, and 'there' as predicate. Chomsky (1986) argues that the post-verbal NP is the subject and that the coda is the predicate. The lack of agreement makes you wonder whether ET sentences are really subject-predicate (SP) after all.

According to Szekely, they aren't. Her view is that 'the existential *there* sentence does not map to the subject-predicate form at all' (2015: 46). Even more emphatically: 'I mean that subject and predicate expressions… are not *in any sense* constituents of the proposition that the *there*-sentence expresses' (42). The ET is a completely different *kind* of sentence. It is a feature-placing (FP) sentence, not an SP sentence.[12] A preliminary statement of what kind of difference this is:

> **[SP]** The subject is an item, or a class of items, which (in context) has already been introduced.[13]
>
> The predicate ascribes a property, or relation, or activity, to this item/class.
>
> The sentence is true if the item/class has the property ascribed to it.
>
> **[FP]** An item/class is introduced by specifying a feature (a kind, a general description).
>
> The feature is said to be ('is placed') at a particular location.
>
> The sentence is true if an object instantiating this feature is found at the designated location.

Stripped down even more:

> **[SP]** The X is Y.
>
> (X has *already* been introduced)
>
> **[FP]** There is an X at L.[14]
>
> (X is *thereby* introduced)

Some examples might be useful:

(22) The squirrel is eating the fat balls. (SP)

(23) There is a squirrel in the garden. (FP)

(24) Tigers are an endangered species. (SP)

(25) There are tigers in the garden. (FP)

In SP, the X is already known about. It has already been 'introduced'. In (22), *The* squirrel is a squirrel already mentioned. I know which squirrel you're referring to. In (24), I already know about tigers (in that sense, they've been 'introduced' already), but you are giving me some new information. In FP, the X is being introduced into the conversational context for the first time. In (23), there is *a* squirrel – one previously unmentioned – in the garden. In (25), an unspecified number of tigers are being introduced, and placed in a location.[15] Examples (22) and (24) are true if the specified objects have the property attributed to them. Examples (23) and (25) are true if objects instantiating the description are found at the designated location.[16]

On this account, the locative is intrinsic to ET sentences. They are, after all, described as feature-*placing*. There is 'something fundamental about the role of location in feature placing' (Szekely 2015: 11); and, more emphatically,

> Location and existence are inextricably bound together for ordinary entities – as the saying goes, to be is to be *somewhere* – and it has often been claimed that we understand the existence of more *abstract* entities by analogical extension from concrete ones.[17]
>
> *(106)*

However, the reason for this inextricable togetherness does not, in Szekely's view, have anything to do with 'there' as a locative adverb. She regards the existential 'there' as an expletive: it does not have any semantic content, despite the fact that it occurs in the syntactic subject position. It is not, as she says, 'there' that does the placing. Instead, this function is carried out directly by the locative coda.

This view raises two interesting questions. First, if the locative is essential to ET sentences, what about those that don't *have* a locative coda (called 'bare existentials' in the literature)? Second, how can abstract entities be 'placed'? How can they be 'located' in the way that squirrels, tigers, and unicorns can be? The first question is one I'll deal with in the next section. Here, I'll say something about locating abstract entities.

Some things which are clearly not physical objects can nevertheless be located in the spatio-temporal, physical world; for example, events, processes, and mental states:

(26) There's a game at Wembley tomorrow.

(27) There is political change in Westminster.

(28) There is anger in Philadelphia this morning.

Imagine any of these sentences without the locative coda. 'There is a game'; 'There is political change'; 'There is anger.' If you heard or read any of these, the first question in your mind would be 'Where?'. You would obviously want other details as well, but would consider yourself not properly informed if the game, the political change, and the anger were not given a physical location. In some cases, the coda has a temporal dimension as well as a spatial one (26, 28). But this is just another form of location: a 'placing' in time, as well as in three-dimensional space.

With nouns further along the spectrum of abstraction, which cannot obviously be placed or timed, we still find codas which, by analogy, can be regarded as locative. Some examples:

(29) There's a flaw in your argument.

(30) There are weird ideas in quantum physics.

(31) There is a prime between 7 and 13.

(32) There is luck in every board game.

(33) There are facts in that statement, but not many.

Again, remove the coda from any of these, and we're going to feel underinformed, or not informed at all. 'There's a flaw.' Right, well, if I'm aware of the context in which this is said, I can probably work out where the flaw is supposed to be (and notice the use of locative 'where'). But with the coda being present, I know that the flaw is allegedly in my argument – not yours, or hers, or his calculations, or the boss's plan, or this dinner plate, or that piece of wood. 'There is a prime.' Of course. Lots of them. But when the coda is included, I know exactly where in the sequence of natural numbers you're referring to. And so on.[18]

We establish the truth, or otherwise, of an ET sentence by confirming that an object with the specified features can be found at the designated location. Sometimes, we have to count. 'There are three cats in the garden.' In this example, 'three instantiations of the feature *cat* in the garden are required for truth' (Szekely 2015: 87). Either way, we have to check. How about 'There are multiple cats in the garden'? Now, counting is not required: all we have to do is determine whether there is more than one cat in the specified location. Straightforward enough.

In Section 5.5, I'll take up a comparable but less straightforward question. Not single versus multiple cats, but single versus multiple realities.

5.4 Bare existentials

'There's coffee and biscuits.' I've just walked in, five minutes before the meeting starts. I look round and, sure enough, on the table by the window are cups, a plate of biscuits, and what I take to be a pot of coffee. The locative coda, in this case, is unnecessary. My informant obviously does not mean 'There's coffee and biscuits in the café across the road', or 'in my house', or 'in Brazil'. If he did, he would have said so. Omitting the locative implies that the coffee and biscuits are somewhere in the vicinity. This is the sort of context-related inference that both speaker and hearer are familiar with. It's like 'It's raining'. Without the locative, the natural inference is 'It's raining here', not 'It's raining in Steeple Bumpstead' (unless, of course, 'here' *is* Steeple Bumpstead).

So any locative-less ET statement – a 'bare existential' – makes us ask what the context implies about the whereabouts of the feature it refers to. Start with the most obvious, and work out from there. If the conversation so far has been about the Royal Albert Hall, and someone says 'There's a King Crimson concert tonight', the default understanding is that she means 'tonight at the RAH'. If it turns out that she meant 'at the Symphony Hall, Birmingham', we'll remain puzzled, pending further explanation. Why was that a relevant comment, given the conversational context? [19]

The existence of bare existentials is quite consistent with Szekely's claim that 'location and existence are inextricably bound together for ordinary entities'. This is why, when the coda is missing, we turn to the context for clues as to the intended location. This, as we've seen, is also true for post-verbal NPs that refer to abstract entities. 'There is a prime.' 'There is political change.' 'There is anger.' 'There is luck.' 'There is a flaw.' All these prompt the question: Where? Whose? In what?

But some bare existentials don't seem to prompt the question, at least not in the same way. Look at (35), for example. 'That sentence will be true if a location can be produced at which the feature "wombats" is instantiated by an item in the world… "somewhere" or "anywhere"' (Szekely 2015: 54). So now we're not checking a specific location to see whether the feature is instantiated *there*; instead, we're looking to see if there is *anywhere* in the world where it is instantiated. Szekely calls this 'place-featuring', rather than 'feature placing'. Sentence (35) says that, *somewhere* in the world, the 'wombat' feature is instantiated – but doesn't specify a more precise location. The same is true of (36). It claims that, somewhere in the world, the ivory-billed woodpecker feature is instantiated. But note: somewhere *in the world*.

(34) There are trees.

(35) There are wombats.

(36) There are ivory-billed woodpeckers.

(37) There is a god.

(38) There are unicorns.

(39) There is a Santa Claus.

Examples (34) to (39) are listed, very roughly, in order of the degree of doubt there might be about the existence of the entities concerned. With (34), there is presumably no doubt at all, and it is difficult to imagine any circumstances in which it would be spoken. You read it, and immediately you're searching for a locative. Trees where? Somewhere unexpected, presumably. In the Gobi Desert? On the moon? There is no real doubt about wombats, either. But with (36), there *is* doubt. Ivory-billed woodpeckers had been thought extinct, the last attested sighting being in 1944. But recent photographs suggest that there might be some in Louisiana (Millman 2022). The point is: where there is no doubt (34, 35), it is unlikely that the sentence would be uttered. The greater the doubt, the more likely it is that someone, somewhere, will make the relevant claim, often with stress on the verb. 'There *is* a god!' 'There *are* unicorns!' 'There *is* a Santa Claus!'

It's crucial to recognise that, even, with sentences like (34) to (39), the locative link remains. *Somewhere in the world*, ivory-billed woodpeckers can be found. *Somewhere in the world*, you'll find unicorns. But what does this 'somewhere in the world' signify? Well, for example, it entails '*not* in my dream', '*not* in heraldry', '*not* in mythology', '*not* in fiction'. Crudely and unphilosophically, it means 'in the real world', 'in reality'. Sentences like (37) to (39) can therefore be paraphrased as: 'God is *real!*' 'Unicorns are *real!*' 'Santa Claus is *real!*'[20]

In this context, 'the world' is not necessarily limited to the Earth. One version of what it signifies is: 'the sum of all entities spatio-temporally related to a given entity' (the speaker could be the 'given entity').[21] This covers everything from the house next door, to the planet as a whole, and on to the entire universe, including stuff 46 billion light-years away. In other words, all of space and time.[22] If you found a couple of unicorns on M51-ULS-1b, the exoplanet in the M51 galaxy, 28 million light-years away, then (38) would be true (although there would be questions about how the unicorns got there and where they came from). Still, there would definitely be *unicorns*. Somewhere in the world, somewhere in reality.[23]

At which point, we can expect the special pleading to start. Not so much with respect to Santa Claus or unicorns, but certainly with respect to God. There *is* a God, but He (?) is not *in* 'the world', not *in* 'the universe', not *in* space-time. If that's what the implied locative in bare existentials amounts to, then God gets a free pass. He's the one exception. By definition. By fiat. Because.[24]

I won't say much about God in the rest of this chapter, though there might be the odd mention. Instead, I'll return to the vexed question of how many realities there are, ontologically speaking. I suspect there will be some special pleading on that one, too.

5.5   Reality and realities

The widespread view in linguistics is that existential sentences are closely related to sentences ascribing location to an individual; and, more specifically, that the locative coda is essential to the ET construction. Language represents location and existence as aspects of the same concept. To be is to be *somewhere*.[25] The primary source of disagreement concerns the linguistic basis for the existence/location connection. My own sympathies, as I've suggested, lie with Szekely's account; and in the rest of the chapter, I'll take her version as read. At the same time, though, I want to emphasise the locative/ existence link more generally, irrespective of whether Szekely's explanation of it is the right one.

Back, then, to the ontological claims of qualitative metaphysics. We can take the usual examples 'There is a single reality' [SR] and 'There exist multiple realities' [MR]. Start with a comparison:

(40) There is a single electron in a hydrogen atom.

(41) There are multiple electrons in a hydrogen atom.

To determine which of these is correct, we have to do some tricky empirical work. It's not like looking in the garden to see whether there's a single cat or multiple cats. On the other hand, the principle is the same. So how do you determine whether MR or SR is correct?

Reader: Well, for starters, 'correct' is not a term I would use in this context. Neither is 'true'.

Me: Okay, I'll rephrase. What are your criteria for theory choice? I'm assuming you don't just toss a coin.

Reader: My criteria reflect what I understand about the world. I select MR because I don't think there is a reality independent of our perceptions. Each person experiences from their own point of view, so each person experiences a different reality.[26]

Me: So your criterion for choosing an ontological theory – MR in this case – is that it repeats another ontological theory that says exactly the same thing.

Reader: No, I'm suggesting that people experience things differently.

Me: Yes, okay. We can agree about that. But I'm curious about the inference. 'People experience things differently; *therefore* each person experiences a different reality.' But somebody else might infer: 'People experience things differently; *therefore* each individual experiences the same reality, but in a different way.' Now we have two more ontological beliefs: 'different realities' *vs.* 'same reality'.

Reader: So? We already know people have different ontological assumptions.
Me: So the same question we started with. What are your criteria for choosing between 'different' and 'same' reality? Because all you've done so far is go round in an ontological circle.

Let's get back to the locative question: 'Where?' We check the garden to see whether there's a single cat there, or multiple cats. We check the hydrogen atom to see whether there's a single electron there, or multiple electrons. What do we check to see whether there's a single reality or multiple realities? I'll assume that (42) and (43) don't apply:

(42) There are multiple realities in mythology.

(43) There are multiple realities in fiction.

In which case, if we're not talking about 'non-reality' domains, are we talking about the default option: somewhere in the real world? Do we examine the real world to see whether there are multiple realities in it, or a single reality? There is obviously something rather odd about this. First, there is the implied singularity of 'the real world'; and claiming that multiple realities exist in the one reality is not, without further explanation, fully intelligible. In any case, second, where in space-time would we look for multiple realities (or the single reality)? Third, suppose we paraphrase (as in Section 5.4): 'There are Xs' becomes 'Xs are real.' In this case, we would get: 'Multiple realities are real' and 'The single reality is real.' Again, this is slightly odd. Multiple realities are real *whats*? [27] I can't think of a sensible answer to that. 'Multiple realities are real realities.' Any takers?

Still, perhaps sense can be made of it. [28] One option is to paraphrase again. 'Multiple realities exist.' But this doesn't really help. Wombats exist, ivory-billed woodpeckers exist, unicorns exist, and Santa Claus exists. If these claims are true, then the wombats, the ivory-billed woodpeckers, the unicorns, and Santa Claus exist… somewhere. To exist, is to exist somewhere. With God, we expect the special pleading. It looks as if 'reality' and 'realities' are going to need some special pleading, too.

5.6 Special pleading

So let's specially plead. It's all very well pointing out that existence claims for things like wombats and unicorns have locative inflections (says the special pleader). They're physical objects, so obviously they have to exist somewhere 'in the world'; that is, somewhere in spatio-temporal reality. But it's different for claims about the existence of realities, or claims about their singularity/multiplicity. *Obviously*, the single reality doesn't exist *inside* 'spatio-temporal reality'. Ditto multiple realities. So what's to stop us saying that the locative connection simply gets suspended when we talk about reality/realities as a whole? Yes, it's there when we refer to physical objects; but surely everyone understands that it's not activated when the reference is to reality itself (/realities themselves). In that context, it's just existence-pure-and-simple that's at stake, not existence-somewhere. As in: something exists or it doesn't.

This, of course, merely restates the claim that MR and SR escape the locative connection. It's not an argument for that view. If a certain construction – in this case, ET – has a condition attached to it; and if we find a sentence which appears to be an example of the construction, but which does not comply with the condition; then there are two possibilities. Either (a) in this particular sentence, the condition is for some reason suspended; or (b) the sentence is in some way inadmissible. The special pleader has opted for (a) but has not yet explained why. 'Surely everyone understands that the condition is not activated when the reference is to reality itself.' This is not an argument, it's a rhetorical device. 'Surely' tries to elicit agreement on the basis that 'this is familiar' and 'everybody else gets it'.

In any case, what is the 'existence-pure-and-simple' that is contrasted with 'existence-somewhere'? The distinction is made as if everyone were familiar with it, and we all understood what 'existence-pure-and-simple' means. But in the absence of any explanation, it's only a form of words covering a gap. Here is another chess analogy. A chess move involves a certain kind of locative: transferring a piece from the square it currently occupies to a different square. Suppose someone wanted to talk about 'chess-moves-pure-and-simple': that is: moves that *don't* involve the locative transfer. 'Existence-pure-and-simple' is like that. It's an attempt to invent-by-subtraction a new concept, while passing it off as a familiar one.[29]

Is this the best the special pleader can do? Say that 'existence-pure-and-simple' is a form of existence that does *not* involve location? Define something by reference to an absence? This is problem solving by fiat, argument-by-assertion. 'How can there be existence without location? Well, there just can. I'll call it "pure-and-simple". So now the non-locative existence question has an answer. It's possible for there to be existence without the locative condition because there is, after all, such a thing as existence-pure-and-simple.' This has a distinctly theological ring to it. It's like defining God as the uncaused causer, in order to get rid of the otherwise irritating question: 'Where did God come from?'[30]

The special pleader encourages us to assume that ET sentences consist of a 'pure-and-simple' existence claim, *plus* a locative; as if the locative were an optional add-on. But Szekely's view is that existence claims are *essentially* locative. In effect, existence *is* location. To be is to be somewhere. So you can't just subtract the locative and say: 'All I've done is remove the optional locative dangling from the pure-and-simple existence claim.' Location isn't a dangler. It's not an appendage. It's an essential part of the business of existing.

Come at the same train of thought from a different angle. If something exists, it's *part of* reality. So you *can't* ascribe existence to reality itself (or realities themselves). If you insist on doing so, you're saying that reality is part of reality (or that multiple realities are). And that's heading rapidly towards nonsense. Let me emphasise: this is *not* to say that SR and MR are false. They are neither true nor false. They don't *say anything*. They are referentially unsuccessful. 'Pure-and-simple existence', abstracted from location, is part of a metaphysical illusion.

A third different angle. Back to the question of single versus multiple. One cat on the lawn or several? One electron in the hydrogen atom or more than one? One god, or a pantheon? This kind of question makes sense for things that are somewhere in the world, things that are 'part of reality'. Existence, location, and single-or-multiple all hang together. But once you start looking at reality-as-a-whole, the world-as-a-totality, the question of one-or-multiple is no longer intelligible.

There is a distant echo here of Kant's antinomies (Kant 1996). Questions that can be asked about things *in* reality – before and after, cause and effect, inside and outside, singularity and multiplicity – can't be asked about reality itself.[31] It's like asking what is outside space, what happened before time began, or what brought the relations of cause-and-effect into being. There's a 'what time is it on the sun?' kind of contradiction in these questions. They ask about a possibility that, in the specified circumstances, has by definition been revoked. There isn't anything *outside* space. Nothing could happen *before* time began. Nothing *caused* cause-and-effect. Reality is *everything*. It is the totality of things that can be counted.[32] How, then, can it be 'single' or 'multiple' itself?

Reader: Hang on. Suddenly, we're only talking about 'reality'. What happened to 'realities'? Aren't you just begging the question? Quietly smuggling the positivist single reality back in?

Me: No. I'm arguing against singularity as well as multiplicity. Reality can't be singular for the same reasons it can't be multiple. The choice we are offered between a single reality and multiple realities is illusory. Admittedly, a fuller answer to your question depends on ideas I'll be discussing in the next chapter.

Reader: H'm, well, we'll see. But you're still assuming that the only things that exist are physical objects. Countable entities, and stuff consisting of grains, molecules, atoms, or what-have-you.

Me: Actually, I'm not. What gets included in 'reality' (or 'realities', for that matter) is anything that can be located in space-time. So as well as physical objects, you get events, situations, processes, thoughts, hopes, beliefs, observations, plans, promises, problems, experiences…

Reader: But you're still pushing the idea that 'existence is intrinsically spatio-temporal', even though you haven't proved that there's no such thing as existence-pure-and-simple.

Me: But that's not the kind of thing that can be *proved*. The only thing I can do is try to make you feel a bit less comfortable about just assuming that there *is*.

To conclude the chapter, I want to return to the earlier discussion of existence claims which introduce things that don't appear to have spatio-temporal location (Section 5.2). I have in mind examples such as: 'There's only one even prime', 'There's a theory that…', 'There's a possibility that…', and 'There's a reason why…'. These look like non-locative abstractions. So might examples of this kind be a route to existence 'pure-and-simple'?

5.7 Non-locative existence

The easy bit is that theories, possibilities, and reasons *are* located in space-time. Have a look at some examples:

(44) There's a theory that the moon landings never happened.

(45) There was a theory that combustion was phlogiston escaping.

(46) There's a possibility that mammoths will become de-extinct.

(47) There's a reason why the ice caps are melting.

(48) There is only one even prime number.

Examples (44) to (47) are located in spatio-temporal regions. In (45), there *was* a theory… It existed in the 17th and 18th centuries and was located on Earth. The possibility of mammoths becoming de-extinct (46) also applies to the Earth, and could not arise prior to them becoming extinct in the first place, or before DNA was extracted from a frozen mammoth in Siberia. The reason why the ice caps are melting (47) applies to the period in which this has been happening, and is again specific to our own planet.

Numbers are rather different. Sentence (48) does not *refer* to a theory, belief, or possibility, all of which would be locative. Still, numbers do belong to what Strawson calls a 'system of relationships', by means of which 'non-particulars' – in effect, things that aren't physical objects – come to be treated as locatable items in the way particulars are. The latter are ordered in space-time, the spatio-temporal framework constituting the *original* system of relationships in which such objects can be located. But 'non-particulars, too, may be related and ordered among themselves; they may form systems; and the structure of such a system may acquire a kind of autonomy, so that further members are essentially identified by their position in the system' (Strawson 1959: 233).

The special pleader will be unimpressed. Numbers do form a system of relationships in which any given number can be 'located', but the locating isn't spatio-temporal. The number system is *analogous* to the spatio-temporal system, but that's neither here nor there. The point is, it's not *identical* with it. So might existence 'pure-and-simple' be something like the non-locative existence attributed to numbers? Could saying 'There are multiple realities' be *something* like saying 'There are multiple numbers'?

Well, we shouldn't rule it out. But there's at least one reason why we might hesitate to make this claim. 'There are multiple numbers' refers to something considerably less than a totality. Suppose that numbers do exist in a pure-and-simple sense. They are still part of a much wider 'world', including space-time. It's not as if one is saying: 'The sequence of numbers is *all* there is.' So a comparison with the totality implied by both 'single reality' and 'multiple realities' is lacking in that respect. We're still modelling the existence of the *whole* on the existence of a *part*. And that's what lands you with antinomies.

However, there's another option. Strawson argues that the words referring to the non-particulars which belong to a 'system of relationships' can, in certain cases, be thought of 'as a unit of meaning in a rule-governed member of a language system' (1959: 234). In this comment, there is more than an echo of Carnap's 'language frameworks' (see Section 4.3). Can't qualitative metaphysicians borrow Carnap's suggestion about the introduction of language frameworks, and get 'multiple realities' up and running that way? Is there anything to stop them proposing a 'multiple realities' language? The idea being that pure-and-simple existence, without any locative implications, can be built into the framework.

Answer: no, there isn't anything to stop them. But there are two implications which can't be ducked. The first concerns the distinction between internal and external questions. Inside the 'multiple realities' MR language framework, 'There exist multiple realities' is a truism (just as, within the 'numbers' language framework, 'There are numbers' is a truism). However, the external question 'Do multiple realities *really* exist?' is a pseudo-question (just as 'Do numbers *really* exist?' is a pseudo-question). The same applies to the 'single reality' SR language framework, and the question 'does a single reality *really* exist?'.

The second implication is Carnap's condition.

Everyone is at liberty to build his own logic, i.e. his own form of language, as he wishes. All that is required of him is that, if he wishes to discuss it, he must state his methods clearly, and give syntactical rules instead of philosophical arguments.

(Carnap 1937, §17)

So rules for the use of the expression 'multiple realities' must be spelt out (see Section 4.5), together with a clarification of the means by which one 'reality' can be differentiated from another. For example, questions like the following need to be answered to get the MR language up and running.

When do new realities pop into existence? Does Jenny's reality come into being when she is born, or at a later stage? Are 'realities' centred on particular phenomena rather than particular people? Is there any overlap between different 'realities'? If Amiria's experience of an event, V, is different from Bankole's experience of the 'same' event, does V belong to a reality they share? Or does it bifurcate into two non-overlapping realities? If so, in what sense do Amiria and Bankole interpret the 'same event'? If they don't, how can the two experiences be compared in the first place, given that they take place in two distinct, non-overlapping 'realities'? How do Amiria and Bankole know that they're attaching different meanings to the same thing? These questions all concern the conditions in which, within the 'multiple realities' framework, we say: 'Here's one reality. Here's a different one.'[33]

Comparable questions will need to be answered for the SR language framework. For example: is the 'single reality' exclusively spatiotemporal, or does it include abstract entities, virtual reality, God, the past? Does it include macroscopic objects, or are its constituents fundamental particles and/or wave functions? Are mental states included, or does accepting the 'single reality' entail reductionism? In what way does the 'single reality' language deal with the patchwork disunity of the sciences? Does it imply a form of holism, with every 'façade' connecting seamlessly to the others? How does it reconcile the 'single reality' with scientific models referring to non-existent entities, impossible properties, and idealisations? What kind of 'singularity' is consistent with models each of which is indispensable, but which contradict each other?[34]

Without this detailed spelling out of terms and conditions, we can have no idea what the expressions 'single reality' and 'multiple realities' refer to. You might just as well say 'There is a single deltub' or 'There are multiple deltubs', for all the sense that MR and SR would make in the absence of a clear specification of the rules-of-use. Protesting that you were using 'single' and 'reality' – or 'multiple' and 'realities' – in their usual senses would be of no help because (I'll suggest) these senses are *not* their usual ones.

5.8   Linking remark

However, this last statement will be strongly resisted. Obviously. So it is at this point that we need to move on to a consideration of how the terms 'reality' and 'realities' are actually used, both in ordinary discourse and by methodologists such as Lincoln and Guba. I said at the outset that this chapter and the next are not easy to keep separate, and we have now reached the buffer zone. So we'll cross the border which divides the EXISTENTIAL THERE part of the ontological sentence from the post-verbal noun phrase. The next chapter discusses the meaning of 'reality', 'realities', 'a single reality' and 'multiple realities'.

Notes

1 It is conventional to place expressions referring to particular constructions in small caps. See Hilpert (2014).
2 The same is not true of mainstream philosophers. In particular, there has been a vigorous debate about 'quantifier variance'. Questions from this debate: Is 'exists' univocal, or does it have different senses in different ontological languages? If one philosopher says Xs exist, and another philosopher says that Xs don't exist, could they just be speaking different languages? Can both claims be true? (We can take this question into the qualitative research context: if one author says there exists a single reality, and another says there exist multiple realities, might they be talking past each other, employing different senses of 'exist'?) See Hirsch (2002) for a defence of quantifier variance, and Sider (2009) for a classic counter.
3 My account of EXISTENTIAL THERE draws on Lakoff (1987), Freeze (1992), McNally (1997), Milsark (2014), Szekely (2015).
4 Both Szekely (2015) and Moltmann (2013) note that 'to be' covers a wider range of options than 'to exist'. For example: 'There are tame tigers that don't exist' (in children's fiction). 'There are historic buildings that no longer exist.' So perhaps: 'There are multiple realities *[in fiction]* which don't exist.'
5 The asterisk attached to (10) is a conventional sign indicating that the sentence is ungrammatical.
6 There are several other syntactic differences between DEICTIC and EXISTENTIAL 'there'. For example, the latter can be negative ('There isn't a cat in the garden') and can take tag questions ('There is a cat in the garden, isn't there?). The former can't ('There aren't the boys in the garden!'; 'There are the boys in the garden, aren't there?').
7 'Introduced' in the sense of being an item which (in context) is *not* inferable, familiar, presupposed, previously mentioned, commonly recognised or, in some other way, a known point of departure.
8 It first appears in the *Physics* IV, 208a30. For details, see Morrison (2002).
9 Transformation rules were originally associated with the early forms of transformational grammar (Chomsky 1957), although accounts of their function and significance have changed over time. See further in the Glossary.
10 This is a jocular suggestion by Kimball 1973. He's just dramatising the point.
11 This is just one of the arguments against *there-insertion*. There are others. For example, if the *there-insertion* rule is correct, then 'There is a god' must be derived from 'A god is'; and it's generally agreed that this doesn't work. (But notice that deriving 'There exists a god' from 'A god exists' *does* work.) Likewise, 'There is a single reality' would have to be derived from 'A single reality is'. Which doesn't really seem plausible.
12 Szekely takes the expression 'feature-placing' from Strawson (1959), especially Chapter 7. Strawson is clear that 'in a feature-placing language the subject-predicate distinction has no place'.
13 'Already introduced' in the sense of being an item which (in context) is inferable, familiar, previously mentioned, presupposed, or commonly recognised. See note 7, and Quirk *et al.* (1985) section 2.47.
14 Strictly speaking, a 'feature' is not an entity of the kind referred to in SP structures. It is something *instantiated* by an item to be found at the designated location.

15 Of course, it's more complicated than this, because there are different ways of construing 'subject' and 'predicate': as logical concepts, or as grammatical concepts. *Grammatically*, a sentence can have an indefinite NP as its subject: '*A squirrel is eating the fat balls.*' But, *logically*, a subject is a (previously introduced) individual or class. For Strawson (2016), the paradigm case of the subject is a *definite* spatio-temporal particular. But an *indefinite* subject can be regarded as an 'extension' of the paradigm. In the text, I focus on the basic distinction between (a) attributing a property to an *already-introduced* entity and (b) *introducing* an entity by placing a feature at a location.

16 By the same token, they are false if such entities are *not* found in that location. Conversely, negative FP sentences are true if the location contains none of the required entities. 'There are no unicorns in the garden' is true if, after searching, we find no unicorns in the garden. It is false if we find at least one.

17 I'll get to abstract entities in a moment, and again in Section 5.7.

18 Strawson (1959) discusses the way in which 'non-particulars' – in effect, things that aren't physical objects – come to be treated as locatable items, by analogy or extrapolation, in the way particulars are. More on this in Section 5.7.

19 On relevance, see Sperber and Wilson (1995). When processing speech or writing, the audience begins with the assumption that what has been said is, in context, relevant. If its relevance is not immediately obvious, there will be a search for a context in which it *would be* relevant. See Chapter 4, note 16.

20 They can also be paraphrased as 'God exists', 'Unicorns exist', and 'Santa Claus exists'. However, as Szekely observes, 'exists' can only be used in an ET sentence when there is no explicit locative coda. 'There are unicorns in the garden', but not 'There exist unicorns in the garden'.

21 See Lewis (1986) for a definition of this kind.

22 The 'visible' universe is about 46.5 billion light years in any direction from a point centred on Earth. If any unicorns turn up on a planet situated further away than that, we'll never know about them.

23 In practice, of course, 'in the world' doesn't extend anywhere near this far. 'All the tears in the world won't help you now.' 'Not a single judge in the world would believe you.' These are not references to the M51 galaxy. The precise limits of what 'in the world' includes on any particular occasion are rarely specified; but, unless 'the world of mythology', 'the world of fiction', or some other 'non-real' world is nominated as the locative, a relatively local region of the space-time framework will be assumed, even if its precise boundaries are left undefined. van Fraassen (2002), Lecture I, is good on this.

24 One shouldn't be too hasty with this free pass, though. The God described in many Old Testament passages is apparently corporeal, rather than not-being-this, not-being-that, and not-being-the other (Stavrakopoulou 2021). So *that* god, at least, is/ was a spatio-temporal being. Divine non-corporeality was a later invention.

25 It's not just linguists. According to a German philosopher: 'Something exists only when it is found in the world' (Gabriel 2015: 12).

26 The words used here to justify the choice of MR are drawn from Krauss (2005).

27 Moltmann (2013: 56) points out: 'Taking a closer look at its linguistic behavior, it appears that *real* is an adjective that is in fact not that felicitous on its own, but more naturally occurs as a modifier of a sortal noun as in *real object*, *real person*, or *real watch*.' However, with doubted entities such as God and unicorns, 'real' on its own looks perfectly legitimate, especially with emphasis: 'Unicorns *are* real!' Perhaps, then, we can imagine someone protesting that: 'Multiple realities are *real*!'. But this is purely rhetorical: italicising-to-persuade, rather than making an assessable claim. If it's intended literally, we have to ask, as I do in the text: 'Real *whats*?'

28 The 'unless and until' proviso. See Section 4.4.
29 Compare inventing-by-subtraction with inventing-by-addition. This is what Ayer does in the sense datum debate (Section 3.7). He introduces a new expression 'directly perceive' (rather than 'perceive' on its own) and discusses it as if it were a familiar concept that needs no explanation.
30 For a review of the cosmological argument, see Reichenbach (2021).
31 'We are allowing ourselves to assume an application for the concept of *the series as a whole*, without considering whether we may legitimately do so' (Strawson 1966: 158). In talking of echoes of Kant, I am, of course, vastly over-simplifying. However, the antinomies do turn on there being concepts which are applicable to the *parts/elements* of a series/whole, which are not applicable to the *series/whole* itself. Helpful accounts include Bennett (1974), Wood (2010), and Strawson (1966).
32 'What about mass nouns? Water can't be counted.' No, but molecules of water can be. So, too, bodies of water. However, for anybody seriously worried about this, I'd recommend Chierchia (1998), whose Inherent Plurality Hypothesis proposes that mass nouns 'come out of the lexicon with plurality already built in' (53).
33 Guba has a stab at answering questions like these in *The Constructivist Credo*. I discuss his attempt in Chapter 7.
34 On the 'patchwork' of science, see Cartwright (1999). For 'façades', see Wilson (2006). For models and idealisations, see Massimi (2022). I say more on these topics in Chapter 11 and the Epilogue.

References

Bennett, J. (1974). *Kant's Dialectic*. Cambridge, UK: Cambridge University Press.

Carnap, R. (1937). *The Logical Syntax of Language*. London: K. Paul, Trench, Trubner & Co.

Cartwright, N. (1999). *The Dappled World: A Study of the Boundaries of Science*. Cambridge, UK: Cambridge University Press.

Chierchia, G. (1998). Plurality of mass nouns and the notion of 'semantic parameter'. In S. Rothstein (Ed.), *Events and Grammar* (pp. 53–103). Dordrecht: Kluwer.

Chomsky, N. (1957). *Syntactic Structures*. The Hague: Mouton.

Chomsky, N. (1986). *Knowledge of Language: Its Nature, Origins and Use*. New York: Praeger.

Freeze, R. (1992). Existentials and other locatives. *Language, 68*(3), 553–595.

Gabriel, M. (2015). *Why the World Does Not Exist*. Cambridge, UK: Polity Press.

Hilpert, M. (2014). *Construction Grammar and its Application to English*. Edinburgh: Edinburgh University Press.

Hirsch, E. (2002). Quantifier variance and realism. *Philosophical Issues, 12*, 51–73.

Kant, I. (1996). *Critique of Pure Reason. First published 1781* (P. Guyer & A. W. Wood, Trans.). Cambridge, UK: Cambridge University Press.

Kimball, J. P. (1973). The grammar of existence. *Proceedings from the Annual Meeting of the Chicago Linguistic Society, 9*(1), 262–270.

Krauss, S. E. (2005). Research paradigms and meaning making: A primer. *The Qualitative Report, 10*(4), 758–770.

Lakoff, G. (1987). *Women, Fire, and Dangerous Things: What Categories Reveal About the Mind*. Chicago: University of Chicago Press.

Lewis, D. (1986). *On the Plurality of Worlds*. Oxford: Blackwell.

Lyons, J. (1968). *Introduction to Theoretical Linguistics*. Cambridge, UK: Cambridge University Press.

Massimi, M. (2022). *Perspectival Realism*. New York: Oxford University Press.

McNally, L. (1997). *A Semantics for the English Existential Construction*. Abingdon, UK: Routledge.

Millman, O. (2022). Back from the dead? Elusive ivory-billed woodpecker not extinct, researchers say. *The Guardian*, 13th April 2022.

Milsark, G. L. (2014). *Existential Sentences in English*. Abingdon, UK: Routledge.

Moltmann, F. (2013). The semantics of existence. *Linguistics and Philosophy*, *36*, 31–63.

Moro, A. (1997). *The Raising of Predicates: Predicative Noun Phrases and the Theory of Clause Structure*. Cambridge, UK: Cambridge University Press.

Morrison, B. (2002). *On Location: Aristotle's Concept of Place*. Oxford: Oxford University Press.

Quirk, R., Greenbaum, S., Leech, G., & Svartvik, J. (1985). *A Comprehensive Grammar of the English Language*. London: Longman.

Reichenbach, B. (2021). Cosmological argument. *Stanford Encyclopedia of Philosophy*, https://plato.stanford.edu/entries/cosmological-argument/#NeceBein

Sider, T. (2009). Ontological realism. In D. J. Chalmers, D. Manley, & R. Wasserman (Eds.), *Metametaphysics* (pp. 384–423). Oxford: Oxford University Press.

Sperber, D., & Wilson, D. (1995). *Relevance: Communication and Cognition*. Second Edition. Oxford: Blackwell.

Stavrakopoulou, F. (2021). *God: An Anatomy*. London: Picador.

Strawson, P. F. (1959). *Individuals*. London: Methuen.

Strawson, P. F. (1966). *The Bounds of Sense: An Essay on Kant's Critique of Pure Reason*. London: Methuen.

Strawson, P. F. (2016). *Subject and Predicate in Logic and Grammar*. Abingdon, UK: Routledge.

Szekely, R. (2015). *Truth without Predication: The Role of Placing in the Existential There-Sentence*. New York: Palgrave Macmillan.

van Fraassen, B. C. (2002). *The Empirical Stance*. New Haven: Yale University Press.

Williams, E. (1996). The subject-predicate theory of *there*. *Linguistic Inquiry*, *37*, 648–651.

Wilson, M. (2006). *Wandering Significance: An Essay on Conceptual Behavior*. New York: Oxford University Press.

Wood, A. W. (2010). The antinomies of pure reason. In P. Guyer (Ed.), *The Cambridge Companion to Kant's Critique of Pure Reason* (pp. 245–265). New York: Cambridge University Press.

6

'SINGLE REALITY', 'MULTIPLE REALITIES'

Here is one response to what I've said so far.

Reader: 'A single reality', 'multiple realities'. I don't see what all the fuss is about. All this 'spelling out the rules of use' and 'specifying the application conditions'. The words which make up both expressions are perfectly familiar. We know what they mean. If I claim that 'there is a single reality', or alternatively that 'there are multiple realities', I am using the words in their usual senses. You know the difference between 'single' and 'multiple', and you know what 'reality' refers to. So what exactly is the problem? You're trying to create a difficulty where there isn't one. Either there's a single cat, or multiple cats. Either there's a single reality, or multiple realities. That's it. The 'locative' stuff is just smoke and mirrors. Obviously, a reality isn't *in* reality. It's not part of itself. But everybody knows that. Tell them there are multiple realities, and they don't ask 'Where?'. They say: 'Oh, right. Interesting.' It's the same if you tell them there's a single reality. No-one is confused by any of this. And that's because they understand English, and know what 'single', 'multiple', and 'reality' mean.

The first half of this chapter questions the assumption that, in talking about a 'single reality' or 'multiple realities', the relevant words are being used in their ordinary, familiar senses. This *is* just an assumption, and I've never seen any evidence to support it. (I think a further assumption is that it doesn't need any.) In contrast, I present evidence to show that this assumption is misguided.

DOI: 10.4324/9781003306382-8

It's a special case of the idea that, if it's the same word, it must have the same meaning; 'as if the meaning were an aura the word brings along with it and retains in every kind of use' (Wittgenstein 2009: §117).[1]

Although the expressions 'single reality' and 'multiple realities' start to appear in their current context – as key phrases in the ontological premises underpinning research – some time after 1970, both were in regular use before that date. Section 6.1 examines the use of 'a single reality' prior to 1970; Section 6.2 examines the use of 'multiple realities' in the same period. In neither case is there any obvious overlap with the 'ontological underpinnings' use. Section 6.3 turns to the use of 'reality' and 'realities', without 'single' or 'multiple', using corpus examples since 1970. Again, the connection with the 'ontological' use is at best tenuous.

The second half of the chapter takes a close look at how, in *Naturalistic Inquiry*, Lincoln and Guba (1985) introduce the expression 'multiple realities'. I've already provided a quick sketch of this in Section 3.7; but here I go into more depth and detail, showing how L&G specify a rule for the use of the expression – as, in Carnap's view, they are perfectly entitled to do – and then promptly forget it.[2] The chapter ends by returning to the idea that there are illusions of thought in philosophy (Cappelen 2013). Believing that there are 'multiple realities' is an example of such an illusion. So, too, is believing that there is 'a single reality'.

6.1 'A single reality': pre-1970

Before 1970, the phrase 'a single reality' occurs in theological discussion, sociological and economic literature, literary criticism, and reference to psychedelic experience. The expression is nearly always used to suggest that two (sometimes more) apparently disparate things *form a unity*, or are just *aspects of a unity*. Some examples:

(1) Law and grace are two aspects of a single reality.

(2) Scripture and tradition are two formalities of a single reality.

(3) For Niebuhr, theology and politics are merely two perspectives of a single reality.

(4) The Old Testament message is that man and the universe form a single reality,

(5) For social work, theory and practice merge into a single reality.

(6) In crisis situations class psychology and consciousness merge into a single reality.

(7) 'Mental activities' and 'material things' are both part of a single reality.

Contrast these examples with the metaphysical sentence 'There is a single reality.' Four points, I think, are particularly noteworthy.

First, in each case the apparently disparate elements/aspects are specified. Law and grace, theory and practice, 'mental activities' and 'material things'. The theme is the discrepancy between 'appearance' (dissimilar, separate items) and 'reality' (underlying unity). This is an idea wholly lacking from 'There is a single reality' as an ontological underpinning.

Second, there are a number of variations. In some cases, the disparate elements are part of, or *form*, a unity. They are, so to speak, *already* a unity (4, 7). In others, they *merge* into a unity (5, 6), implying that they can, in other circumstances, remain separate. In a third group, they are *views* of, or *perspectives* of, the unity (1, 3). One example here is unclear: 'formalities' (2).

Third, (1) to (7) are all subject-predicate in form, contrasting with the feature-placing, ET structure of 'There is a single reality.' In each case, the subject of the sentence is the set of two disparate elements, and the predicate describes them as belonging to a single reality.

Fourth, the expression 'a single reality' varies in what it refers to. It is entirely dependent on the things-specified-as-disparate by the subject. Whatever it is that 'single reality' refers to in (2) – something that encompasses scripture and tradition in a unity – it is not the same as whatever 'single reality' refers to in (5), a unity which merges theory and practice in social work. Similarly, the 'single reality' of (4), the unity of 'man and the universe', cannot be the same as the 'single reality' of (6), the merging of class psychology and consciousness. The expression refers to a different kind of 'reality', and a different kind of 'singleness', in each case. The 'single reality' predicate is not, in every instance, describing its subject in the same way.

Although the appearance/reality theme runs through all the examples, it is not clear in most cases what precisely is being said. In some instances, the author expands. For example, Gessert (1960), having told us that Law and grace are two aspects of a single reality, adds that the 'single reality' in question is 'the reality of God's existential relation to man' (259). He then asks: 'How can Law and grace be two aspects of a single reality?' His answer, as he admits, involves metaphor: 'Grace can be compared to a fluid and Law to the vessel that contains it. Without the glass, the water cannot be conveyed to the lips… Without the water, the empty glass… will quench no thirst'. What he says about water and glass is no doubt true, but I don't myself see why this makes the 'glass-of-water' a 'single reality' or a 'unity'.

More to the point, if (for Gessert) this metaphor serves as an explanation of what he means by 'a single reality', then it's clear that this cannot possibly be the sense the qualitative metaphysician has in mind. What, in the sentence 'There is a single reality', is the equivalent of the water and the glass? What does the metaphysician imagine is being united when she writes that sentence? Gessert's metaphor may be a bit feeble (to my ear, anyway), but at least what he's aiming at is relatively clear: to quench your thirst, you need *both* the liquid *and* the glass. In the claim 'There is a single reality' [SR], what is needed to achieve what? Without an understanding of that, it's impossible to see why the 'single reality' in SR has the same sense as the 'single reality' in (1). Nor is it clear why the sense in (1) would be described as the 'usual' or 'ordinary' sense. Similar questions and difficulties arise with the other examples.

It is evident from these examples that the sense of 'a single reality' is context-dependent. Although the theme of 'appearance vs. reality' is broadly consistent, what the expression is used to convey depends on the nature of the disparate elements. 'Law and grace' do not form a 'single reality' in anything like the same way that 'theory and practice' do. And in none of these examples does the expression refer to what we might call the 'number' of realities. We are not 'counting' realities in any of these sentences. Instead, we are saying that X and Y, while they may appear to be separate, are in fact aspects of the same thing. There is no sense in which the singularity or multiplicity of reality-as-a-whole, or realities-in-general, is even vaguely at issue.

So the *Reader's* claim to be 'using the words in their usual sense' is already questionable. First, the pre-1970 sense turns on a broad distinction between disparate 'appearances' and an underlying 'unity'. This disappears in the qualitative metaphysical use. Second, beyond that distinction, there is little consistency in how 'a single reality' is used pre-1970. It is certainly not used to refer to the *same* unity, and precisely what is being said is entirely context-dependent. Third, the relation between the disparate elements and the underlying 'unity' is not always of the same kind ('form', 'merge', 'aspect of'). Consequently, there is no 'usual' or 'ordinary' sense before 1970 that post-1970 writers can adopt or conform to.

The assumption that what 'a single reality' means is obvious simply doesn't hold up. On the evidence so far, the sentence 'There is a single reality' is a metaphysical sentence which, in Balaguer's (2021) terms, is 'catastrophically imprecise'.

6.2 'Multiple realities': pre-1970

References to 'a single reality' prior to 1970 are not confined to any particular discipline or theory; nor do they cite any key author(s). In contrast, virtually every discussion of 'multiple realities' before 1970 cites Schutz (1945), and sometimes James (2018). In this instance, then, we can reasonably assume, at least initially, that the authors concerned are all talking about the same idea.

Schutz's essay begins with an account of James' analysis of 'our sense of reality'. The key idea is that 'there are several, probably an infinite number of various orders of realities, each with its own special and separate style of existence' (Schutz 1945: 533). Some examples James refers to are: the world of sense or physical things, the world of science, the world of religion, the world of abstract truths, the world of individual opinion, the world of 'idols of the tribe' (illusions and prejudices). Other 'worlds', or 'realms', mentioned by Schutz include the worlds of everyday life, dreams, theatre, jokes, fiction. The main aim of Schutz's essay is to clarify 'the relationship between the world of daily life and that of theoretical, scientific contemplation'. The expression Schutz uses to describe all these 'worlds' is 'finite provinces of meaning'. He uses the term 'multiple realities' only once – in his title.[3]

Benţa (2018) compares the relation between the finite provinces of meaning (FPMs) with the rooms in a house, each of which is 'lived in' differently (dining room, bedroom, bathroom). What Schutz refers to as everyday life (EDL), or sometimes the 'world of working', is associated with the living room. It is the 'paramount reality', the central point of reference, the room one returns to after visiting the others. For Schutz, the 'totality of the finite provinces of meaning constitute the life-world' (Benţa 2018: 50). On this view, 'life-world' and 'everyday life' are not the same. Everyday life is just one room, even if it is the most important room in the house. The life-world is the house itself, even if it is of infinite extent.

The idea of a series of FPMs is contrasted with the idea that the social world is a 'unique and coherent reality'. This is clearly a multiple/single distinction, but it is not the same as the distinction alluded to in qualitative metaphysics. The 'unique and coherent reality' would be a house in which every room is the same. The 'uniqueness' does not refer to the 'one reality'. It refers to the sameness of rooms. To believe in the 'unique coherence' would be to imagine that every aspect of life was identical and that there was just one mode of thought and behaviour applying to all of them.

Another respect in which Schutz's multiple/single distinction is different from that of the constructivist metaphysicians is that these 'worlds', these realities, are *shared*. Continuing with the house analogy, I can be in the EDL room while you are in the room of fiction. Or the reverse can be true. Or we can both be in the same room. The world of daily life is an 'intersubjective world which existed long before our birth, experienced and interpreted by others, our predecessors, as an organized world' (Schutz 1945: 533). 'We experience this world as ours (*i.e.*, with a certain sense of both ownership and belonging), but we know we created neither the world nor its meanings' (Benţa 2018: 28).

It is possible to inhabit two or more provinces at the same time. It's not just that, in EDL, I can perform actions whose 'final purposes' are located in a different FPM, the world of leisure, say, or the world of religion. It's that 'I, this psycho-physiological unity, live in several of these realms simultaneously' (Schutz 1970: 9-10). In fact, FPMs are rarely experienced independently. Writing an academic text, for example, is an activity that spans several provinces. At the very least, it involves the world of working (writing) and the world of theoretical contemplation.

Schutz provides a relatively clear account of how finite provinces of meaning are differentiated from each other. He gives us a sense of where one 'reality' stops and another starts, and discusses the psychological shifts involved in crossing the threshold between one 'reality' and the next. There are ambiguities in his account

(Hammersley 2020), which he tweaked and tinkered with over a period of years. But he does not use the expression 'finite provinces of meaning' without *any* attempt to articulate and explain the rules governing his use of this expression. In Carnap's terms, he introduces a language, 'states his methods reasonably clearly, and gives syntactical rules instead of philosophical arguments'.[4]

The multiplicity to which Schutz refers is not defined by reference to individual or cultural differences, let alone ontological ones. It is a multiplicity that a single individual experiences: 'My mind may pass during one single day or even hour through the whole gamut of tensions of consciousness, now living in working acts, now passing through a day-dream, now plunging into the pictorial world of a painting' (Schutz 1945: 568). However, as Hammersley (2020: 292) observes, the phrase 'multiple realities' has often

> come to be interpreted… in ways that are at odds with [Schutz's] discussion, being taken to refer to socially constituted "realities" or to "multiple cultures"; sometimes with the suggestion that each of these is true in its own terms, and that it is impossible for people (including researchers) to extricate themselves from their own particular sociocultural niches so as to attain an objective viewpoint.

It is clear, then, that there is no standard, or obvious, or ordinary, or familiar sense of 'multiple realities', handed down (so to speak) from Schutz to post-1970 sociologists and metaphysicians. So the *Reader's* claim to be 'using their words in their usual sense' is again questionable. The lesson of this section and the last is that you can't just spray the word 'reality' around without explaining how you're using it, or how one 'reality' differs from another (if you claim there's more than one). Schutz makes a decent fist of explaining the difference between 'realities' – finite provinces of meaning – and does so in a way that would embarrass many qualitative metaphysicians, who scarcely bother. However, it's just possible that 'reality' as a count noun has acquired a 'standard', modern meaning. This is the possibility I examine in the next section.

6.3   Corpus: 'reality' and 'realities'

'Reality' is much the more common word of the two. In COCA, it has 91,451 occurrences; 'realities' has only 9,351. What's interesting, though, is that their (1, 0) adjectives are quite similar. Here's the top 20 for both:

Reality: virtual, augmented, political, physical, social, harsh, objective, alternate, economic, ultimate, historical, sad, stark, grim, external, current, everyday, material, unfortunate, underlying.

Realities: political, economic, new, harsh, social, different, alternate, hard, practical, physical, market, spiritual, current, historical, multiple, financial, grim, cultural, changing, virtual.

Ten of these adjectives occur on both lists: political, virtual, physical, social, harsh, alternate, economic, historical, grim, current. Of those that don't, several have a similar flavour: sad, stark, unfortunate, hard, practical. I won't say anything about 'virtual', 'augmented', and 'alternate', except in this note.[5] Setting those aside, most of the remaining adjectives belong to one of two families: a negative-valence family (sad, grim, harsh, etc.) and a problem-source family (political, economic, physical, and so on).[6] In both cases, the theme is: *restriction*.

Negative-valence examples:

(8) The harsh reality is not everyone who wants to be back next season will be.

(9) The sad reality is that voter integrity issues are boring for most people.

(10) The stark reality is that bullying will never be completely eliminated.

(11) Poets face the harsh realities of the market place.

(12) The hard realities of making a living leave little time for cultural pursuits.

(13) At Christmas take a break from the grim realities of life and believe in love and dreams.

Both the singular and the plural are used primarily to mark an implicit contrast between (a) 'how things *are*' and (b) 'how things seem', or 'how one would like things to be', or 'how things would ideally be', or 'how they are said to be'. In each case, the how-things-are is much less pleasant than the alternative of that-would-be-nice. Voter integrity issues would ideally be interesting to the majority of people (9); in fact, they're not. The *restriction* theme is apparent in both singular and plural cases. It would be good if bullying could be completely eliminated, but the stark reality is that it won't be. It would be pleasant to have more time for cultural pursuits, but the hard realities of making a living make this impossible.

Problem-source examples:

(14) The economic reality is that Scexit would be much worse than Brexit.[7]

(15) She repeats ad nauseam pointless positions which have zero political reality.

(16) Astrology is a lot of made-up nonsense with no basis in physical reality.

(17) This is an idealist perspective which ignores all the practical realities.

(18) The policy will need to be changed to accommodate new market realities.

(19) Laura doesn't understand even the most basic financial realities.

Again, both singular and plural imply a contrast between 'what we'd like' and 'how things actually are'. There is a slight difference, however, in that (in these examples) the contrast has to be mined rather more energetically than in cases (8) to (13). Many Scots believe that independence would be survivable, or better, from an economic point of view. The author of (14), however, suggests that independence would be far worse than the optimists claim. This is the 'reality'. In (19), Laura has put together a business plan based on naively unrealistic assumptions. She hasn't taken account of the 'realities' that an experienced entrepreneur would factor in routinely.

All examples, as with the negative-valence family, exhibit the *restriction* theme. Physical reality is at odds with what astrology says about the influence of planetary alignments on personality. In this sense, reality – as represented by the findings of astrophysics – limits what can sensibly and accurately be said about the sources of human behaviour. The new market realities in (18) circumscribe the formulation of a policy if the latter is to have any chance of achieving its aims.

This account of the use of 'reality' and 'realities' – the contrast between 'how things seem', or 'how we would like them to be', and 'how things in fact are' – has something in common with Reynolds' (2006) account of 'really'.[8] Reynolds construes this term (and its cognates) as a discourse marker indicating a transition from discourse about how things are *represented* as being to discourse about how things *are*. 'How things are represented' includes reports of what people say or believe, exaggerated talk, fiction, descriptions of dreams, comments on illusions, and so on. In the second half of his paper, Reynolds uses this idea to provide an interpretation of the difference between realism and anti-realism. I won't follow him down this path, but in the next section I'll ask what my own view implies for the two sentences: 'there is a single reality' [SR], and 'there are multiple realities' [MR].

6.4   Implications of the contrast/restriction view

The first thought is that, given the analysis of the count noun, 'reality', just outlined, SR does not make a lot of sense. It does, at the very least, require elucidation. Similarly for the claim MR. It's not at all obvious how the determiners 'single' and 'multiple' get any traction with the 'contrast/restriction' view. Of course, the noun occurs in both the singular and the plural, exercising a similar function in each case; but this cannot be what the qualitative metaphysicians have in mind. There is a singular word, 'reality', and a plural word, 'realities'. Pointing out this morphological fact certainly doesn't count as making an ontological statement; and it's not as if we have to make a choice between the two.

Still, I can think of two ways of parsing SR and MR in such a way that they do make a kind of sense. The only trouble is that, on the first, MR is a truism and SR is a falsism. On the second, it's the other way round. Ontological statements are not generally regarded as truisms or falsisms. They're supposed to be fundamental descriptions of what the world is like.

First way. In the previous section, I listed some of the 'realities' which are routinely referred to: 'new', 'market', 'economic', 'political', 'practical', 'physical'; and I noted that these 'realities' apply to many different kinds of situation. So *obviously* there are multiple realities – 'economic' ones, 'political' ones, 'physical' ones, and so on – and an indefinitely large number of contexts in which these expressions are applied. This is a truism. By the same token, SR looks like a falsism. With so many types of 'reality', and so many different contexts, it seems obviously wrong to say that there's only one.

Second way. I also suggested that both the singular 'reality' and plural 'realities' were used to mark a distinction between (a) 'how things *are*' and (b) 'how things seem', or 'how one would like things to be', or 'how they are said to be'. For this reason, one might say that the count noun has a single primary function; and one might express *that* by saying: 'there is a single reality'. This would be a grammatical remark, in Wittgenstein's sense,[9] rather than an onto-logical claim. If one did want to talk this way, then SR would be a truism, and MR would be a falsism.

Neither of these ways of parsing will appeal to the qualitative metaphysicians. The latter need a sense of 'reality' and 'realities' that makes SR and MR intelligible in an ontological context. The *Reader's* comments at the beginning of this chapter implied that the required sense was ordinary, usual, familiar. The discussion since then, however, has shown that this claim is not self-evidently true.

I think we are left with two options. One is that the required sense of 'reality' is *not* ordinary, but rather a special and indefinable sense. This is, in effect, the position set out by Fine (2001), who argues that the metaphysical notion of 'reality' is not to be confused with ordinary, everyday uses of the word 'reality'. Instead, it signals a special, metaphysical sense. Moreover, this sense is *primitive*. It can't be defined in terms of more ordinary concepts like 'fact' or 'truth'. This is, as Hofweber (2009) points out, a highly esoteric kind of metaphysics: 'To know what this sense is gives you entrance into the discipline, but it takes a metaphysician to know this sense' (270). In any case, how do we check that the metaphysician really *does* know the sense, or whether she is mistaken? Presumably, other metaphysicians will tell us. (Metaphysicians as initiates of a secret society.) Adopt this line in qualitative metaphysics, and only a few writers (I imagine) will understand what it *means* to say 'There are multiple realities' or 'There is a single reality.' The rest of us, including the novice researchers who read these sentences, will have to take what they say on trust, because we – the uninitiated – have no idea what they mean. In which case, how is an informed choice between them possible?

The second option brings us back to Sections 3.8 and 4.5. It is perfectly legitimate, according to both Wittgenstein and Carnap, to propose a new sense of an expression, or even to introduce a new language, provided you explain the rules of use, the application conditions. This, as it turns out, is what Lincoln and Guba (1985) actually do. At least initially. The problem is: having introduced rules of use for 'multiple realities', they promptly forget them, and switch to ontology mode. In Carnap's terms, this represents an abrupt and unacknowledged shift from 'internal' to 'external'. It's what we'll see happening in the next two sections.

6.5   Lincoln and Guba: introducing 'multiple realities'

I commented on Lincoln and Guba's (1985) understanding of 'paradigm' and 'positivism' in Chapter 2, and it's not necessary to repeat those comments here. Instead, I will pick up the thread of *Naturalistic Inquiry* at Chapter 3. In this section, I'll show how the first half of that chapter introduces discourse about 'multiple realities' through a series of linguistic and rhetorical associations. In Section 6.6, I'll show how the second half of the chapter makes an abrupt, unexplained jump from linguistic discourse to ontological claims. At no point is any attempt made to justify this jump. Indeed, Lincoln and Guba (L&G) seem unaware that they have introduced rules-for-use, and then immediately broken them.

The first half of the chapter (pp. 70–81) consists of a series of scenarios which illustrate differences of opinion, perspective, perception, or interpretation. Let me give some examples.

[1] The first concerns the 'different perspectives on the same book evinced by two reviewers' (71). One condemns it, the other finds it admirable. The book itself, and the reviewers, 'represent perspectives, or what would be called "multiple realities"' (72). Interestingly, L&G don't specify *who* would describe perspectives as 'multiple realities'. I imagine plenty of people wouldn't. The point, however, is that L&G do not attempt to justify this comment. It is the first of several passages in which the expression 'multiple realities' is juxtaposed to some other way of describing a situation, the effect being to create a series of associations. In this case, it is an association between 'multiple realities' and 'perspectives', with the implication that these are just alternative ways of describing the same scenario ('perspectives, or what would be called…').

[2] Books by Carlos Castañeda,[10] say L&G, 'provide the reader with extensive "reality disjunctions" on virtually every page' (74). They don't explain, explicitly, what they mean by 'reality disjunctions', but their discussion makes it clear that the issue is: 'What are we to believe about these writings?' Are they true? Are they fictions? Are they based on drug-induced hallucinations? Castañeda's readers will have different views.

Some will believe Castañeda's narrative, others won't. L&G express this thought in the following way: 'One person's reality will undoubtedly be another's mystical allegory, and still another's hogwash' (75). So an association is created between 'what a person *believes*' and 'a person's *reality*'. In this case, the association is supported by the assertion that the reason why readers disagree is that people have different 'belief structures'. Those with belief structure A will believe what Castañeda says, those with structure B won't. L&G provide no evidence at all for this claim. So the main achievement of the scenario is to create a juxtaposition of 'what I believe' and 'my perspectival creation of reality'.

[3] Another example is taken from a discussion by Emery (1978: 39), which includes the sentence: 'We literally create a reality that reflects our view of the world and who we are in relation to it.' Note (i) the use of 'literally', without explanation; (ii) the singularity of 'the world' and 'it'; (iii) the juxtaposition of 'created reality' and 'our view'. The question to which this inevitably gives rise is: what is the relation between the realities 'literally created' by multiple individuals and the single 'world' of which they have a 'view'? This is not a question to which Emery provides an answer. Nor do L&G. So, again, the point is the juxtaposition of 'create a reality' and 'view of the world'.

[4] Shere Hite is also said to provide some 'interesting examples of constructed realities' (74). Hite's books are based on questionnaires which elicit 'attitudes and practices of individual sexuality'.[11] L&G continue: 'reading even snippets of responses lends a sense of variety of experiences and constructions placed on such intimate human contact'. Here again, 'variety of experience' is juxtaposed with people's 'constructed realities', creating an association between differences in attitude and perception (on the one hand) and distinct 'realities' (on the other other).

[5] Stake (1977), say L&G, 'took on "truth" (and therefore reality)'. It's another interesting inference ('truth', and therefore reality), and this time it is accompanied by Stake's own comment (19): 'In any circumstances the truth might be but a single truth – but evaluators are certain not to find it. What they can find are multiple truths, multiple understandings.' The casual equation of 'multiple understandings' and 'multiple truths', implying that multiple understandings of 'what-is-true' is the same as multiple 'what-is-trues', is itself a further example of L&G's association rhetoric.

[6] Bogdan and Taylor (1975) report on ward attendants' perspectives in a state hospital. L&G suggest that 'the realities of ward attendants' and the 'perspectives of administrators' are very different, and 'demonstrate that reality is indeed a construction' (79). They add that: 'reality as

experienced by ward attendants is not reality as experienced by residents is not reality as experienced by sociologists' (80). The sequence of associations here is remarkable. First, the *realities* of ward attendant are compared to the *perspectives* of administrators. Second, this contrast *demonstrates* that 'reality' is a *construction*. Third, another expression is introduced – 'reality as experienced by' – which creates an ambiguity of its own: that between 'different experiences of reality' and 'different realities'.

In summary, the first half of Chapter 3 is a series of casual juxtapositions and associations, in which the expression 'multiple realities' is assimilated to other expressions referring to the differences in people's views, experiences, opinions, interpretations, construals, constructions, perspectives, beliefs, perceptions, meanings, understandings, frames of reference. It's important to see that none of these assimilations is argued for, which is why I have referred to the 'rhetoric' of association. Indeed, the sheer, argument-free casualness of the juxtapositions is the key to their persuasiveness. The reader is seduced into a sense that this is all familiar, routine, uncontroversial. She is, in effect, invited to adopt a new language in which a variety of opinions, perspectives, beliefs, and experiences is referred to as 'multiple realities'.

But we know from Part I that this is, within certain limits, perfectly legitimate. Carnap says that we can adopt a new linguistic framework, provided only that we state our methods clearly, and give syntactical rules instead of philosophical arguments (Section 4.5). This is how I read the first half of Chapter 3. L&G present a series of scenarios – examples of differences in how people 'see' the world – and grant us a licence to refer to such situations as 'multiple realities'. It's like a rule that says:

'Whenever people disagree in their views, opinions, perspectives… , you are licensed to refer to this circumstance as an example of 'multiples realities'. And vice versa: 'Whenever you see the expression "multiple realities", understand this as a reference to people's views, perspectives and experiences being different.'

There is absolutely no problem about this, as long as you stick to the rules you have set out. If you do, you will have created a new language framework, which your audience will understand because they know what the rules of use are. The internal question, 'Are there multiple realities?', is answered: 'Yes, of course.' The external question 'Are there *really* multiple realities?', or 'Do multiple realities *really* exist?', will make no sense. Unless and until.

Similarly, Wittgenstein says that it's fine to introduce a new use of a word or expression, as long as the application conditions are made clear, and are not subsequently ignored, forgotten, or disregarded (see Sections 3.7). If, at some point, it begins to look as if they *have* been disregarded, this is a *prima facie* reason to question the new use, while recognising that the writer/speaker may be able to explain it. This is the equivalent of Carnap's challenge (Section 4.4). In the absence of such an explanation, the new use can provisionally be described as nonsense. Unless and until.

6.6   Lincoln and Guba: the switch to ontology

The reading of 'There are multiple realities' in Section 6.5 makes it a truism. In the first half of the chapter, L&G tie 'multiple realities' to examples of people seeing things differently. But has anyone, ever, not tumbled to the fact that people don't always agree? Has anyone, ever, not noticed that failing-to-see-eye-to-eye happens a *lot*? If not, then virtually everyone will recognise that the statement 'There are multiple realities' is an accurate summary of (an aspect of) the human condition. Not because it's an 'ontological' truth, but because it's a bona fide anthropological generalisation. By the same token, 'There is a single reality' is wrong, because it's not true that people always agree about everything.

But, in the blink of an eye, L&G reframe all this as a piece of ontology. Turning the page, and entering the second half of the chapter *(The philosopher's viewpoint)*, we learn that it is not just 'the person on the street and social scientists' who have come to grips with 'the question of reality' (82). Philosophers, it appears, have 'introduced arguments asserting that "reality" might exist at any one of four levels'.

This is immediately puzzling. The introduction to this section strongly implies that there has been no change of subject. The discourse of social scientists and persons 'on the street' was discussed in the first half of the chapter. However, in the course of that discussion no sense was given to the expression 'the question of reality'; nor was there scope for the idea that 'reality' (or 'realities') might 'exist' at various 'levels'. The earlier part of the chapter just set out the rules of use for the expression 'multiple realities', licensing it as a way of referring to circumstances in which people have different views, experiences, and understandings. On the face of it, no 'question of reality' has been raised. This looks suspiciously like a shift, in Carnap's terms, from the 'internal' discourse of 'reality'/'realities' to an 'external' question: Do multiple realities really exist? Or does a single reality really exist?

Still, this may represent an imprecision on L&G's part; and it's possible that the apparent discontinuity of topic here is only that: apparent. So let's see what the four levels are.

L&G call these levels 'objective reality, perceived reality, constructed reality, and created reality for the purpose of discussing them as ontological positions' (82). This seems to confirm that they have jumped the tracks. We have moved, in an unacknowledged way, from the proposal to introduce a new language framework – through a series of juxtapositions and associations – to reviewing 'ontological positions' as possible answers to an 'external' question.

[1] *Objective reality.* 'This stance has also been called naïve realism.'[12] Realism, L&G say, is the view that 'the world of which we have knowledge exists independently of our knowledge of it'. This is an ontological claim. It ignores the syntactic rules for using the expression 'multiple realities', and instead proposes an answer to Carnap's 'external' question of *existence.* The first half of the chapter introduced the language of 'multiple realities', used to refer to the fact that people frequently disagree about stuff. Once you agree to use this language, its implicit converse, 'there is a single reality', becomes obviously false. Abruptly, however, in the second half of the chapter, this linguistic proposal is transposed into the idea that something called 'reality' *really, objectively,* exists, and that this 'objectively existing reality' is the only one of its kind. L&G make no attempt to explain or justify this transposition.

[2] *Perceived reality.* Both naïve realists and perceptual realists 'adopt the ontological position that there is a reality out there, a "real reality", if you will' (83). Or a 'reality that *really* exists', if you prefer. So we're still talking about existence rather than the rules for the use of the expression 'multiple realities'. L&G's account of the difference between 'naïve realists' and 'perceptual realists' is barely intelligible. It confuses four different questions. (i) Can reality be known *fully*? (ii) Can it be known to *everybody*? (iii) Can *one* individual, or one group, know *all* of it? (iv) Does reality *really* exist? As far I can judge, the naïve realists supposedly answer 'yes' to the first three questions; the perceptual realists supposedly answer 'no'. But they agree that the answer to question (iv) is 'yes'. Again, there is no connection at all between this account and the discussion in the first half of the chapter.

[3] *Constructed reality.* 'Those who see reality as a construction in the minds of individuals asserts [*sic*] that it is dubious whether there is a reality. If there is, we can never know it.' This is one of the oddest sentences in the book. 'Those who see *reality* as a construction… doubt whether there is a *reality*…' 'Reality' is used to refer to *both* 'a construction in the mind' *and* something that probably doesn't exist. Alternatively, it is used to refer to *both* 'a construction in the mind' *and* something that can't be known. L&G attach the word, almost randomly, to a series of different conceptions. It's like a linguistic pinball; but they never acknowledge the ricochets, even when one occurs in the same sentence, as here.

There is, in this ontological position, always an infinite number of constructions that might be made, and hence there are multiple realities.' Setting aside the first six words, this reverts to the linguistic licensing arrangement: attaching the expression 'multiple realities' to the anthropological truism that there are multiple construals, understandings, and interpretations. Internal. However, that part of the sentence is welded on to the claim that this is an 'ontological position'. External.

The paragraph continues: 'Any given construction may not be (and almost certainly is not) in a one-to-one relation (or isomorphic with) other constructions of the same (by definition only) entity.' So people construct *the same entity* differently, where 'same entity' is identified by the word used to 'define' it? Does that mean that *words* straddle all constructions? It seems to. A little later, they say: 'None of these things... [Watergate, nursing homes, the middle ages, communism, God, and many more] ... exists in a form other than those constructed by the persons who "recognize" the term.' But doesn't that mean that the terms, which they all 'recognize', *do* exist in a non-constructed, independent form? Otherwise, how could they recognise the *same* term? In which case, words do *really* exist, 'out there'; but the things they refer to only exist in constructed realities. You've got to say: that's pretty mixed-up.

Then another change of tack. 'Of course, constructed realities (or constructions) are often related to, and equally often inseparable from, tangible entities.' So 'tangible entities' are not *included* in constructed realities? This sounds like another reversion to the first half of the chapter. The *constructed realities*, it is now said, are the meanings 'ascribed to these tangible phenomena in order to make sense of them'. So we're back to square one. 'Constructed realities' and 'multiple realities' are merely ways of referring to the fact that we make sense of 'tangible phenomena' differently. So why all this talk about existence? Why, earlier, do L&G say that nursing homes and Watergate *do not* exist *except* in constructed realities? What exactly *is* this 'ontological position'?'

[4] *Created reality.* 'The fourth and final ontological position is there is no reality at all.' But having made that statement, L&G unexpectedly tell us what reality *is*. 'Reality is best understood as a standing wave function that is not realized... until some observer "pops the qwiff".' From which we can infer that this position makes more than a nod to quantum mechanics (QM).[13] The passage includes a long description of 'Schrödinger's Cat', and a discussion of Zukav's (1979) *The Dancing Wu-Li Masters.* The 'created' bit arises from the idea that when you 'pop the qwiff', the wave function collapses, and the 'reality' comes into being. In that sense 'you *create* the reality' (86).[14] So this position, according to L&G, says: (a) there is no reality at all; (b) reality is a standing wave function; (c) you create reality by causing the wave function to collapse. You pays your money, and you takes your choice.

That's basically it. L&G don't resolve the apparently contradictory claims about 'reality', but they say that Schrödinger 'first posed the problem of activating several realities at once' (85). This, together with a reference to the 'many worlds' interpretation of QM, is yet another sense L&G give to 'multiple realities'.[15] It's confusing stuff, but the use of QM to support the existence of 'multiple realities' does turn up occasionally in the qualitative metaphysics literature. I'll discuss it further in Section 6.7.

Decision time. L&G, while attracted to position [4], opt for position [3]. The two are said to be similar in that both of them assume reality *'doesn't exist until either* (1) it is *constructed* by an actor or (2) it is *created* by a participant' (87). This is all very odd. How, for example, does it square with the 'out there', independent-of-construction existence of words in position [3]? How is it reconciled with the idea that reality is best understood as a standing wave function in position [4]? And if reality doesn't exist until it is constructed/created by an actor/participant, where on earth did the actor/participant come from? Is she not part of reality herself? It's pretty confusing. 'Reality' and 'realities' bounce around like linguistic pinballs, bumping against one concept after another, with no consistent account of what exactly they are referring to.

In this section I've skated past the references to 'constructed realities'. But that expression, along with 'socially constructed realities', will be discussed more fully in Chapter 7.

6.7   The implications of quantum mechanics

Lincoln and Guba are not the only writers on qualitative metaphysics to have played footsie with quantum mechanics. Attempts are occasionally made to connect the behaviour of electrons and photons with the behaviour of human beings (Pernecky 2016 devotes a whole chapter to the topic). This strikes me as unexpectedly reductionist, coming from authors who are usually averse to reductionism. If you think QM has implications for social science (via its 'indeterminism', for example), you are surely being as reductionist as the 'positivists' who had the same thought about classical physics (via its 'determinism'). But this is a relatively trivial point. There are more serious problems facing anyone who sets out to assess the ontological implications of QM, with a view to plugging them into qualitative metaphysics.

There is a major puzzle at the heart of QM, and it's essential to understand what (and why) it is before asking about QM's implications for 'reality'. Like classical physics, QM makes it possible to explain and predict the behaviour of things, both macro and micro, by using mathematics. It explains even the weird stuff: the interference patterns created by firing electrons at the screen with two slits, and the mysterious correlations exhibited by entangled particles. At least, it explains them in the sense that the mathematics of wave mechanics predicts the patterns created by the two slits, while the mathematics of matrix mechanics predicts the 'spin' correlations of the entangled particles.[16] However, QM is arguably unique in the history of science. 'It is a theory in which we have no idea what we are talking about, because we have no idea what (if anything) the basic mathematical structures of the theory represent' (Lewis 2016: 22).[17]

In classical physics, and other sciences, we know what the mathematical expressions represent. In QM, we don't. The equations include at least some expressions that don't represent anything, at least nothing that can be coherently described. There is no makes-sense physical interpretation of the entangled state in terms of the *properties* of electrons, whether individually or in aggregate. Nor is there any physical interpretation of the wave function – as a wave, a particle, or something else. QM 'is radical precisely because it does not say how the world is' (Healey 2017: 4). However successful the mathematics may be in terms of prediction, we cannot provide a coherent *explanation* of quantum phenomena.

Nevertheless, explanations are attempted. To 'interpret' QM is to have a stab at describing the world in a way that makes quantum mechanics intelligible. There are plenty of interpretations to choose from. Bell (2004) identifies six, Lewis (2016) describes about a dozen (but the number, he says, is indefinite). It's a smorgasbord. Or a Rorschach blot. And there's something in it for everybody. For the moralist, there is the suggestion that free will is not only safeguarded but metaphysically fundamental. For the spiritually minded, there's the promise that the physical world may depend on consciousness rather than the other way round. For the theologian (and sundry others), there is the possibility of a 'relational ontology'. For the qualitative methodologist, there's the assurance that realities really *are* constructed.

The possibilities excite the imagination and suggest handholds for your favourite view of the universe. It's possible to decide what you'd *like* the implications of QM to be, and then choose an interpretation that gives you *that*. But it's as well to be clear. There are no ontological implications of QM as such. There can only be ontological implications of this or that interpretation.[18] 'Metaphysical claims of the form "Quantum mechanics shows that…" need to be treated very carefully, and in their full generality are likely to be false' (Lewis 2016: 182).[19]

To make an informed assessment of the 'ontological implications' of QM, therefore, it is essential to be familiar with the maths; and to understand, for each interpretation, the problems it is designed to solve, the strategy it adopts in trying to solve them, and the various arguments against it. Very few experienced qualitative researchers, and even fewer novices, are in that position.

Yet one occasionally finds methodologists appealing to QM in their metaphysical pronouncements. I looked at Lincoln and Guba's discussion in Section 6.6, but here is a more recent example. Like most qualitative writers,

Pernecky (2016) argues that the researcher has to know what her ontological and epistemological views are. In order to do this, he suggests, she must ask herself whether she agrees with a series of philosophical statements. One of them is (192):

> Quantum mechanics undermines the notion of the thing-in-itself and also the possibility of absolute and universal truths.[20]

'Quantum mechanics', Pernecky says, 'can be included in the overall philosophical deliberations when considering the essence of things, objectivism, absolutism, and universalism.' I find it impossible to take this seriously. Does he really expect the novice researcher to evaluate the QM literature, and work out what its ontological implications are? A task which has defeated physicists and philosophers alike, and about which there is nothing resembling a consensus? It's a crazy idea, and one which almost counts as a *reductio ad absurdum* of the whole 'underpinnings' doctrine.[21]

Not that I favour any particular interpretation myself, given that I'm not competent to make an informed judgement. For what it's worth, I incline towards Healey's (2017) view that QM is not in the business of *representing* the world. Its success lies in the universal accuracy of its predictions. It gives us nothing that can be used to build an ontology. It tells us nothing about 'reality'.[22]

6.8 Concluding thought

The chapter began with *Reader* saying that: 'I am using the words in their usual senses. You know the difference between 'single' and 'multiple', and you know what 'reality' refers to. So what exactly is the problem?' This is very like Wittgenstein's interlocutor saying:

> 'You surely know what "It's 5 o'clock here" means; so you also know what "It's 5 o'clock on the sun" means. It means simply that it is just the same time there as it is here when it's 5 o'clock'.
>
> *(Wittgenstein 2009: §350)*

The problem, in that case, was that 'on the sun' can't be slotted into the O'CLOCK construction in the way that 'in London' can be. There is a similar problem here. As I suggested in the last chapter, the locative coda of the EXISTENTIAL THERE construction is not an optional extra; so 'reality' (or 'realities') *as a whole* cannot be slotted into it. In this chapter, I've asked whether 'single reality' and 'multiple realities' have established uses (they don't), or special uses introduced by Lincoln and Guba (a special use is introduced for 'multiple realities' in the first half of Chapter 3, but it is forgotten immediately).

So once again, we are confronted with the question: Why do people think 'There is a single reality', or 'There are multiple realities?' are intelligible statements? Why do they think they believe one of them? This question has cropped up before and will crop up again. I will keep giving it the same answer, looked at from different angles. We're dealing with what Cappelen (2013) calls an 'illusion of thought'.

Carnap's expressivism offers an alternative way of understanding these sentences, one which offers a partial explanation of the illusion. They are not ontological claims but ritual phrases which signal a commitment. They are part of a creed enacting the decision to join a research culture, a research community (Section 4.7). This commitment is key to what sustains the illusion that these are intelligible, referentially successful statements which can be believed. 'There are multiple realities.' To *believe* that is an expression of the commitment, but it *feels* like recognising a fundamental truth. And, of course, one is encouraged to assume that it is.

Perhaps, though, the insertion of 'constructed' or 'socially constructed' makes a difference. Perhaps these terms help to tease out the meaning of 'There exist multiple realities', resolving it intelligibly. Perhaps they form part of the required explanation – an elucidation of the application conditions – for Lincoln and Guba's proposed usage. This is a possibility I consider in Chapter 7.

Notes

1 Wittgenstein provides several 'pictures of language' which are opposed to the 'aura' image. One I particularly like is from Wittgenstein (2009: §18): 'Our language can be seen as an ancient city: a maze of little streets and squares, of old and new houses, and of houses with additions from various periods; and this surrounded by a multitude of new boroughs with straight regular streets and uniform houses.' This applies to language in general, but also to individual words and expressions.
2 I will resort to 'L&G' as a convenient abbreviation on several occasions during this chapter and the next two, most commonly in Sections 6.5 and 6.6.
3 James doesn't mention 'multiple realities' at all. For a comparison of James's and Schutz's accounts of what James calls 'sub-universes', see Geniusas (2020).
4 See Section 4.5. I think it is instructive to see Schutz's discussion as providing syntactical rules rather than philosophical arguments. His general orientation was towards Husserlian phenomenology; but he remained 'outside the circle of "orthodox" phenomenologists' (Benţa 2018: 25). In an earlier discussion of everyday life, Schutz says: 'we do not claim to outline a "phenomenology of reality" or to make any contributions to "phenomenological philosophy"' (Schutz 1996: 25–26).
5 Virtual reality/worlds and augmented reality have been the subjects of numerous qualitative research studies, and there are textbooks describing suitable methods (e.g. Plesner & Phillips 2014); but I've not seen any suggestion that they contribute to the metaphysics underpinning qualitative methods. However, a recent book might prompt a debate about virtual reality that will eventually be taken up by qualitative methodologists. Chalmers (2022) argues that: 'Virtual reality is genuine

reality. Or at least, virtual realities are genuine realities. Virtual worlds need not be second-class realities. They can be first class realities… What happens in VR really happens. The objects we interact with in VR are real' (xvii). Can you get from 'virtual realities are real' to 'there are multiple realities' ('multiple realities' as Lincoln and Guba understand the expression)? I'm sceptical. Still, you wouldn't bet against the possibility of such an argument turning up in future textbooks.

6 'Social' and 'multiple' don't belong to either family, of course. They belong, as one might say, to the qualitative metaphysics family, to which the book as a whole is devoted. 'Multiple' will be discussed in Sections 6.5 and 6.6. 'Social' will be discussed in Chapter 7.

7 Brexit: the United Kingdom's departure from the European Union. This actually happened. Scexit: Scotland's possible departure from the United Kingdom. This hasn't happened but might if the Scots were to vote for independence in another referendum.

8 It also echoes Dilman's (1996) distinction 'between what is real and what is illusory, bogus or a false imitation. These distinctions do not come to the same thing in different areas of discourse: what we mean by *reality* depends on the grammar within which the question whether something is real or not arises' (191). This view traces back to Austin (1962), and the idea that 'real' has one primary job which is performed in countless different circumstances, so that its 'sense' is a function of which type of 'not-real' it is contrasted with on any given occasion. See Laugier (2018), especially section 5.

9 See Chapter 3, note 12.

10 For example, Castañeda (1977).

11 Hite (1976), Hite (1981).

12 L&G identify 'objective realism' with naïve realism, but it's quite possible to be an 'objective' realist without being a 'naïve realist'. In philosophy, the latter is a theory of perception, and it's taken seriously by a number of philosophers (see the review by Genone 2016). When qualitative writers dismiss 'naïve realism', the view they are rejecting is usually 'the belief that there is a single, unequivocal social reality or truth' (Mays & Pope 2000), usually with the implication that this reality can be known.

13 The expression 'qwiff' stands for 'quantum wave function'. 'Popping' it is to cause the wave function to collapse by making an observation. It's not obvious why the standing wave function isn't itself real; why it isn't part of 'reality'. In fact, a view called 'wave function realism' has recently been canvassed in the literature (though it was first suggested by Schrödinger). The theory interprets the quantum wave function as a field on an ultra high-dimensional space, and all objects – however three-dimensional they appear to be – are constituted out of it. See, for example, Ney (2021).

14 If you create reality by making an observation, are you yourself part of the reality you create? Or are you somehow 'outside' reality? Or are you in a 'wider' reality than the one you create? This last option seems, marginally, to be the least paradoxical. But then there would seem to be a (single?) reality – the 'wider' one – which encapsulates narrower realities, presumably located where the observation is made. Would it be these narrower realities that are 'multiple'? If so, how does that square with either half of L&G's chapter? A fourth option is that the 'you' who does the creating is just your conscious self, not your bodily self. This line of thought can lead to the view that minds exist outside the material world. It's a form of dualism which tempts some neurophysiologists (Eccles 1994) as well as some physicists (Stapp 2017). Or, for some social scientists, it can lead to panpsychism (Wendt 2015). Further thoughts on the relevance (or not) of QM in the next section.

15 The 'many worlds' are, of course, nothing like the differing perspectives ('or what would be called "multiple realities"') described in the first half of L&G's chapter.
16 Wave mechanics and matrix mechanics were shown to be equivalent by Schrödinger; but it is usually easier to apply wave mechanics to interference patterns and matrix mechanics to entangled electrons.
17 For example, if we ask 'What physical states do the noneigenstates of a given operator represent?', no answer is forthcoming. It doesn't really matter if you don't understand the question. The point is: it has no answer. The theory doesn't tell us what these mathematical expressions refer to.
18 DeCanio (2017: 127) makes the same point: 'While the Babel of quantum interpretations can be taken as making room for one's own favored interpretation, that is not the same thing as saying that it requires or even favors a particular ontology.' A similar view: 'Accepting quantum theory does not commit one to believing there is a multiverse of countless other physical worlds, that there is instantaneous action at a distance, or that consciousness has peculiar effects on matter' (Healey 2017: 12).
19 As will be evident, my account here draws particularly on Lewis (2016), Healey (2017), and Baggott (2020). The first two are philosophers, the third a science writer with a background in chemical physics. I should add that there are compelling arguments against *every* interpretation. So there is no consensus, and many physicists are apparently reluctant to speculate. The phrase 'Shut up and calculate!' (Mermin 1989) has come to signify, in a jocular way, this reluctance.
20 To decide whether she agrees with this statement, the researcher not only has to understand QM, she also needs to have understood Kant. Fortunately, Pernecky provides a chapter on German idealism.
21 Risjord (2010: 212) makes a similar point about the other philosophical debates that researchers are expected to resolve. He refers to the way in which researchers are asked to make up their minds about 'philosophical questions such as whether humans have free will or whether psychology can be reduced to biology'. These are important questions, he agrees, but the answers to them have no bearing, in his view, on methodological decision making.
22 There is further discussion of QM in Sections 8.9 and 8.10.

References

Austin, J. L. (1962). *Sense and Sensibilia*. Oxford: Clarendon Press.
Baggott, J. (2020). *Quantum Reality: The Quest for the Real Meaning of Quantum Mechanics - A Game of Theories*. Oxford: Oxford University Press.
Balaguer, M. (2021). *Metaphysics, Sophistry, and Illusion: Toward a Widespread Non-Factualism*. Oxford: Oxford University Press.
Bell, J. S. (2004). *Speakable and Unspeakable in Quantum Mechanics*. Cambridge, UK: Cambridge University Press.
Benţa, M. I. (2018). *Multiple Realities: Alfred Schutz's Sociology of the Finite Provinces of Meaning*. Abingdon, UK: Routledge.
Bogdan, R., & Taylor, S. (1975). *Introduction to Qualitative Research Methods*. New York: John Wiley.
Cappelen, H. (2013). Nonsense and illusions of thought. *Philosophical Perspectives, 27*, 22–50.
Castañeda, C. (1977). *The Second Ring of Power*. New York: Simon & Schuster.
Chalmers, D. J. (2022). *Reality +: Virtual Worlds and the Problems of Philosophy*. London: Allen Lane.

DeCanio, S. J. (2017). What is it like to be a social scientist? *Critical Review, 29*(2), 121–149.

Dilman, I. (1996). Existence and theory: Quine's conception of reality. In R. L. Arrington & H.-J. Glock (Eds.), *Wittgenstein and Quine* (pp. 173–195). London: Routledge.

Eccles, J. C. (1994). *How the Self Controls its Brain*. Berlin: Springer-Verlag.

Emery, S. (1978). *Actualizations: You Don't Have to Rehearse to be Yourself*. Garden City, NY: Doubleday.

Fine, K. (2001). The question of realism. *Philosophers' Imprint, 1*(1), www. philosophersimprint.org/001001/

Geniusas, S. (2020). 'Multiple realities' revisited: James and Schutz. *Human Studies, 43*, 545–565.

Genone, J. (2016). Recent work on naïve realism. *American Philosophical Quarterly, 53*(1), 1–25.

Gessert, R. A. (1960). The integrity of faith: The meaning of law in the thought of John Calvin. *Scottish Journal of Theology, 13*(3), 247–261.

Hammersley, M. (2020). On Schutz's conception of science as one of multiple realities. *Journal of Classical Sociology, 20*(4), 281–297.

Healey, R. (2017). *The Quantum Revolution in Philosophy*. New York: Oxford University Press.

Hite, S. (1976). *The Hite Report*. New York: Macmillan.

Hite, S. (1981). *The Hite Report on Male Sexuality*. New York: Alfred A. Knopf.

Hofweber, T. (2009). Ambitious, yet modest, metaphysics. In D. J. Chalmers, D. Manley, & R. Wasserman (Eds.), *Metametaphysics: New Essays on the Foundations of Ontology* (pp. 260–289). Oxford: Oxford University Press.

James, W. (2018). *Principles of Psychology, Vol II*. Tempe, AZ: New Classics Books. First published 1890.

Laugier, S. (2018). The vulnerability of reality. In S. L. Tsohatzidis (Ed.), *Interpreting J L Austin: Critical Essays* (pp. 119–140). Cambridge, UK: Cambridge University Press.

Lewis, P. J. (2016). *Quantum Ontology: A Guide to the Metaphysics of Quantum Mechanics*. New York: Oxford University Press.

Lincoln, Y. S., & Guba, E. G. (1985). *Naturalistic Inquiry*. Beverly Hills, CA: Sage.

Mays, N., & Pope, C. (2000). Assessing quality in qualitative research. *BMJ, 320*(7226), 50–52.

Mermin, N. D. (1989). What's wrong with this pillow? *Physics Today, 42*(4), 9.

Ney, A. (2021). *The World in the Wave Function: A Metaphysics for Quantum Physics*. New York: Oxford University Press.

Pernecky, T. (2016). *Epistemology and Metaphysics for Qualitative Research*. London: Sage.

Plesner, U., & Phillips, L. (Eds.). (2014). *Researching Virtual Worlds: Methodologies for Studying Emergent Practices*. New York: Routledge.

Reynolds, S. L. (2006). Realism and the meaning of 'real'. *Noûs, 40*(3), 468–494.

Risjord, M. (2010). *Nursing Knowledge: Science, Practice, and Philosophy*. Chichester, UK: Wiley-Blackwell.

Schutz, A. (1945). On multiple realities. *Philosophy and Phenomenological Research, 5*(4), 533–576. Reprinted in Schutz, A. Collected papers, Vol 531: 207–259.

Schutz, A. (1970). *Reflections on the Problem of Relevance*. New Haven: Yale University Press.

Schutz, A. (1996). *Collected Papers IV*. Dordrecht: Springer.

Stake, R. E. (1977). Some alternative presumptions. *Evaluation News, 3*, 18–19.

Stapp, H. P. (2017). *Quantum Theory and Free Will: How Mental Intentions Translate into Bodily Actions*. Cham, Switzerland: Springer Nature.

Wendt, A. (2015). *Quantum Mind and Social Science: Unifying Physical and Social Ontology*. Cambridge, UK: Cambridge University Press.

Wittgenstein, L. (2009). *Philosophical Investigations: Revised 4th edition by P. M. S. Hacker and Joachim Schulte*. Malden, MA: Wiley-Blackwell.

Zukav, G. (1979). *The Dancing Wu-Li Masters*. New York: Bantam.

7

'CONSTRUCTED', 'SOCIALLY CONSTRUCTED'

Switcheroo 'One commits a switcheroo by starting with a hypothesis that's amenable to a range of interpretations, giving arguments that support a weak version, and thenceforth pretending that one of the stronger versions has been established.' (Kukla 2000: x)

'Switcheroo' is another way of looking at Lincoln and Guba's treatment of 'multiple realities': the weaker version, supported by numerous examples, is 'people construing things differently', an anthropological truism. The stronger version is an ontological thesis: it is dubious whether there is a reality; or we can never know it; or there is no reality at all; or it doesn't exist until created by an actor (Lincoln & Guba 1985: 83–87). We'll find more switcheroos turning up in this chapter.

One of the problems in discussing 'constructed' and 'socially constructed' is the large number of -isms that congregate round those expressions: constructivism, constructionism, social constructivism, social constructionism, communicative constructivism, cognitive constructivism, radical constructivism, post-constructivism, empirical constructivism, interactive constructivism, perhaps more.[1] It's a terminological jungle out there. Approach with caution.

The various -isms, as such, don't particularly interest me (and it would take a complete book to untangle them). But a few distinctions would be helpful.

DOI: 10.4324/9781003306382-9

7.1 What, who, how?

Three questions. According to constructionists/constructivists of various stamps and stripes:

[A] What is it that is constructed?

[B] Who or what does the constructing?

[C] How is the constructing achieved?

Or, in Mallon's (2019) terms: What is constructed? What constructs? What is it to construct?

[A] Different writers give different answers to all these questions. The range of options is particularly wide with [A]. Hacking (1999) exclaims: 'What a lot of things are said to be socially constructed!'. He lists: emotions, gender, the child viewer of television, quarks, serial homicide, technological systems, women refugees, danger, illness, and reality, among many others. More recent additions to the list include self-esteem (Hewitt 2021), male infertility (Hanna & Gough 2020), Asian migrant women in the United States (Moon 2021), systemic risk (Maskrey et al. 2023), popular female music stars (Lieb 2019). These are *social* phenomena, the product (as we'll see in a moment) of people acting in concert. It's not possible to provide a similar list for what is just 'constructed' – that is, 'constructed' without the 'socially' – since these are *individual* constructions, not necessarily recognised by other people.

[B] There is a spectrum of possibilities here, but the key distinction is that between the individual-as-constructor and a collective-as-constructor. By 'collective', I mean a group, a network, or a community; or something slightly more abstract: a society, a culture, a tradition, or a language. The people involved in such a collective might be aware that they are acting in concert, but then again they might not. They don't have to know each other and may be separated in time. But they have all made a contribution in some sense. The social construction of quarks was carried out by a community of physicists; the social construction of gender was/is carried out by a society, or by dominant groupings within it.

Given that the work of construction, when carried out by a collective, is 'social' in a way that the work of construction carried out by an individual is not, we might reserve the expression 'social construction' for this possibility, omitting the 'social' when referring to construction by individuals. This is not, as we will see, a convention universally adhered to, but I'll adopt it here. In the same vein, I'll reserve 'social constructionists', or sometimes just 'constructionists', for those who view 'construction' as a collective enterprise, and use 'constructivists' to refer to those who focus on the individual-as-constructor.

The 'multiple realities' which result from these constructing activities will be of two main sorts. Where the constructing agents are individuals, they will be 'centred' on the individuals concerned. 'Centred' is not an ideal word, largely because accounts of the relation in question are deeply unclear. However, if Agnes has constructed one reality, Bruno has constructed a different one, and Colette has constructed a third – even with respect to just a single phenomenon – then the realities concerned (however else we describe them) are in some ill-defined way attached to, identified with, centred on, the individual who did the constructing.[2] In contrast, where the constructing agents are groups or societies, the resulting 'multiple' realities will 'belong' to the groups/societies concerned. If Society *S* has constructed one reality, which all or most of its members share; and if Society *T* has constructed a different reality – again, shared by all or most of its members – then we have two 'realities', each 'centred' on the society in question. In the first case, we have multiple individuals with their respective realities. In the second case we have multiple societies, with *their* respective realities (shared by individual members).

[C] The process of construction is not always described very clearly, but there appear to be two basic methods. First, there is a *non-causal* process which involves something usually described as *attaching meanings*, or 'understanding', or 'defining'. The meanings are attached to 'phenomena' or sometimes words. For example, Lincoln and Guba (1985) say that a common term is 'understood (or constructed) differently by different individuals'. Harvard University, the middle ages, God, realpolitik as practised by Henry Kissinger, and good manners, all mean 'something quite different to different individuals'.[3] 'None of those things exists in a form other than those constructed by the persons who "recognize" the term' (84). On the face of it, then, we construct a 'reality' by 'interpreting' or 'defining' an expression in a way that's different from how the next chap defines it. It's a fuzzy idea, but we'll come back to it.

The second method consists of almost any form of *action*: what people do, make, say, write, legislate for; how they decide, adjudicate, persuade; the way they argue and evaluate; the assumptions they make, the policies they adopt, the institutions they create, the habits they acquire, the routines they put in place. All these contribute to the bringing into existence of a 'phenomenon', an 'idea', or a 'reality'. Whether the 'X' is a quark, female pop stars, illness, self-esteem, or 'facts', the construction of an 'X' involves a lot of work and, usually, a lot of people. It doesn't happen *merely* by 'defining' or 'attaching meanings' (though these are certainly involved). To emphasise the difference further, we can say that this form of construction is *causal*. The work involved includes creating, building, organising, and influencing; and these, in a harmlessly non-ontological way, are all examples of causation.[4]

To make explicit what I've already implied, the *non-causal* process is associated with *individuals*, while the *causal* process requires *collectives*. The constructivist's 'multiple realities' are the result of different individuals defining things differently. The social constructionist's 'X' is created through many people's combined efforts, leading to a generally recognised 'thing', whether gender, serial homicide, or quarks. For the constructivist, reality is 'a construction in the mind of individuals' (Lincoln & Guba 1985: 81). 'Change the individual and you change the reality.' In contrast, the social constructionist explains how a specific social 'phenomenon' came to exist.[5] The 'X' in question is not inevitable; it is not set in tablets of stone. It 'was brought into existence or shaped by social events, forces, history, all of which could have been different' (Hacking 1999: 7). It's entrenched, but contingent. For the constructivist, however, there is no single 'reality'; so, equally, there is no entrenched, widely recognised 'phenomenon'. Every different interpretation generates another reality, centred on the interpreting individual.

So constructivists think individuals create 'realities' by the non-causal attaching of meanings to things. Social constructionists think groups, networks, and societies create 'phenomena', or ideas, by the causal processes involved in collective work. This is too glib a summary, but it gives a broad-brush impression of the terrain. We're nearly ready to get down to the main business, but first some remarks on the book whose title started it all.

7.2 The Social Construction of Reality

In the beginning was *The Social Construction of Reality: A Treatise in the Sociology of Knowledge* (Berger & Luckmann 1967). It's the first book to have 'social construction' in the title. Indeed, Eberle (2019: 131) suggests that it was not 'the content of this book but its title that had the greatest impact... it was a thesis in itself'. The title certainly created an instant academic meme. As the 'social construction' label caught on, different authors attached it to different projects. 'I suspect the main role of the Berger & Luckmann book was as a resource that was not read closely but treated as a kind of programmatic statement... We all read the book, and in it we could find support for our project' (Pinch 2019: 154).

Still, the opening pages do seem clear enough. The book is a contribution to sociology, not philosophy – and, specifically, the sociology of knowledge. '[T]his treatise is a sociological analysis of the reality of everyday life, more precisely, of knowledge that guides conduct in everyday life'. Its purpose 'is *not* to engage in philosophy' (33; italic original).

The clarification ('more precisely…') is significant. The key point is that the 'reality of everyday life' is identified with the taken-for-granted, 'common-sense' knowledge that the members of a society *share*. Berger and Luckmann are less bothered about 'ideas' in an intellectual sense. They emphasise that: '*The sociology of knowledge must concern itself with everything that passes for "knowledge" in society*' (26). For example, I and millions of others know that Tuesday comes after Monday. We also know that dropped objects will fall to the ground. This is the kind of 'knowledge' B&L have in mind. It just *is* the 'reality of everyday life'. The job of the sociology of knowledge is to determine how that 'knowledge' arose, and how individuals acquire it.[6]

This represents a departure from earlier understandings of the sociology of knowledge, which portrayed it as the study of ideologically produced 'distortions'. It was, in effect, a 'sociology of error', explaining how we 'go wrong', but making no attempt to explain how we acquire 'correct' beliefs. B&L go beyond this. In making 'everything that passes for knowledge' the topic of enquiry, they open up the possibility of sociologically explaining beliefs which are 'true' – or which no-one seriously questions – as well as beliefs that have been shown, or are suspected, to be 'false'. On the face of it, this has no ontological implications. It merely extends the range of things-to-be-explained-sociologically.

However, as several authors have pointed out, *The Social Construction of Reality* contains a number of ambiguities, making it difficult to determine precisely what Berger and Luckmann's view is. For example, they appear to hedge between the claim that what-is-socially-constructed is *whatever passes for reality* (in a given society) and the claim that what-is-socially-constructed is *reality itself*. The first of these is what Collin (1997: 69) calls 'sociology-of-knowledge neutralism', an empirical project with no obvious ontological commitment. The second looks like a form of cultural relativism, since different societies may construct different realities (as opposed to having different views about what's real and what isn't). It has even been argued that Berger and Luckmann can be categorised as 'social constructivists', despite the fact that they 'steadfastly rejected' this label themselves – associating it, as they did, 'with a mindset of postmodern arbitrariness' (Pfadenhauer 2019: 1).[7]

In summary, Berger and Luckmann argued for the sociological study of everything that the members of society take themselves to know, especially the taken-for-granted knowledge that constitutes the warp and weft of everyday 'reality'. This is, intrinsically, shared knowledge (in the society concerned); so the 'reality', too, is shared. In this context, 'multiple realities' refers to Schutz's finite provinces of meaning (Section 6.2), which everybody experiences. B&L see this as an expansion in the scope of the sociology of knowledge. They do not think they are doing philosophy.[8]

It is not difficult to understand why *The Social Construction of Reality* should have created a platform for the kinds of 'social construction' project Hacking discusses. 'Social construction of X' projects take specific examples of taken-for-granted 'knowledge' and explain how they arose. Such knowledge might extend to society as a whole (illness, danger, pop stars); or to more defined populations (technological systems, quarks, legal grievances, serial homicide); and in some cases it might not strictly be 'taken for granted' at all (parapsychology: Collins & Pinch 1982). Yet, in all cases, the 'X' will have been brought into existence through a *causal historical* process, necessarily involving a range of people (politicians, historians, activists, scientists, journalists, philosophers, the judiciary) over a period of time.

L&G-style constructivism is in marked contrast. Lincoln and Guba don't generally use the expression 'socially constructed realities'.[9] They talk about 'multiple constructed realities', without the 'socially'; and it is clear (most of the time) that individuals do the constructing. They show no interest in 'everyday reality', or in the *work* people have to do – as opposed to 'interpreting' or 'meaning attaching' – in order to bring an 'X' into existence. They do suggest that constructions can be 'shared', but this is just a matter of individuals happening to have the *same* construction. It is not a matter of constructions being intrinsically pooled or public.[10] Nor is it a question of the 'constructing' process itself being 'joint' (so to speak). Their version of 'construction' is explicitly, and very much, *not* social.

Even so, constructivism and social constructionism are often conflated. Perhaps this is because 'socially constructed' has become such a routine trope in qualitative methods writing. An example is Merriam and Tisdell's (2016: 9) account of what they call the 'interpretivist' ontology:

> Reality is socially constructed; that is, there is no single, observable reality. Rather, there are multiples realities, or interpretations of a single event.

Read slowly, this can appear self-contradictory. Reality (*singular*) is socially constructed. *So* there is *no* single reality. The implication seems to be that, *because* reality is socially constructed, there are multiple realities. At the very least, this doesn't follow. It would make rather more sense to say: because 'reality' is *individually* constructed, there are multiple realities, with *individuals* having different interpretations of events.[11] But perhaps Merriam and Tisdell regard 'socially constructed' as a synonym of 'constructed by people', rather than having the 'joint', 'in common', or 'collective', B&L sense.

The conflation of constructivism and social constructionism, in addition to making the terminological thicket even denser, has made it harder to untangle the conclusions which supposedly follow from the fact that 'construction' occurs. In the rest of the chapter, I will attempt to *un*-conflate, and treat these arguments separately. In Sections 7.3–7.7, I will deal with L&G's constructivism; in Sections 7.8 and 7.9, I'll turn to two versions of social constructionism.

7.3   The Constructivist Credo: the Presumptions

The Constructivist Credo is the most recent statement of L&G's version of constructivist metaphysics, published after Guba's death (Lincoln & Guba 2013). The main text, after introductions by Yvonna Lincoln and Thomas Schwandt, is largely written by Guba himself. He notes: 'what I do here may be thought of as poetic, because most of the passages that I set out strike me as metaphors for something that's in my head but which I cannot express with precision' (29). Even so, the text is organised, very approximately, as a logical system, reflecting Guba's conviction that constructivism and constructivist inquiry '*may be derived* – at least in the form of reasonable conjectures – from a small number of metaphysical presumptions, ontological, epistemological, axiological and methodological in nature, which I have [arbitrarily?] taken as axiomatic' (28: italics and brackets in original).[12] So the main text comprises a set of four metaphysical 'presumptions', from which are derived 133 'conjectures', divided into 13 categories.

My aim in this section and the next three is to clarify, if possible, the relation between certain key terms in Guba's account, particularly 'constructed', 'construction', 'reality', 'real', 'exist', 'meaning', 'social', 'socially', 'know' and 'known'. In doing so, I focus on the *Presumptions* (this section) and the first three *Conjecture*-categories.

The Presumptions are answers to 'four fundamental questions', the first of which is (37):

> The *ontological* question: "What is there that can be known?" Or, to rephrase the question, "What is the nature of reality?"

The equating of these two questions is puzzling. Both of them may be valid and reasonable, but they are clearly not the same. The second is not merely a 'rephrasing' of the first. On the face of it, all kinds of things can be 'known' (I know that Tuesday follows Monday, and that I'm using a keyboard to type this sentence); but these facts don't have anything to do with 'the nature of reality'. So Guba is already using his terms in an unexplained way.

Reader: Oh, come on. You know perfectly well that Tuesday following Monday is not what he's talking about.

Me: Do I? How do I know that? He hasn't said anything about using 'known' in an unusual, non-standard way. And if we're using the word as it's normally used, then the fact that Tuesday follows Monday is the kind of thing that can be known.

Reader: Yes, but in the context of a philosophical discussion, everybody knows that 'what can be known' isn't a reference to Mondays and Tuesdays.

Me: Ah, well, I obviously didn't get the email.

Reader: Yeah, right. You know as well as I do what he means.

Me: I wish you would stop assuming that.[13] But, okay, if it doesn't mean Tuesdays following Mondays, what does it mean?

Reader: It means: 'What *kinds* of thing can be known?'

Me: But that's a linguistic matter. A question about how we use the word 'know'. We talk about knowing facts, knowing people, knowing places, knowing stuff, knowing secrets, knowing the ropes... Those are all kinds of thing that can be known.

Reader: There you go again. Deliberately missing the point. It's not a matter of how we use the *word*. It's a matter of what can be *known*.

Me: I've just given you a *list* of things that can be known. Why is that missing the point?

Reader: Because you're ignoring the philosophical context. According to some writers, all knowledge is 'empirical', what can be observed/measured. Guba says the only things that can be known are constructions, and these exist only in the minds of the persons contemplating them.

Me: But that's clearly not true in any ordinary sense of 'know' and 'known'. So I come back to my earlier point. Guba is obviously not using those words in their ordinary sense. So now I want to know what this *non*-ordinary sense is. How does it work? What are its rules of use? Unless you or Guba can tell me that, how can I understand what it is you're trying to say?

Guba goes on to adopt a 'relativistic' view (38):

> What if reality is conceptualized as not being real in the usual sense, but relative to its observer/definer? Is there a class of entities worth inquiring into that would fit this definition? We believe it to be the case that all entities commonly included within the purview of the human sciences are of this kind... [They] exist only in this non-concrete, intangible form.[14]

So social *entities* are 'real' only relative to an observer/definer. This is the intangible form they *exist* in. However, by the end of the same paragraph, Guba is saying (38; my italics):

> the *meaning of entities* such as "school", "personality", "values", "intelligence", "morality", "leadership", "poverty", "democracy", "race"... depends entirely on the definer.

There is a switcheroo here.[15] First, Guba says that *entities exist* relative to the definer, in a non-concrete, intangible form. This is definitely wow!-worthy. But then he says that the *meaning* of entities depends entirely on the definer.

Which is much less wow!-worthy. It's not implausible to say that the *meaning* of entities depends on the definer – that is, the person who 'attaches the meaning'. But that's a far cry from suggesting that the *existence* of entities depends on the definer. Perhaps this is why Guba places inverted commas round his examples. To say that *schools* exist only in a non-concrete form might elicit scepticism. To suggest that *'school'* exists only in a non-concrete form fudges it, because it's not clear what it means. Does it refer to schools, the word 'school', the meaning of 'school', the connotations of 'school', or…?

This is a ubiquitous theme in *TCC*. Guba never distinguishes between *entities*, the *existence* of entities, the *meaning* of entities, the *reality* of entities and, often, the *words* that refer to entities. He switches between them almost at random, usually – as here – in ways that get him from something that is almost a truism (the meaning of entities depends on the meaning attacher) to something ontologically surprising (the existence of entities depends on the definer). For example, later on the same page he says: 'Change the individuals and you change the reality.' But if the *meaning* of entities depends on the definer, what he presumably should say is: 'Change the individuals and you change the meaning.' You could at least make a decent case for that.

The formal statement of the ontological presumption (39) is as follows:

> In the human sciences, entities are matters of definition and convention; they exist only in the minds of the persons contemplating them. They do not "really" exist. That is, they have ontological status only insofar as some group of persons (frequently, social scientists, but often the rest of us, also) grants them that status.

Guba's list of 'entities' above includes many 'intangible' examples: 'personality', 'morality', 'values'. But it also includes an institution, 'school'; and Guba might well sanction the addition of others: 'bank', 'church', 'hospital', 'university', and so on. None of these, it seems, 'really' exist. They 'exist only in the minds of the persons contemplating them'. Again, the conflation of entities and meanings is clear. The *meanings* of 'church', one might plausibly argue, 'exist only in the minds of those contemplating them'. But to argue that *churches* 'exist only in the minds of those contemplating them' is more of a stretch.[16]

The problem that Guba never acknowledges is that words like 'school' and 'church' can refer to an idea, a building, an institution, a community, an experience (being at school, being in church), and more.[17] The experience may be non-concrete, intangible, and dependent on the definer. The building isn't.

7.4 Conjectures: A – In the Beginning

'Human beings experience an inchoate world, a buzzing, bumbling confusion, a confounded surround, that challenges their very survival' (Lincoln &

Guba 2013: 44). The 'buzzing, bumbling confusion' is an echo of a remark attributed to William James, who described the sensory-perceptual world of infants as a 'blooming, buzzing confusion'.[18] But that was babies. Guba is talking about adults. He continues (44):

> There is no compelling reason to believe, a priori, that this surround has any existence apart from the individuals who encounter it, that is, to believe it to be objectively independent of the sense mechanisms of the individuals who experience it. Encounters within the surround – with objects, events, and life forms including other persons – provide a store of sensory memories which the individual processes into forms that seem to "make sense", that is, forms that organize – reconstruct – sense experiences and make them meaningful. This world is made sensible... by the order that human beings impose on events, situations and circumstances.

There are a number of peculiarities in this passage. For example, it's not clear that individuals can be said to 'encounter' something which doesn't exist separately from them. But this is probably semantic trifling. More seriously, the implication seems to be that each individual has their own 'surround', on which they impose order: there is not a 'single' surround which is ordered in different ways by different individuals. If there were, presumably it would have existence independently of at least *some* of those individuals (remove one individual, and the surround would have to remain for the others). So there is a one-to-one correspondence between individuals and surrounds.

So now consider 'encounters within the surround', encounters with objects, events, and other persons. If the surround has no independent existence apart from the individual to whom the surround belongs, then presumably those objects, including the people, have no independent existence either. Their existence is dependent on the individual-doing-the-encountering. There is, in Guba's terms, no compelling reason to believe, a priori, that they have any existence apart from her. This view – it's a kind of solipsism – is strange enough, but it gets even stranger when you realise that it must apply to *all* individuals. Jack has no existence apart from Jill (who encounters him within her surround), but Jill has no existence apart from Jack (who encounters her within *his* surround). Specifically, she has no existence independently of Jack's sense mechanisms (and vice versa).[19]

Here's another puzzling question: *how* do individuals impose order on the 'surround', or on the events, situations and circumstances they 'encounter' within it? The surround itself is a buzzing confusion, so it will not, itself, contain any resources. So where do the categories, the constructions, the orderings, come from? Well, from the individual. But where did she get them? What repository of 'meanings' does she draw on? Is she born with them, or does she somehow conjure them from... well, what? Guba says she does it by 'utilizing the constructive character of the mind', 'limited only by the imagination'. But 'the constructive character of the mind' just tells us that the mind *can* construct; it doesn't tell us how.[20] As for the imagination, how does the individual acquire one? Not from the bumbling and buzzing. So we're back to 'born with' or 'conjuring'. In any case the imagination must have some raw material to work with. It's not just a random-concept generator, pulling categories out of the ether. And how is it that different individuals often produce meanings which, while they may not be identical, don't seem to be radically divergent either? You can't appeal to 'society' or 'interaction' here, because 'society' is itself an 'ordering' concept, and the 'interaction' is interaction in only a very eccentric sense. For example, Jill 'interacts' with Jack – but Jack has no existence apart from Jill's surround.

So the origin of these orderings is a bit mysterious.

There is another ambiguity built into Guba's account of the surround and the encounters within it. If the surround is a 'bumbling buzzing confusion', then presumably one does not 'encounter' an *object* within it. Jill does not 'encounter' Jack as a *part* of the confusion. Rather, 'Jack' is the result of Jill imposing an order on the surround, or a segment of it. He is a *construction* of Jill's. Yet Guba sometimes talks as if Jill *does* encounter Jack, in all his Jackness, as an item in the surround, and as if the order she imposes on him is related to intangibles: his character, abilities, emotions, and so on. But if that's right, how did the surround 'acquire' something identifiable as Jack *before* Jill's imposition of order? Guba doesn't answer the question, of course; but that's ultimately irrelevant, for the question is almost pointless. If the surround has no existence independently of Jill's sense mechanisms, then Jack's existence is dependent on her, whether he is the result of imposing order on the surround, or whether he 'originates' (as it were) in the surround, pre-ordering. And in the same way, Jill's existence is dependent on Jack's. So this only intensifies the mystery rather than resolving it.

7.5   Conjectures: B – Constructions

In the second set of conjectures, Guba explains what constructs and constructions are.

[A] A construct is a mental realisation – "a making real" – of an apparently singular, unitary entity or relationship; an element of a construction.

[B] A construction is a coherent, articulated set of constructs – a pattern or web of constructs and their interconnections – that makes sense of some aspect (some "chunk") of the constructor's surround…

The 'apparently singular, unitary entity' in A is presumably the *result* of the mental act of 'realisation'. It is not something 'prior' on which that act was carried out (given that there *are* no prior entities in the bumbling, buzzing surround). However, the use of the word 'entity' suggests the conflation of meanings and objects which is endemic to Guba's use of the term 'construct'.

The act of 'sense-making' creates a construct-as-concept, a way of organising experience. There's nothing problematic about this. But Guba implies that the 'entity' – the thing the concept is *applied to* – is also 'created' by the same act. Unless he explains how this works, how an 'entity' is manufactured out of the inchoate surround, it is perfectly reasonable to reserve judgement. The reference to 'the constructor's surround' in B confirms that every individual has their own surround; so the implication is that Jack and Jill each create their own unique universe of 'entities'.

[C] Constructions are the end products of individual (and sometimes group) efforts at sense-making, and hence they are inherently subjective.

[D] The scope of constructions (especially their form) is limited, for a given constructor, by the forms of representation (verbal, emotional, artistic, performative, and others) which he or she has previously learned and with which he or she feels comfortable.

Constructions, which are organised sets of constructs, are inherently subjective, according to C, since they are products of sense-making. This is not objectionable. All it says is that concepts, ideas, thoughts, interpretations, and theories are all, in a colloquial sense, 'mental'.[21] Human beings create them. If there were no human beings, there would be no constructs, no constructions. (It would be another switcheroo if Guba were now to suggest that *entities* were 'created' and subjective.)

The outstanding puzzle here is the reference in D to the forms of representation 'which he or she has previously *learned*'. In view of what Guba has already told us, how does this learning take place? Each individual has a 'confounding surround', bumbling and buzzing. So she can't have learned anything of use from that.[22] On the other hand, everything she 'encounters' is encountered *within* the surround; and there is 'no compelling reason to believe, a priori, that this surround has any existence independently of the individual who encounters it'. So what she has 'previously learned' *must* come, ultimately, from the surround; and every instance of 'making sense' must depend on her previous 'encounters' and the sense she has made of them. She 'makes sense', in other words, by learning from her 'previous' sense-making. Which makes you wonder how the 'sense-making' process got started, given that we seem to be on the edge of an infinite regress here. Guba says a bit more about this (48):

I. Constructions need not be developed de novo by every individual; they may be developed jointly with other individuals or learned from them… Culture itself is also a powerful transmitter of constructions, and some of the constructions we carry around with us are "inherited" from our culture.

But the individuals you 'learn from', or 'develop constructions jointly with', were encountered in the surround; and the surround has no existence apart from the individual to whom it 'belongs'. Moreover, these 'other individuals' are the result of previous sense-making. They are constructions that *must* have been developed de novo – because, before you 'encountered'/'created' them, these 'other individuals' did not exist. So there is no escape from the solipsistic universe in which the individual finds herself. The 'people' she 'learns from' are themselves constructions from within her own unique surround. As for 'culture', where did that come from? Isn't that just another construction, with which the individual 'makes sense?' How does she 'inherit' anything from that? It's almost as if Guba thinks that culture pre-dates the individual and passes its constructions on to her. Yet earlier, in the first set of conjectures, he appears to reject this idea (46):

> Sense making, or the creation of constructions, is independent of any social foundational reality (if such in fact exists).

Of course, it's not clear exactly what he means by 'social foundational reality'; but this does sound like scepticism concerning the existence of any reality that is 'prior' to the individual, or which is capable of 'transmitting' constructions to her.[23] There is, at the very least, a tension here, which Guba doesn't seem to recognise.

K: Personal as well as cultural identities are formed and understood through interactions between and among multiple individuals situated in the same, or metaphorically or vicariously similar, surround. It is also the case, however, that personal and/or cultural identities may be formed and understood through interactions between and among multiple individuals and groups situated in *radically different surrounds*, as, for instance, when individuals travel to culturally strange, exotic and different places. (49)

This conjecture suggests that individuals may be situated in the 'same surround'. Recognising the fact that, earlier, Guba has strongly implied that each individual has her *own* surround, this is immediately qualified: individuals may be situated, not in *literally* the same surround, but in a '*metaphorically* or *vicariously* similar' one. This claim is a long way from being clear. What is 'a vicariously similar X'? I've never come across this expression before, and I don't understand what it means in this passage.

The talk of 'interaction' is compromised, as before, by the solipsistic nature of 'encounters with others'. Even 'metaphorically' or 'vicariously' similar surrounds would still be numerically different, ensuring that each individual remains locked in her own. The fact that Jack's surround is 'similar' to Jill's does not mean that he can 'interact' with her as an independently existing person: for she only exists as a constructed item encountered *within* his surround (and he only exists as a constructed item encountered within hers).

7.6 Conjectures: C – Shared constructions

Moving beyond 'metaphorically' or 'vicariously' similar surrounds and 'interaction' with others, Guba now suggests that constructions may be shared (53):

G: Shared constructions require shared experiences, and shared experiences require shared constructions; efforts at common sense-making require some base of prior experience/construction commonality.

This conjecture gets close to suggesting that any attempt at 'commonality' requires prior 'commonality'. So how does 'commonality' get started? There can't be an initial instance of it, because even an 'initial' instance would require a prior instance. It's a little dizzy-making.

I'm not hanging a lot on this observation. It's not an argument in itself (or, if it is, it's the sort people tend to be suspicious of). However, it does draw attention to the fact that Guba's text is seriously short on explanations of how *anything* happens. We have individuals who, according to some passages, have their own surrounds, and who encounter other people only within those surrounds; and we have people who, according to other passages, can have the 'same' surround – or at least 'metaphorically' similar, or 'vicariously' similar surrounds – and who can therefore 'interact'. Now we have people 'sharing' their constructions and 'sharing' their experiences. But whether this is in virtue of the fact that they have the 'same' surround, or a 'vicariously similar' surround – or whether they can share constructions despite having their own unique surrounds, and if so how – is completely unclear.

K: Shared constructions, especially among larger groups of individuals, become reified over time to become part of the sociocultural milieu. They may be jointly reviewed, edited, and stabilised; physical, historical, social, and cultural "realities" are thereby rendered tangible and concrete... Nevertheless, constructions, even when shared as part of the sociocultural milieu, are not reality but continue to be mental assemblages of semiotic signs and symbols, of meanings and meaning sets (54).

Now, I'm even more confused. Through shared constructions, 'realities' can be rendered tangible and concrete... nevertheless, these constructions are not reality'. This is odd because, in earlier passages, the expression 'tangible and concrete' is used to refer to the 'out there' view of reality (37):

Traditionally reality has been believed to be concrete and tangible, 'out there'.

However, because reality (as L&G understand it) is 'relative to its observer/ definer', 'entities commonly included in the purview of the human science' are not like this (i.e. not concrete and tangible)… 'We would argue that every social/psychological/cultural entity… exists *only* in this non-concrete, intangible form' (38; italics mine). Yet K says social and cultural realities *can* be made 'tangible and concrete'. This, according to the earlier passages, should qualify them as part of 'out there reality' (as traditionally understood). But apparently it doesn't.

Even here, though, there is ambiguity. Shared constructions are not (out there?) 'reality' but continue to be 'mental assemblages'. Yes, but this is part of another switcheroo. Constructions – concepts, theories, ideas – are, we could agree, 'mental assemblages'. Fine. How, then, can 'cultural and social realities' be rendered 'tangible and concrete', when tangibility and concreteness imply (according to Guba's earlier statements) that they are part of an 'out there' reality? In whatever way you try to unpick this tangle, you still have an apparent contradiction between the claim that social and cultural entities exist *only* in a non-concrete, intangible form, and the claim that they *can* be rendered tangible and concrete. And we still have a bewilderingly arbitrary array of uses of the words 'reality' and 'realities' – sometimes in inverted commas, sometimes not.

7.7   The Constructivist Credo: assessment

As I've said, Guba admits: 'what I do here may be thought of as poetic, because most of the passages that I set out strike me as metaphors for something that's in my head but which I cannot express with precision' (29); and a close reading of passages from the *Credo* confirms that it's often difficult to make sense of what he says. The book is full of non-sequiturs, ambiguities, apparent inconsistencies.[24] There is his inability (or reluctance) to distinguish between entities, the meaning of entities, and the existence of entities. There is the puzzle of the 'surround': does every individual have their own, or is it possible for several individuals to have the same one? If not, what are 'metaphorically similar' and 'vicariously similar' surrounds? Is order of *every* sort imposed on a surround's 'bumbling, buzzing confusion' by the individual concerned? Or does the surround contain items – such as persons – whose existence is *not* dependent on other people's orderings? If the latter, what exactly is the relation between surrounds and individuals? If the former, how are 'interaction', 'learning' and 'sharing' possible? Does Guba think that social entities exist *only* in non-concrete, intangible form (38)? Or does he think that social and cultural 'realities' can be rendered concrete and tangible (54)? Is there any way of reconciling these apparently inconsistent possibilities? Does social reality, in some sense, pre-exist the individual, or doesn't it?

It's a long list, and this is just the edited highlights. Although one reviewer says that 'the *Credo* works best as a foundation to clarify the paradigm's approach' (Fram 2014: 599); and while another suggests that 'the first 85 pages of *The Credo* help make the paradigm clearer' (Repass 2013), I've found it impossible to determine how Guba's metaphysics are supposed to work. If *this* is constructivism, then I have no idea how to describe it. I have no idea what Guba *means* by 'construct' or 'construction'. I have no idea what his ontological position is.

Of course, that might just be me. But I'd like to see a detailed exegesis of what's going on in this text, explaining all the metaphysical wrinkles, and filling in the ontological gaps. So far, I have not been able to find one.

7.8 Language versus reality

Moving on to the social constructionist end of the spectrum, I want to consider another way to approach the idea that, in Guba's terms, entities 'do not "really" exist'. They are real 'only relative to the definer'. For the constructivist, 'definers' are individuals. For the constructionist, they are collectives: networks, societies, traditions, languages. But, in both literatures, we find variations on the argument that, if things are only 'real' relative to a 'defining' agent, then there is no such thing as an 'objective' reality – that is to say, a reality that exists independently of the 'definitions'. Or, if there is such a reality, then we have no 'access' to it, and cannot know it. There are *only* 'constructed realities'; and it is literally impossible to compare them to a non-constructed, 'real', 'out there' reality.

Burr (2015), for example, frames the argument in terms of language and 'discourse'. 'All that language can do', she says, 'is to refer to itself'. She continues (94):

> There is no way out of this into the 'real' world that might exist beyond language. Whatever the nature of the 'real' world, we cannot assume that the words in our language refer to it or describe it. Social Constructionism seems to lead to the claim that nothing exists except as it exists in discourse.

The idea that one cannot 'step outside' language in order to check on 'unlanguaged reality' is a popular one.[25] As with most qualitative metaphysics, it seems to generate a major result on the basis of a simple truism. The truism is this: we can't refer to anything without employing language. All apparent counter-examples, such as pointing at things, are just different forms of language.[26] The major result is: 'We can never break out of this system into the 'real' world outside of discourse' (Burr 2015: 103). Suddenly, we are 'imprisoned' in language, with no means of checking whether it accurately reflects the 'real' world or not. Suddenly, we find reality receding beyond the 'veil' of language: inaccessible, unreachable, for ever hidden. That's a pretty impressive conclusion to base on such an obvious premise.

Burr conflates 'refer' and 'define'. She begins by saying: 'If I was asked to *define* a "tree", I could only do this by contrasting the concept "tree" with other concepts, to demonstrate the category…' (94). She continues:

> But all I'm doing here is *referring* to other signs (animate, sentient, shrub) which themselves can only be *defined* in terms of yet more signs from the same language system… Whatever the nature of the "real" world, we cannot assume that the words in our language *refer* to it or describe it (my italics).

The argument boils down to this: 'We can only define words by using other words; so we can't use words to refer to anything except words.' It's a massive non-sequitur, based (apparently) on the assumption that 'defining' and 'referring' amount to the same thing.[27]

What does Burr mean when she says: 'All that language can do is refer to itself'? The claim that 'we can only refer to things by using language' (which is clearly true) is not the same as the claim that 'language can only refer to *itself*' (which clearly isn't). If I say 'The tall American has left', I'm referring to the tall American. I'm using language to do it – obviously – but the language I use is not referring to *itself*. It's referring to the tall American. When we use the word 'refer', that's what we mean. 'The tall American' is a *referring expression*. It refers (in this case) to the person who has just left.

Language *can* refer to itself, of course. 'Language' is a word in the language, and here I'm using it to refer to language. But words referring to other words is like words referring to tall Americans. Words and tall Americans are both the kind of thing that language can refer to. So the idea that words can *only* refer to other words is clearly wrong. 'Referring' is using language to pick out something, whether it's an American, a tree, or another bit of language. If you don't understand that, then you don't understand the word 'refer'. And if you don't understand 'refer' – if you think it means the same as 'define' – then you might imagine that the sentence 'All language can do is refer to itself' says something sensible. It doesn't. Unless and until Burr justifies her apparent belief that 'refer' and 'define' are synonymous.[28]

Come at this another way. Burr's discussion implies that language and 'reality' are, in a sense, separate. 'Language can only refer to itself', 'You can't step outside language', 'Reality independent of language is unknowable', and so on. But language is *part* of reality. It's marks on paper, it sounds, it's Braille, it's signing. Language is one bit of reality being used to refer to another. The idea that language-as-a-whole either 'mirrors' reality or 'creates' reality-as-a-whole doesn't make a lot of sense. Language is a *part* of reality.

Reader: Just a minute. Words on paper, sounds, Braille, signing… these are already constructions.

Me: Constructed by what? Language?

Reader: Yes, sure. You're confusing language with its physical manifestations.

Me: So what *is* language, then?

Reader: Language is the system of possibilities. The possible ways of classifying and describing that create a 'reality'.

Me: Is 'create' the same as 'construct'? Because, if it is, you're saying that reality is constructed by something that constructs reality. Can't fault the logic, but it's not very informative.

Reader: Look, all I'm saying is this: language is a system of relations. It predates and shapes the only 'reality' we can be aware of.

Me: But language is either part of 'reality' or it isn't. If it is, how can it 'pre-date' itself? If it isn't, where does it come from? Where does it hang out? Does it just float around in the ether?

Reader: You can try to be funny, if you like. But I think you're just being deliberately obtuse.

Me: Yes, I know. And not for the first time.

One advantage of accepting that language is *part* of reality is this: 'construction' becomes possible. You can use one part of reality to talk about – or construct – other parts. That's how reality works. Language is a set of tools, like a hammer or a potter's wheel. It can be used to construct, modify, or build things. If it's not part of reality, if it's a network of relations 'separate from' and somehow 'prior to' reality, then it's just not possible to understand how any of this happens. One bit of reality affecting another bit? Yes. Sure. Routine. Something that's not part of reality affecting reality? Eh? How? What are you on about?

7.9 'Language' and 'reality' as names

A major part of the problem here is that the terms 'reality' and 'language' have been turned into names, each of them designating a sort of 'whole thing'. This makes it harder to see that language is itself part of reality, not something separate which exists nowhere in particular, but which somehow manages to 'construct' the reality it is apparently distinct from. Both terms – along with 'fact', 'truth', 'knowledge', and others – are what Hacking calls 'elevator words'.[29] They don't just permit us to talk about *the world*. They permit us to talk about *how we talk about the world*. 'Language' gives us the ability to generalise about what is said, what is written. 'Reality' gives us a way of referring to the differences between how we'd like things to be, or how things seem, and how they are. But these are linguistic functions. The two words are additional tools, supplementing the range that's already available.

But even though they are nouns, they are not *names*. They don't designate one thing called 'reality' and another called 'language'.[30] The problem is, that's the picture people have. Nouns as naming words. 'Reality', on its own, outside any real-life linguistic context, can appear to be a name for 'the whole caboodle', an entity-which-comprises-everything. Putnam (1994: 452), for example, talks about the common 'philosophical error of supposing that "reality" must refer to a single super thing'. Chuck in 'language' as the name of another 'single, super thing', an abstract system of signs which is (at least by implication) different from 'reality', and suddenly you have a major philosophical problem: what is the relation between reality and language? But the problem is a mirage.

The two main solutions to this philosophical 'problem' are supposed to be: (a) Language 'mirrors' reality. It is, in that sense, 'transparent'. It is used to reflect the structure of the world, corresponding to how the world *is*. (b) Language 'constructs' reality. It constructs people. The

> person cannot pre-exist language because it is language that brings the person into being in the first place… [language] provides us with a way of structuring our experience of the world and ourselves… we should guard against the common sense assumption that language is nothing more than a clear, pure medium.
>
> *(Burr 2015: 53–54)*

Given that the problem is a mirage, neither 'solution' makes much sense; and both disintegrate once you recognise that language is itself part of reality. As a part of reality – as a set of tools – language (a) is not a 'transparent' window on the world, the 'clear, pure medium'. As part of reality, it (b) cannot 'predate' reality and bring it into being. The *use* of language can help to create new ideas and new phenomena;[31] but it can also describe, represent, report.

It can do plenty of other things as well, as I've observed before. We can ask questions, make jokes, issue instructions, enact rituals, tell stories, and lots more. None of these would be possible if language were not *part* of 'reality'. The idea that it is a 'super thing', detached from this other 'super thing' ('reality') – either as a 'mirror', or as the agent of its construction – is a misleading picture prompted by our inability to understand our own use of words (see Section 3.1).

7.10   Concluding remark

Language mirrors reality – but only in the sense that what we say and write can tell others about the situation in this or that corner of the world. Language also constructs reality – but only in the sense that linguistic tools, combined with social activity, can help to create new ideas, new objects. But it can only do this because these tools are themselves part of 'reality'. We are not in a zero-sum ontological game, a metaphysical either/or. Rather than arguing about -isms, we have to re-examine our use of these words, and how they connect up with words like 'define' and 'refer'. If we can do that, we'll have a chance of seeing that a 'theory' of the relation between 'language' and 'reality' is not in fact necessary.

Notes

1 Even if we restrict attention to just one of these, we find enormous variation. Here, for example, is a well-known author reviewing 11 books in the Sage series *Inquiries in Social Construction*: '[T]he "ism" in social constructionism becomes virtually impossible to pin down… no two contributors share exactly the same set of concerns and background assumptions… different contributors will use similar terms in ways that diverge fundamentally from each other' (Danziger 1997: 400-1).

2 I realise that this is an unsatisfactory account, but I'll be saying more later. The difficulty is trying to make sense of writing which is itself ambiguous, metaphorical, and not always consistent – exhibit A being *The Constructivist Credo* (Sections 7.3–7.7).

3 These five examples are taken from a much longer list. See Lincoln and Guba (1985: 84). I haven't put inverted commas round them because Lincoln and Guba don't, even though they are referring to 'terms'.

4 For those suspicious of this claim, I'll discuss causality at length in Chapter 10. As I've said before, it's impossible to discuss any of the topics in Part II without reference to the others.

5 Note that I'm using 'phenomenon' as a superordinate term intended to cover everything on the list. It's a bit like 'thing'. This usage has no theoretical or philosophical connotations. It has nothing to do with phenomenology.

6 The idea that *shared* knowledge forms the warp and weft of 'reality' is obviously very different from Lincoln and Guba's view. Berger and Luckmann do refer to 'multiple realities'; but, as I note later in the text, this is Schutz's sense (see Section 6.2), not L&G's.

7 Several of the essays in Pfadenhauer and Knoblauch (2019) address this question; but see especially Eberle (2019). Evidence of the 'steadfast rejection' includes an interview with Luckmann: '[W]hen Berger and I were being labeled "social constructivists" we were both very much annoyed. We never thought of ourselves as constructivists' (Dreher & Vera 2016: 31). However, Luckmann's comment presupposes a particular understanding of 'social constructivism', one which many authors don't share. The terminological jungle again.

8 Prior to their 'core argument', they conduct what they describe as 'philosophical prolegomena', in the form of 'a phenomenological analysis of the reality of everyday life' (7). However, they regard this as a 'purely descriptive method and, as such, "empirical" but not "scientific"' (34). The analysis also refrains from 'assertions about the ontological status of the phenomena analysed'. The account draws on Schutz (1945), and especially Schutz and Luckmann (1973), and plays roughly the same foundational role for sociology as phenomenological psychology plays for empirical psychology (Husserl 1999: 322-327).

9 Once (that I've seen). In Lincoln and Guba (2013) they refer to two forms of 'reality': physical reality, and socially constructed realities. In context, it's clear that 'social reality' or 'social realities' would be closer to what they intend. They are not talking about a construction *process* that is 'social' rather than 'individual'; they are talking about different 'types' of reality, physical and social.

10 This statement applies to Lincoln and Guba (1985) but must be qualified for some of the later work. As we'll see in Section 7.6, Lincoln and Guba (2013) get themselves into a major tangle over this.

11 Plenty of other questions could be asked. For example, in which 'reality' is the what-is-interpreted a *single* event? If different interpretations create multiple realities, then there must be *multiple* events…? Either that, or there *is* a single event, belonging to the region formerly known as 'the single reality'; and that is the single event interpreted differently by different individuals. In that case, the 'no single reality' ontological claim collapses.

12 Note the 'arbitrarily?', and refer back to the discussion in Section 2.4. It is worth adding that *TCC* is 'the result of a thirteen-year conversation' between the two authors (7), and the published version is the 'fifteenth iteration' (31). So we can assume that this account is close to being definitive.

13 I genuinely don't understand Guba's 'ontological' question. If it was 'What is there that can be known *by*…?', plus a method, it would make sense. 'What is there that can be known by intuition, scientific experiment, logic, qualitative research…?' No problem. Or if it was 'What is there that can be known *about*…?', plus a subject. That would make sense, too. 'What is there that can be known about ivory-billed woodpeckers, Rameses II, the Higgs Boson…?' Any of those, fine. But 'What is there that can be known?' On its own? If Tuesdays following Mondays isn't one possible answer to that, then I'm sorry, but I've no idea what it means.

14 Make a note of this last sentence. It makes an unexpected return in Section 7.6.

15 See the quote from Kukla (2000) at the beginning of the chapter. Guba switches between claiming that the *meaning* of entities depends on the definer, and claiming that the *existence* of entities depends on the definer.

16 There's also a question about the implications of 'contemplating'. Does it, in this context, imply active thinking about whatever-it-is? Does the church, or the meaning of 'church,' cease to exist when the person concerned *isn't* actively think about it? Or is 'contemplating' intended to cover 'having the concept of'? This seems more likely, but makes me wonder why the word 'contemplate' was chosen.

17 Technically, these expressions can display 'copredication'; that is, they can be accompanied by radically mismatched predicates. 'The book was interesting enough, but too heavy to pack.' The 'was interesting enough' predicate refers to *the book* as information. The 'too heavy to pack' predicate refers to *the book* as a physical object. See Collins (2023) for this and other examples.

18 Gregory (1990) asks whether James ever actually said this: 'Though this is often quoted, I have not come across it' (703). In any case, 'many neuroscientific findings and the results of carefully designed perceptual tests now give us good reason to believe that such a characterization is very far from the truth' (Hamer 2016: 96).

19 As I noted in Section 7.3, Guba does say: 'what I do here may be thought of as poetic, because most of the passages that I set out strike me as metaphors for something that's in my head but which I cannot express with precision' (29). The thought conveyed in this passage is not, on my reading, expressed with precision. I'm not sure I think of it as poetic, though.

20 'Why does opium induce sleep?' 'Because it has a sleep inducing character.' This is borrowed from Molière's 1673 satire, *The Imaginary Invalid*. Compare: 'How does the mind construct?' 'By using its constructive character.'

21 Guba notes that constructions 'may be simple or complex, lower-level or higher-level, small-scale or large-scale, ranging from simple naming of entities to complex theories and paradigms' (48).

22 Unless the surround somehow contains identifiable entities, *prior* to the imposition of order. See the last paragraph of Section 7.4.

23 In contrast, Berger and Luckmann are clear that society *does* pre-date the individual. Human beings create society, but they are also born into the society created by their predecessors. For B&L, culture 'transmitting' constructs to individuals isn't a problem.

24 None of which, incidentally, are mentioned in the reviews. For example: Fram (2014) and Travers (2016) are both mildly critical of some aspects of the book, but neither of them suggests that it's almost impossible to make sense of significant chunks of it.

25 It is a modern version of 'veil of perception' theories. These theories argue that we do not 'directly perceive' actual objects. Rather, we 'directly perceive' some sort of

intermediary: ideas, images, sense data, which 'represent' objects (see the discussion in Section 3.7). It follows – or so it is claimed – that we cannot 'step beyond' the veil of perception in order to determine the relation between sense data and the world. We can't compare sense data with non-sense-data-reality because all we can ever (directly) perceive is sense data.

26 Or more generally, forms of representation. Woolgar (1988): '… as if gestures were any less a manner of representation than spoken or written language' (57). Woolgar suggests that even 'physical assaults constitute a form of representation/communication'. It's interesting that he assimilates representation and communication. A punch in the face (his example) could be construed as a form of communication, but it might be harder to make the case for it being a form of representation.

27 Woolgar's case for the claim that 'representation constitutes objects' is based on a version of the same argument: it's impossible to demonstrate the existence of any object without recourse to representation. 'Students quickly see the difficulty of the task. Indeed, no one has thus far succeeded in demonstrating the antecedent existence of a fact or a thing independent of some representative practice' (57). Well, of course they haven't. This is trivial. But the conclusion Woolgar draws from this spurious exercise is just as inflated as Burr's.

28 It's ironic that methodologists who claim that language creates reality make so little effort to examine the detailed workings of language. You might imagine they would analyse it closely, take a particular interest in linguistics, consult the literature on philosophy of language, and so on. But there's very little evidence of any of this.

29 See Hacking (1999), Chapter 1.

30 Austin says something similar about 'concept' in 'The meaning of a word' (Austin 1961). He suggests that concepts are 'fictitious entities', but that the word 'concept' is an important linguistic tool, which is used to describe various aspects of our life with words.

31 The word 'help' here is important. Language rarely 'constructs' on its own. See Section 7.1.

References

Austin, J. L. (1961). *Philosophical Papers*. Oxford: Clarendon Press.

Berger, P. L., & Luckmann, T. (1967). *The Social Construction of Reality: A Treatise in the Sociology of Knowledge*. Garden City, NY: Doubleday.

Burr, V. (2015). *Social Constructionism*. Third Edition. Hove, UK: Routledge.

Collin, F. (1997). *Social Reality*. London: Routledge.

Collins, H., & Pinch, T. (1982). *Frames of Meaning: The Social Construction of Extraordinary Science*. London: Routledge & Kegan Paul.

Collins, J. (2023). Copredication as illusion. *Journal of Semantics*, https://doi.org/10.1093/jos/ffad1014

Danziger, K. (1997). The varieties of social construction. *Theory and Psychology*, 7(3), 399–416.

Dreher, J., & Vera, H. (2016). *The Social Construction of Reality*, a four-headed, two-fingered book: an interview with Thomas Luckmann. *Cultural Sociology*, 10(1), 30–36.

Eberle, T. S. (2019). Variations of constructivism. In M. Pfadenhauer & H. Knoblauch (Eds.), *Social Constructivism as Paradigm? The Legacy of The Social Construction of Reality* (pp. 131–151). Abingdon, UK: Routledge.

Fram, S. (2014). Review of *The Constructivist Credo*. *American Journal of Evaluation*, 35(4), 597–599.

Gregory, R. L. (1990). Editorial: perceptions of William James - at the centenary of *The Principles of Psychology*. *Perception, 19*, 701–704.

Hacking, I. (1999). *The Social Construction of What?* Cambridge, MA: Harvard University Press.

Hamer, R. D. (2016). The visual world of infants. *American Scientist, 104* (March-April), 96–101.

Hanna, E., & Gough, B. (2020). The social construction of male infertility: a qualitative questionnaire study of men with a male factor infertility diagnosis. *Sociology of Health and Illness, 42*(3), 465–480.

Hewitt, J. P. (2021). The social construction of self-esteem. In C. R. Snyder, S. J. Lopez, L. M. Edwards, & S. C. Marques (Eds.), *The Oxford Handbook of Positive Psychology*. Third Edition (pp. 309–318). New York: Oxford University Press.

Husserl, E. (1999). Transcendental phenomenology and the way through the science of phenomenological psychology. In D. Welton (Ed.), *The Essential Husserl: Basic Writings in Transcendental Phenomenology* (pp. 322–336). Bloomington, IND: Indiana University Press.

Kukla, A. (2000). *Social Constructivism and the Philosophy of Science*. London: Routledge.

Lieb, K. J. (2019). *Gender, Branding, and the Modern Music Industry: The Social Construction of Female Popular Music Stars*. 2nd Edition. New York: Routledge.

Lincoln, Y. S., & Guba, E. G. (1985). *Naturalistic Inquiry*. Beverly Hills, CA: Sage.

Lincoln, Y. S., & Guba, E. G. (2013). *The Constructivist Credo*. New York: Routledge.

Mallon, R. (2019). Naturalistic approaches to social construction. *Stanford Encyclopedia of Philosophy*, https://stanford.library.sydney.edu.au/archives/win2019/entries/social-construction-naturalistic/

Maskrey, A., Jain, G., & Lavell, A. (2023). The social construction of systemic risk: towards an actionable framework for risk governance. *Disaster Prevention and Management, 32*(1), 4–26.

Merriam, S. B., & Tisdell, E. J. (2016). *Qualitative Research: A Guide to Design and Implementation*. Fourth Edition. San Francisco: Jossey-Bass.

Moon, D. J. (2021). Dependents and deviants: the social construction of Asian migrant women in the United States. *Affilia, 36*(3), 391–405.

Pfadenhauer, M. (2019). Introduction. The reality of social constructivism: introductory remarks. In M. Pfadenhauer & H. Knoblauch (Eds.), *Social Constructivism as Paradigm? The Legacy of The Social Construction of Reality* (pp. 1–17). Abingdon, UK: Routledge.

Pfadenhauer, M., & Knoblauch, H. (Eds.). (2019). *Social Constructivism as Paradigm? The Legacy of The Social Construction of Reality*. Abingdon, UK: Routledge.

Pinch, T. (2019). The social construction of technology: where it came from and where it might be heading. In M. Pfadenhauer & H. Knoblauch (Eds.), *Social Constructivism as Paradigm? The Legacy of The Social Construction of Reality* (pp. 152–164). Abingdon, UK: Routledge.

Putnam, H. (1994). Sense, nonsense, and the senses: an inquiry into the powers of the human mind. *The Journal of Philosophy, 91*(9), 445–517.

Repass, M. (2013). Words of wisdom… for now: *The Constructivist Credo*. *The Qualitative Report, 18*(37), 1–2.

Schutz, A. (1945). On multiple realities. *Philosophy and Phenomenological Research, 5*(4), 533–576. Reprinted in Schutz, A. Collected papers, Vol 531: 207–259.

Schutz, A., & Luckmann, T. (1973). *The Structures of the Life-World*. Evanston, IL: Northwestern University Press.
Travers, M. (2016). Review of *The Constructivist Credo*. *Qualitative Research, 16*(2), 245–246.
Woolgar, S. (1988). *Science: The Very Idea*. Chichester, UK: Ellis Horwood Limited.

8

'THE KNOWER' AND 'THE KNOWN'

'The knower and the known are interactive, inseparable.'[1]

Here is another metaphysical claim, seeming to state how things *necessarily* are. It's obviously not an empirical generalisation. No-one has made a study of examples of 'knowing', and inductively inferred that this interactive inseparability typifies every case. Nor is it a 'generic', to use a term in linguistics.[2] Nobody thinks the knower is 'usually', 'typically', or 'for the most part', interactive with/inseparable from the known. Nor is it a tautology. We don't imagine that it is true purely in virtue of the meanings of 'knower', 'known', 'interactive', and 'inseparable'. It's not like 'A bachelor is an unmarried man.' So it must be reality-describing, necessary, universally true, and established on the basis of... well, it's not clear what. But that's what you get with metaphysical claims. Information whose provenance is not self-evident.

Reader: Well, that's what philosophy is for, isn't it? Coming up with fundamental truths that aren't empirical, or generic, or tautological.

Me: It doesn't bother you that it's not clear *how* a metaphysical truth is established?

Reader: Isn't that what metametaphysics is supposed to work out? In any case, I'm more interested in the methodological implications.

Me: Okay, so does 'the knower and the known are inseparable' apply to all forms of knowledge?

Reader: Of course. That's the point.

Me: So if you ask me whether I know anyone in Philadelphia, and I say 'Yes, I know Richard Kaplan', you infer that Richard Kaplan and I are inseparable?

Reader: Now you're just being silly. You know perfectly well I don't mean that.

DOI: 10.4324/9781003306382-10

Me: Well, in this case I am 'the knower' (I assume), and Richard is 'the known'. According to you, the knower and the known are inseparable, so...

Reader: You're confusing two different senses of 'inseparable'. Obviously, the knower and the known aren't inseparable in the sense of 'never being apart'.

Me: Ah, right. You should have said.

Initial thought. 'The knower and the known are interactive, inseparable' is not an 'axiom', though that's what Lincoln and Guba sometimes call it. Really, it's little more than a slogan. However, L&G's account of epistemology is consistently framed in terms of the relation between 'knower' and 'known', so it's perfectly reasonable to ask: in what sense *are* 'the knower' and 'the known' inseparable and interactive? What, for that matter, is a *knower* and what is a *known*? What other ways are there of expressing this epistemological claim? Are they any more precise? Is the so-called 'positivist' version – 'Knower and known are independent, a dualism' – any more transparent? In this chapter, I tackle these questions, and attempt to work out what precisely qualitative epistemologists are trying to say about the relation between 'known' and 'knower'. Sneak preview: I won't succeed.

8.1   'The knower'

'The knower' is not the most familiar of expressions: 93 occurrences in COCA ('know' has more than 2 million), 50 of them academic. So it doesn't come with a clear sense of what it means. It doesn't, for example, refer to a single individual ('The Knower'?). If you think it's *obvious* what it means, you may be overlooking some tricky questions:

i   So far we've got three negatives. First, 'the knower' is not a particular individual. Second, it's not people who know other people (Richard Kaplan, say). And, third, given that 'the knower and the known are interactive, inseparable' *isn't* a generic, it's not 'people who know things' typically, or for the most part. So if it's not any of those, to whom *does* it apply? *Which* people who know *what*?

ii Plenty of people know that Julius Caesar was assassinated on the Ides of March – people who haven't studied ancient history as well as those who have. Do they all count as 'knowers' in the relevant sense? Does 'the knower' apply to them all? Does each of them have the same interactive/inseparable relationship with 'the known'? There's also a question about what 'the known' is in this sort of case, but I'll come to that in a moment. Whatever 'the known' turns out to be, is every 'knower' inseparable from it? In the same way, and to the same degree?

iii   As Azzouni (2020: 17) observes, '"We" know things that, in fact, only some or very few of us – as individuals – understand much about.' For example, we know that there is a super-massive black hole at the centre of the Milky Way.[3] Who is the 'we' in this example? Is it everyone who is aware of this fact? Do they all count as 'knowers' in the relevant sense? Or does it only apply to those who understand *how* we know? Does 'second-hand' knowledge not count? If not, why not? If the claim 'Knower and known are interactive' does apply in this case, who in particular does it apply to?

8.2 'The known'

There are a number of expressions in which a past participle is used as a noun, preceded by the definite article. The chosen, the damned, the fallen. They belong to a wider group of similar expressions in which an adjective, rather than a participle, is used as a noun. The poor, the young, the elderly, the left. Ironically, 'the known' is not the best known of these and barely occurs outside academic discussion. So its meaning is not immediately transparent, although some qualitative metaphysicians apparently assume it is.

So what counts as 'the known'? A useful starting point is to look at some of the constructions in which 'know' occurs, and at the range of things which, if only grammatically, can be described as 'objects of knowledge'. Here's a brief selection:

(**1**) Everyone in Naphill knows Trevor.

(**2**) Manoela knows Lisbon very well.

(**3**) I'm saying this because I know men.

(**4**) Do you know the work of Johann Friedrich Herbart?

(**5**) We know that the average distance between Earth and the Sun is about 93 million miles.

(**6**) Liz knows how to fix the economy.

(**7**) We all know what happened next.

(**8**) Look, you should know that!

There is a consistent thread in these examples. The verb 'to know' is followed by: a person's name (1), a place name (2), a sortal noun (3), a noun phrase (4), a noun clause (5-7), or a demonstrative pronoun (8), all of which function as the grammatical object. Grammatically speaking, then, 'the known' is a nominal expression following the verb. At first sight, it would appear that these expressions can refer to a variety of object-types: a person, a place, a group, an idea/theory, a fact, an ability, a situation or event, a rule or a norm. So the question arises: do claims about the relation between 'the knower' and 'the known' – their independence or inseparability – apply equally to all of these? This question comes up again in Section 8.4.

8.3 'Know'

'Knower' and 'known' are inflections of the verb 'to know'. 'Knower' is a 'participant' (or 'agentive') nominaliser, on a par with *writer, builder, climber*, and so on (Lieber 2016), but less frequently used. 'Known', as already noted, is a past participle used as a noun. While qualitative metaphysicians have plenty to say about 'knower', 'known', and 'knowledge', they don't talk much about 'know', or how it is used in everyday situations.[4]

'Know' is the tenth most commonly used verb in English.[5] The other top ten verbs (*be, have, do, say, go, can, get, would, make*) all have a wide variety of uses, and 'know' is unlikely to be very different in this respect. For example, consider some of the possible continuations of 'Do you know....?':

… where I put my phone?	… how to get this open?	… why you're here?
… that there isn't a largest prime?	… Joanne Fleet?	… how wicked that is?
… what the consequences will be?	… 'Over The Rainbow'?	… the solution to 15 down?
… the atomic number of gold?	… if this is effective?	… your multiplication tables?
… the time?	… that you're acting weird?	… about Charles and Fiona?
… what 'metonymy' means?	… if that's an orchid	… what her real worry is?

Now imagine, for each of these, the reply: 'Yes...', and the kind of explanation that would follow. 'Yes, I can see it in your back pocket.' 'Yes, I'm nervous.' 'Yes, I'm a chemist.' 'Yes, I have met her several times.' 'Yes, I've read the systematic review.' 'Yes, I always sing it in the bath.' The circumstances are different, the reasons offered to support the knowledge claims are diverse. It appears that the criteria for the legitimate use of 'know' vary greatly with the context.[6]

The point is not just that many different things can be 'the known' but that there are 'multiple ways of knowing' (as one might put it). Each example involves a different kind of evidence, a different history of how the 'knowledge' comes about. In each case, there is a different *reliable process* that is generally, but not infallibly, sufficient to support the claim. Keen observation, relevant reading, a wide vocabulary, a good memory, self-awareness, a flair for mathematics, psychological insight, and so on. 'Know', says Azzouni (2020: 9), is a vague word 'because the (tacit) standards for knowledge are vague… For the same reason, a reliable process that's suffi-cient for knowledge for an agent in some circumstances won't be sufficient for knowledge for another agent in other circumstances.' Learning to use 'know' correctly involves getting a sense of the standard appropriate to each type of circumstance.

8.4 'Ways of knowing'

Just now, I used the expression 'multiple ways of knowing'. I intend this in a particular sense. Suppose I say: 'There are multiple ways of playing.' This may be rather puzzling until it is pointed out that we talk of playing dumb, havoc, golf, the fool, Metallica, dirty, hard to get, a hunch, the oboe, along, truant, fast and loose, hell, and lots more, all of which are 'played' in different ways. 'There are multiple ways of playing' is a slightly fanciful way of saying that. Similarly with 'There are multiple ways of knowing.' I think of it as a slightly fanciful way of saying that there is a wide variety of ways in which things can be 'known'; just as there is a wide variety of ways in which things – golf, tru-ant, havoc – can be 'played'.[7]

The idea that 'the knower and the known are interactive, inseparable' seems curiously orthogonal to all this. 'I know Joanne Fleet.' But she and I are not inseparable. We've been 'interactive' in the sense that we've met on a few occa-sions, but the 'interaction' isn't constant. Is occasional interaction enough to imply that I (the knower) and Ms Fleet (the known) are interactive? 'Lynda knows where I put my phone.' One might suggest that Lynda and I are interactive, inseparable. She is my partner, after all. But that's not the point. What Lynda knows, in this example, is not me but where-I-put-my-phone. Are Lynda and where-I-put-my-phone interactive, inseparable? 'Hansa knows the solution to 15 down.' So Hansa and the solution to 15 down are interactive, inseparable?

As I say, orthogonal. Not *obviously* relevant. Throwing no light. If anything, muddying the waters. Still, we must bear in mind that it aims to articulate something more profound than the mere facts of usage, something whose nature has yet to be made clear. Something metaphysical. We'll get to that. For now, I'll just say this: if the claim about 'inseparability' makes such little contact with the general pattern of usage, perhaps 'know' and 'known' are not being employed in their ordinary senses.

Reader: Why do you insist on dancing round the periphery? All this Joanne Fleet, 15 down, where I put my phone, stuff isn't germane. What we're really interested in is *knowledge*. Research-based knowledge. Serious knowledge. Not off-the-cuff remarks about crosswords.

Me: You said earlier that the epistemological pronouncement applied to all forms of knowledge.

Reader: Well, yes, but I meant proper knowledge. Not knowing some bloke in Philadelphia.

Me: So on what basis do you make that distinction? You presumably don't deny that the verb 'to know' is used in the ways I've suggested?

Reader: No, but most of those are subsidiary uses. Non-central. Knowing *that…* is what counts.

Me: Why are the other uses non-central?

Reader: Because they're just at-the-time comments. We want to know about *knowledge*, not transient uses of the verb 'to know'.

Me: But why is knowing-that the only construction that points to 'proper knowledge'?

Reader: I would have thought that was obvious. Epistemology has always been about how we know *that* such-and-such. It's never been about knowing Joanne Fleet or where your phone is.

Me: So you're saying that claims about the relation between 'the knower' and 'the known' apply *only* to knowing-that. Other uses aren't invited to the party.

Reader: That's pretty much it, yes.

The assumption that *knowing-that* is the most significant kind of 'knowing' for epistemology is widely held. However, according to Ayers (2019), it 'is fundamentally misguided. The different formulations of knowledge-ascription have complementary functions… and the epistemological task is to explain their interrelations, not to pick one as philosophically the most satisfactory for the purposes of "analysis".'[8] (96). This is what *Reader* has done here: picked out a single use of 'know', a single construction, and said that it's the *only* one that counts in epistemology.[9]

This stipulation – and a stipulation is what it is – gets rid of a lot of (what *Reader* regards as) peripheral uses of 'know', but it leaves earlier questions unanswered. 'We know that the average distance between Earth and the Sun is about 93 million miles.' Who is included in the 'we' here? Anyone who happens to be aware of this fact? Or only those with an understanding *how* we know? What is 'the known' in this example? The Earth? The Sun? The combination of the two? The average distance? The proposition that the average distance is 93 million miles? The fact that this is the case? Are 'we' – whoever is included – interactive with, or inseparable from, *any* of these? If so, are we all interactive/inseparable in the same way, and to the same extent? The answer, in each case, is far from clear. If you don't like the example because it's too science-y, and we're only interested in the social world, take a look at an alternative in this note.[10]

8.5   Key features of 'know that'

Here's one key feature. If you realise that something you thought you knew is wrong, you withdraw the knowledge claim ('I thought I knew that *p*; but *p* is false, so I was mistaken'). This is what philosophers mean when they say that 'know' is *factive*. We only use the KNOW THAT construction when what-we-know is assumed to be true, or when there is definitive evidence of a relevant kind ('I know your phone is in your pocket. I can see it.' 'I know there isn't a largest prime. I can show you the proof.') If it turns out that it *isn't* true, we retract the claim to 'know'.[11]

As I implied in Section 8.3, the 'relevant' kind of evidence will vary from situation to situation. Being able to see the phone in your pocket is massively different from being familiar with, and understanding, the population-based epidemiological studies which show that there is no causal link between the measles, mumps and rubella vaccine and autism, and both are different from proving that there is no largest prime number. Moreover, it is in the nature of knowledge claims that they can be challenged – in many different ways ('That's not my phone, it's a pack of cards.' 'The atomic number of gold isn't 89. It's 79.') It's impossible to delineate 'relevant evidence', or 'grounds for challenge', in a way that covers all cases. 'Relevant evidence' is context-bound, and contexts vary *wildly*. What counts as 'relevant' in different types of context is something we have to learn, and in everyday circumstances we usually agree about what's relevant and what isn't. But there are lots of cases, too – including academic cases – where it remains a matter of dispute.

'Context-bound' does not mean 'anything goes'. The relevant evidence in any particular situation will be based on a method which in a general sense is reliable, but not infallibly so. The point is that what is generally reliable in one type of circumstance is unlikely to be reliable in another. 'I saw it with my own eyes' works, probably, for the phone-in-the-pocket case but not the atomic number of gold case. 'Fiona told me' will generally work for the Charles-and-Fiona case, but not for the largest-prime case (unless Fiona is a mathematician). 'I recited them constantly as a child' explains how I know my multiplication tables, but it's useless if I want to explain how I know the solution to 15 down.

One distinction is especially significant here: that between knowing something as a result of expertise or personal experience, and knowing something as a result of being informed by an authoritative source. 'I know there is a super-massive black hole at the centre of our galaxy because I worked with Ghez at the W.M Keck Telescope.' 'I know there is a super-massive black hole at the centre of our galaxy because I read about it in *New Scientist*.' 'I know Charles and Fiona had a major row because I was there when it happened.' 'I know Charles and Fiona had a major row because Fiona told me.' These examples suggest a distinction between what we might call 'first-hand' and 'second-hand' knowledge. It is the distinction between being a witness or participant and learning from someone who is a reliable (but not infallible) informant.

A great deal of what we take ourselves to know is, in this sense, 'second-hand'. If Carla and Paulo can both be legitimately described as knowing that *p*, their reasons (method, evidence) won't always be the same. Carla knows that *p* because she was a witness. Paulo knows that *p* because he was told by Carla, or by someone else in a position to know already. It's clear that second-hand knowledge depends on a spectrum of relations including trust, assessments of expertise, deference to epistemic authority, and so on. If you are happy to accept knowledge that has been 'passed along', it's because you believe your source is reliable. This is another 'method', like seeing it for yourself, studying chemistry or botany, possessing a watch (that works properly), being self-aware, having a history of reciting multiplication tables, or being able to prove that there isn't a largest prime.

Inevitably, then, there is a certain vagueness in our use of 'know'. Azzouni (2020) says that the word is governed by two necessary conditions, one of which is: 'If S know(s) *p*, then S has come to know *p* by a process that is, *to some extent*, reliable. The vagueness, I've argued, is ineliminable… it's vague because the (tacit) standards for knowledge are vague' (388: italics mine). This is one reason why philosophers have sometimes suggested that we'd be better off ditching the word 'know' altogether, or at the very least re-engineering it (Quine 1987, Papineau 2021).

So we have a verb whose use:

(A) is factive: it is retracted if it turns out that what was 'known' is in fact untrue;

(B) requires a cognitive process which is broadly reliable, but not infallibly so;

(C) is consistent, therefore, with fallibility;

(D) is predicated on wildly varied standards, which are themselves vague and contestable;

(E) can be based on 'first-hand' *or* 'second-hand' evidence, subject to the reliability condition.

All five features have provided some philosophers with what they regard as reasons for abandoning or re-engineering 'know'. And yet – despite this – it is *still* the 10th most commonly used *verb* and the 59th most commonly used *word* in English. It is obviously not a term that English speakers don't really know what to do with, or for which they have no use. It appears to have an essential, one might think pivotal, function. So it's not unreasonable to assume that these features *enable* that function rather than hinder it.

So what is the function in question? Reliable second-hand information is indispensable to any society. It would be impossible for *all* reliable information to be first-hand for *everybody*. I know that fossas are a species of carnivorous mammal native to Madagascar, but I didn't need to take a degree in zoology, or visit Madagascar, in order to learn this. I read it in a recent book, written by an expert, Nick Garbutt.[12] The most interesting thing about 'know'

is that we use the same word when talking about reliable first-hand information *and* when talking about reliable second-hand information. If asked *how*
we know, Mr. Garbutt and I will cite different reasons, but we're both entitled
to say: 'I know'. If I subsequently pass this knowledge on to Emily, she will
also be entitled to say 'I know' (assuming she thinks I'm a reliable source). If
the question 'What is a fossa?' comes up in a quiz, she'll be able to answer
correctly. And the same again, if she passes it to Judy. The social world is
dense with 'know'-chains.

Because the same word is used for each link in the chain, there is a ripple-
outwards effect if it transpires that what the expert thought was true… isn't.
The retracting goes outwards from him, to me, to Emily, to Judy. This wouldn't
happen if we used 'know' only for first-hand links in the chain, and 'kwon'
(say) for second- and third-hand links. Nick Garbutt would have to retract
'know', but I would still 'kwon' that fossas are carnivorous mammals native to
Madagascar. Given that this is roughly equivalent to: 'I received this information at second-hand from a generally reliable source', it's still true. The
immense value of 'know' lies in the fact that it is not restricted to first-hand
cases. Instead, it forms these factive, fallible, contestable, but to-a-certain-
extent-reliable chains across many different epistemic contexts.[13]

8.6   The expressivist take

'The knower and the known are interactive, inseparable.' I conceded at the outset that this sentence is little more than a slogan, even if it is assumed to make a
metaphysical claim.[14] So far I've argued that, taken seriously, it raises several
questions to which there appear to be no satisfactory answers: How do we identify a 'knower'? To what does 'the known' refer? How does the metaphysical
claim, construed as a reality-describing statement, accommodate different
'ways of knowing'? How does it explain the distinctive pattern of usage associated with the verb 'know'? In this section, I'll turn to the expressivist option
again and suggest that we construe the sentence, not as metaphysical-reality-
describing but as a resolution or recommendation, a proposed new rule.[15]

The new rule imposes a condition on the use of 'know'. It says that the
word can only be employed in certain circumstances. In effect, and adopting
the terms introduced in Section 8.5, the use of 'know' will be restricted to
cases of first-hand information. Nick Garbutt has studied Madagascar mammals in the wild. Assuming this counts as interaction with – and possibly
inseparability from – 'the known', he is entitled to say: 'I know fossas are
carnivorous mammals native to Madagascar.' In contrast, *I* acquired this same
information by reading Garbutt's book. There is no sense in which I am (or
have ever been) interactive with, or inseparable from, the mammals of
Madagascar. So, according to the new rule, *I* do not *know* that fossas are carnivorous mammals native to Madagascar.

This is a fairly clear-cut example. However, before the new rule can be introduced, further clarification is required. For example: if I was present when Charles and Fiona had their row, I presumably 'know' about it. If I wasn't present, but Fiona told me later, does that count? Let's say it does: after all, I'm now interacting with Fiona. On the other hand, if I mention the row to a friend – she was neither present, nor does she know the couple – the new rule says that she cannot be described as 'knowing'. No interaction, certainly no inseparability.

Another clarification would have to resolve the question as to whether the new rule applies to *all* forms of knowledge, or whether it applies only to knowledge of the human/social world. It *could* be applied in the non-human sciences. Garbutt has observed fossas in person, so he *knows* they are carnivores native to Madagascar. Equally, given that they have first-hand experience of observation, experiment, and calculation, we can say that astronomers really *do* know that the average distance between the Sun and the Earth is 93 million miles, and that chemists really *do* know that gold has an atomic number of 79. Alternatively, we might restrict the 'interaction' to personal contact with other people. Still, this is a matter for those promoting the new rule to decide. What we *can* say, either way, is that those who *only* get their information from books do not *know*.

So another way of looking at the new rule: a proposed ban on 'know'-chains.[16] It's not clear, of course, what verb, if any, can be used in second-hand cases. However, the authors who talk about the relation between 'the knower' and 'the known' don't see what they are doing as promoting (in Carnap's terms) a new language framework. They think they're drawing attention to a metaphysical truth. Fundamentally, this is how things *are*. So why would they suggest an alternative word for second-hand circumstances in which, according to the current language framework, the use of 'know' is perfectly legitimate?

There is a long tradition of narrowing down what counts as 'knowledge'. Plato did it, Descartes did it. A popular move has been to argue that 'know' requires infallibility. Descartes, for example, restricted its use to cases in which 'knowledge' was certain and unerring.[17] Lincoln and Guba belong to this 'narrowing down' tradition, except that their criterion is not infallibility but 'interactiveness'/'inseparability'. There may be good reasons for introducing this alternative 'know' language (though I'm sceptical). But one of those reasons is *not*: 'We have no option because this, metaphysically, is how the world is.'[18]

8.7 Inquiry

Borrowing from Lincoln and Guba, qualitative authors sometimes refer to 'the inquirer' and 'the object of inquiry' (or 'the inquired-into') instead of – or often in addition to – 'the knower' and 'the known'. This represents a major, though usually unacknowledged, shift. Claims are now being made about somebody *undertaking inquiry*, rather than just anyone *who knows*. On the face of it, we can now put aside worries about second-hand knowledge, because we're dealing with a researcher (of some kind), not people who have acquired the information from books, the internet, or word of mouth. At the same time, 'the object of inquiry' refers to something *to be studied* instead of something (already) *'known'*. We've shifted the *mise-en-scène* from 'post-inquiry' to 'pre-inquiry' (or 'peri-inquiry').

The downside is that this is no longer epistemology. Instead of making pronouncements about the nature of knowledge, or the metaphysics of 'the knower' and 'the known', we're talking about the relationship between observable, independently identifiable things. Consider the so-called 'positivist' version: 'The inquirer and the object of inquiry are independent.' And the constructivist: 'The inquirer and the object of inquiry interact to influence one another.' *Both* of these can be true. An inquirer who is independent of the object of inquiry can still interact with that object (it/her/him/them). Indeed, 'interaction' is only possible between things that *are* independent. Otherwise, what is interacting with what?

Suppose I'm a police officer, inquiring into the death of Enoch. The 'death of Enoch' is the object of my inquiry. Do 'I' and 'the death of Enoch' interact? Well, yes, obviously. The death 'influences' me, in the sense that I am enquiring into it, so it's engaging my time and attention. But this is a truism, not an epistemological insight. Am 'I', and 'the death of Enoch', independent? Well, yes, obviously. I had nothing to do with Enoch's death. I'm merely trying to find out who was responsible for it. That's another truism. In no sense does the death depend on me, and I don't depend on it. (Okay, it's my job to crack the case, but that's not an epistemological profundity either.) So in this example, as well as thousands of others, the inquirer and the object of inquiry are independent. But they *also* interact.

The shift from 'knowers' to 'inquirers', and the emphasis on interaction, is a reminder that the primary focus of these discussions is research in the human sciences, and in particular interview-based studies. But throughout the Lincoln and Guba oeuvre there is a persistent ambiguity. Are they talking exclusively about the social sciences, or about 'inquiry' in general? The fact that they take themselves to be *doing epistemology* suggests the latter. Their comments on the relation between 'the knower' and 'the known' by implication generalise to 'knowledge-in-general', with the problematic consequences I have outlined. But their emphasis on interaction between 'the inquirer' and the 'object of inquiry' implies the former. Consider Lincoln and Guba (2013), for example. On the one hand, they adopt (as far as one can judge) a *general* ontological relativism; on the other, and only a page later, they suggest that their presumptions and conjectures 'apply only to the human sciences' (39). It's difficult to see how they can have it both ways.

Interaction, whether in a police investigation or a qualitative study, is endemic. But that, as I've noted, is not an epistemological claim. Interviews, with witnesses or with research participants, are 'interactive' and mutually 'influencing'. I ask a question, the witness/respondent replies. Her answer might suggest another question (although in both cases the interviewer has an 'agenda'). It's one variation on dealings with other people. There appears, at first sight, to be nothing here that has any metaphysical bearing.

8.8 Mind-dependence

Still, these clunky claims are trying to say *something* that doesn't just boil down to 'In an interview, two people interact'. I think it's a bit of unfinished business from Chapter 7. Here's a passage from Lincoln and Guba (2013: 39), where they are explaining the epistemology 'presumption':

> The relationship between the knower and the knowable (to-be-known) is highly person- and context-specific. The 'realities' taken to exist depend on a transaction between the knower and the 'to-be-known'… That transaction is necessarily highly subjective… Knowledge is not 'discovered' but rather *created*.

The clunkiness is still there. Does anyone think knowledge is 'discovered'? ('Guess what I've just found in the garden. A piece of knowledge!') The hardest of hard scientists have to work punishingly hard to 'create' knowledge.[19] Nobody imagines it's just 'there', waiting to be unveiled. Another comment from the same book features the same tortured logic: 'The categories we choose for sense-making purposes are not "givens" from the cosmos. We *create* those categories.' (51) Again, does anyone, working in any of the sciences, believe that the cosmos *provides* the categories for us? So what is it Lincoln and Guba are trying to convey with these puzzlingly worded observations?

We create the categories and concepts we use to talk about the world – although it should be noted that the 'We' here includes previous generations. The language *I* learn is not something *I* created. Still, it's true that it has human origins. Where else can it come from? So whenever I refer to anything, whenever I describe anything, I must use either concepts I have learned (most of the time) or concepts I have invented for myself (rarely, but it happens). So far, this amounts to nothing more than the toe-curlingly obvious. Yet some authors appear to be hypnotised by it, and imagine it to be chockful of metaphysical import. It shows that 'the knower' and 'the known' are *not* independent, since the only way we can refer to 'the known' is by using concepts that we, as 'knowers', have brought to the party. 'The knower' and 'the known' really are inseparable in *this* sense. We can *only* describe the 'known' by using 'knower' concepts.

It's difficult, I've found, to convince people that this is *still* a truism. All it says, in effect, is: to describe things we need language. It's only when you draw the conclusion that reality – that is, the reality we can 'know' – is mind-dependent that you find yourself in Metaphysics-Land.[20] Because *that* conclusion is a non-sequitur. It's not *reality* that's mind-dependent; it's *our understanding of reality*. But what else did you expect? 'Reality is mind-dependent.' Seriously? Including the 13.7 billion years before our species came into existence? 'Our understanding of reality is mind-dependent.' Yes, of course. Obviously. So we're back to truisms.

The banality of these claims – that we can only refer to things by using concepts/language – is concealed by contrasting them with claims implicitly attributed to 'positivists': 'Knowledge is *found*.' 'The cosmos itself *provides* us with categories.' 'We can arrive at knowledge with *certainty*.' Given a choice between such impossibilities and something that is sensible (if trivial), the reader naturally opts for the latter; and then, as like as not, walks into the metaphysical trap. The 'reality-we-know' is mind-dependent; if there *is* a 'reality-as-it-is-in-itself', then it is unknowable.

Hofweber (2023) distinguishes between 'reality' as the totality of *things*, and 'reality' as the totality of *facts*. Reality-as-the-totality-of-facts is mind-dependent. Unfortunately, reality-as-the-totality-of-things isn't. The universe, all 13.7 billion years of it, is the totality of things. Things exist. Facts, in Hofweber's view, *obtain* but do not exist. 'We are central to the totality of facts: our forms of thought are limiting what facts do and can obtain… we might have nothing to do with what there is, but we are central for what is the case'(134). Hofweber's distinction is between what we clearly have 'constructed' and what we clearly haven't.

'Fact', 'proposition', 'statement', 'truth', 'sentence', 'describe', 'reference', 'language', 'reality'. It is a series of linguistic devices which permit us to talk about how-we-talk-about-the-world.[21] They don't name entities, as 'door', 'fossa', and 'planet' do, but they enable discussion of – and inference about – the way we use language. They form an inter-related system, a sort of meta-language, which makes it possible to say (for example) that: 'Facts are what true propositions state.' This is, in Wittgensteinian terms, a note on grammar. It's neither metaphysics nor linguistics, but an indication of how the constituent words are used. All of this comes from us. It's mind-dependent. The totality of things, the universe, is not.

8.9 Uncertainty, measurement, observation

There is another family of arguments used to support constructivist epistemology. They are based on an appeal to quantum mechanics. Lincoln and Guba (1985) refer to Heisenberg's Indeterminacy Principle. Lincoln and Guba (2013) refer to the Heisenberg Uncertainty Principle (HUP), as well as to something called the 'social Heisenberg effect'.[22] I'll talk about the HUP, because that's the usual term, and L&G appear to be referring to the same idea in both books. They suggest, in 1985, that the Principle is one of several 'emergent conceptual/empirical formulations' which 'positivism falls short of being able to deal with'. What it states, they say, is that:

> It is impossible to determine both the mass and the momentum of a particle simultaneously, for measuring either one will render the other immediately and forever indeterminate. Here was the ultimate instance of observer disturbance!
>
> *(Lincoln & Guba 1985: 97)*

This extract doesn't fit with my own understanding of the quantum mechanics literature, and there is at least one outright error. The variables which cannot be 'determined simultaneously' are *position* and momentum, not *mass* and momentum. Still, this may just be a slip on Lincoln and Guba's part.[23]

The passage just quoted appears to confuse two different, though related, quantum phenomena. One is HUP, as it applies to position and momentum; the other is the 'measurement problem'. Here's a clear exposition of the HUP.[24]

> It is important to understand that the uncertainty principle is much stronger (and *stranger*) than the statement that we just can't physically measure, say, both position and momentum because measuring one property disturbs the other one and changes it. Rather, in a fundamental sense, the quantum object *does not have* a determinate (well-defined) value of momentum when its position is detected, and vice versa. This aspect of quantum theory is built into the very mathematical structure of the theory, which says in precise logical terms that there simply is no yes/no answer to the question about the value of a quantum object's position when you are measuring its momentum.
>
> *(Kastner 2022: 5; italics original)*

Both position and momentum can only be specified as a range of possibilities. If the object's position is within a narrow range of possibilities, its momentum will be within a wide range of possibilities. If, on the other hand, the momentum is within a narrow range, the position will be within a wide range. Put another way, the more determinate the position, the less determinate the momentum, and vice versa.[25] This, it must be emphasised, is an inherent property of the quantum system concerned. It's not the result of 'observer disturbance'. Measuring one of these variables will not *render* the other 'immediately and forever indeterminate'.

The measurement problem in quantum mechanics starts with the indeterminacy described by HUP. If this indeterminacy is an intrinsic feature of quantum states, how is it that the world of our everyday experience contains objects that are determinate and clearly defined? For example, how is it that, when we measure the position of an electron, it acquires a determinate location, apparently as a result of the measurement process itself? If, prior to measurement, the electron's position can only be defined in terms of possible outcomes, each weighted for probability, how is it that, on being measured, it resolves into a single outcome? One of the weird things about quantum physics – perhaps the weirdest – is that the theory does not tell us. It tells us, prior to measurement, that the position of the electron might be A, B or C; but it doesn't say which of these will be realised; 'nor does it provide any reason for *why* only one of these is actually observed' (Kastner 2022: 11). It would appear that measurement literally brings about the outcomes we observe.

I don't think either HUP or the measurement problem apply to qualitative research.[26] Human beings are not characterised by pairs of properties akin to position/momentum, although individual properties may be indeterminate, at least temporarily. For example, it may not be clear, sometimes, whether I'm angry or not – meaning, not that I don't *know*, but that there is no fact of the matter one way or the other. But this is a rare circumstance; it does not apply universally, as HUP applied to position/momentum does in quantum mechanics. By the same token, indeterminate states do not resolve into determinate ones post-measurement. Again, something *like* this may be true very occasionally. The question of my anger may be indeterminate until I'm asked whether I'm angry – at which point it becomes clear that, actually, yes I am. But this is not the standard case. My anger does not normally resolve as a determinate, definable emotion only *after* I've been asked about it, or after my neurological state has been measured.

What Lincoln and Guba are really interested in is what they describe as 'observer disturbance'. Any sort of observation/measurement of the world, including any sort of research activity, will have an effect on what is observed/measured. L&G appeal to quantum mechanics because they imagine that it represents the 'ultimate instance' of this. But, in the first place, their understanding of quantum physics is deficient; and, in the second place, they don't actually *need* quantum mechanics to justify the claim that observation makes a difference (or, if you prefer, precipitates a 'disturbance'). They could get that from classical physics (Baclawski 2018), everyday experience, or casual conversation (fast forward to Section 8.11). Like a number of other writers – including Tranel (1981), whom they quote, Patton (1980), Bretz (2008), and Pernecky (2016) – they assume that HUP is an example of the observer effect; and, given the status of quantum mechanics,[27] they want to co-opt it. But they're barking up the wrong tree. HUP tells us nothing about the epistemology of qualitative research, or the epistemology of anything else, for that matter. As Barad (2007: 118) observes: 'The common public conception of the uncertainty principle is (at best) the epistemic version that Heisenberg himself retracted.'

8.10 Quantum mechanics and scale

HUP is not the only way quantum mechanics has been used to support the claim that there is 'lack of inherent separation between knower and known' (Barad 2007). Different writers come at this from different angles. Wendt (2015), for example, appeals to 'quantum consciousness' and panpsychism. Kirby (2011) sees a 'resonance' between entanglement and deconstruction. Barad derives her 'onto-epistemology' from a reading of Bohr.[28] Pernecky (2016), writing expressly for qualitative researchers, suggests that quantum mechanics 'has a place in the formulation of philosophical assumptions' (176).

The key premise is the idea that quantum mechanics makes some kind of difference to the everyday, macroscopic, world. Pernecky suggests:

> When we consider that [quantum mechanics] underpins the appearances and phenomena to which we are accustomed, quantum reality must form an inevitable part of the ontological and epistemological landscape… If we accept that the objects we perceive in our everyday life are composed of subatomic particles, which in turn are subject to quantum behavior… then it behoves us to include it in the overall metaphysical/ontological picture.

This is disappointingly vague. How does quantum mechanics 'underpin' everyday phenomena? In what way must quantum reality be part of the onto-logical/epistemological landscape? How do we include it in the overall met-aphysical picture? Pernecky answers none of these questions. Instead, he leaves it to the qualitative researcher to answer them, inviting her to decide whether 'Quantum mechanics undermines the notion of the thing-in-itself and also the possibility of absolute and universal truths' (192).

We can compare Pernecky's 'underpinning' move with Barad's (2007) claim that 'no evidence exists to support the belief that the physical world is divided into two separate domains' (110).[29] The implication of this is that, whatever ontological or epistemological sense we make of quantum mechanics, the same metaphysical framework must apply – if not so transparently – to the macroscopic world. If this is right, classical mechanics is obsolete. 'Quantum physics does not merely supplement Newtonian physics – it supersedes it' (110). So we must abandon the idea that 'Newton's laws are the physical laws that govern the macroscopic world'. Quantum mechanics represents 'a final renunciation of the classical idea of causality, that is, a strict determinism' (129). 'Newtonian physics… is a flawed physical theory' (423-4).

The most interesting thing about this view is that it adopts a 'universalising' (or 'totalising', or 'monist', possibly even 'reductionist') position.[30] If the world at quantum level has certain features, then the world at every level must have the same features, or at least features which can be derived from the quantum level. If quantum physics is 'right', Newtonian physics is 'wrong' (well, 'flawed'). Barad generalises from quantum mechanics to science as a whole. The possibility that *scale* – the very small contrasted with the medium-sized, the large, and the very large – might make a significant difference is one that she dismisses. As Woods (2017: 208) observes, 'the assertion that there are no fundamental rifts among scale domains repeats throughout *Meeting the Universe Halfway*'.

Woods himself argues against this 'scale invariance', drawing particularly on examples from biology and ecology. He cites essays by Haldane and Gould explaining why insects cannot grow to the size of a mammal, and mammals cannot shrink to the size of an insect. Fleas can't be 'scaled up', elephants can't be 'scaled down'. Some biological properties *are* scale invariant, but many aren't. It is possible 'to put large and minute organisms in quite separate baskets; there is a fundamental rift between the living worlds of the large and the very small' (Bonner 2006: 40). The reason for this is the effect of gravity, 'which becomes progressively insignificant the smaller an organism, while molecular forces come to the fore and play an increasingly important role'. Scale variance, it turns out, is the rule rather than the exception, at least in zoology.

What about physics? Barad argues that there are three reasons why 'quantum effects are not commonly evident in the realm of our everyday experience' (279), but cites quantum tunnelling and macroscopic quantum decoherence as evidence that they do occur. However, as the biological examples suggest, the fact that scale invariance applies to *some* macroscopic phenomena does not entail that it applies across the board. In fact, it appears that scale variance is also the rule rather than the exception in physics and engineering, with 'multiscalar architectures' being routine (Wilson 2006, 2017, 2022).

Consider, for example, a bar of steel measuring a millimetre. If subject to stretching and compression, this bar obeys the same 'rules' – conforms to the same equations – as it would if it had had a length of one metre, or any length in between. At a length of 0.1 millimetre, however, its behaviour changes: it 'responds to pushes and pulls in a different manner' (Wilson 2017: 11). If we now continue to descend through 'levels of length', its behaviour changes again, and it exhibits a complex hierarchy of responses at ever lower levels, right down to the molecular lattice.

It's impossible to trace this process by working upwards from the molecular scale. We can't calculate how steel will behave at the macro levels on the basis of how it behaves at the molecular level. Instead, a series of models and sub-models, arranged in a 'multiscalar scheme', is employed to make computation possible. Each sub-model focuses on the behaviour characteristic at the relevant size level, leaving the job of tracking disturbances at other levels to other sub-models. The computations at the different levels are scrutinised for self-consistency, and interscalar corrections are introduced as necessary, a sequence that can run through many iterations.

As Wilson's work shows, this kind of 'multiscalar hierarchy' is the norm. The idea that physics is just a matter of employing the same handful of equations at every different level, in a 'deterministic' way, is a myth. Scale variance, as in biology and ecology, is entirely typical. So the 'reductionist', or 'totalising', assumption that quantum mechanics can be 'scaled up' to macroscopic levels – on the basis of a small number of 'breakthrough' examples like quantum tunnelling – cannot be justified. At least, not yet. And, despite Barad's description of it as a 'flawed' theory, Newtonian mechanics will continue to be used at the appropriate level (or, rather, levels) in the scalar hierarchy.[31]

8.11   Observer effects

Let's get one canard out of the way first. Barad (2007) says: 'classical mechanics also holds that when you observe things, you disturb them... The fact that things are disturbed when we measure them is not a startling new result of quantum physics – this point already follows from classical physics'. It would seem that quantum phenomena are not uniquely subject to observer effects.[32]

Barad talks about the observer effects in terms of 'disturbance'. Lincoln and Guba (2013: 65) suggest that the inquirer's 'intrusion' into a local context will 'necessarily disturb and disrupt it'; Tranel (1981: 427) says that 'in physics one cannot observe without distorting the object of observation'. Disturb, disrupt, distort. These words don't have the same connotations. You can disturb something without disrupting or distorting it. So we might ask what it is, precisely, that these authors are referring to.

At its simplest and crudest, the idea is that research (in any discipline) is likely to have an effect on what is studied. In observing and measuring, we interact causally with the thing being observed or measured, and this may affect the thing's behaviour and/or its properties. The crucial idea rests on a counterfactual: the difference between the situation-as-represented-by-measurement (call this M), and the situation-as-it-would-have-been-if-it-hadn't-been-measured (call this N). This difference is a result of the interaction between the object to be measured and the measuring apparatus – or, more generally, between the-what-is-observed and the mechanism of observation.[33]

Some of the time, (M) effects can be ignored because they are much too small to be significant. Visible objects are constantly being bombarded with photons, but it's not something we're aware of because the impact is negligible, relative to the observation or measurement we're making. 'For example, we don't notice the furniture being rearranged in the room when we turn a light on in a dark room, although this is strictly the case' (Barad 2007). Nor are we aware of a mercury-in-the-glass thermometer affecting the temperature of what it is being used to measure. But we notice when we use an ordinary tyre pressure gauge, which in the act of measuring the pressure in the tyre inevitably lets some of the air escape, with the result that the pressure is reduced. Again, though, the reduction is negligible – at least in everyday cases – because the difference between the (*N*) pressure and the (*M*) pressure is small.

If 'distortion' occurs in physics, Tranel added, it 'must occur when both the observer and the observed are human persons about whom predictability is precluded by virtue of the uniqueness of each'. I am rather doubtful about Tranel's reasons for saying this, but it's true that observer effects figure strongly in the social sciences. We've had the Hawthorne effect – although there are several different accounts of what this is (Oswald *et al*. 2014), and for some writers the idea is based on a myth (Kompier 2006). Now we have 'reactivity' (Zahle 2023), acting as a constraint on qualitative data collection.

Two of us in a room. I ask you a question, you answer. This may be an interview or casual conversation. Either way, you wouldn't have said anything if I hadn't been there. So I have modified your behaviour already. If somebody else had asked you the same question, you might not have answered in the same way. If I'd used alternative phrasing, you might have given me a subtly – perhaps a radically – changed reply. If I'm somebody you've not met before, you might respond cautiously, not replying with total candour. If we are old friends, you may be less guarded. And so on, through almost limitless variations. If I want information, I have to engage in some sort of causal interaction. And that makes a difference that 'disturbs'. The information you gave me when asked might be different from what you would have said (on the same subject) if I hadn't been there to ask you. The counterfactual strikes again.

There are many ways in which qualitative researchers react to all this, and there are several strategies designed to increase the likelihood that the difference between (*M*) and (*N*) is minimal. They fall into a number of groups. For example: unobtrusive measures, and naturalistic measures (Potter *et al.* 2020);[34] minimally specific questions avoiding researcher categories; triangulation in various forms, including member checks; auditing the researcher, including 'bracketing' and intersectionality analysis (Zhang *et al.* 2021). Some of these have been researched – I mean empirically researched – many haven't. There is a lot of work still to do.

But we're no longer talking metaphysics. The interaction between inquirer and inquired-into – between observers and what they observe, between measurers and what they measure – is an empirical question. To observe is to be at one end of a certain kind of causal interaction. Any attempt to acquire empirical data must involve some kind of causal process, and any causal process has the potential to modify the property we want to observe, whether by a large or a small amount. This applies to interviewing and observation as much as it does to using a tyre pressure gauge, or a mercury-in-the-glass thermometer. If qualitative writers are to study observer effects, it is not by 'going ontological' via quantum mechanics. It is by doing empirical research on the methods of empirical research.

8.12 Concluding comments

The relation between the inquirer and inquired-into is different from the relation between 'the knower' and 'the known'. It is a purely empirical matter, and concerns the causal relation between the methods of observation and the effect they have on what-is-observed. It starts from the anthropological truism that there *is* such a relation and continues with studies of the relevant causal chains. The 'knower and known' relation brings us to Epistemology Hall, with Azzouni's (2020: 25) comment above the door: 'Epistemology, dangerously but unavoidably, relies on facts of usage… Epistemological theorizing has to yield to usage, not the other way round'. My own take on this appears in the first half of the chapter.

Given the facts of usage, constructivist pronouncements about the inseparability of 'the knower' and 'the known' can be construed as a proposal to introduce a new, Carnapian language in which the use of the verb 'know' is severely restricted. This proposal is fine provided that: (a) you explain the new rules adequately, (b) you don't pretend that it's based on an unevidenced claim about the fundamental nature of reality, and (c) you resist the urge to declare that 'the knower' *really is* inseparable from 'the known'. If you comply with these conditions, can I be the first to wish you the best of luck with your project?

Notes

1 The best-known constructivist version of an epistemological 'basic belief', from *Naturalistic Inquiry*. The 'positivist' version: 'Knower and known are independent, a dualism.' These are not, of course, the only formulations of their epistemological 'axioms', and I will be discussing others later in the chapter.
2 An example: 'Dogs bark.' This has the form of a generalisation, but it's a generalisation of a certain kind. It doesn't say that *all* dogs bark', and pointing to a dog which never barks wouldn't disconfirm it. But it does imply 'usually', or 'typically', or 'for the most part'. In linguistics, such statements are known as 'generics', which 'allow for exceptions, whereas universally quantified propositions do not' (Papafragou 1996: 4).
3 It's called Sagittarius A*, and it's about 14.6 million miles in diameter. It has a mass 4.3 million times that of the sun.
4 'We must first learn what to count as knowledge by paying attention to uses of "know" and related terms in ordinary conversation' (Reynolds 2017: 4).

5 And the 59th most commonly used *word* in English (Pinillos 2012: 193).
6 'If I was asked what knowledge is, I would list items of knowledge and add "and suchlike." There is no common element to be found in all of them, because there isn't one' (Wittgenstein, MS 302, 'Diktat für Schlick' 1931–33. Cited by Stern 2004: 14).
7 Strictly speaking, I think there are multiple ways of *coming to know*, or (even better) multiple, context-dependent *criteria for the legitimate use* of the verb 'to know'.
8 Lehrer's classic text on epistemology (1990) starts with a list similar to mine: 'I know the way to Lugano, I know the expansion of pi to six decimal places. I know how to play the guitar. I know the city. I know John. I know about Alphonso and Elicia.' Yet he goes on to say that only propositional knowledge is the main concern of epistemology. See Chang (2022), as well as Ayers, for scepticism about this.
9 Austin (1962: 83) observes that it is fatal to 'embark on explaining the use of a word without seriously considering more than a tiny fraction of the contexts in which it is actually used.' Years later this still needs repeating: 'The behavior of our definitionless words is more subtle and constrained than most philosophers *still* realize – especially epistemologists' (Azzouni 2020: 30). This is especially true 'with a word as complex in its usage as "know(s)".' Qualitative methods writers are no more sensitive to this than 'most philosophers'.
10 We know that the tense structure of languages correlates with future-oriented behaviour. Speakers of languages with 'weak' future tenses ('It rains tomorrow') are more likely to save money, avoid smoking, and exercise regularly, than speakers of languages with 'strong' future tenses, like English ('It will rain tomorrow'). See Chen (2013). The same questions arise. What exactly is 'the known' here, and who is included in the 'we-who-are-knowers'? On what grounds do we propose an answer to either question?
11 Like any other use of language, this can be abused. Liars say 'I know that *p*', when they are aware that *p* is untrue. That's what lying *is*.
12 Garbutt (2023).
13 For more on this line of thought, see Azzouni (2020), especially Chapter 9.
14 They may be ageing slogans, but the same language, or minor variations on it, is still used. Smith *et al.* (2012), Staller (2012), Yilmaz (2013) are examples. Kostere and Kostere (2022) say that one of the 'axioms of the naturalistic paradigm' is: '*Epistemology* (the relationship of the knower to the known): Naturalists believe that the knower and the known are inseparable' (5).
    There is a potential terminological snafu here. Kostere and Kostere use 'naturalists' to refer to those who adopt the 'naturalistic paradigm', Lincoln and Guba's original term for constructivism. However, some writers regard *positivism* as a form of naturalism, and refer to interpretivist alternatives as 'anti-naturalism' (Bevir & Blakely 2018).
15 It is also, as I suggested in Sections 1.8 and 4.7, an enacting: a joining of the research community that promotes this new language.
16 I quoted Azzouni in Section 8.1. 'We know things that, in fact, only some or very few of us – as individuals – understand much about' (Azzouni 2020: 2). The restriction imposed by the new 'know' rule would make this claim untrue.
17 At least, he has generally been interpreted as doing this. Pasnau (2017) demurs.
18 The basic belief of so-called 'positivist' epistemology is in the same boat. 'Knower and known are independent, a dualism.' Although qualitative methodologist regard it as a reality-describing claim – a false one, presumably – the expressivist takes it as an alternative proposal, to the effect that we reject the 'new rule', and stick more or less with the language we've got. In making this proposal, we do *not* add: 'And we should do that because metaphysical reality is like *this*.'
19 Whether they are theoreticians, data analysts, or model builders. All three groups are featured in the 2020 film, *Black Holes: The Edge of All We Know*, produced by Peter Galison. It follows a four-year project involving several multidisciplinary

teams, responsible in 2019 for the first pictures of a black hole. If you want to know what one form of modern science looks like, it's worth watching.

20 And/or draw the conclusion that something called 'reality-as-it-is-in-itself' is inaccessible because, by definition, it is 'beyond' language (and we cannot step 'outside' language to take a look at it).

21 Hacking's 'elevator' words again. See Section 7.9.

22 This is a terminological minefield. Heisenberg's key paper was written in 1927. In most of that paper, he refers to 'indeterminacy' (*Ungenauigkeit*), but in the endnote he prefers 'uncertainty' (*Unsicherheit*). 'Uncertainty' became the standard English way of referring to the Principle, although the real issue, as Heisenberg later acknowledged, is indeterminacy.

There are a few scattered references to the 'social Heisenberg effect' in the 1990s, for the most part in the literature of decision science and technology. An example of the effect is said to be the conversation changing when a manager walks into the room.

23 Position/momentum is just one of the 'conjugate' pairs of variables to which HUP applies. Another is the time/energy pair, which refers to the fact that a quantum state which exists only for a short time can't have definite energy.

24 Two more useful quotes on HUP.

> It's nothing to do with measuring apparatus… the position and momentum cannot even be precisely defined for such objects… The property of momentum and the property of position cannot exist, in the sense of being measurable with infinite precision at a given instant of time. So it is not a failure of experiment. It's not a failure or a lack of resolution or technology. It's an intrinsic property of nature for these objects.
>
> *(Balakrishnan 2009)*

> The modern version of the uncertainty principle proved in our textbooks today… deals not with the precision of a measurement and the disturbance it introduces, but with the intrinsic uncertainty any quantum state must possess, regardless of what measurement (if any) is performed.
>
> *(Rozema* et al. *2012: 1)*

25 The most helpful explanation I have come across is a video by Brian Greene (2020), at least for the first ten minutes. After that the maths start to pile up.

26 They're not even analogies. If anyone were to claim that they are, I would want a clear explanation of how the analogy is supposed to work.

27 The belief that positivism could not accommodate quantum mechanics – see Section 2.6 – also plays a role here.

28 There is, as I observed in Section 6.7, no consensus about how to 'interpret' quantum mechanics. To that extent, the accounts of Wendt, Kirby, Barad, and others are basically speculative. Pick the one you find most congenial. Nobody can prove you're wrong, but neither can you demonstrate that you're right.

29 Barad's understanding of quantum physics is more sophisticated than Pernecky's, and she answers the questions posed in the previous paragraph in a way he doesn't. However, the basic idea – that quantum mechanics in *some* sense scales up to the visible, macroscopic world – is the same.

30 There is at least an irony here. Critics of positivism often complain that scaling the 'determinism' of classical physics up to the human world is 'reductionist'. But some of them seem willing to scale the indeterminism of quantum mechanics up to the human world. Why isn't this reductionist as well? See Section 6.7.

31 In any case, it's not clear what 'Newtonian' or 'classical' mechanics refers to. 'Throughout our educations, we have been encouraged to speak of 'classical

mechanics' as if it represented a unitary and well-understood doctrine. 'Tain't so… in fact, such terminology can be readily applied to deeply incompatible doctrines' (Wilson 2009: 173).

32 Barad makes it clear that she's 'not interested in drawing analogies between particles and people'. She rejects the 'all-too-popular and mistaken invocations of the uncertainty principle, as in "of course people will behave differently if you watch them".' She cites an example from NPR: 'Corporate executives are like subatomic particles; their behavior changes when you observe them.' This is all kinds of wrong.

33 If anyone is bothered by my use of 'causal' here, I will have to defer further discussion to Chapter 10. As I've said several times before, it's impossible to discuss any of the topics in Part II without referring to the others.

34 Yet another sense of 'naturalistic'. This has nothing to do with Lincoln and Guba's *Naturalistic Inquiry*, or the 'naturalism' opposed by Bevir and Blakely. The expression 'unobtrusive measures' goes back to a book published by Webb *et al.* (1966). The methods described in that book are now outdated, but Potter *et al.'s* investigations 'in the wild' are, very roughly, a modern equivalent.

References

Austin, J. L. (1962). *Sense and Sensibilia*. Oxford: Clarendon Press.

Ayers, M. (2019). *Knowing and Seeing: Groundwork for a New Empiricism*. Oxford: Oxford University Press.

Azzouni, J. (2020). *Attributing Knowledge: What it Means to Know Something*. New York: Oxford University Press.

Baclawski, K. (2018). The observer effect. Paper presented at the *IEEE International Multi-Disciplinary Conference on Cognitive Methods in Situation Awareness and Decision Support (CogSIMA) Boston*. 10.1109/COGSIMA.2018.842398

Balakrishnan, V. (2009). Lecture 1. Introduction to quantum physics: Heisenberg's uncertainty principle. *Department of Physics, Indian Institute of Technology, Madras*, https://www.youtube.com/watch?v=TcmGYe39XG30

Barad, K. (2007). *Meeting the Universe Halfway: Quantum Physics and the Entanglement of Matter and Meaning*. Durham, NC: Duke University Press.

Bevir, M., & Blakely, J. (2018). *Interpretive Social Science: An Anti-Naturalist Approach*. Oxford: Oxford University Press.

Bonner, J. T. (2006). *Why Size Matters: From Bacteria to Blue Whales*. Princeton, NJ: Princeton University Press.

Bretz, S. L. (2008). Qualitative research designs in chemistry education research. In D. M. Bunce & R. S. Cole (Eds.), *Nuts and Bolts of Chemical Education Research* (pp. 79–99). Washington, DC: American Chemical Society.

Chang, H. (2022). *Realism for Realistic People: A New Pragmatist Philosophy of Science*. Cambridge, UK: Cambridge University Press.

Chen, M. K. (2013). The effect of language on economic behavior: Evidence from savings rates, health behaviors, and retirement assets. *American Economic Review*, *103*(2), 690–731.

Garbutt, N. (2023). *Handbook of Mammals of Madagascar*. Princeton, NJ: Princeton University Press.

Greene, B. (2020). Heisenberg uncertainty principle. *Britannica.com*. https://www.britannica.com/science/uncertainty-principle/images-videos

Hofweber, T. (2023). *Idealism and the Harmony of Thought and Reality*. Oxford: Oxford University Press.

Kastner, R. E. (2022). *The Transactional Interpretation of Quantum Mechanics: A Relativistic Treatment*. Second Edition. New York: Cambridge University Press.

Kirby, V. (2011). *Quantum Anthropologies: Life at Large*. Durham, NC: Duke University Press.

Kompier, A. A. J. (2006). The "Hawthorne effect" is a myth, but what keeps the story going? *Scandinavian Journal of Work, Environment and Health, 32*(5), 402–412.

Kostere, S., & Kostere, K. (2022). *The Generic Qualitative Approach to a Dissertation in the Social Sciences: A Step by Step Guide*. Abingdon, UK: Routledge.

Lehrer, K. (1990). *Theory of Knowledge*. Boulder, CO: Westview Press.

Lieber, R. (2016). *English Nouns: The Ecology of Nominalization*. Cambridge, UK: Cambridge University Press.

Lincoln, Y. S., & Guba, E. G. (1985). *Naturalistic Inquiry*. Beverly Hills, CA: Sage.

Lincoln, Y. S., & Guba, E. G. (2013). *The Constructivist Credo*. New York: Routledge.

Oswald, D., Sherratt, F., & Smith, S. (2014). Handling the Hawthorne effect: The challenges surrounding a participant observer. *Review of Social Studies, 1*(1), 53–73.

Papafragou, A. (1996). On generics. *UCL Working Papers in Linguistics, 8*, https://www.phon.ucl.ac.uk/publications/WPL/96papers/papafrag.pdf

Papineau, D. (2021). The disvalue of knowledge. *Synthese, 198*, 5311–5332.

Pasnau, R. (2017). *After Certainty: A History of Our Epistemic Ideas and Illusions*. Oxford: Oxford University Press.

Patton, M. Q. (1980). *Qualitative Evaluation Methods*. Beverly Hills, CA: Sage.

Pernecky, T. (2016). *Epistemology and Metaphysics for Qualitative Research*. London: Sage.

Pinillos, A. (2012). Knowledge, experiments, and practical interests. In J. Brown & M. Gerken (Eds.), *Foundations of Metacognition* (pp. 192–219). Oxford: Oxford University Press.

Potter, J., Hepburn, A., & Edwards, D. (2020). Rethinking attitudes and social psychology: issues of function, order, and combination in subject-side and object-side assessments in natural settings. *Qualitative Research in Psychology, 17*(3), 336–356.

Quine, W. V. O. (1987). *Quiddities*. Cambridge, MA: Harvard University Press.

Reynolds, S. L. (2017). *Knowledge as Acceptable Testimony*. Cambridge, UK: Cambridge University Press.

Rozema, L. A., Darabi, A., Mahler, D. H., Hayat, A., Soudager, Y., & Steinberg, A. M. (2012). Violation of Heisenberg's measurement-disturbance relationship by weak measurements. *Physical Review Letters, 109*(10), 100404, corrected 189902.

Smith, B., Sparkes, A. C., Phoenix, C., & Kirby, J. (2012). Qualitative research in physical therapy: a critical discussion on mixed-methods research. *Physical Therapy Reviews, 17*(6), 374–381.

Staller, K. (2012). Epistemological boot camp: the politics of science and what every qualitative researcher needs to know to survive in the academy. *Qualitative Social Work, 12*(4), 395–413.

Stern, D. G. (2004). *Wittgenstein's Philosophical Investigations: An Introduction*. Cambridge, UK: Cambridge University Press.

Tranel, D. D. (1981). A lesson from the physicists. *Personnel and Guidance Journal, 59*, 425–429.

Webb, E. J., Campbell, D. T., Schwartz, R. D., & Sechrest, L. (1966). *Unobtrusive Measures*. Chicago: Rand McNally.

Wendt, A. (2015). *Quantum Mind and Social Science: Unifying Physical and Social Ontology*. Cambridge, UK: Cambridge University Press.

Wilson, M. (2006). *Wandering Significance: An Essay on Conceptual Behavior*. New York: Oxford University Press.

Wilson, M. (2009). Determinism and the mystery of the missing physics. *British Journal for the Philosophy of Science, 60*, 173–193.

Wilson, M. (2017). *Physics Avoidance: Essays in Conceptual Strategy*. Oxford: Oxford University Press.

Wilson, M. (2022). *Imitation of Rigor: An Alternative History of Analytic Philosophy*. New York: Oxford University Press.

Woods, D. (2017). Scale variance and the concept of matter. In S. Ellenzweig & J. H. Zammito (Eds.), *The New Politics of Materialism: History, Philosophy, Science* (pp. 200–224). Abingdon, UK: Routledge.

Yilmaz, K. (2013). Comparison of quantitative and qualitative research traditions: epistemological, theoretical, and methodological differences. *European Journal of Education, 48*(2), 311–325.

Zahle, J. (2023). Reactivity and good data in qualitative data collection. *European Journal for Philosophy of Science, 13*(10). https://doi.org/10.1007/s13194-13023-00514-z

Zhang, B., Chang, B., & Du, W. (2021). Employing intersectionality as a data generation tool: Suggestions for qualitative researchers on conducting interviews of intersectionality study. *International Journal of Qualitative Methods, 20*, 1–9.

9

'OBJECTIVE'

It is important to understand what objectivity *is*. A traditional and widely held view says that it's the absence, inhibition, or cancellation of everything subjective: values, emotions, opinions, prejudices, assumptions, and so on. If this *is* what objectivity is, we can ask whether it is possible to attain it. Most constructivist writers say it isn't.

Alternatively…

The words 'objective' and 'subjective' represent one *possible* way of marking a series of non-identical but closely related epistemic distinctions. They can be used to refer to one or more of these distinctions, but they don't have to be. In fact, for several reasons, not using them is probably the better bet. On this second view, objectivity is not, in itself, anything. The philosophical task is to identify these epistemic distinctions, show how they are related, and illustrate the different contexts in which reference is made to them.

I will sketch aspects of this latter task later in the chapter. First, I need to do some scene setting.

9.1 The constructivist legacy

Like everything else, the words 'objective' and 'objectivity' have a history. I'll start by cutting into this history at a particular point: qualitative methods writing from the late 1990s to the mid-2000s. Here are some typical passages from that period:

DOI: 10.4324/9781003306382-11

Within this paradigm, the neutrality of the researchers is emphasized as they must confine themselves to examining *what is* – what is objective – and dislodging themselves from all bias, emotion, values, or anything *subjective* that would compromise the objectivity of the research.

(Sciarra 1999: 39)

Findings are inevitably influenced by the researcher's perspective and values… making it impossible to conduct objective, value-free research.

(Snape & Spencer 2003: 17)

Scientists, like all men and women, are opinionated, dogmatic and ideological. Therefore, the idea of objectivity loses its meaning.

(Streubert Speziale & Carpenter 2007: 12)

Objectivity is a chimera: a mythological creature that never existed, save in the imaginations of those who believe that knowing can be separated from the knower.

(Lincoln & Guba 2000: 181)

The last one, of course, is the grandaddy. It has been quoted repeatedly and is still cited in the recent literature. Arguably, it's little more than a colourful, hyperbolic soundbite; but that is probably a major part of its appeal.[1]

It's not difficult to see the common thread in these extracts. The basic idea is that all researchers have certain attributes that make objectivity impossible. Because they are human beings, they cannot help but have opinions, emotions, values, biases, feelings. They make assumptions, including political and cultural assumptions; they're dogmatic; they're ideological. In short, like everyone else, they are replete with a human subjectivity from which they cannot escape. Cancelling this subjectivity, or 'detaching' oneself from it, is impossible. And that means that objectivity is impossible, too.

For this argument to go through, objectivity has to be conceived as a putative *psychological state*. It has to be assumed that being 'objective' requires the researcher to somehow disengage from the attributes just listed. If there is such a thing as objectivity – if the idea is even to make sense – there has to be a sort of psychic scouring, an absence or suppression of the psychological fixtures and fittings that make us human. And because that can't be done, objectivity is not an option. It's impossible. It's a chimera. It 'loses all meaning'.

So objectivity, if such a thing exists, is a psychological state, one identified with the absence of certain mental attributes. Anyone who believes that scientists can attain this state, when in fact it is impossible, has an 'arrogant belief in human objectivity' (Campbell 2001: 60); and it is the non-existence of this objectivity which has caused 'the fall of empirical science from its supremacy among the paradigms of knowing' (*ibid*). But is this 'absence', this suppression, really what 'objectivity' means? Is the capacity for mental self-purging really what being 'objective' requires?

Well, we'll get to that. First, though, I want to acknowledge that recent years have seen a slight shift. There is greater reluctance to assert, outright, that objectivity is not possible. Rather, the aspiration to objectivity is assigned to quantitative researchers, who think that 'values can be suspended in order to understand, and "true objectivity" (or something very close to it) is possible as long as the researcher adopts a distant, detached, non-interactive posture' (Sparkes & Smith 2014: 12–3). All this is rejected by qualitative researchers, who are *'subjectivist, transactional, and constructivist'*, and believe that 'values always mediate and shape what is understood'. The upshot: 'The difference between qualitative and quantitative researchers in how they answer the questions about ontology and epistemology actively influence how they develop their methodologies' (Sparkes & Smith 2014: 13). Methods are determined by, or 'aligned with', metaphysical assumptions, including beliefs about objectivity.

There is no declaration here that objectivity is a chimera. The commitment to objectivity is relegated to being just another difference between quantitative and qualitative researchers, or between positivists and interpretivists. This relegation is, at least partly, the result of 'mixed methods', the development of which was always inevitable. Indeed, a recognition of its sheer, obvious usefulness prompted efforts to find a suitable 'paradigm',[2] and the dismissals of 'positivist' objectivity became somewhat less strident.

However, the concept of objectivity hasn't changed. It is still about suspending, disengaging, purging, and evacuating. It is still ascribed to 'positivist' and/or 'quantitative' researchers, while 'subjectivist, transactional, and constructivist' authors express scepticism about its viability – reject it, in fact – just as they express scepticism about other 'positivist' and 'quantitative' metaphysical views.

9.2 Popper on objectivity

In the last section, I asked whether objectivity could be identified with a form of psychological self-purging. According to Popper, the answer is 'no'. He emphasises this point on several occasions. Here is an example:

> The naïve view that scientific objectivity rests on the mental or psychological attitude of the individual scientist, on his training, care, and scientific detachment, generates as a reaction the sceptical view that scientists can never be objective. On this view their lack of objectivity may be negligible in the natural sciences where their passions are not excited, but for the

social sciences where social prejudices, class bias, and personal interests are involved, it may be fatal. This doctrine… is based on the naïve view that objectivity depends on the psychology of the individual scientist… [However,] if we had to depend on his detachment, science, even natural science, would be quite impossible.

(Popper 1961: 155)

Interestingly, Popper and the constructivists agree about one thing. *If* objectivity is defined as a matter of psychological self-purification, *then* there is no such thing as objectivity. What they disagree about is what comes next. The constructivists accept the premise. That's exactly what objectivity is. So there is no such thing. Popper, however, doesn't accept the premise. That's precisely what objectivity *isn't*. The constructivist view is 'naïve'. So the argument fails. Objectivity, *not* defined as psychological self-purification, is still alive and kicking. Not a chimera.

The obvious question is: if objectivity *isn't* self-suppression or psychic self-scouring, what is it? As the preamble to this chapter will have implied, my response to this isn't that it's X (or Y, or Z), but instead: 'It's the wrong question.' So I'll defer Popper's answer until Section 9.12, and in the meantime develop a different approach, starting somewhat obliquely. Initially, I'm going to talk about visual illusions.

9.3 Visual illusions

The Müller-Lyer illusion is the best known, and the most thoroughly studied, of all visual illusions (Gregory 2015). For those jaded by its familiarity, I've used an alternative version (Figure 9.1). The point of the illusion is, of course, that the line in segment L does *look* shorter than the line in segment R; but in fact the two lines are… no, not of equal length, in fact. In this version, the L line is 16% *longer* than the R line. Even after you've checked the measurements, this is difficult to believe.

Four features of this illusion in particular are worth noting. First – and putting philosophy to one side for a moment – there is a clear distinction between 'how it looks' (R > L) and 'how it really is' (L > R). Second, we determine how it really is by adopting a particular procedure, measurement, which involves the use of a certain instrument, a ruler. Third, it is generally accepted that this

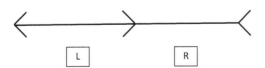

FIGURE 9.1   The Müller-Lyer illusion.

is an appropriate method of settling the question of which line is longer. Fourth, provided they carry out the procedure correctly, anyone using this method will obtain the same result.[3]

Implicit in these remarks is a sort of 'ordinary language epistemology', which reflects the simplicity of the illusion itself. The first feature suggests that we cannot always trust an initial judgement, and that it sometimes turns out that this judgement is wrong. The second indicates that the difference between *how it is* and *how it looks*, and our ability to discriminate between the two, depends on the use of a method. The third suggests that the connection between the method and the *is/seems* distinction is conditional on an agreement between interested parties. And the fourth adds a primitive notion of reliability. They appear to be, to some extent, interdependent. For example, unless the fourth condition holds, the third condition will not do so; and if the third doesn't, neither can the second.

I'll say more about what I mean by 'ordinary language epistemology' in Section 9.4. Meanwhile, here's another optical illusion (Figure 9.2).

This is one of the most astonishing of visual illusions, devised by the psychologist Edward Adelson. Remarkably, the squares labelled A and B are exactly the same colour and shade. It is difficult, if not impossible, to believe this without checking. The best way to do this is to photocopy the diagram, and then use a marker pen to efface all but the two squares concerned. It will then be clear that they are indeed identical.[4] The effect is created by the way in which our expectations that alternate squares on a checkerboard are dark and light interact with the way we visually compensate for what appears to be a shadow cast over the board.

FIGURE 9.2 Checkerboard: Edward H Adelson.

Once again, we cannot trust our initial judgement, and it turns out that there is a discrepancy between *how it is* and *how it looks*. In this case, though, there isn't a ready-made instrument, like the ruler, so we have to devise a procedure to determine whether A and B are the same shade or not. However, it is a method which people will probably agree to, and which produces the same result, irrespective of who carries it out. As with the Müller-Lyer, using the procedure does nothing to dispel the illusion. Squares A and B still look completely different. Checking has no impact on the visual conviction that they can't possibly be the same. The illusion is resistant to evidence that they are.

9.4 An ordinary language epistemology

Using visual illusions as an initial point of reference, I have suggested that they have four features that can be construed as a minimalist 'ordinary language epistemology' (OLE). They are:

(1) There is a distinction between 'how it looks' and 'how it is'.

(2) 'How it is' is determined by adopting a particular procedure.

(3) The procedure in question is generally accepted as an appropriate method.

(4) Anyone using the procedure will obtain the same result.

In suggesting that these four features embody an OLE, I want to be clear about why. What I *don't* mean is 'epistemology' in the metaphysical sense, or the kinds of pronouncement that Lincoln and Guba make. People in everyday life don't talk about 'epistemology', or 'the knower', or 'the known'. They *do* talk about 'how it looks', and they'll say something about what 'in fact' is the case if that diverges from the look of the thing. OLE is a way of referring to this kind of talk, using a bit of philosophy-speak.

A similar idea was broached in Section 6.3, where I suggested that the words 'reality' and 'realities' are used, in everyday contexts, to mark a contrast between (a) 'how things *are*' and (b) 'how things *seem*', or 'how things would ideally be', or 'how one would like things to be', or 'how they are said to be'. In this chapter, the OLE contrast has, so far, been a narrower one: between 'how it is' and 'how it *looks*'.

A distinction between 'objective' and 'subjective' is embodied in the OLE. I'm not going to suggest that anyone says: 'Well, subjectively L is shorter than R, but objectively L is longer'. Or: 'Subjectively, squares A and B are different colours, but objectively they're the same'. It's more likely that a person will say: 'Well, it does *look* as if R is longer than L, but I've measured them, and *in fact* L is longer than R.' Or: 'It looks as if A is a different colour from B, but I've checked by blanking out all the other squares, and in fact they're exactly the same.' Even so, 'subjectively this, but objectively that' would be an intelligible way of marking this kind of discrepancy.

We have various options. We can argue that a distinction between 'objective' and 'subjective' is being discussed here. Or we can follow Hacking (2015), and just not talk about 'objectivity' at all. In which case, we can suggest that OLE is a preferable substitute. If the terms 'objective' and 'objectivity' are used, it is purely in their capacity as what Hacking calls 'elevator words' (see the brief discussion in Section 7.9). Or I might decide to call OLE an 'epistemology of checking', and say: 'If I do talk about objectivity, that should be taken as a reference to the checking procedure'. The thing is, though: in OLE, the ordinary language distinction between 'how it is' and 'how it looks' is what's important, together with the methods we adopt in order to tell the difference. How we describe all this abstractly – if we're doing philosophy – is secondary.

In the rest of this chapter, I'll extend the OLE to cover cases beyond visual illusions. First, I'll give some examples of (what have been called) 'cognitive illusions', after which there will be another stock-taking exercise at Section 9.6. From there, I'll move on to cognitive biases, and then proceed to non-illusory, non-biased circumstances, both everyday and scientific. Finally, I'll come back to Popper.

By way of anticipation: I'll be offering a choice between three philosophical pictures. One in which we would have to self-purge in order to be 'objective'. Another in which 'objectivity', or something like it, involves *checking*. And a third in which we do loads of checking, and don't worry overly much about 'objectivity'.

9.5 Cognitive illusions

The term 'cognitive illusion' has been adopted by analogy with the expression 'optical illusion' (Pohl 2017: 3). As Piatelli-Palmarini (1996: 17) suggests: 'Phenomena identical to optical illusions exist in the world of thought'. These illusions are not 'mistakes' of judgement, any more than our perception of Adelson's checkerboard is a visual 'mistake'. Three reasons for this. First, illusions are systematic and predictable. Second, like visual illusions, some cognitive illusions are resistant to evidence that they *are* illusions; this, too, isn't typical of everyday mistakes.[5] Third, we're more likely to make ordinary mistakes in certain circumstances: for example, when we're tired, preoccupied, or drunk. Cognitive illusions, like optical illusions, can occur when we're awake, focused, and sober.

There is a wide variety of such illusions, ranging from the simple to the complex. Here is a homely example. Which of the following four statements is false?

(5) Cows are more closely related to horses than to whales.

(6) Cardiff is west of Edinburgh.

(7) Rome is south of New York.

(8) There are more words beginning with 'r' than words that have 'r' as their third letter.

These all look true, and most people have no reason to doubt them. But they are all false. The reasons why they seem true are interesting. They are all forms of attribute substitution (Kahneman & Frederick 2002). For example, in (6) we tend to substitute the attribute 'to the left of, on the map' for the attribute 'west of'. In the majority of cases this works, but with Cardiff and Edinburgh it doesn't. Scotland runs roughly NNW/SSE rather than N/S, with the result that the centre of Edinburgh is actually just west of Cardiff. This, by all accounts, occasions a certain amount of disbelief.[6] However, it is something that can be *checked* by consulting an atlas, specifically the respective longitudes of the two cities.

Attribute substitution applies to the other examples as well. Cows look more like horses than they do whales, but they're more closely related, genetically, to the latter. It's certainly easier to think of words beginning with 'r' than it is to think of words whose third letter is 'r'; but that doesn't mean there are more of them. With (7), I suspect people substitute climate for latitude.

One type of cognitive illusion, more significant than the trivial examples we have considered so far, has been studied systematically during the past 40 years. These are illusions arising from the widespread tendency to get-it-wrong with probabilistic reasoning (Gilovich *et al.* 2002). Assessment of risk, including medical risk, is one important field in which probability judgements are made, and it has been shown that health professionals routinely succumb to illusions of this kind, even when evaluating the results of tests (Whiting *et al.* 2015).

An entertaining example of a probability illusion is the so-called Monty Hall Problem.[7] In this problem, a game-show contestant is invited to choose one of three doors, behind one (but only one) of which is 'tonight's star prize'. Once a door has been chosen, the host (Monty) opens one of the two remaining doors and shows that there is no prize behind it. He then tells the contestant she can either stick with her original choice or switch to the third door. Most contestants, it appears, stick to the original choice (Falk & Lann 2008); but to most people it's obvious that, in fact, it's just a 50/50 bet.

Except that it's not 50/50. Why not? The question went viral (as we'd now say) in 1990 when it was discussed by Marilyn vos Savant in a popular weekly magazine. vos Savant argued that your chances of winning were 2/3 if you switched, but only 1/3 if you stuck. Her article provoked a nationwide debate and a front-page article in the *New York Times*. vos Savant received over 10,000 letters, the vast majority from people convinced that she was wrong (among them a number of mathematicians). After two more articles, though, the majority of her readers were persuaded she was right. But there was a substantial minority of diehards, including one scientist who wrote: 'I still think you're wrong. There is such a thing as female logic' (Tijms 2022).[8]

Here's why vos Savant was right. Call the three doors A, B, and C. Suppose that the prize is behind door C (as the contestant, you don't know this, of course, but Monty does). You have three initial options. Suppose you adopt a switching strategy. On that basis, let's go through what happens with each of your possible choices:

- Choose A. Monty opens B, and invites you to stick or switch. You switch. You win.
- Choose B. Monty opens A, and invites you to stick or switch. You switch. You win.
- Choose C. Monty opens B, and invites you to stick or switch. You switch. You lose.

Three possibilities, and with the 'switching' strategy you will win two of them. Now we can try it with a sticking strategy.

- Choose A. Monty opens B, and invites you to stick or switch. You stick. You lose.
- Choose B. Monty opens A, and invites you to stick or switch. You stick. You lose.
- Choose C. Monty opens B, and invites you to stick or switch. You stick. You win.

Again, three possibilities, but this time you win only one. So switching wins 2/3 and sticking wins 1/3. The same will happen, obviously, if the prize is behind one of the other two doors. The illusion – and it is a very powerful one – that the stick-or-switch choice is 50/50 is based on the assumption that, when you have two doors, the prize is equally likely to be behind either of them. But it's not. After the initial choice, the probability of the prize being behind one of the *other* two doors was 2/3. But one of them has now been eliminated, which means that the 2/3 probability is attached to just one door rather than two. Monty, in opening one of the doors – and he obviously won't open the one with the prize behind it – has actually done you a favour.

In this example, then, a readily understandable type of judgement is clearly related to probability theory. Not only do the vast majority of people get this judgement wrong, but the incorrect answer often strikes them as 'obvious', and it can take several runs through the procedure adopted above to convince them otherwise. Once again, an initial judgement proves unreliable, and we need a procedure – in this case, a series of simulations of the game – to *check* whether it is correct or not.

9.6 Variations on the checking theme

The scenarios I have used, and will be using, to illustrate the OLE run through a number of variations. They are not all illusions. I've started with illusions for two main reasons. First, the four OLE features map neatly on to each scenario without arousing any philosophical controversy.[9] Second, they are (to my mind) entertaining. They're also thought-provoking, to the extent that they are examples of things that can look *obviously* right, yet still turn out to be wrong. For me, this is true particularly of Adelson's checkerboard and the Monty Hall problem.

However, the scenarios in the rest of the chapter are not illusions. Though they still (as I argue) fit the OLE template, they vary on several axes.

Resistance. Visual illusions are often resistant to correction by checking. Even when you've measured the two segments of the Müller-Lyer, it still *looks* as if R>L. But it's not clear if this applies to the case of the cows and whales. Some of the new scenarios I'll be describing have this 'resistant to evidence' feature, others don't.

Confidence. Our confidence varies by degrees. 'I mean, obviously the choice between the two doors is 50/50, but I'm not actually sure whether I locked the front door when I left home.' So I go back and check. Very often, when we're sure about something, the question of whether we *should* check doesn't even arise, unless we're prompted.

Stakes. Whether the situation we check on is high stakes or low stakes is another variation. Nothing important hangs on Adelson's checkerboard, but a lot might hang on whether I've locked the front door. High stakes might make us more inclined to check.

Type of method. The checking procedure varies from case to case. For example, there's a difference between the Müller-Lyer illusion and Adelson's checkerboard. One is quantitative, the other isn't. One involves a standard measuring instrument, the other requires an improvised solution. In addition, we've had molecular genetics, longitude and latitude, counting dictionary words, and simulations of a game show.

Accessibility of method. There's a difference between scenarios where it's pretty obvious *how* to check, and scenarios requiring thought. How do we know if R>L? Get a ruler. How can we check if squares A and B are the same shade? A bit of thought required. Same with Monty Hall. This is the most interesting difference of all: where we have to devise a *new* method in order to check. A lot of science is like that.

The OLE template remains the same for all variations, though in some cases subject to provisos. The main adjustment is, as I've just suggested, for situations where a new method has to be devised from scratch. Adelson's checkerboard is a simple example of this, but there are far more complicated ones. Any new procedure will have to comply, at a minimum, with the requirement that everybody using it obtains the same result. If it does so, then there is a reasonable chance that it will eventually become generally accepted as an appropriate method of discriminating between 'how it is' and 'how it seems'. This is still the primary distinction at the centre of OLE.

9.7   Cognitive bias

'Bias' is arguably an unfortunate term, as it is easily confused with prejudice or a lack of impartiality. However, *cognitive biases* are not prejudices, and the term does not signal a deliberate lack of fairness or open-mindedness. Instead, it refers to a set of usually unconscious cognitive mechanisms which are triggered by circumstances of various kinds, and which can lead to 'suboptimal decisional outcomes' (Korteling *et al.* 2018). Numerous types of cognitive bias mechanism have been identified. The book edited by Pohl (2017) describes 24, sorted by three categories: thinking, judgement, and memory. I give two examples in this section, and one more in Section 9.8.

Self-serving bias. If you give an account of yourself that shows your behaviour in a more positive light than is warranted, you could be subject to self-serving bias. 'Researchers have repeatedly demonstrated that people on average tend to think they are more charitable, cooperative, considerate, fair, kind, loyal, and sincere than the typical person, but less belligerent, deceitful, gullible, lazy, impolite, mean, and unethical' (Epley & Dunning 2000). Most of us think that we are more intelligent than our peers, better looking, more ethical, less biased, more likely to go to heaven. We are also better than average drivers, have a better than average sense of humour, and a better than average ability to get along with others (Myers 2002).[10] Ironically, most of us think that we're less self-serving than other people, and that we're less susceptible to bias in general (Pronin *et al.* 2004).

Venturing into the realm of people-descriptions – as opposed to looking up longitudes and gauging probability – raises the question of method fairly strongly. There are no people-rulers, no humour calculators, and no atlases listing characteristics. But if someone says you're not as clever, or as funny, or as good a driver as you think you are, OLE looks around for some means of checking these claims. We can do this in general terms. If the majority of people think they are more skilled drivers than the average person (Svenson 1981), we know some of them *must* be wrong. But how about the individual? Well, there are various ways in which this might be tested, some of them fair and reasonably accurate (though the individual concerned might not share this view if a test showed her to be less skilled than average). So there may be a level of precision that methods for evaluating such characteristics cannot attain. But that's not a reason for declaring that 'objectivity' is a 'chimera'.

OLE still thinks there's a distinction between 'how it seems (to the driver)' and 'how it (probably) is'.

Belief bias. A form of attribute substitution, in which 'Do I believe this conclusion?' is substituted for 'Is this conclusion valid?' It is usually illustrated
by a syllogism like the following (Stanovich 2003):

All living things need water.

Roses need water.

Therefore, roses are living things.

This is an invalid inference, though most people are initially inclined to
think it valid, including 70% of university students (Sá *et al.* 1999). What
happens is that they recognise the syllogism's conclusion as something
they already believe to be true, but confuse believability with validity, and
therefore assume that the inference is valid. If this syllogism is compared
with another, the point becomes obvious:

All insects need oxygen.

Mice need oxygen.

Therefore, mice are insects.

The form of inference is similar to the first example, but now the fallacy
is easier to spot, because the believability of the conclusion is not a distrac-
tion. As Stanovich (2003: 292) says: 'prior knowledge does not get in the
way'. The possibility of belief bias generalises to other kinds of inference.
For example, the methodological appraisal of scientific studies can be
compromised by prior beliefs about the findings (Koehler 1993). This has
been demonstrated in the context of clinical trials (Resch *et al.* 2000,
Kaptchuk 2003). Well-designed studies are criticised if they indicate that
an unconventional treatment is effective (or that an established treatment
is ineffective), and poorly designed studies are accepted because their
findings appear to confirm widely held opinions.

The 'roses are living things' inference is yet another variation on the difference between 'how it seems' and 'how it is'. What kind of procedure can
check the validity of the inference? There's no alternative to learning some
rules of logic, for the same reason that we learn the multiplication tables, the
rules for addition and subtraction, and how to do long division. It's unlikely
that people will say: 'Subjectively, the inference is valid, but objectively it's
not.' What they *will* say is: 'It *looks* valid, and it's tempting to think it *is* valid…
but, in fact, it isn't. So, once again, they give expression to the OLE template.

9.8 Preceded, therefore caused

I will offer one more example of a cognitive bias, this time linked to a significant health care issue of recent times. Many people believe the claim that the measles, mumps and rubella (MMR) vaccine causes autism. One reason for this is personal experience. For example, consider some below-the-line comments on a *Daily Telegraph* article, 9th July 2007.[11]

> I think MMR causes autism. My son is autistic. He was diagnose shortly after him having his MMR jab. I noticed a change in him after him having the jab, he started to arrange his toys and would not talk. Sometimes he wouldn't talk for up to 5 hours. Before his injection he was a bright loving normal boy.
>
> Whether there is a proven link between MMR and autism or not – all you cynical, scientifically inclined individuals need to just shut your 'politically correct' ranting and listen to parent's concerns. My son too, was developing normally and had started talking but soon after having his MMR jab, stopped talking completely. Now, almost 2 and half, he still does not speak. Unless you have a child that you have to watch painfully trying to communicate, don't talk about how 'safe' the MMR jab is as you are none the wiser!

In these cases, as in many others, the conviction that there is a causal link between MMR and autism is a result of the diagnosis being made, or changed behaviour being observed, soon after the vaccination. This is an extraordinarily powerful experience. If Y follows X, then obviously X must be the cause of Y, particularly if Y is an emotionally loaded life event. The conviction is a consequence of the fact that there seems to have been no other cause of Y.[12] The autism must have had a causal trigger, the trigger must have occurred shortly before the autism became apparent... and the only candidate for the trigger is the MMR. Therefore, the MMR *must* have caused the autism. There can be no other explanation. This kind of certainty is impervious to arguments based on statistics. I *know* that X caused Y; therefore, conclusions based on statistics are wrong.

But MMR does not cause autism. Demonstrating this, conclusively, requires some fairly sophisticated statistical techniques. However, the key idea is straightforward. The belief that there is a connection is usually based on a single case (the parent's own child), or a small number of cases (other children who developed autism shortly after being vaccinated with MMR). These are all X-then-Y cases. Once the suspicion that X-caused-Y has been formulated, there tends to be a search for further X-then-Y cases in order to substantiate it (confirmation bias). The trouble is, this approach ignores all the cases in which there was X but no Y, and all the cases in which there was Y but no

X. In other words, it ignores all the cases in which the MMR vaccination was not followed by autism, and all the cases in which autism was diagnosed even though the child was not MMR-immunised. If it can be shown that children who have had the MMR vaccine are no more likely to be diagnosed with autism than children who have not had MMR; and if it can be shown that children with autism are no more likely to have had the MMR vaccine than children who do not have autism… the claim that there is a causal link is disconfirmed, however convincing personal experience may be.

In this example, as in many others, *how it seems* can be completely convincing… yet still at odds with *how it is*. In a large population, it's inevitable that there will be *some* cases in which autistic behaviour began, or was diagnosed, very shortly after getting the MMR.[13] This *is* just a coincidence. However, for the person to whom it happens, it cannot possibly be.[14] Unfortunately, however, the checking process in this case is not as accessible as in the Müller-Lyer example.

9.9   Everyday checking

In her discussion of cognitive biases, Gendler (2010: 124) notes that the discrepancy between an initial judgement and the evidence that it is mistaken is not 'an anomalous or idiosyncratic feature of arcane or unusual cases' but a 'central feature of our mental lives'. The plausibility of this observation will be apparent from the examples so far, even if we exclude the startling, but presumably relatively rare, cases of visual illusion. But in this section I'll run through a few everyday scenarios in order to give a sense of how routine the various types of checking procedure are.

[1] I'm going shopping. I'm think there's plenty of detergent left, but I look in the cupboard just to be sure. Turns out I'm wrong. I check the adjacent cupboard. It's not there either. I add detergent to my shopping list.

[2] 'You know that Charles and Fiona have split up?' says Mike. 'No, surely not.' I reply. 'That can't be right. I saw them only last week. They were fine.' I phone Charles that evening. Apparently he and Fiona have separated.

[3] I'm taking the train into London today. I'm pretty sure the train leaves at quarter past the hour. But it's been quite a while since I did this trip, and my memory isn't what it once was. I check my copy of the timetable. I was right. Quarter past the hour.

[4] I wake up not feeling particularly well. It feels as if I might have a fever, but it's hard to be sure. I get the medical thermometer and check. It reads 38°C. I think that counts as fever.

[5] I want to quote the 'chimera' remark by Lincoln and Guba, but I can't remember what page it's on in *Naturalistic Inquiry*. I search the book. It's not there. What *is* there is the claim that *generalisation* is a chimera. I have obviously misremembered.

[6] A friend and I are playing the board game *Babylonia*. She makes a move which I think is illegal. She's sure it's permissible. We dig the rule book out. She's right. It is.

So checking comes up rather a lot. A few further points are worth noting. First, with OLE, 'objectivity' and quantitative methods aren't glued together. Most of these examples don't even involve counting, let alone measuring or calculating. Second, and relatedly, checking has to be of the relevant kind. Phoning Charles would be of no use in any scenario but [2], unless he was familiar with the rules of *Babylonia*, say, or the railway timetable. Third, and most importantly, challenges to the checking procedure are almost always possible. In [1], my partner says: 'You looked in the wrong cupboards. Check the one under the sink. In [3], my niece says: 'You do realise that timetable's two years out of date? Check online.' I do. The times have changed. In [4], I read later that some home thermometers are off by as much as 0.83°C, so it's possible my temperature is lower by that much. And so on.

Reader: More footling about. What has any of this got to do with objectivity?

Me: I'm discussing the various methods we ordinarily use to check whether 'how it seems' is really 'how it is'.

Reader: So I ask again. What's that got to do with objectivity?

Me: It might have nothing. Depends what you have in mind. But there's a distinction here which is at least comparable to the distinction between 'subjective' and 'objective'.

Reader: It's not the *same* as 'subjective'/'objective', though, is it?

Me: Well, okay, if you say not. But in that case I think you should explain what you mean by 'subjective' and 'objective', and why *that* distinction is more important than the one I've been talking about.

Reader: Objectivity is about being neutral and detached. It's about being free of values, assumptions, and prejudices.

Me: Right, so that's an interesting difference. I give you several examples, with diverse, context-relevant methods of checking 'how it is'. You give me a definition.

Reader: What's wrong with that? At least I'm clear about what 'objectivity' means.

Me: A definition imposes bogus uniformity. According to yours, there's only *one way* of being objective. It's a matter of emptying yourself of values, emotions, opinions, everything.

Reader: Exactly. And that can't be done. So there's no such thing as objectivity.

Me: But why choose to define it in such a way that – by definition – it's impossible? And why insist that the 'emptying' picture is the only one that counts?

Reader: Look, nobody thinks objectivity refers to checking the rules of a board game.

Me: Well, that's one reason why I prefer not to talk about 'objectivity'. It's more informative to talk about specific examples, and to ask whether, in a particular case, the most appropriate checking procedure has been used.

As I suggested in Section 9.4, 'objectivity' is an 'elevator' word (Hacking 2015), like 'fact', 'truth', and 'reality'. These words do have a use, provided we avoid the rabbit holes. They allow us to talk about how we talk about the world. A statement like 'True statements are those which correspond to reality' is just a 'grammatical remark'. It indicates, broadly, the relation between how we use 'reality' and how we use 'true'. But some people can't leave it alone. They get agitated about 'correspondence *theories* of truth' and demand to know how we can step outside language to get 'access to reality'. They attach metaphysical significance to 'truth' and 'reality'. They search for one-size-fits-all theories – what truth is, what reality is – and 'generate grandiose important-sounding but idle controversies' (Hacking 2015: 24). They have a similar obsession with 'objective'. There must be something that objectivity *is* – the voiding of self – and it must apply to *everything*. The 'craving for generality' again.

9.10 Scientific checking

The examples of everyday checking set out in the previous section all start with not wanting to act on an assumption, an initial judgement, a memory, an inference, that might be in error. They all represent ways in which we might, in the absence of checking, go astray. This does not mean that, having checked, I can no longer go astray. It turns out that I did in [1], [3] and [4]. But the point of checking is to minimise the risk that I will fall into inferential error: about the detergent, about my fever, about the whereabouts of 'chimera' in *Naturalistic Inquiry*. The same kind of thing happens, at a more elaborate, stringent, and often labyrinthine level, in the sciences.

Haack (2003) puts this succinctly: 'There is less to scientific method than meets the eye. Is scientific inquiry categorically different from other kinds? No. Scientific inquiry is continuous with everyday empirical inquiry – only more so' (94). The ways in which this 'more so' is realised are, Haack says, 'astonishingly various' (95). Three examples. First, 'observation' routinely depends on instruments of all kinds – microscopes, computers, DNA sequencers, spectrometers, interviews – just as my attempt to determine whether I have a fever in scenario [4] depends on the thermometer. Second, findings are not purely up to the individual but are open to scrutiny by other members of the scientific community; non-scientific, everyday examples of this can be seen in scenarios [1] and [3]. Third, the circumstances of observation are not fortuitous or freewheeling; they are rather 'deliberate, contrived, controlled'.

The history of science, according to Mayo (1996, 2018), is the history of the development of methods for inquiring into error. As science grows, so does the range of recognised sources of error, along with a repertoire of procedures for identifying and eliminating them. When a new source of error is spotted, a procedure for recognising it, and controlling for it, is devised. The range of possible errors into which canonical inquiries are routinely carried out is extensive and familiar to any researcher. They include errors which arise when association is mistaken for cause; errors which occur because various design assumptions fail to hold; errors resulting from misconceptions about how the instruments work; errors caused by instruments not working properly; and lots more. The repertoire of procedures for checking whether such errors have been made, in a range of research situations, is equally familiar. The point is that, when the evidence generated by a research protocol is in accordance with what a hypothesis under examination predicts, *and* a series of canonical inquiries (tests) have failed to identify error, then the evidence can be taken as decent grounds for (provisionally) accepting the hypothesis.

This position, in effect, generalises the stripped-down structure of OLE. Any procedure that has proved successful as a way of checking for a specific form of error is incorporated into the methodological canon, which is a series of reliable tests recognised by the scientific community. However, in one sense, Mayo's view is even more minimalist than the pared-down OLE version. Instead of a distinction between *how it seems* and *how it really is*, she adopts a distinction, inherited from Popper and Neyman (Neyman & Pearson 1967), between 'how it seems (but isn't)' and 'what we can (for the time being) accept'. The error is identified, the illusion is dispelled, but the *how it really is* hypothesis is accepted only provisionally; it is not *assumed* to be true, and it may be rejected later following further tests.

Mayo (1996) is about experimental research, so the identification of error is predicated on the use of quantitative techniques: statistics are required to establish whether an error is being made in accepting or rejecting an experimental hypothesis. Understandably, then, Mayo refers to her approach as an error-statistical philosophy. However, this is not quantification-for-the-sake-of-it. There is a purpose in the use of statistics (in this context) which can be defined without any reference to numbers. Mayo views *'statistical inference as severe testing'* (Mayo 2018: xii italics original). Her point is that, for any type of enquiry at all, 'if little or nothing has been done to rule out flaws in inferring a claim, then it has not passed a *severe test'*. And she sets out a characterisation of 'severe testing', as follows (*ibid*):

> A claim is severely tested to the extent it has been subjected to and passes a test that probably would have found flaws, were they present.

No mention of numbers. Where an enquiry necessarily involves measurement in some form, statistical procedures can (often) provide a severe test, as understood according to this characterisation. But if an enquiry does not involve measurement, we can look for a non-quantitative severe test.

We can see this in rudimentary form even in the everyday cases of Section 9.9. In [1], for example, if I'd looked in every cupboard of the house – not just two – and if I *still* hadn't found detergent, that would have been a far more severe test (of the hypothesis that 'there's plenty left') than the test I carried out. Similarly, in [5] it depends how thorough the search was. If it was a general skim, that presumably wouldn't count as a severe test. I've been known to miss stuff before. But if I did a line-by-line, proof-reading-style search, that would be as severe a test as I could make it. (Almost. I could give the book to other people to check as well.) In neither case is an accurate result *guaranteed*. But that's equally true in the sciences. Notice that Mayo refers to: 'a test that *probably* would have found flaws', if any had been present. This lack of certainty is endemic. But a severe test is still better than a non-severe one. The more severe the check, the more confidence we can have in the conclusion we draw. This applies to both the ordinary and the scientific. Everyday checking and experimental severe tests are on a rough continuum.

9.11   Three pictures

There's more than one way of coming at this. A first way is to insist – as *Reader* does in Section 9.9 – that objectivity is something over and above all this talk of checking. Nobody thinks of objectivity as checking the rules of a board game. Checking doesn't count as 'being objective' because, as long as the researcher has values and assumptions, prejudices, and preferences, her conclusions will inevitably be an expression of her subjectivity. And because she cannot simply toggle her presuppositions to 'off', objectivity is unachievable.

A second way of approaching it might be to say that checking and severe tests *do* count as 'objective', or as objective as it's possible to be. They represent an alternative way of construing 'objectivity', an alternative picture. They have one advantage over the first approach: that of being possible. Checking can be less or more thorough, tests can be less or more severe. Objectivity, on this interpretation, is no longer 'yes-or-no', 'on-or-off'… an all-or-nothing chimera. It's more like a sliding scale.

A third way, the one I've attributed to Hacking, is to suggest that we stick to the detail of actual cases, describe and evaluate tests, and quietly forget about the elevator word 'objectivity'. Ordinary language, as I've said, seems to favour this option. It distinguishes routinely between 'how it seems' and 'how it is', and makes plenty of references to checking. It does sometimes refer to 'objective' and 'subjective', too; but it does so in a manner that is consistent with the second approach, not the first.

These are three different pictures of objectivity, or three different ways of using the relevant words. In Carnap's terms, three alternative languages. Which you adopt is up to you. Provided you're clear about the rules you're recommending, and as long as you don't suppose that your preferred option is justified on the basis of 'how things metaphysically are', you're free to use the language of 'objectivity' (or not use it) as you see fit. You might, of course, argue that one of the three pictures is more useful, and less likely to mislead – Carnap would certainly welcome this – but that would be an empirical claim, and it would need to be evidenced.

Personally, I find it hard to determine what usefulness the first option might have. What value does a distinction have if one of its terms can never be applied? If you say that it will encourage researchers to recognise that objectivity is a chimera, you'll just be going round in linguistic circles. The rules of your language *define* 'objective' in such a way that there can be no such thing. Which is fine if that's how you want to use the term. But you'll have to show that this usage results in a language that's practically useful (compared to the alternatives).

Even on its own terms, there's something slightly off about the first approach. 'If complete success in the self-purging department can't be achieved, then there's no such thing as objectivity.' I think this is reminiscent of those who argue: 'You can never attain absolute equality (so there's no point trying to reduce *in*equality).' Both are all-or-nothing. It's like saying: 'I'll never be able to run a marathon in two hours. So there's no point trying to improve the time I *can* run it in.' As Mayo (2018: 221) observes: 'Whenever you come up against blanket slogans such as "no methods are objective" it is a good guess that the problem is being trivialized into oblivion.'

Giving up on this approach means relinquishing some powerful rhetorical tropes. Objectivity represents the 'dominant discourse', the arbitrary 'privileging' of an Enlightenment prejudice, positivism, realism, scientism, materialism, determinism, empiricism, Cartesianism, reductionism, rationalism, and lots of other 'outdated' ideas. But what you get in exchange for abandoning these tropes is something with no metaphysical pretensions. Something not in the business of defining 'reality'. Something which refers only to a variegated, ever-expanding array of methods designed to minimise the risk of succumbing to inferential error. If you reject this offer, and stick with the rhetorical tropes, you might just as well – it sometimes seems to me – stick with the view that Edinburgh is east of Cardiff, and that squares A and B on Adelson's checkerboard are different colours.

9.12   Back to Popper

I suggested in Section 9.2 that Popper and the constructivists agree that: '*If* objectivity is defined as a matter of psychological self-purification, *then* there is no such thing as objectivity.' They differ in this respect: the constructivists accept the premise, so assent to the conclusion; whereas Popper rejects the premise, so is not obliged to agree to the conclusion. Popper has a different understanding, a different definition, of 'objectivity'. On his view, it is *not* defined as self-purification, so it's still viable.

The alternative to the self-purification view – the one I've proposed, anyway – is modelled on everyday checking and severe tests. Whether this is pitched as an alternative definition of objectivity, or whether it represents a change of subject – let's talk about checking and severe tests, and quietly forget the word 'objective' – doesn't really matter. Either way, it's a reflection of ordinary language epistemology. We could call it a 'procedural' view.

However, the two views do have something in common. They both regard subjectivity as antithetical to something. The *self-purification* view portrays it globally. It is the complete range of mental states and processes, all of which must be suppressed if objectivity is to be achievable. An impossibility. The *procedural* view portrays subjectivity as something that, on specific occasions, expresses itself as misperception, cognitive bias, defective judgement, first impressions. On these occasions, subjectivity stands in the way of seeing clearly. Checking procedures and severe tests are designed to minimise the likelihood of being deceived.

Both views recognise that subjectivity is inescapable. The purveyors of purging take that as a knock-down argument against the impossible dream of objectivity. The proponents of procedure take it as a reason why the checking function is necessary. The former imagine that subjectivity must be purged or banished, while the latter think it can be bypassed. Instead of having to expunge subjectivity, we accept that expunging isn't an option, and find a route around it. The purifiers think that the only way to deal with the boulder blocking the road is to get rid of it (sadly, this cannot be done). The procedurals look for a detour. Subjectivity is unavoidable. So we have to devise a procedure for making it irrelevant, for taking it out of the loop. This is a crude and overly simple image. But it conveys the basic idea.

Popper was less inclined to fanciful imagery, but he insisted that objectivity was not dependent on the psychological state of the individual scientist. Instead, the scientist goes to an independent tribunal, the court of science as an institution. She retains the partiality, passions and preconceptions that make her human, but submits her theories to 'the *friendly-hostile co-operation of many scientists'* (Popper 1966, p. 217). 'A scientist may offer his theory with the full conviction that it is unassailable. But this will not impress his fellow-scientists' (p. 218). Where I have emphasised the procedures which scientists – and all of us, in everyday contexts – adopt, Popper emphasises the institution which incorporates them into the canon. Procedures become canonical when the scientific community accepts them as such.

9.13 Concluding thought

Yet there is something not entirely wrong about the idea that objectivity has something to do with self-discipline. The word 'objectivity' has been associated with many threads in the history of science, and according to Daston and Galison (2007), detachment *is* one of them. During the 19th century, various forms of scientific discipline were developed which became part of what it meant to be 'objective', and this discipline was identified with what might be called 'technologies of the self' (Foucault 1988). The practices which implemented the 'scientific self' did not require self-purging, nor did they involve the suppression of one's humanity. But they did involve a kind of self-restraint, one which accepted that (in Popper's terms) your personal convictions do not impress other scientists.

Karl Pearson proposed that the scientist 'has above all things to aim at self-elimination in his judgments' (cited Daston & Galison: 196). But what he meant was that he had 'to provide an argument which is as true for each individual mind as for his own'. What *I* find convincing will not necessarily persuade others, so I must adopt a regime that can produce evidence others will be able to accept. This included training in observation, keeping journals of laboratory work, drawing specimens, channelling attention, and monitoring one's own hypotheses – not in order to 'put them out of play', or to make a show of 'bracketing' them, but in order to anticipate what the scientific community, Popper's 'many scientists', will make of my arguments and evidence. This is not a purging of the self. It is, rather, the adoption of a third-person point of view. It is an acquiring not a divesting, an addition not a subtraction. It does not require of me that I deny my own humanity.

Notes

1 Claiming that *knowing* can't be separated from the knower is, of course, different from claiming that the knower and the *known* are inseparable.
2 This debate continues. See, for example, Molina-Azorin and Fetters (2020), an editorial introducing a special issue on 'paradigms in mixed methods research'. For most of the articles in this issue, the task seems to be finding a way of reconciling mixed methods with the notion of a 'paradigm'. The latter is, apparently, still too entrenched to think about giving it up altogether.

3 Where 'same' is 'same within a reasonable margin'. Two measurements, in milli-metres, differing at the third decimal point (to take an extreme example) would obviously count as 'the same'.

4 Alternatively, google 'Incredible shade illusion', and watch the video.

5 Many cognitive illusions, however, can be mitigated, or even eliminated, at least for some people, some of the time, in some circumstances.

6 An article in the Bristol Post (3rd January 2018) reported that a Channel 4 presenter had 'dropped a geographical bombshell' – that Edinburgh is west of Bristol. People were described as 'dumbfounded', 'shocked', and 'mind-blown'. A man posted on Twitter: 'The fact that Edinburgh lies further west than Bristol has caused me to run around my house shrieking.' (Cardiff is, of course, even further west than Bristol.) There is a similar surprise awaiting anyone who assumes that Los Angeles is west of Reno.

7 The problem is based on the show 'Let's Make a Deal', whose host was apparently named Monty Hall.

8 Tijms' article on the Monty Hall problem is short, entertaining, and instructive. Worth digging out.

9 At any rate, I have never heard anyone argue: 'The claim that L>R is an objective fact is rooted in positivist assumptions about measurement and the separation of knower and known. Objectivity is a chimera.'

10 Some of these findings could be out of date by now, of course, but self-serving bias is still studied by psychologists. Myers (2002) has an entertaining romp through the literature (93-98). And here's a nice quote from the humourist Dave Barry: 'The one thing that unites all human beings, regardless of age, gender, religion, eco-nomic status or ethnic background is that deep down inside, we all believe that we are above average drivers' (Barry 1998).

11 Unfortunately, the web page is no longer available.

12 This is a version of the fallacy known as 'post hoc ergo propter hoc', or 'after this, therefore because of this' (Manninen 2018). It can be seen as another example of attribute substitution, with the attribute 'caused by' replaced by 'closely following'.

13 This has been demonstrated in numerous studies. One of the statistically more approachable ones is Smeeth et al. (2004). For a more recent study, see Hviid et al. (2019). It must be emphasised that there are many reasons for vaccine hesitancy and/or resistance (Lane et al. 2018). They are all independently discussable. Statistical studies have no direct bearing on any of the others.

14 The theme of 'it can't be a coincidence' turns up frequently in the posts from the Daily Telegraph website. 'After the MMR he had a fever then stopped talking. Is this coincidence?' 'I am absolutely sure that the MMR jab is the trigger for my son's autism. He was developing normally until the jab. Within ten days of receiving it he became brain damaged; the coincidence is too great.'

References

Barry, D. (1998). *Dave Barry Turns 50*. New York: Crown.

Campbell, J. K. (2001). Inside lives: the quality of biography. In R. R. Sherman & R. B. Webb (Eds.), *Qualitative Research in Education: Focus and Methods* (pp. 59–75). Abingdon, UK: Routledge.

Daston, L., & Galison, P. (2007). *Objectivity*. New York: Zone Books.

Epley, N., & Dunning, D. (2000). Feeling "holier than thou": Are self-serving assess-ments produced by errors in self- or social prediction? *Journal of Personality and Social Psychology*, 79(6), 861–875.

Falk, R., & Lann, A. (2008). The allure of equality uniformity in probabilistic and statistical judgment. *Cognitive Psychology*, *57*, 293–334.

Foucault, M. (1988). Technologies of the self. In L. H. Martin, H. Gutman, & P. H. Hutton (Eds.), *Technologies of the Self* (pp. 16–49). Amherst: University of Massachusetts Press.

Gendler, T. S. (2010). *Intuition, Imagination, and Philosophical Methodology*. New York: Oxford University Press.

Gilovich, T., Griffin, D., & Kahneman, D. (Eds.). (2002). *Heuristics and Biases: The Psychology of Intuitive Judgment*. Cambridge, UK: Cambridge University Press.

Gregory, R. L. (2015). *Eye and Brain: The Psychology of Seeing*. Fifth Edition. Oxford: Oxford University Press.

Haack, S. (2003). *Defending Science Within Reason: Between Scientism and Cynicism*. Amherst, NY: Prometheus.

Hacking, I. (2015). Let's not talk about objectivity. In F. Padovani, A. Richardson, & J. Y. Tsou (Eds.), *Objectivity in Science: New Perspectives from Science and Technology Studies* (pp. 19–33). Cham, Switzerland: Springer.

Hviid, A., Hansen, J. V., Frisch, M., & Melbye, M. (2019). Measles, mumps, rubella vaccination and autism: A nationwide cohort study. *Annals of Internal Medicine*, *170*, 513–520.

Kahneman, D., & Frederick, S. (2002). Representativeness revisited: attribute substitution in intuitive judgment. In T. Gilovich, D. Griffin, & D. Kahneman (Eds.), *Heuristics and Biases: The Psychology of Judgment* (pp. 49–81). Cambridge, UK: Cambridge University Press.

Kaptchuk, T. J. (2003). Effect of interpretive bias on research evidence. *BMJ*, *326*, 1453–1455.

Koehler, J. J. (1993). The influence of prior belief on scientific judgments of evidence quality. *Organizational Behavior and Human Decision Processes*, *56*, 28–55.

Korteling, J. E., Brouwer, A.-M., & Toet, A. (2018). A neural network framework for cognitive bias. *Frontiers in Psychology*, *9*, https://doi.org/10.3389/fpsyg.2018.01561

Lane, S., MacDonald, N. E., Marti, M., & Dumolard, L. (2018). Vaccine hesitancy around the globe: Analysis of three years of WHO/UNICEF Joint Reporting Form data 2015–2917. *Vaccine*, *36*(26), 3861–3867.

Lincoln, Y. S., & Guba, E. G. (2000). Paradigmatic controversies, contradiction, and emerging confluences. In N. K. Denzin & Y. S. Lincoln (Eds.), *Handbook of Qualitative Research*. Second Edition (pp. 163–188). Thousand Oaks: Sage.

Manninen, B. A. (2018). False cause: post hoc ergo propter hoc. In R. Arp, S. Barbone, & M. Bruce (Eds.), *Bad Arguments: 100 of the Most Important Fallacies in Western Philosophy* (pp. 342–345). Hoboken, NJ: Wiley Blackwell.

Mayo, D. (1996). *Error and the Growth of Experimental Knowledge*. Chicago: University of Chicago Press.

Mayo, D. (2018). *Statistical Inference as Severe Testing: How to Get Beyond the Statistics Wars*. Cambridge, UK: Cambridge University Press.

Molina-Azorin, J. F., & Fetters, M. D. (2020). Virtual special issue on 'paradigms in mixed methods research'. *Journal of Mixed Methods Research*, *14*(1), 6–10.

Myers, D. G. (2002). *Intuition: Its Powers and Perils*. New Haven, CT: Yale University Press.

Neyman, J., & Pearson, E. S. (1967). *Joint Statistical Papers*. Berkeley, CA: University of California Press.

Piatelli-Palmarini, M. (1996). *Inevitable Illusions: How Mistakes of Reason Rule Our Minds*. Chichester: John Wiley & Sons.

Pohl, R. F. (Ed.) (2017). *Cognitive Illusions: Intriguing Phenomena in Thinking, Judgment and Memory*. Abingdon, UK: Routledge.

Popper, K. R. (1961). *The Poverty of Historicism*. London: Routledge & Kegan Paul.

Popper, K. R. (1966). *The Open Society and Its Enemies, Volume 2*: Fifth Edition. London: Routledge.

Pronin, E., Gilovich, T., & Ross, L. (2004). Objectivity in the eye of the beholder: Divergent perceptions of bias in self versus others. *Psychological Review, 111*, 781–799.

Resch, K. I., Ernst, E., & Garrow, J. (2000). A randomized controlled study of reviewer bias against an unconventional therapy. *Journal of the Royal Society of Medicine, 93*, 164–167.

Sá, W., West, R. F., & Stanovich, K. (1999). The domain specificity and generality of belief bias: searching for a generalizable critical thinking skill. *Journal of Educational Psychology, 91*, 497–510.

Sciarra, D. (1999). The role of the qualitative researcher. In M. Kopala & L. A. Suzuki (Eds.), *Using Qualitative Methods in Psychology* (pp. 37–48). Thousand Oaks, CA.

Smeeth, L., Cook, C., Fombonne, E., Rodrigues, L. C., Smith, P. G., & Hall, A. J. (2004). MMR and pervasive developmental disorders: A case-control study. *Lancet 364*, 963–969.

Snape, D., & Spencer, L. (2003). The foundations of qualitative research. In J. Ritchie & J. Lewis (Eds.), *Qualitative Research Practice: A Guide for Social Science Students and Researchers* (pp. 1–23). London: Sage.

Sparkes, A. C., & Smith, B. (2014). *Qualitative Research Methods in Sport, Exercise and Health: From Process to Product*. New York: Routledge.

Stanovich, K. (2003). The fundamental computational biases of human cognition: heuristics that (sometimes) impair decision making and problem solving. In J. E. Davidson & R. J. Sternberg (Eds.), *The Psychology of Problem Solving* (pp. 291–342). New York: Cambridge University Press.

Streubert Speziale, H. J., & Carpenter, D. R. (2007). *Qualitative Research in Nursing*, Fourth Edition. Philadelphia, PA: Lippincott Williams & Wilkins.

Svenson, O. (1981). Are we all less risky and more skillful than our fellow drivers? *Acta Psychologica, 47*, 143–148.

Tijms, S. (2022). Monty Hall and 'the Leibniz Illusion'. *Chance, 35*(4), 4–14.

Whiting, P. F., Davenport, C., Jameson, C., Burke, M., Sterne, J. A. C., Hyde, C., & Ben-Shlomo, Y. (2015). How well do health professionals interpret diagnostic information? A systematic review. *BMJ Open, 5*, e008155.

10

'CAUSE' AND CAUSAL LANGUAGE

Schematically, here is an argument frequently presented to the reader of qualitative methods texts:[1]

    (a) There is a choice between X and Y approaches to research.

    (b) X researchers assume that people's actions are caused.

    (c) Causal laws are immutable, deterministic, mechanistic, outside time and space.

    (d) Human behaviour cannot be understood in those terms.

    (e) So you should adopt Y.

Underlying this argument is the assumption that 'causation' refers to causal laws, and that causal laws are as described in (c). Just possibly, however, there might be alternative theories of causation. If there are, a different inference might look like this:

    (f) Z is a theory of causation, as described in (c).

    (g) Z is clearly bonkers if applied to people.

    (h) So causation can't be applied to human behaviour.

It's an obvious non-sequitur. If Z is bonkers, then it's Z as a *theory* of causation that should be rejected, not causation as such. Perhaps there is some other

DOI: 10.4324/9781003306382-12

theory of causation which *can* be applied to human behaviour. 'Cause' might not, in itself, be a problem. Maybe it's the immutable, deterministic, outside-time-and-space thing that's the problem. Perhaps this whole gloomily rigid picture is a mistake.

10.1 The argument

The idea of 'causal law' attracts some of the most forceful rhetoric in the literature:[2] fixed, context-free, linear, deterministic, mechanistic, immutable, prediction, control, necessary connection, beyond space and time. The messaging here is transparent: to speak of 'causal laws' is to speak of the exceptionless. If A causes B, there's no escape. A *always* causes B, whatever the circumstances. You can't avoid, deflect, divert, detour, alter, prevent. Free will goes out the window. People acting purposively – on the basis of reasons, motives, goals, and meanings – gets knocked on the head. This is one of the reasons why many authors argue that causality *cannot* apply to human affairs. The *cannot* here is the metaphysical 'cannot' (Thomasson 2020). It allegedly tells us something fundamental about people-in-the-world. At the ontological baseline, human beings aren't causal.[3]

Qua physical objects, of course, people *are* subject to causation. Why did this person die? She fell from a balcony. She had a brain tumour. She drowned. These are, uncontroversially, causal explanations. Why did she donate money to the cystic fibrosis charity? Her son has cystic fibrosis. She is an altruistic person. She was virtue-signalling to her friends. Uncontroversially, these are not causal explanations. Except that, as we'll see in Section 10.5, quite possibly they are. Still, anti-cause metaphysicians do draw a line somewhere in this vicinity. People falling off balconies: causal. Gravity. People contributing to a cystic fibrosis charity: not causal. Altruism.

My strategy in this chapter will be slightly different from the one adopted in the other chapters of Part II. Up to now, I've suggested that qualitative metaphysical sentences don't make sense unless they are construed as expressivist commitments rather than reality-describing statements. Here, I will suggest that 'human beings aren't causal' makes sense, but that (construed as reality-describing) it's absurd. It is so clearly at odds with the way we talk, think, and behave that it's difficult to see why anyone would regard it as plausible. Language is dense with causal verbs and connectives (Gilquin 2010). The 'human cognitive system is built to see causation as governing how events unfold' (Sloman & Lagnado 2015: 224). Causal language, sometimes unrecognised as such, is constantly used in the social sciences, even in qualitative studies (Maxwell 2021). When you abandon ontological dogmatism and (as Wittgenstein suggests) just look – assembling reminders – you can't fail to notice the stream of constant causality which flows through everything we do, including how we make sense of each other (Campbell 2020).

But of course people do fail to notice. If they didn't, we wouldn't be having this conversation. So am I attributing that to widespread ontological dogmatism? Yes and no. Yes, in the sense that 'non-causal' claims in qualitative methods writing are often made by authors who don't provide much in the way of argument. No, in the sense that 'just looking' isn't as easy as it sounds. People use causal language – with respect to human beings – all the time, but don't realise they're doing it. As I've said before, we have no difficulty using language, but we're not so good at understanding and describing that use.[4] And if you have a lopsided idea of what causes *are*, or how the word 'cause' is used, or what other causative constructions look like… well, none of that's going to help. Which is why 'assembling reminders' is necessary.

Assume that causal language and causal inference, with respect to human behaviour, really is in current and constant use (obviously, I haven't provided evidence for this yet, but that's coming in Sections 10.3 and 10.4). That does not mean that qualitative metaphysicians cannot say: 'human beings aren't causal', or 'causal concepts cannot be applied to human thought and action'. But if they do say it, I'll construe it – in a Carnapian way – not as a reality-describing statement, but as a resolution, a recommendation, a proposal. I introduced this kind of expressivism in Section 4.6, and in Section 10.6 I'll discuss it in the context of causation. The key point is that, if you're going to give up causes for Lent, then you need to be clear about how exactly that can be done. This is Carnap's proviso. If you're going to adopt a new language (in this case, a non-causal language), you must specify the rules you'll be using; which means (in this case) specifying what kind of causal concepts *won't* be allowed. Immutable laws outside time and space, it goes without saying.[5] But what else?

Before proceeding, I should acknowledge that there isn't a consensus about causation in the qualitative methods literature. Some authors are hostile to the very idea, usually on 'ontological' grounds. Others seem to regard it as a concept that qualitative researchers aren't really interested in. A third group sees causal questions as perfectly legitimate. A fourth is bothered about 'causal *laws*', but they're not always clear about where they stand on non-law causal concepts.[6] It's primarily the first group of authors I'll have in mind, as writers in the other groups have no 'ontological' objection to causality. As for 'laws', I'll be arguing that there are plenty of causal statements in which they have no role at all.

10.2 Three assumptions

The qualitative methodologists who describe causation in such hostile terms make several assumptions which are rarely queried. In this section, I'll discuss three.

[1] There is just *one theory of causation*. I've already alluded to this assumption in the preamble to the chapter, implying that there are several different theories.

[2] The *causal relation is always the same*. If it is true that *A causes B* and *X causes Y*, the A/B relation is the same as the X/Y relation, even if we're not sure how this relation is to be defined.

[3] *Causal statements are generalisations* (including those identified as 'laws'), by definition. Singular causal claims are hardly ever mentioned.

Assumption [1] is straightforwardly false. There is, in fact, a range of different theories of causation, at least five of which are regularly discussed in the literature.[7] Assumptions [2] and [3] are more open to debate, but many philosophers reject both. 'Causal pluralism' – which is the converse of [2] – has been growing in popularity during the last 20 years. As for [3], it is universally recognised that there are singular causal statements ('This particular event, *M*, caused this particular event, *N*'), as well as causal generalisations. The debate here concerns the relation between them. Which is more 'fundamental'? Do singular or general causal statements have some kind of 'priority'?

10.2.1 Theories of causation

In the Z theory of causation, which many qualitative methodologists appear to regard as the only one, causes are identified through causal laws, which are context-free, deterministic, immutable, mechanistic, are aimed at prediction and control, and involve necessary connection. Where to start? There are, in fact, several theories of causation, usually classified into groups, each group consisting of variations on a core concept. For example, we have regularity theories (Mackie 1980), probabilistic theories (Suppes 1970), causal process theories (Dowe 2000), mechanistic theories (Glennan 2009), counterfactual theories (Lewis 1973), causal power theories (Mumford 2009), and interventionist theories (Woodward 2003).[8]

None of these theories has the full set of features rejected by qualitative methodologists. Regularity theories don't involve necessary connection, and they're not mechanistic. Probabilistic theories are similar – not mechanistic, and no necessary connection – but they're also not deterministic. Causal process theories don't involve causal laws, they're not deterministic, and they're not context-free either. Mechanistic theories arguably incorporate a form of necessary connection, but they're not deterministic or context-free. Counterfactual theories are also not context-free or deterministic, nor do they involve causal laws. Interventionist theories say that something is a cause if manipulating it results in a change to something else; but they're not context-free, and don't involve necessary connection. Causal power theories attribute causation to powers of things, so don't involve relations between events. Powers may be fixed, but they don't entail laws, and (once again) they're not context-free or deterministic. None of these theories implies 'immutability'; but, on the other hand, it's not entirely clear what this is supposed to mean.

It's difficult to see where the Z theory comes from. It does not seem to correspond to any theory that has actually been held, at least not recently;[9] but it sounds like a regularity theory combined with a dash of unsophisticated mechanism, plus a few bolt-ons. It's a compilation of things-that-will-make-you-feel-queasy – designed, less with the aim of providing a clear and attributable account, and more with a view to frightening the horses.

10.2.2 Causal pluralism

Most philosophical accounts of causation, including all those listed above, are based on the 'straitjacket' assumption: the view that 'there is a single, unified and all-encompassing metaphysical story to be told as to what causation is' (Psillos 2010: 80). There is no consensus about what that story looks like, but all agree that 'causation' refers to just one kind of relation. It's just that views differ as to the *nature* of that relation. The problem is this: 'there is no theory of causation that is counterexample-free' (Psillos 2010: 134). Each theory states that causation always and necessarily has such-and-such a feature. That's what causation *is*. But in every case – and this is widely acknowledged – it is possible to identify examples of causality that don't fit the theory. In one respect or another, then, all these theories fail.[10]

No surprise, then, that the 'straitjacket' assumption has been questioned, especially in the last 20 years. Perhaps there isn't just a *single* (kind of) thing that causation universally *is*. Perhaps there is more than one causal concept. Perhaps the words 'cause' and 'effect' straddle several different types of relation. Perhaps we have to come to terms with 'causal pluralism' (Godfrey-Smith 2009). And, of course, there are different accounts of what that implies. We have 'causal pluralism' pluralism, so to speak (de Vreese 2010). Still, the basic idea – that causation isn't a singular thing/process/concept/relation – is common to all these accounts.

Here, I will draw on one particular form of pluralism, which can be traced back to Anscombe (1971). In a key passage, Anscombe suggests that possessing the concept *cause* 'presupposes the mastery of much else in the language' (93):

[T]he word 'cause' can be *added* to a language in which are already represented many causal concepts. A small selection: *scrape, push, wet, carry, eat, burn, knock over, keep off, squash, make* (e.g. noises, paper boats), *hurt*. But if we care to imagine languages in which no special causal concepts are represented, then no description of the use of a word in such languages will be able to present it as meaning *cause*.

On this view,[11] the word 'cause' is a way of referring, in general, to different kinds of 'bringing about'. It is a bit like 'common cold', a 'rather loose condition with no single underlying nature' (Psillos 2010: 131), or the term 'pet', a very broad classification referring to different species: cats, hamsters, goldfish, budgies… even snakes. As with 'pet' and 'common cold', the word 'cause' is an extremely useful term, even if it doesn't refer to any one particular type of thing. It permits generalisations of various kinds; it can act as a placeholder for more specific causal verbs (which may not even exist in English); it can be used when we don't know exactly what form of 'causing', what sort of mechanism, was responsible for an outcome; and so on. If this analysis has any traction, it justifies Cartwright's (2004) title, 'Causation: one word, many things', and her claim that 'there is an untold variety of causal relations'.[12]

10.2.3   Singular causal statements

No-one denies we routinely make causal claims referring to single events and sequences. If I say that, last night, I curdled the sauce by adding lemon juice to hot milk, I'm reporting on a particular occasion, and suggesting that (on this occasion) the lemon juice caused the milk to curdle. Of course, it's also true, as a generalisation, that adding an acidic substance to an emulsion can cause curdling, especially if the emulsion is at a high temperature. So we have a causal law (acidic substances curdle hot emulsions), and we have a singular causal claim: last night I curdled the sauce by adding lemon juice to warm milk.

'At the height of the gale, the harbour master radioed a coastguard on the spot and asked him to estimate the wind speed. He replied he was sorry, but he didn't have a gauge. However, if it was any help, the wind had just blown his Land Rover off the cliff.'[13] This is another singular causal statement, but there is no recognised 'law' that gales cause Land Rovers to be blown off cliffs. However, it is generally true that very strong winds can cause even heavy objects to be blown away, or move, or fall, or tip over. So there is often some kind of link between a singular causal event and a general 'lawlike' statement.

Some philosophers think 'singular causal relations obtain because they are instances of a general causal regularity or law'. Others think that

> 'singular causal relations can obtain even if they are not instances of causal regularities or laws, and what makes causal generalizations true, when they are true, is that they correctly describe a pattern of singular instances of causally related events'.
>
> *(Glennan 2011: 789)*

The Z theory seems to imply the first option, claiming that reality is governed by immutable natural laws, with never any mention of singular causal statements, or how they might be justified.

Anscombe (1971) takes issue with this view. It is generally assumed, she says,

> that any singular causal proposition implies a universal statement running 'Always when this, then that'; often assumed that true singular causal statements are derived from such 'inductively believed' universalities... Even a philosopher acute enough to be conscious of this, such as Davidson, will say, without offering any reason at all for saying it, that a singular causal statement implies that there is such a true universal proposition – though perhaps we can never have knowledge of it.

Anscombe argues that singular causal events can be observed (unlike causal laws). For example, the coast guard *saw* his Land Rover being blown off the cliff by the wind. This was not an inference based on knowledge of a general law. And we can *see* things being scraped, pushed, broken, knocked over.[14] It might be doubted whether we can observe comparable events in the social sciences, but we do make singular causal claims about the actions of ourselves and other people (Campbell 2020). 'My financial problems prompted me to close my account.' 'The abuse scarred her for life.' 'He did it because he was jealous.' I will return to this topic in Sections 10.4 and 10.5.

So in contrast to Theory Z, we can say: (i) There are several different theories of causation, including theories that don't talk about deterministic, context-free, immutable laws. (ii) Theories of causation which aim to identify the one universal relation that causality *is* … don't work. There is a variety of different causal relations. (iii) Everyday discourse includes singular causal claims, which are discussed in philosophy, but which don't merit a mention in most qualitative methods texts.

10.3   The language of causation

The aversion to causality that is a feature of some qualitative methods writing seems to be derived, at least in part, from a lack of interest in the linguistics literature. It overlooks the ubiquity of causal language in everyday discourse. As Solstad and Bott (2017: 619) observe, 'Natural languages display a great range of devices that allow us to speak of causal relations.' In this section, I will briefly review some of these devices. A discussion of the uses of the word 'cause' itself is postponed until the next section, for reasons that will emerge.[15]

10.3.1   *Causally specific lexical verbs*

Anscombe's examples (see Section 10.2.2) are *scrape, push, wet, carry, eat, burn, knock over, keep off, squash, make, hurt*. However, there are plenty more, including *move, stop, change, create, build, cut*. According to Schwenkler and Sievers (2022), the latter examples all appear in the top hundred most commonly used English verbs. Moving to the slightly less common, but still very familiar, we can mention *throw, crank, drag, lift, shove, open, close, press, squeeze, crush, gouge, soak, swallow, kick, switch on, pull, break*, and so on.[16] Most of these refer to physical causings; but, importantly, there are plenty of social and psychological verbs too: *frighten, disappoint, amuse, irritate, upset, worry, please, delight, annoy, disgust, embarrass, excite, surprise, anger, astonish*, and lots more.

Causally specific verbs are almost always used in singular causal statements. They tend not to turn up in anything that could be described as a 'causal law'. Verbs of physical causing refer to events in which the causal process can be observed: 'she threw the ball over the fence', 'he dragged the sofa into the corner'. Arguably, the same is true of at least some of the psychological verbs: 'he frightened his little brother by pretending to be a ghost', 'she astonished her father by announcing her engagement'. Some readers will, again, be unwilling to accept that these are causal claims. However, Sections 10.4 and 10.5 will return to the question of the relation between causes and reasons/motives/meanings/beliefs.

10.3.2 General causal verbs

The physical verbs listed in the previous section are 'specialist': they are intrinsically causal, referring to (usually visible) changes, contacts, movements, pressures, and the exercise of force. However, there is a more general group of verbs – they are again very common – which *can* be used in this way, but which are also used in other, non-causal, ways. For example:[17]

(1) Beth *had* a milkshake. (She drank it, moving it from glass to gut)

(2) Jim *got* the keys out of the drawer. (He moved them from one place to another)

(3) Annie *sat* the doll in the chair. (She placed it there, in a sitting position)

Other general verbs that can be used causally include *put, give, use, keep, begin, turn, start, bring, pay, stand, add, send*. All of these are in the top hundred most frequently used English verbs, though most of them are not used to denote causal processes all that often. For example, 'sit' is usually intransitive – Annie sat down, or is sitting on the sofa – but can be transitive, as in (3).

A few psychological verbs also have this dual role: sometimes causal, more often not.

(4) I talked him into it.

(5) She joked her way into the meeting.

(6) They laughed him off the stage.

In these examples, it's not just talking, joking, or laughing. It's bringing about an effect, or triggering a process, by acting in a certain way. These are atypical uses of the verbs concerned, but they are instantly intelligible to anyone with an idiomatic understanding of English.

10.3.3 Periphrastic causative constructions

These are constructions in which a causative verb governs a non-finite complement clause, which can be either an infinitive or participle.[18] The most common verbs used in these constructions are: 'get', 'have', 'make', 'cause'. Two examples:

(7) The teacher made the student extinguish the cigarette.

(8) The teacher got the student reading poetry.

In this construction, 'made' is the CAUSATIVE VERB, and 'the student' is the CAUSEE.[19] A complete list of verbs which can serve as periphrastic causatives has been provided by Wolff and Song (2003). It falls into two groups. The first group includes *block, cause, enable, force, get, help, hinder, impede, hold, leave, let, make*. All of these can be used in constructions where the CAUSEE is either sentient or non-sentient. The second group includes *bribe, compel, convince, incite, influence, inspire, push, prompt, restrict, discourage, persuade*. These can only be used in constructions where the CAUSEE is sentient, and usually human.

All these verbs can be used in periphrastic constructions to signal different causal processes. Consider some examples from Nadathur and Lauer (2020):

(9) Gurung made the children dance.

(10) Gurung had the children dance.

(11) Gurung got the children to dance.

These, as Nadathur and Lauer (3) point out, 'do not describe the same situation or chain of causation'. For example, (9) implies that Gurung used force or authority, and further suggests that the children did not want to dance. In (10), it seems that the children complied with a straightforward instruction or request, without offering resistance. (11) implies that Gurung had to overcome some kind of obstacle in order to achieve his aim. As with the two earlier categories, there are many different types of causal chain that can be referred to, providing further evidence against the view that causes are always of the same kind, and that a singular causal statement always entails a generalisation or 'law'.

10.3.4 Causal suffixes

Verbs can be created morphologically out of nouns and adjectives by using (among other possibilities) suffixes such as *-ise, -ate, -ify, and -en*. The majority of such creations are not causal, but many are, and especially those with *-ise* and *-ate*. Some causal *-ise* verbs are *bowdlerise, lobotomise, vaporise, pulverise, vandalise, cauterise, magnetise, moisturise*. Some *-ate* verbs are *manipulate, incapacitate, defibrillate, refrigerate, exterminate, liberate, obliterate, suffocate*. There are somewhat fewer *-ify* and *-en* causal verbs: *modify, electrify, solidify, crucify, shorten, thicken, strengthen, flatten*.

The examples above all refer to physical causings, but in each case we can identify psychological verbs of causing: *mesmerise, traumatise, familiarise, infantilise; captivate, irritate, disorientate, fascinate; horrify, terrify, gratify; gladden, frighten, dishearten*. Finally, in some cases, but mainly with *-ise*, we find verbs that refer to social causings: *industrialise, criminalise, nationalise, industrialise, privatise*.

10.3.5 Causal connectives

The principal causal connective in English is *because*, but there are several others: *since, as, owing to the fact that, for the reason that*, and so on (there are comparable prepositions such as: *due to, thanks to, because of, as a result of*). These are all 'backward-looking', the specification of the cause following the specification of the effect in the sentence (X happened because Y happened). Additionally, there are 'forward-looking' connectives, such as *so, hence, resulting in, as a result, consequently*. With these, the sentence order is reversed (Y happened, so X happened).

All of these expressions are used non-causally as well as causally. Some languages (French and Dutch have been particularly studied) have rather more specialised connectives, each allocated to a different context.[20] However, the use of 'because' is extremely flexible. This has occasioned considerable debate about different uses of the word, and about different kinds of 'causal' relation. For example, we might distinguish between:[21]

(12) Frank broke his wrist because he slipped and fell.

(13) Liz booked the tickets because she particularly wanted to see Othello.

(14) Benjiro came back because he loves her.

(15) Hiba was angry because her wife had been unfaithful.

Here, I'm tiptoeing round the difference between reasons, motives, and goals, and the question as to whether any of these count as 'causes'. But only for the moment. I will return to such issues in Section 10.5. But it's worth noting, in the meantime, that many writers will accept (12) as genuinely causal, but not (13), (14), or (15), because reasons, motives, and goals are not causal: their relation to the action concerned, or to the state of mind, is of a different kind. Such writers might refer instead to a non-causal response, grounded in webs-of-belief, 'meanings', interpretations, cultural norms, or social expectations.

10.3.6   Disposition ascriptions

There are many English words (I will focus on adjectives, but many have corresponding nouns) which ascribe a disposition: *soluble, indelible, immovable, combustible, fragile*. To assign a disposition to something is to refer to the possibility of its participation in a causal process. To suggest that an object is fragile, for example, is to claim that it is likely to break if dropped or struck. 'Every disposition has a causal basis' (McKitrick 2004: 111).

In addition to terms for physical dispositions, there are numerous adjectives which are applied to people: reserved for 'ascription only to things with minds' (Mumford 1998: 2). A short selection: *shy, friendly, brave, irascible, honest, untrustworthy, truthful*. There are also several which can be applied either to physical things or – let's say metaphorically – to people's psychological characteristics: *flexible, robust, resilient*, and so on. Ryle (1949) thought that *all* mental ascriptions were disposition ascriptions, so that beliefs, desires, and sensations would also count as dispositional, but this is not a popular view now.

The literature on the metaphysics of disposition is extensive; but my primary objectives here are, first, to draw attention to the 'pervasive nature of dispositional discourse' (Mumford 1998: 3) and, second, to show that there is a 'prima facie case for accepting that dispositions and causes are deeply interrelated' (Handfield 2009: 3). As with other aspects of causal language, this raises the question of whether beliefs and actions can be explained causally. On the face of it, the use of disposition terms suggests they can, but this is by no means the consensus view.

10.4   'Cause' and corpus

The word 'cause' is itself part of causal language, and recent philosophy has taken considerable interest in how it is used in everyday discourse by people other than philosophers. In particular, there have been a number of experimental ('x-phi') studies designed to identify the criteria governing this use.[22] One unexpected finding from these studies is that the ordinary use of 'cause' appears to have a normative dimension. It is more likely to be used when the outcome to be explained is problematic in some way, and/or when someone is deemed to have behaved wrongly or inappropriately. The precise significance of these findings is still being debated, but there seems to be little doubt that many ordinary uses of the word 'cause' are sensitive to 'outcome valence' (that is, they are prompted by undesirable or unusual events and circumstances).

Sytsma *et al.* (2019) add corpus evidence from COCA to the experimental studies. They looked at the nouns occurring most frequently after the phrase 'caused the…'. I undertook a similar analysis more recently and got pretty much the same result (although the number of 'hits' varies slightly from those identified by Sytsma *et al.*). The top ten are *death, problem, accident, crash, deaths, explosion, fire, crisis, collapse,* and *loss*. So I agree broadly with Sytsma *et al.* that 'cause' is frequently directed at negative outcomes: 'outcome valence has a substantial effect on ordinary causal attributions' (219).[23]

We get a similar result when looking at the nouns following 'cause of the', with 'cause' as a noun rather than a verb. The top ten hits are *problem, crash, fire, accident, disease, explosion, war, crisis, problems, death*. This is an almost identical list. So the conclusion that one main function of 'cause' is its use with negative outcomes appears to be justified, irrespective of whether 'cause' is a verb or a noun.

The adjectives commonly preceding the noun 'cause' also exhibit a pattern. Some of these adjectives are relevant to the sense of 'cause' as a project or campaign (*good, lost, worthy, noble*). If we set these aside (with 'probable cause', a legal term), the top ten hits are *leading, major, underlying, primary, main, real, possible, proximate, exact, likely*. These all refer to an item that is being singled out – from a range of other possible contributing factors – as particularly significant. For example, there are a number of factors which contribute to global warming, but 'mankind is the primary cause of that warming' (web source, COCA). Similarly, psychological factors exacerbate palmar hyperhidrosis, but 'it is generally accepted now that the underlying cause is physiological' (COCA). So the combination of one of these singling-out adjectives with the word 'cause' is used to identify the most causally salient factor.

One further point of interest from Sytsma *et al.* (2019). They compared the COCA profiles of 'caused the' and 'was responsible for the'. The two profiles are similar, but they differ in one respect. 'Caused the' is used mainly where something non-human brought about the outcome, while 'responsible for the' is more likely to be used when the causal agent is a person, group or organisation. 'Thus, it is relatively rare that people make claims such as "the malfunctioning brakes are responsible for the accident" but rather speak of malfunctioning brakes causing accidents' (223). This might well be another reason why some writers resist the idea of causation in human affairs: they associate 'cause' with inanimate factors like malfunctioning brakes.

In summary, empirical studies suggest that the use of the word 'cause' is associated with circumstances in which (i) the outcome is negative, and/or (ii) there is reason to identify the 'underlying' or 'primary' factor, and/or (iii) the causal agent is not sentient. These are not hard-and-fast rules but rather usage preferences. It is not as if 'cause' is strictly reserved for situations in which all three boxes are ticked, and there are plenty of circumstances in which none of them are. For example, consider the question:

(16) What caused Scrooge to change his mind?

This was, of course, a positive change of mind: from selfish and miserly to generous and charitable, so it's not a negative outcome. Nor does the question imply a single 'underlying' cause; there were, in fact, several contributing factors (three ghosts, for a start). Moreover, the question of whether the relevant factor(s) involved a 'what?', or a 'who?', or both, is left entirely open. So the three usage preferences *are* preferences. They are not a set of conditions definitively nailing down the 'meaning' of 'cause'.

Moving on from Scrooge to the case of Doris and Violet, what do we make of these?

(17) What Doris said caused Violet to change her mind.

(18) Doris got Violet to change her mind.

(19) What Doris said persuaded Violet to change her mind.

(20) What Doris said made Violet change her mind.

(21) Violet changed her mind because of what Doris said.

As with Scrooge, the change of mind might not be negative, and the responsible agent is a person. Some writers might object to (17), but these statements all appear to be narrating the same kind of process: Doris saying something that resulted in Violet's change of mind. Unlike (17), examples (18) to (21) do not include the word 'cause', but that doesn't mean that the process being described isn't causal. (19) is an example of a causally specific lexical verb (Section 10.3.1), while (18) and (20) are examples of the periphrastic causative construction (Section 10.3.3).

So we can speak of 'causal processes' and 'causation' in sentences like these, even if the use of the word 'cause' is generally associated with circumstances that meet one or more of the three conditions. On this line of thought, 'causation' is simply a way of referring to all these different types of 'bringing about' (a superordinate term, as Anscombe suggested). We *can* talk about causes without using the word 'cause', because language provides us with a wide range of devices for describing many different types of causal process.

10.5   Reasons and causes

It has been said (Millikan 1993) that one of the few achievements of contemporary analytic philosophy is the acceptance of Davidson's (1994) thesis that reasons *are* causes.[24] Davidson's view has recently been challenged by several writers, including Alvarez (2010), Tanney (2013), and Schumann (2024); but a majority of philosophers think that suggesting a reason why someone acted as they did is, as Davidson argued, to make a causal claim.

But it's still worth asking: are reasons causes or not? It's not clear what the question amounts to. If we're asking whether the *word* 'cause' would be used when referring to reasons… well, it might or it might not. 'Cause' *tends* to be reserved for certain kinds of circumstance, as explained in Section 10.4: negative outcome, primary/underlying factor, or non-sentient agent. But these are not hard-and-fast rules. They are sociolinguistic observations. Alternatively, if we're asking whether attributing reasons is a form of causal language, the examples in Section 10.3.5 suggest it could be, given that 'because' is used in a variety of explanations, including those which (apparently) explain-by-giving-a-reason.[25] But it's not obvious what would count as confirmation of this.

So split the question into two. [A] In what circumstances might we use 'cause' to refer to someone's reasons? [B] Do reasons figure in causal language?

[A] Reasons are ascribed to human agents, so of the three conditions in which 'cause' is routinely used – negative outcome, primary/underlying factor, non-sentient agent – the third does not apply. To what extent, then, might the other two conditions justify the use of 'cause' in reason-giving? Consider:

(22) Why did Asami push Kaia off the cliff?

It makes a considerable difference whether the push was prompted by Asami's well-known loathing of Kaia, or whether it was self-defence when Kaia attacked her. In such a case, it does make sense to ask what caused Asami to push Kaia off the cliff. In other words, what was the primary contributing factor. Was she motivated by malice? Or was it fear, and the desire to prevent Kaia assaulting her? Perhaps we'll never know. Still, in this case at least, it seems there's an argument for saying that Asami's reason for acting in the way she did is the action's cause. From among the possible reasons she may have had, *this* was the one that counted.

That's one kind of situation in which we might be inclined to talk of 'cause'. Another is where there is evidence that the person concerned is genuinely mistaken about what she believes to be her reason for an action, belief, or decision. There is plenty of evidence to suggest that this kind of situation is not as rare as one might imagine (Miyazono & Bortolotti 2021). One influential paper by Nisbett and Wilson (1977) is still cited. It reports on a study in which a majority of participants offered a demonstrably inaccurate account of their reasons for preferring one type of stocking, compared to three other types.[26] In fact, all four types were identical, but the participants still explained their choice by reference to greater softness, superior knit, and so on. The four types of stocking were arranged in piles, and the selections overall showed a marked right-hand preference. If we call the furthest left A, and the furthest right D, the distribution of choices across participants was: A = 12%, B = 17%, C = 31%, D = 40%. So the question as to what prompted the choice is intriguing, but possibly it had something to do with left-right ordering (although, when participants were asked later whether position had played any part in their preference, the suggestion was routinely rejected). So:

(23) Why did Francine choose the stockings in pile D?

Here again, we have circumstances in which we might use the word 'cause'. What *caused* Francine to make the choices she did (23)? We're interested in the 'real' or the 'underlying' cause; and the factor which looks as if it might have prompted Francine's selection – display order – is something she was not aware of. She was aware only of 'quality' considerations, apparently confabulated, when asked to give a reason for her choice.[27]

So there do seem to be circumstances in which we use 'cause' to refer to someone's reasons – generally, where we want to ask what the primary, or underlying, precipitating factor was. Asami claims she was motivated by self-defence. Francine says she preferred the sheerness of the D-stockings. But are these claims warranted? Do they identify the *real* cause? Do they identify the *underlying* cause?

[B] Consider (24). There are several different ways of conveying the same information:

(24) Financial problems prompted Danielle to close her account.

(25) Danielle closed her account because of financial problems.

(26) Danielle's reason for closing her account was financial problems.

(27) Financial problems were the reason Danielle closed her account.

(28) Why did Danielle close her account? Financial problems.

(29) Financial problems caused Danielle to close her account.

Again, there might be philosophical resistance to (29), but it's not something that would excite comment in ordinary circumstances. As for the other alternatives, there is little to choose between them. At most, there are some delicate nuances; and, generally, they seem indifferent to any proposed distinction between 'cause' and 'reason'. In all cases, the account-closing is attributed to an antecedent state of affairs. 'Was it a cause? Was it reason?' What's the difference? One thing resulted in another thing.[28]

Now compare:

(30) Trevor has taken his umbrella because it's been raining all morning.

(31) The pavement is wet because it's been raining all morning.

Are we going to say that (30) refers to a reason, but (31) refers to a cause? The syntax does not appear to make any such distinction. In both cases, one state of affairs is attributed to another state of affairs. In both cases, the rain has resulted in a change of condition. The pavement is now wet, where before it was dry. Trevor is now with umbrella, where before he was without.

Reader: Look, (24) to (28) all refer to Danielle's reasons. It's just that some of them use what you call 'causal language' to do it. The syntax is immaterial. (30) states Trevor's reason. (31) refers to a cause. How it's expressed is neither here nor there.
Me: What about (29)?
Reader: That's an imprecise way of talking about Danielle's reason. I wouldn't put it that way myself.
Me: So on what basis do you distinguish between a sentence that's referring to a cause, and one that's referring to a reason?
Reader: If we're talking about somebody's action, decision, or belief, then it's a reason. Pavements getting wet is causal.
Me: So this is a metaphysical *fiat*. If it involves mental states, it's a reason. If not, not.
Reader: Well, *fiat* begs a few questions, but I make the distinction on metaphysical grounds, yes.[29]
Me: Okay, but in both (30) and (31), we have an antecedent circumstance leading to a different state of affairs. So there's a relation of *some* kind between the rain and the later situation. But presumably the 'reason' relation is different from the 'cause' relation?
Reader: Yes. Exactly that.
Me: So can you explain what that difference is?
Reader: Well, to start with, a decision on the basis of a reason is a consequence of how the individual concerned interprets the situation. The meaning she assigns to it.
Me: But all you've done there is redescribe the antecedent circumstance (the interpretation) and the new state of affairs (the decision). And you've called the latter the 'consequence' of the former. But you haven't explained *how* the first leads non-causally to the second.[30]

Reader: But they're *obviously* different. A cause is inanimate. It's a force. A push, a pull, a chemical reaction. Something like that. A reason is when you have beliefs, desires, interpretations, and meanings.

Me: But I haven't denied that there are different ways of getting from an antecedent circumstance to a new situation. The wind blew the Land Rover off the cliff, Danielle closed her account owing to financial problems, Violet was persuaded by Doris. What I'm asking about is the process that gets you from A to B when it's a *reason*; and why *that* process isn't 'causal'. You can say reasons are different if you like. But you still haven't explained how.[31]

Qualitative writers who stick with the cause/reason distinction are a bit vague about the answer to the question posed here. If *this* explanation specifies a *reason*, what's the relation between the antecedent circumstances and the subsequent decision/action? The interpretation or the meaning is antecedent, and the change of state is the action. But how exactly does the one lead, non-causally, to the other?

One author says that the 'interpretive position assumes the social world is constantly being *constructed* through group *interactions*, and thus social reality can be understood via the perspectives of social actors *enmeshed* in meaning-making *activities*' (Hesse-Biber 2017: 6; my italics). Here, Hesse-Biber goes full-on causal. Or, if you disagree, you have to explain how construction, interaction, being-enmeshed, and activity can be construed non-causally. Another example (my italics again):

> [E]xplaining a given belief or action requires citing the other beliefs that *inform* it. This means viewing human behavior as the *product* of a *process* of *creative agency* or *(weak) reasoning*. But the explanation of beliefs *in light of* reasons is logically incompatible with the determinism of general causal laws.
>
> *(Bevir & Blakely 2018: 35)*

Here we have two causal terms, 'product' and 'process', and several vague ones: 'inform', 'creative agency', '(weak) reasoning', and 'in light of', each of which could also be construed causally.

So my answer to the question 'Do reasons figure in causal language?' is: 'Yes, of course'.[32] Indeed, to refer to reasons is to refer to one type of causality. The antecedent circumstances which causally bring about the new state of affairs are immensely varied. There can be many different types of 'external' situation: the rain that prompts umbrella-taking, the remarks that prompt a change of mind, the joke that prompts laughter, the financial problems that prompt account-closing. Or we can switch to 'internal' states – attitudes and dispositions – and talk about the dislike of getting wet that prompts umbrella raising, the fear of assault that brings about the pushing, the gullibility that leads to a change of mind, the sense of humour that laughs at *that*... and thousands more.[33]

Perhaps the linguistic devices that 'allow us to speak of causal relations' (Solstad & Bott 2017) should rather be described as devices that refer to 'bringing about relations'. After that, it doesn't really matter whether you say *this* bringing-about is a reason, or whether you say *that* bringing-about is a cause. Only those with an 'ontological' reason for doing so will want to insist on one or the other.

10.6   Expressivism and causal language

The language of causation cannot be applied to human beings, at least as far as their beliefs, decisions, intentions, reasons and actions are concerned. In one respect, the key word here is *cannot*. It's use here shows that this is a metaphysical claim – it's certainly not an empirical one – more specifically a modal metaphysical claim. 'Debates in metaphysics often revolve around questions about what could, must, or could not be the case... These are all modal questions' (Thomasson 2020: 1). For a neo-Carnapian like Thomasson, modal claims 'do not function to describe or track special modal features of reality... Instead, they serve as perspicuous ways of mandating or enforcing, reasoning with, and renegotiating rules' (6). The fact that the italicised claim above is in the indicative doesn't mean it's a description of anything. It does not refer to 'reality', not even 'modal reality'. The 'force of a speech act... is not to be read off its mood, whether imperative, indicative, or interrogative' (Langton 2015: 6). Modal claims included. 'Descriptive' cannot be inferred from 'indicative'.[34]

So, if not a description of 'modal reality', then what? A resolution, a recommendation, a proposal. A bid to change the rules of the game. Recall Carnap's concept of a language framework. What I've tried to do in Sections 10.3 to 10.5 is provide evidence for the claim that causal language is ubiquitous, even in the context of human thought and action. But supposing that's true, it doesn't prevent someone adopting a different language, or recommending that the rest of us should. In this case, the proposal is that a new language – free of causal terms and other reference to causality – should be adopted by qualitative researchers, at least in the context of thoughts, beliefs, reasons, actions. The fact that this proposal is couched in the indicative, with the modal 'cannot', does not entail that it is a description of 'ontological' reality. It's more like saying: 'Tell you what... let's ban castling in chess.'

There is one proviso. You have to explain how this will work. If you're going to adopt a non-causal language (in the context of thought and action), you have to specify the proposed new rules clearly. The key question is going to be: what causal terms and concepts will not be allowed? An obvious first move is presumably to ban any reference to causal *laws*, or anything that smacks of the deterministic and the invariant. That won't be a problem: most of this chapter has been about singular causal statements (we can let philosophers worry about whether those *entail* 'laws' or not). So what else?

We presumably have to rule out certain kinds of enquiry. Like asking: 'What prompted the selection of stockings in pile D?' This looks like a question about cause, in which case it would be off the agenda. 'The participant said that she chose pile D because the stockings were softer. That's her experience, that's her interpretation. That's all we're interested in.' What *caused* her to select that pile, under the new rules, is not an askable question. The same would go, presumably, for why Asami pushed Kaia off the cliff. Wishing Kaia harm is understandable, given her web of belief and previous experience, even if it's not morally justifiable. On the other hand, pushing Kaia in self-defence is understandable too. But which of these motives was the primary cause, the real cause, the underlying cause, is not something we're interested in. This is qualitative research, not a court of law.

More generally, we have to rule out studies which leave open the possibility that the researcher's view of the participant's 'real' motives (reasons, intentions) will ultimately diverge from the participant's own view. This restriction is consistent, of course, with the preference for participants' 'meanings' as the source of thought and action; but in Carnap's terms, that's exactly what it is – a preference. It can't be justified ontologically. It is derived, not from a metaphysical truth, but from the researcher's wish to abandon 'causal' talk and limit herself to 'meaning' talk. It's a self-denying ordinance. The point of the ontological 'arguments' is to pressure others into adopting the same self-imposed restrictions.

Abstaining from certain kinds of research question, and from 'positivist' methods, is the easy part of adopting the non-causal Carnapian framework. There's a fair amount of work to be done on the detail as well. To what extent do those adopting the non-causal framework permit themselves the use of causally specific lexical verbs, causal suffixes, periphrastic causal constructions, causal connectives, and disposition terms (Section 10.3)? A ruling will have to be made. Can all of these be reinterpreted as non-causal? If so, on what basis?

The word 'cause' itself will obviously be steered clear of.

10.7 Concluding remark

The non-causal preference is associated with certain values. Qualitative researchers are those who 'trust' participants, who acknowledge their 'free will', who don't seek to 'predict and control' them, who don't engage in 'deception'. All of which is fine. It's not that I regard these principles as wrong, or that I want to prevent researchers from proceeding in whatever manner they see fit. But I don't think any of this can be justified 'metaphysically'; and I don't think other people should feel obliged, on so-called 'ontological' grounds, to adopt the same restrictions. If you want to go ahead with a non-causal ball and chain round your leg, that's okay by me (though I suspect it will be harder than you imagine). But don't badger me with 'metaphysical' reasons why I should do the same.

Notes

1 It goes something like this. Quantitative research is based on positivism. Positivists adhere to realism. They believe that a single, uniform, objective reality exists 'out there'. This invariant reality is governed by immutable laws, outside time and space. It is deterministic and mechanistic. Positivists assume that every science has to establish general causal laws. They believe that the researcher's aim is to discover these laws in order to control and predict. This implies finding necessary causal connections. But human behaviour cannot be subsumed under immutable, mechanistic causal laws.

This is a mash-up of Sparkes & Smith (2014), Ou *et al*. (2017), Bevir & Blakely (2018). Qualitative methods for sports science, nursing, and political science, respectively. Here, I'm not really bothered by the f-positivist assumptions attributed to... well, no-one in particular. I covered all that in Chapter 2. My interest now is in the structure of the argument.

2 In fact, it's hard to escape the impression that much of the hostility to causal laws, and causation in general, is based on imagery more than argument. Take 'mechanistic', for example. This word is used without reference to the recent literature on 'the new mechanical philosophy' (Glennan 2017), and on its own it has a scary feel. People hear the sound of clanking. Similarly for 'predict and control'. In the absence of further elaboration, it sounds authoritarian. And then 'uniform', 'invariant', 'immutable'. Images of serried ranks, all dressed in the same way and doing the same thing. Little wonder students opt for something less spartan.

3 See, for example, Bevir & Blakely (2018). It's worth observing, though, that 'in practice, almost all qualitative researchers implicitly make causal claims, for example about what factors have "influenced", "shaped", "formed", "brought about", etc. some outcome' (Hammersley 2012: 72).

4 See section 3.1.

5 It's not obvious what 'outside time and space' means in this context. Does it just mean that causal laws are unchanging? Or does it mean that they are non-spatio-temporal 'entities', like God? Or does it mean that they are abstractions? If the latter, then other things are also 'outside time and space': propositions, numbers, relations, concepts, and so on. Since I don't really understand what writers who say that causal laws are 'outside time and space' are getting at, I will quietly forget about it.

6 That is, causal concepts that do not obviously implicate laws or regularities. These will be discussed in the sections that follow, especially 10.2.3.

7 A good introduction is Illari & Russo (2014).

8 Beebee *et al*. (2009) is an excellent and comprehensive anthology.

9 Moreover, references to the philosophy of causation originating later than the 1960s are scarce. For example, Bevir & Blakely (2018) cite Ayer, Hempel, and Davidson; and that's about it. Honourable exceptions include Hammersley (2012), Mason (2018), Maxwell (2021).

10 'We can find objections and counterexamples to show that any given account fails to capture at least some situations that we would consider causal' (Illari & Russo 2014: 249). The 'straitjacket' assumption is another version of Wittgenstein's 'craving for generality': an account that covers *every* case.

11 My own view is akin to Anscombe's, and partially derived from it. See Section 10.5.

12 Some authors have discussed causal pluralism in the context of the social sciences, for example Reiss (2009), Crasnow (2011), and Maxwell (2021).

13 Attributed to the *Aberdeen Evening Express*, but possibly apocryphal.

14 Hume said that a connection between cause and effect is not observable. But the causal connection is not an 'extra thing' – any more than 'beside-ness' is an extra thing that we observe when we see two people sitting beside each other. We don't see: one person + another person + beside-ness. Rather 'we just observe that the first person is beside the second person. Similarly, Ducasse argues, when one event causes a second, we observe the first event, the second event, and the fact that they are causally related' (Glennan 2011). Of course, it's possible to be mistaken about what (we think) we observe, just as it's possible to be mistaken about the length of the lines in the Müller-Lyer diagram (Section 9.3).

15 The literature on the linguistics of causation is extensive, so my remarks will only scratch the surface. My principal aim is to emphasise that causal constructions are ubiquitous in everyday discourse. The idea that human affairs are somehow, and in some respect, *non*-causal seems bizarre once you recognise this. Gilquin (2010) is an accessible text.

16 Many of these verbs are more common than 'cause' itself. 'Break; is an example (Rose *et al.* 2021).

17 These examples are taken from Schwenkler & Sievers (2022).

18 The syntactic difference between this category and the previous one is as follows. In 'He got the keys out of the drawer', the verb 'got' is followed by a direct object and a prepositional *phrase*. In 'He got the student to read poetry', it is followed by a direct object and a non-finite *clause*.

19 See Gilquin (2010) for an extended discussion.

20 See especially Pit (2003).

21 See, for example, Girju & Moldovan (2002), Mulligan (2011).

22 One frequently cited example is Knobe & Fraser (2008), but others include Hitchcock & Knobe (2009), Sytsma *et al.* (2012), and Livengood *et al.* (2017).

23 Sytsma *et al.* compared the nouns following 'caused the', with the nouns following eight expressions such as 'made the', 'led to the', 'precipitated the'. Only the last of these was accompanied by similarly negative outcome words: *crisis, war, decline, conflict, demise,* and so on. 'This means that the effect we recorded for "cause" seems to be rather specific' (221).

24 Davidson's paper was first published in 1963 and was a response to an argument – associated with Melden (1961), among others – implying that reasons are *not* causes. He did not think that psychology is, or can ever be, like the physical sciences. His discussion was based on an analysis of singular causal statements.

25 Skow (2016) thinks that 'because' is ambiguous, with one sense reserved for reasons-for-action, and a second sense reserved for non-reason causes. But I suspect this just boils down to: 'sometimes we use it for one thing, sometimes for another'. It's not clear how he justifies the ambiguity claim.

26 There's an entertaining TED talk by a psychologist who has conducted several similar experiments. See https://www.ted.com/speakers/petter_johansson.

27 'Confabulation' is not only used in cases of pathology. For example, Miyazono & Bortolotti (2021) use it for two different types of situation: those involving 'unusual circumstances', and those which are 'everyday cases'. The Nisbett & Wilson study fits the latter category. See also Hirstein (2005).

28 Similar remarks can be made about sentences (17) to (21) from Section 10.4.
29 As always, 'metaphysical grounds' signals that a preferred rule of grammar is being referred to. 'If we're talking about somebody's action or belief, then it's a reason. Pavements getting wet is causal.' Read this as a proposal about the use of language. If we're explaining someone's action, the word to use is 'reason'. If we're explaining pavements getting wet, it's 'cause'. Not *because* there's an antecedent metaphysical difference. Rather, insisting on the rule creates the *illusion* of a metaphysical difference. 'The apparent "structure of reality" is merely the shadow cast by grammar' (Hacker 2021: 235).
30 This is a version of an argument I associate with Michael Martin (2000), who quotes Charles Taylor explaining why 'interpretation has nothing to do with causality' (165). 'An emotion term like "shame", for instance, essentially refers us to a certain kind of situation, the "shameful", or "humiliating", and a certain mode of response, that of hiding oneself, of covering up, or else "wiping out" the blot. That is, it is essential to this feeling's identification as shame that it should be related to this situation and give rise to this type of disposition. But this situation in its turn can only be identified in relation to the feelings it provokes; and the disposition is to a goal that can similarly not be understood without reference to the feeling experience' (Taylor 1987: 64). As Martin notes (167), this passage 'fairly bristles with causal concepts'. I would cite 'humiliating', 'give rise' and 'provokes' in particular.
31 Davidson's challenge was to explain the 'mysterious' special connection between someone's reason for an action and the action itself 'without invoking the notion of cause' (Glock 2014: 43).
32 A different view is that of Mercier & Sperber (2018), who think reasons are for public consumption, 'a way to establish reputations and coordinate expectations' (143). They *don't* think that beliefs and actions are uncaused. It's just that what drives/precipitates an action is not a reason. Beliefs and actions, on their view, have causes, but they reserve the word 'reason' for an act of self-justification.
33 Campbell (2020): 'We can and do give causal mentalistic explanations, and the notion of causation here is exactly the same as the notion of causation that we use in the physical case' (18).
34 See Section 4.6 for more extensive comments.

References

Alvarez, M. (2010). *Kinds of Reasons: An Essay in the Philosophy of Action*. Oxford: Oxford University Press.
Anscombe, G. E. M. (1971). *Causality and Determination*. Cambridge, UK: Cambridge University Press.
Beebee, H., Hitchcock, C., & Menzies, P. (Eds.). (2009). *The Oxford Handbook of Causation*. Oxford: Oxford University Press.
Bevir, M., & Blakely, J. (2018). *Interpretive Social Science: An Anti-Naturalist Approach*. Oxford: Oxford University Press.
Campbell, J. (2020). *Causation in Psychology*. Cambridge, MA: Harvard University Press.
Cartwright, N. (2004). Causation: one word, many things. *Philosophy of Science*, *71*(5), 805–819.
Crasnow, S. (2011). Evidence for use: causal pluralism and the role of case studies in political science research. *Philosophy of the Social Sciences*, *41*(1), 26–49.
Davidson, D. (1994). Actions, reasons, and causes. In M. Martin & L. C. McIntyre (Eds.), *Readings in the Philosophy of Social Science* (pp. 675–686). Cambridge, MA: The MIT Press.

de Vreese, L. (2010). Disentangling causal pluralism. In R. Vanderbeeken & B. D'Hooghe (Eds.), *Worldviews, Science and Us. Studies of Analytical Metaphysics: A Selection of Topics from a Methodological Perspective* (pp. 207–223). Singapore: World Scientific Publishing.

Dowe, P. (2000). *Physical Causation*. New York: Cambridge University Press.

Gilquin, G. (2010). *Corpus, Cognition and Causative Constructions*. Amsterdam: John Benjamins.

Girju, R., & Moldovan, D. (2002). Mining answers for causation questions. *AAAI Technical Report SS-02-06*, 15–25.

Glennan, S. (2009). Mechanisms. In H. Beebee, C. Hitchcock, & P. Menzies (Eds.), *The Oxford Handbook of Causation* (pp. 315–325). Oxford: Oxford University Press.

Glennan, S. (2011). Singular and general causal relations: a mechanist perspective. In P. Illari, F. Russo, & J. Williamson (Eds.), *Causality in the Sciences* (pp. 789–817). Oxford: Oxford University Press.

Glennan, S. (2017). *The New Mechanical Philosophy*. Oxford: Oxford University Press.

Glock, H.-J. (2014). Reasons for action: Wittgensteinian and Davidsonian perspectives in historical and meta-philosophical context. *Nordic Wittgenstein Review, 3*(1), 7–46.

Godfrey-Smith, P. (2009). Causal pluralism. In H. Beebee, C. Hitchcock, & P. Menzies (Eds.), *The Oxford Handbook of Causation* (pp. 326–339). Oxford: Oxford University Press.

Hacker, P. M. S. (2021). *Insight and Illusion: Themes in the Philosophy of Wittgenstein*. 3rd Edition. London: Anthem Press.

Hammersley, M. (2012). Qualitative causal analysis: grounded theorizing and the qualitative survey. In B. Cooper, J. Glaesser, R. Gomm, & M. Hammersely (Eds.), *Challenging the Qualitative-Quantitative Divide. Explorations in Case-Focused Causal Analysis* (pp. 72–95). London: Continuum.

Handfield, T. (2009). The metaphysics of dispositions and causes. In T. Handfield (Ed.), *Dispositions and Causes* (pp. 1–30). Oxford: Clarendon Press.

Hesse-Biber, S. N. (2017). *The Practice of Qualitative Research: Engaging Students in the Research Process*. Third Edition. Thousand Oaks, CA: Sage.

Hirstein, W. (2005). *Brain Fiction: Self-Deception and the Riddle of Confabulation*. Cambridge, MA: The MIT Press.

Hitchcock, C., & Knobe, J. (2009). Cause and norm. *The Journal of Philosophy, 106*, 587–612.

Illari, P., & Russo, F. (2014). *Causality: Philosophical Theory Meets Scientific practice*. Oxford: Oxford University Press.

Knobe, J., & Fraser, B. (2008). Causal judgments and moral judgment: two experiments. In W. Sinnott-Armstrong (Ed.), *Moral Psychology*, Volume 2: *The Cognitive Science of Morality* (pp. 441–447). Cambridge, MA: MIT Press.

Langton, R. (2015). How to get a norm from a speech act. *Amherst Lecture in Philosophy, 10*, 1–33.

Lewis, D. (1973). Causation. *The Journal of Philosophy, 70*(17), 556–567.

Livengood, J., Sytsma, J., & Rose, D. (2017). Following the FAD: folk attributions and theories of actual causation. *Review of Philosophy and Psychology, 8*(2), 274–294.

Mackie, J. (1980). *The Cement of the Universe*. Oxford: Oxford University Press.

Martin, M. (2000). *Verstehen: The Use of Understanding in Social Science*. New Brunswick, NJ: Transaction Publishers.

Mason, J. (2018). *Qualitative Researching. 3rd Edition*. London: Sage.

Maxwell, J. A. (2021). The importance of qualitative research for investigating causation. *Qualitative Psychology, 8*(3), 378–388.

McKitrick, J. (2004). A defense of the causal efficiency of disposition. *SATS Nordic Journal of Philosophy, 5*(1), 110–130.

Melden, A. I. (1961). *Free Action*. London: Routledge & Kegan Paul.

Mercier, H., & Sperber, D. (2018). *The Enigma of Reason: A New Theory of Human Understanding*. London: Penguin.

Millikan, R. G. (1993). *White Queen Psychology and Other Essays for Alice*. Cambridge, MA: MIT Press.

Miyazono, K., & Bortolotti, L. (2021). *Philosophy of Psychology: An Introduction*. Cambridge, UK: Polity Press.

Mulligan, K. (2011). Because, because, because. In M. Cozzi, M. Herbstritt, & G. Lini (Eds.), *Seventh European Congress of Analytic Philosophy* (pp. 180–181). Milan: Società Italiana di Filosfia Analitica.

Mumford, S. (1998). *Dispositions*. Oxford: Oxford University Press.

Mumford, S. (2009). Causal powers and capacities. In H. Beebee, C. Hitchcock, & P. Menzies (Eds.), *The Oxford Handbook of Causation* (pp. 265–278). Oxford: Oxford University Press.

Nadathur, P., & Lauer, S. (2020). Causal necessity, causal sufficiency, and the implications of causal verbs. *Glossa: A Journal of General Linguistics, 5*(1), 1–37.

Nisbett, R. E., & Wilson, T. D. (1977). Telling more than we can know: verbal reports on mental processes. *Psychological Review, 84*(3), 231–259.

Ou, C. H. K., Hall, W. A., & Thorne, S. (2017). Can nursing epistemology embrace p-values? *Nursing Philosophy, 18*, e12173.

Pit, M. (2003). *How to Express Yourself with a Causal Connective: Subjectivity and Causal Connectives in Dutch, German and French*. Amsterdam: Rodopi.

Psillos, S. (2010). Causal pluralism. In R. Vanderbeeken & B. D'Hooghe (Eds.), *Worldviews, Science and Us: Studies of Analytical Metaphysics. A Selection of Topics from a Methodological Perspective* (pp. 131–151). Singapore: World Scientific.

Reiss, J. (2009). Causation in the social sciences: evidence, inference, and purpose. *Philosophy of the Social Sciences, 39*, 20–40.

Rose, D., Sievers, E., & Nichols, S. (2021). Cause and burn. *Cognition, 207*, 104517.

Ryle, G. (1949). *The Concept of Mind*. London: Hutchinson.

Schumann, G. (2024). *Historical Explanation: An Anti-Causalist Approach*. New York: Routledge.

Schwenkler, J., & Sievers, E. (2022). Cause, 'cause', and norm. In P. Willemsen & A. Wiegmann (Eds.), *Advances in Experimental Philosophy of Causation* (pp. 123–144). London: Bloomsbury Academic.

Skow, B. (2016). *Reasons Why*. Oxford: Oxford University Press.

Sloman, S. A., & Lagnado, D. (2015). Causality in thought. *Annual Review of Psychology, 66*, 223–247.

Solstad, T., & Bott, O. (2017). Causality and causal reasoning in natural language. In M. R. Waldmann (Ed.), *The Oxford Handbook of Causal Reasoning* (pp. 619–644).

Sparkes, A. C., & Smith, B. (2014). *Qualitative Research Methods in Sport, Exercise and Health: From Process to Product*. New York: Routledge.

Suppes, P. (1970). *A Probabilistic Theory of Causality*. Amsterdam: North-Holland.

Sytsma, J., Bluhm, R., Willemsen, P., & Reuter, K. (2019). Causal attributions and corpus analysis. In E. Fischer & M. Curtis (Eds.), *Methodological Advances in Experimental Philosophy* (pp. 209–238). London: Bloomsbury Academic.

Sytsma, J., Livengood, J., & Rose, D. (2012). Two types of typicality: rethinking the role of statistical typicality in ordinary causal attributions. *Studies in History and Philosophy of Biological and Biomedical Sciences*, *43*, 814–820.

Tanney, J. (2013). *Rules, Reason, and Self-Knowledge*. Cambridge, MA: Harvard University Press.

Taylor, C. (1987). Interpretation and the sciences of man. In P. Raboinow & W. M. Sullivan (Eds.), *Interpretive Social science: A Second Look* (pp. 33–81). Berkeley, CA: University of California Press.

Thomasson, A. L. (2020). *Norms and Necessity*. New York: Oxford University Press.

Wolff, P., & Song, G. (2003). Models of causation and the semantics of causal verbs. *Cognitive Psychology*, *47*, 276–332.

Woodward, J. (2003). *Making Things Happen: A Theory of Causal Explanation*. New York: Oxford University Press.

11
'TRUE' AND 'TRUTH'

Can we agree that *everybody* uses the word 'true'? And that this includes qualitative methodologists? So whatever the problem is with truth, it clearly doesn't entail that we can't use sentences such as:[1]

(1) The same is true when beginning a research study.

(2) Many of the same suggestions about the title hold true for the abstract.

(3) This is especially true when making judgements about quality.

(4) … although the opposite could also be true.

(5) Unfortunately, as Metzler… noted, the reverse is also true.

In all these examples, 'true' is written without scare quotes, which qualitative writers often use to signal that they are distancing themselves from the concept of truth. I don't detect any embarrassment when the adjective is used in this way, even when elsewhere in the text 'true' gets the same scare-quote treatment as 'truth'. So I take it that, consciously or not, these authors are happy to describe certain claims as *true*.

One of the key distinctions in this chapter is that between 'truth' and 'true'. Obviously, one of them is a noun, the other an adjective, but they are handled differently in qualitative textbooks. 'Truth' is usually treated with either mistrust or hostility, while 'true' seems to be… well, unavoidable. 'Truth' attracts descriptions designed to put you off. 'True' may be treated with suspicion in the philosophical bits, but in the rest of the book it just breezes by. So there's something slightly odd going on here.[2]

DOI: 10.4324/9781003306382-13

There are other distinctions as well, but I'll explain those when we get there.

11.1   Anaphoric uses of 'true'

You've probably spotted what (1) to (5) have in common. In each case, 'is true' (along with its variants: 'could be true', 'holds true') is used anaphorically. The subject of the sentence refers back to something that has already been said:

'*The same* is true'

'*This* is true'

'*the reverse* is true'

'*the opposite* could be true'

'*Many of the same suggestions* hold true'

In none of the examples are we told explicitly *what* claim, assertion, or suggestion is true. To understand any of them completely, you'd have to read the text immediately before it. For instance, (1) is from the Chapter 4 of Merriam and Tisdell (2016). The first three sentences of this chapter read as follows:

> Rarely would anyone starting out on a trip just walk out the door with no thought of where to go or how to get there. The same is true when beginning a research study. You need some idea of what you want to know and a plan for carrying it out.

So the second sentence is, in effect, claiming that: 'Rarely would anyone starting out on a research study just walk out the door with no thought...'. The third sentence, of course, confirms this. A similar trick is performed in each of the other sentences. The predicate 'is true' is attached to an anaphoric noun phrase, so that the reader can work out what statement is being referred to.

This is one function of 'is true' sentences: they make certain kinds of repetition unnecessary. Here's a simple example:

Alfhild: 'The car is filthy.'
Levent: 'That's true.'

Once again, we have an anaphoric expression ('That') combined with 'is true'. It refers back to what Alfhild said. In this context, 'The car is filthy' is the *antecedent*. It is what the *anaphor*, 'That's true', is referring back to. This construction permits Levent to make the same claim as Alfhild, but without having to repeat it.

But what is Levent doing here? Obviously, he's acknowledging Alfhild's statement, and agreeing with it. In this respect, he could have used several different expressions: 'Yes', 'Quite', 'Exactly', 'Uh-huh', 'Right', or just 'True'. Equally, he could have nodded, shrugged, looked sheepish, made a fist-pumping gesture, and so on. Which of these he selects will depend on how he construes what Alfhild has said (for example: observation, accusation, expectation, resignation), and on what he wants to convey (in addition to agreement) by way of response. 'Uh-huh' might convey indifference. 'Quite' could convey the sense of 'And what are you going to do about it?'. 'Yes', might be followed by '... but I promise I'll clean it tomorrow'. These 'convey-ances' are not built into the meaning of the expression concerned; they are just pragmatic reasons for choosing one option or another.

None of the possible responses in the previous paragraph makes a *state-ment*. They convey agreement, in some cases with a hint of resignation, accu-sation, concession, indifference, or whatever. But no *claim* is made. They are not statement-making sentences. They are not sentences at all. 'That is true', on the other hand, *is* a sentence. It does appear to make a claim, on a par with 'That is red', 'That is bumpy', or 'That is peculiar' – each of which refers to something and describes it. So does it make a statement in the way that a nod, 'Quite' or 'Uh-huh' do not? Does it pick something out and describe it?

Park that question for a minute. I'll return to it in Section 11.2. First, con-sider some further uses of 'true':

(6) 'Fossas are native to Madagascar' is true.

(7) That fossas are native to Madagascar is true.

(8) It is true that fossas are native to Madagascar.

(9) Avogadro's hypothesis is true.

(10) Everything Olena says is true.

In one respect, (6) and (7) are very similar to the Alfhild/Levent example. In all three cases, the speaker is aware of what the antecedent is. Levent uses 'That's true' to refer back to 'The car is filthy.' The speaker in (6) knowingly attaches 'is true' to the sentence 'Fossas are native to Madagascar', while the speaker in (7) attaches it to the proposition that-fossas-are-native-to-Madagascar. Constructions such as (7) are not common in everyday English, but they do turn up in academic writing.

Example (8) is similar again, except that the antecedent now follows 'It is true'. Cataphoric constructions of this kind are very common. 'By the time she arrived, Rebecca was over an hour late.' The antecedent in this case ('Rebecca') follows the cataphoric pronoun ('she'). With (8) we have an inver-sion of (7), the difference being that 'is true' comes first (since English requires a grammatical subject, 'It' is added), and the antecedent proposition follows it. However, in all cases – Alfhild/Levent and (6) to (8) – the antecedent is, so to speak, available. The speaker knows what it is being said, or has been said.

This antecedent 'availability' does not necessarily apply to (9) and (10). You can know that Avogadro's hypothesis is true, even if you're none too sure what the hypothesis is.[3] And, on the face of it, (10) refers to all Olena's statements, including those she has not yet made. In both (9) and (10), the predicate 'is true' is attached to a *noun phrase*, rather than a noun clause, sentence, or proposition. The noun phrase doesn't spell out, explicitly, what it is being described as true. Instead, it refers to a certain claim (9), without actually specifying it; or it generalises to an indefinite set of claims (10), without specifying any of them.

So we've looked at five types of 'is true' statements.[4]

[A] 'That's true', or an equivalent, following an antecedent not specified by the speaker (Alfhild/Levent).

[B] '… is true' attached to a sentence which precedes it (6).

[C] '… is true' attached to a proposition, which may precede or follow it (7, 8).

[D] '… is true' attached to a noun phrase which refers to a single, but unspecified, claim (9).

[E] '… is true' attached to a noun phrase which refers to a set of unspecified claims (10).

We can now return to the question I parked earlier, and ask it about all five types, not just [A]. On the face of it, examples (6) to (10) refer to *something*, and describe it using the predicate 'is true'. But are they really doing the same kind of job as sentences like these:

(11) That's askew.

(12) That fossas are native to Madagascar is well known.

(13) It's well known that fossas are native to Madagascar.

(14) Avogadro's hypothesis is complicated.

(15) Everything Olena says is interesting.

11.2 Predicates and properties

Austin (1975: 1) says that philosophers have long assumed that the business of a 'statement' can only be to 'describe' some state of affairs, or to 'state some fact', which it must do either truly or falsely. In the same vein, Wittgenstein (2009) suggests that we should make 'a radical break with the idea that language always functions in one way, always serves the same purpose' (§304)... 'We don't notice the enormous variety of all the everyday language games, because the clothing of our language makes them all alike' (II xi: 335). They both warn against succumbing to the 'descriptivist fallacy' (Macarthur 2010: 81).

In Section 4.6, I gave some examples of indicative sentences that weren't in the fact-stating or describing business. These were mostly 'rules' of some kind: game rules ('Black moves first'), instructions ('Dowel A is inserted into hole B'), definitions ('A bachelor is an unmarried man'), etiquette ('The bride and her parents are photographed before the groom and his'), and so on. These are all indicatives, with a subject-predicate structure, but they don't *report* on anything.

Here, we're dealing with a slightly narrower idea – subject-predicate sentences of the form:

(NA) NOUN PHRASE + *is* + ADJECTIVE

'Avogadro's hypothesis is complicated.' 'That's askew.' 'Everything Olena says is interesting.' In cases like (11) to (15), the predicate is used to ascribe a property to a subject. Complicatedness to Avogadro's hypothesis. Being askew to *that*. Being interesting to everything Olena says. So the parked question is slightly modified: does the predicate 'is true' ascribe the property of truth? If 'The road is bumpy' ascribes the property of bumpiness to the road, does '"Fossas are native to Madagascar" is true' ascribe the property of truth to the claim that fossas are native to Madagascar?

In one sense, clearly yes, given that '...is true' is a predicate, attached (in this case) to 'Fossas are native to Madagascar'. So, obviously, it's saying that this sentence is true. But the critical question is this one: is being-true a *property* of something in the way that being-bumpy is?

Come at this question, initially, from a different angle. Consider some expressions that are, colloquially, the 'opposite' of 'is true', especially those that start with 'That is...'. We can say 'That's not true', of course, or 'That's false'; but there are plenty of more idiomatic options: 'That's baloney', 'That's tripe', 'That's rubbish', 'That's cobblers', 'That's poppycock', and several less savoury ones. These are all NA constructions, but do they all ascribe a property to what 'That' refers to (usually something somebody said)? Obviously, a number of these expressions are non-literal. If you say 'That's tripe', or 'That's cobblers', I don't expect to see the stomach of a cow, or a collection of shoe repairers. But does either of them ascribe a *property* (however metaphorically identified) to what I said? Doesn't it seem more natural to take them as expressions of disagreement? In which case, isn't it equally natural to take 'That's true' as a similar kind of expression: expressing agreement, rather than property-ascribing?

Reader: Okay, so all these expressions are figurative. Big deal. They're all equivalent to 'That's false' or 'That's not true'. The first ascribes the property of falseness, while the second says that the property of truth can't be ascribed.

Me: Ah. Your craving for generality is still in good working order, I see.

Reader: I don't think a craving for generality is unreasonable. It's a test of a theory that it works for all the relevant cases. Better than having exceptions all over the place.

Me: Equally, I could argue that acknowledging exceptions is better than customising the data to fit the theory.

Reader: All I'm saying is, I don't think the 'poppycock' paragraph is much of an argument.

Me: It's not an argument. It's an object of comparison. It's there to plant a seed of doubt. To jump-start the thought that there might be an alternative way of thinking about 'is true'.

Reader: I see. Jump start. Well, maybe you need to up the voltage.

The idea that the NA construction is *always* in the business of ascribing a property to the subject is one of the assumptions that Austin and Wittgenstein think is questionable. It is an example of the view that 'language always functions in one way, always serves the same purpose'. If it's true of the majority of NA sentences, it must be true of all of them (there's the craving). Even so, there are three branches of philosophy in particular where doubt has been cast on the idea that NA is always a property-ascribing construction: ethics, truth and aesthetics (aka 'the good, the true and the beautiful').

'That action is morally right.' 'That statement is true.' 'That painting is beautiful.' By analogy with 'That road is bumpy' or 'That shirt is blue', it is easily assumed that being right, being true, and being beautiful are qualities/properties of actions, statements, or artworks. Wittgenstein frequently warns us against this kind of assumption. On the first page of Wittgenstein (1967), for example, he suggests that words such as 'beautiful' and 'good' are liable to be misunderstood. 'Beautiful' is 'an adjective, so you are inclined to say: "This has a certain quality, that of being beautiful".' But once you assume that being-beautiful *is* a property, you are committed to specifying what kind of a property it is: to defining beauty, or making weighty remarks on the nature of beauty, or identifying what all beautiful things have in common.

For Wittgenstein, this sort of thing is a dead-end. He thinks it's more useful 'when discussing a word' to 'ask how we were taught it' *(ibid)*. If you ask how a child learns to use 'beautiful' or 'good', 'you find it learns them roughly as interjections' (2).[5] It's not surprising, then, that many contemporary philosophers influenced by Wittgenstein have adopted various forms of expressivism in relation to truth, aesthetics, and ethics.[6] On views of this kind, predicates such as 'is good', 'is true', and 'is beautiful' do *not* ascribe properties. Instead, they express things, propose things, recommend things, prescribe things.

Here's an image of how that works. Syntax has a limited range of options, the most common in English being subject-predicate indicatives. Everyday language-games, however, have a 'prodigious diversity' (Wittgenstein 1963: Part II, 224ᵉ).[7] We remain unconscious of this diversity 'because the clothing of our language *[the limited syntactical options]* makes everything alike'. Different types of language-game are 'clothed' in the same syntactic dress. We think that we're always describing and referring, because that's what the syntax suggests, but in fact we're not.

On this line of thought, then, we think that we're ascribing a property when we use the predicate 'is true', but in fact we're not.

11.3   Deflationary accounts of 'is true'

The idea that 'is true' does not ascribe a property, but instead does something else, can be classified as a 'deflationary' account. It deflates the assumption that 'X is true' makes a *descriptive claim*. There are a number of different versions of deflationism, some defended by writers who also adopt expressivism (it depends on what kind of 'something else' the 'is true' predicate is said to be doing).[8] In this section I'll avoid technicalities, and give a rough sketch of what deflationism generally entails.

What are often referred to as the 'traditional' theories of truth – correspondence, coherence, pragmatist, and so on – all have one thing in common. They all argue that to say 'x is true' is to claim that 'x has a particular characteristic'. In Horwich's (2010) notation:[9]

[T] 'p' is true ↔ 'p' has such-and-such characteristic

Deflationary theories have a different schema:

[D] 'p' is true ↔ p

To put it roughly: to say that 'p is true' is equivalent to saying 'p'. In saying 'It's true that grass is green' you have said *no more* than if you had said 'Grass is green'. So the predicate 'is true' does not ascribe a property to the sentence (or proposition) 'Grass is green'. Instead, it says exactly the same thing. This is why the schema is 'deflationary'. It knocks the stuffing out of the idea of truth and makes it seem trivial. As Horwich (2010: 4) notes: 'Not surprisingly, those philosophers with a penchant for profundity have found it disappointing.'

However, the equivalence of 'p is true' and 'p' does *not* mean that they have the same *uses*. To employ the first, you need to understand 'is true', which is clearly not necessary for the second; and deflationists usually suggest that 'p is true' has functions over and above what the [D] equivalence with '*p*' directly implies. The equivalence lies, not in their respective functions, but in this: if you believe that *p*, then you also believe that '*p*' is true. And vice versa: if you believe that '*p*' is true, then you also believe that *p*.

This equivalence represents the core of all deflationary theories, since it effectively 'defines' truth for the deflationist. If you adopt one of the 'traditional' theories – correspondence, say – you're claiming that 'is true' ascribes a new property to *p*, namely correspondence with reality. If you favour deflationism, there is *no* new property, and 'corresponds with reality' is not a theoretically rich proposal, but merely a 'long-winded synonym' (Blackburn 2017) for 'is true'. On this view, '*p* is true' states just what *p* alone states, although it will be used in different circumstances. Truth, for the deflationist, is not 'a *deep* concept and should not be given a pivotal role in philosophical theorizing' (Horwich 2010: 16).[10] However, that does not mean that 'is true' isn't a really useful predicate.

We've already seen some of these uses in Section 11.1. The anaphoric use is especially flexible. It can be used to signify agreement in various contexts: a sudden realisation ('Heavens, that's true!'), concessions ('That's true, but…'), confirmation ('She's right, that's true'), emphasis ('It's true!'), conclusions ('That must be true'), and more. But it doesn't have to signify agreement. It turns up in conditionals ('If that's true, then…'), optatives ('I wish it were true'), hypotheticals ('She acts as though it's true'), subjunctives ('That could be true'), and so on. All of these avoid repetition of the sentence/claim concerned.

However, avoiding repetition is not the predicate's only function. For example, there are generalisations ('Everything Olena says is true') and indirect reference ('Avogadro's hypothesis is true'). In such cases, how would we say what we want to say if 'is true' were not available?

With Avogadro, we would have to know what the hypothesis is. The beauty of 'is true' here is that we can assure someone that, whatever the hypothesis is, let's call it *p*… then *p*. And we can do this without knowing, or having forgotten, what *p* actually is. With Olena, it would have to be something like: 'For any claim, "*p*", that Olena makes, *p*.' Or: 'If Olena says that *p*, then *p*.' Expanding on this kind of formula would involve an indefinite series of possible statements Olena might make. 'If Olena says that grass is green, then grass is green.' 'If Olena says King Charles has abdicated, then King Charles has abdicated.' And so, endlessly, on. Here, it's not repetition that's being avoided, as with anaphoric uses, it's awkward logical formulae, or indefinitely long disjunctions of possible statements.

So 'is true' is a really handy expression, which enables us to say succinctly things that would otherwise require awkwardness and/or impossible length. This is its main function. It does not ascribe a property, but it does permit certain kinds of statement. In Carnapian terms, we've been comparing two languages: English as it is, a language that possesses 'true' and its cognates, and an imaginary English that does not possess them. The Carnapian question is: which of the two languages is more useful? The fact that English-with is able to make certain claims more easily than English-without is a *prima facie* reason for supposing that English-with is the better bet. Of course, someone may be able to come up with a reason for thinking that English-without has advantages that outweigh the virtues of English-with. But unless and until that happens, the usefulness question appears to tilt the other way.[11]

Whatever else, on the deflationary view, the value of 'true' has nothing to do with the 'deep' nature of truth, or the importance and weight of the property which 'is true' ascribes. This is nothing more than a very useful linguistic device.[12]

11.4 Uses of 'truth'

I've focused on the adjective so far, but how about the noun? Has it got the weight and depth that, on the deflationary view, 'true' hasn't? The top 30 hits for 'truth' (4,0) in COCA fall into a number of easily recognisable categories. 'Absolute', 'universal' and 'ultimate' I'll deal with in Section 11.5. Meanwhile, comfortably the most common uses are in the context of 'telling the truth', or 'speaking the truth'.

(**16**) You should always tell the truth.

(**17**) Our job is to speak truth to power.

(**18**) I told Martin the honest truth.

These are all variations on what I've already said about 'is true'. Example (16) is a generalisation, that in English-without-truth might be rendered as: 'For any proposition, p: if p, do not deny that p.' Instead of (17) we might say. 'Our job, if p, is to say to those in power: p.' (Our job, if grass is green, is to say to those in power: 'Grass is green'. Our job, if grass is blue, is to say to those in power: 'Grass is blue.' And so on.) With (18), we have a different species of indirect reference. It's equivalent to (19), with 'honest' acting as an intensifier, a sincere assurance that p (where 'p' is what I told him).

(**19**) I said to Martin 'p'; and, honestly, p.

These examples suggest that there is no significant difference between the uses of the noun and the uses of the adjective. They are both linguistic devices for conveying certain types of information more simply and succinctly. We find the same thing with the other main category of 'truth' collocates: seek, search for, discover, reveal, pursue.

(20) She searched for the truth about her childhood.

(21) He revealed the shocking truth about his partner's disappearance.

(22) If you work hard, you will discover the truth about writing.

English-without would deal with (20) by saying: 'She wanted to learn more about her childhood, and to believe "*p*" only if *p*.' As for (21), we might have: 'He asserted '*p*' about his partner's disappearance; and *p*. It is shocking that *p*.' And then (22): 'If you work hard, you will draw a conclusion about writing, namely '*p*'; and *p*.

So, again, English-with-'the truth' is a more economical, less repetitive, and more elegant way of making claims that would otherwise be clumsy and verbose. In this respect, the noun and the adjective have more or less the same job. They can even pull the same trick, illustrated in (21) by 'shocking'. The noun can be qualified by an adjective – 'sad', 'inconvenient', and 'ugly' are the most common, according to COCA – while the adjective can be qualified by an adverb: 'That's true, sadly.' 'That's true, fortunately.'[13]

Surely, however, there are some references to truth which are not consistent with deflationism? Aren't there contexts in which truth really is a 'deep' concept, whatever Horwich says? Don't the sciences aim at something more significant than the 'truth' of 'grass is green'. Something that's supposedly universal, objective, and unchanging? In what sense is *that* kind of truth no more than a linguistic trick, designed to enhance economy and succinctness? Surely truth in the 'objective' sense refers to something which – if it did exist – would be more profound than a mere 'device'? Okay, well, let's see.

11.5   P-truth *versus* C-truth

Objectivity, said Lincoln and Guba, is a chimera. I don't think any qualitative methodologists have been bold enough to make the same claim about truth, although Lincoln and Guba (2013) do describe truth as 'coercive', and there are occasional references to the idea that 'truth claims are a form of terrorism' (Rosenau 1991: 78).[14] Still, qualitative metaphysicians tend to distance themselves from the whole idea, with plentiful use of scare quotes.[15]

Here's a list of the adjectives often applied to the kind of truth that qualitative methodologists are nervous about:

universal, absolute, indisputable, objective, *true*, definitive, generalizable, unchanging, decontextualised, permanent, unshakeable, foundational, ultimate, single, unitary, unified, big-T, with a capital T.

I'll refer to truth described like this as P-truth (the concept of truth attributed to 'positivists'). Now here's a list of the adjectives applied to the kind of truth that is acceptable (probably):

> contingent, situated, local, embodied, partial, personal, special, community, subjective.

I will refer to these as examples of C-truth (the concept of truth endorsed by constructivists and various other qualitative methodologists). The contrast between P-truth and C-truth is frequently alluded to in the qualitative literature. Three examples:

- Narrative researchers are interested in personal truth ahead of objective truth, because for them 'objective Truth' does not exist. (Papathomas 2017: 37–8)
- The data we gather reflect *contingent* moments rather than some 'true' (decontextualised) truth … We argue for the need to grapple more with the question of how we claim the value of the situated, partial, and contingent, in contrast to the 'true truth' (Braun & Clarke 2021).
- Positivist and Post-Positivist perspectives maintain a belief in a singular big-'T' understanding of truth… [Other paradigms] believe in multiple interpretations of a little-'t' understanding of truth (Brennen 2022: 12).

Now, just for a moment, pretend that this isn't the kind of stuff you've read a dozen times before in texts on qualitative research. Imagine that these are not seen-it-all-before tropes – the ones your eyes just slide off as you skim the philosophical bits before we get to methods. And then ask yourself: what on *earth* are these people talking about? Big-T truth, universal truth, unchanging truth, absolute truth, *true* truth? None of these expressions is ever explained. It's just assumed that the reader will understand what 'Big-T truth' (or 'absolute truth', or 'true truth') refers to. It's simply taken for granted that expressions which a philosopher would struggle to decode are instantly intelligible to the research novice.

In the absence of a clear explanation of how these terms are being used, or what they refer to, the most likely impact on the reader is a series of vague mental pictures. A dogma inscribed on stone tablets, a single slab of exceptionless edicts issued by people ('positivists') who never change their minds. These are intimidating images, rather than justifications. They function as deterrents rather than reasons.

It would help if we were given some examples of these single, big-T, absolute, indisputable, unchanging, ultimate truths; but we so rarely are. It would also help if qualitative writers quoted the 'positivists' who allegedly beat the drum for big-T truth, but that rarely happens. However, we're assured that 'positivism has its roots in the nature of inquiry that was developed for the physical sciences, where "truths", "laws", and "axioms" wait to be discovered' (Croker 2009: 6). On this view, 'positivism' and P-truth are derived from an interpretation of the physical sciences.

But isn't there something right about that? Surely, the sciences *do* aim at truth. Don't they aim at truths which are universal across time, across space, and independent of context? [16] Isn't this an eminently justifiable reading of the concept of P-truth, the concept qualitative metaphysicians try to articulate, in order to question or criticise it? Don't physical scientists think their laws of nature are capital-T true?

11.6 Felicitous falsehoods

In a word, no. Science deals in laws that 'lie' (Cartwright 1983), 'rampant and unchecked idealization' (Potochnik 2017), 'false theories' (de Regt & Gijsbers 2017), and 'felicitous falsehoods' (Elgin 2017).[17] These untruths are not occasional exceptions, atypical examples of scientific theories and models. They are run-of-the-mill stuff: ubiquitous, dime-a-dozen. 'The products of science are for the most part not things we believe to be true' (Potochnik 2017: 20). It's not that truth is *never* the aim; it's that science has other aims as well, and truth is frequently an also-ran in the quest for understanding, explanation, or prediction. This may sound slightly mad. From a scientific perspective, don't understanding, explanation and prediction *depend* on truth? Well, it turns out not. In fact, they frequently depend on falsehood.

A few examples:

Idealisations. Scientific laws frequently describe the behaviour of things that don't exist. Across all the sciences, including biology and sociology, there are many idealised 'entities' and 'calculated nonentities' (Azzouni 2017: 108): weightless inextensible cords, infinitely deep oceans, frictionless planes, isolated populations, point masses, and more. For example, the gas laws define the relation between the pressure, volume and temperature of a gas. The ideal gas law is:

$$pV = nRT$$

where p is pressure, V is volume, T is temperature, R is a constant, and n is the amount of gas. The gas presupposed in the ideal law is composed of dimensionless, spherical molecules that do not exhibit mutual attraction. There is no such gas. No molecules are spherical; every object exists in space; and every object is subject to gravitational attraction. 'Nonetheless, the ideal gas model is integral to thermodynamics' (Elgin 2017: 15). Another example: the pendulum discussed in physics textbooks is not subject to either gravity or friction, and it is attached to a string which has zero mass. This is not the case, obviously, with any real pendulums. Scientific laws 'do not hold true for virtually any real systems' (Potochnik 2017: 24).

Ceteris paribus laws. Many, perhaps most, physical laws are not universally true. They have exceptions. They are subject to a *ceteris paribus* clause ('other things being equal'), the clause that says: provided no other factors are involved. Take the law of universal gravitation. This says that two bodies exert a force between each other which varies inversely with the square of the distance between them, and varies directly as the product of their masses. So 'does this law truly describe how bodies behave? Assuredly not' (Cartwright 1983: 57). One reason why not is this: electricity also exerts forces inversely as the square of the distance. Some bodies are electrically charged, so the force between them combines gravitational force and electrical force. So the 'universal' law of gravitation has a *ceteris paribus* clause. It's not true if the bodies concerned are electrically charged.

Approximations. According to qualitative methodologists, 'positivists' think that laws like Newton's second law of motion ($f = ma$) are unchanging, and they also believe that *all* 'truths' are like that. The trouble is, Newton's laws are *not* unchanging. They break down at or near the speed of light, and also in quantum physics. Since Einstein, it has been recognised that they are only approximations. They work well – to a sufficient degree of accuracy – at planetary distances and with bigger-than-particle sizes, but outside those parameters, not so much. 'Decontextualised' they're not. Although Barad suggests that Newton's laws do not 'govern' the macroscopic world (Section 8.10), they are still very much in use – even though they are not true.[18] Any 'positivist', I imagine, would know that. But in the absence of names and citations by qualitative writers, it's hard to be sure. Equally, it's hard to be sure which 'positivists' think *all* truths are like $f = ma$.

Tractability. In some cases, an equation is known which could, in principle, predict the behaviour of a phenomenon – for example, a fluid flowing across a solid object – but which cannot mathematically be solved (i.e. the impossibility of a solution can be demonstrated). Since this equation cannot be used in practice, assumptions *known to be false* are introduced. These permit a mathematically tractable equation to be used instead (Morrison 1999). The solution to this tractable equation is only an approximation, but in certain conditions that is close enough. The approximation works in a way that the 'truth' doesn't and can't.[19]

These examples are all variations on a theme. Approximations, idealisations, assumptions known to be false, and things known not to exist, are an endemic feature of science.

Science routinely transgresses the boundary between truth and falsity. It smooths curves and ignores outliers. It develops and deploys simplified models that diverge, sometimes considerably, from the phenomena they purport to represent… Even the best scientific accounts are not true.

(Elgin 2017: 14)

And the widespread recognition of these transgressions has 'resulted in philosophical investigations of science all but abandoning the conception of laws as universal, exceptionless regularities' (Potochnik 2017: 24). So 'decontextualised truth' (Braun & Clarke 2021) presumably refers to the views of people who haven't abandoned it. I'm not sure who, but send in your suggestions.

So the idea that science always aims at 'big-T-truth' looks unconvincing; and appealing to the 'scientific' concept of truth – single, ultimate, absolute, universal, decontextualised, and so on – is an untenable way of marking the boundary between 'positivism' and constructivism, or between 'positivism' and whatever alternative you happen to favour.

None of this implies that scientists have little interest in truth, although it's true that they don't pay much attention to 'truth' as an elevator word. Think of it this way: science doesn't set out to determine whether it's true that *'p'*; it sets out to determine whether *p*. If you discover that *p*, you have *ipso facto* discovered that *'p'* is true. The hard work goes into finding out what's in the world, how it behaves, how it changes, how it functions. In principle, this is no different from finding out whether there's coffee in the pot, or how a door handle works, or what happens if you plant azaleas in alkaline soil; but it's like that squared, cubed, or tesseracted.

Reader: Here we go again. Coffee pots and azaleas. They aren't relevant to the question of whether there's an objective, decontextualised truth.
Me: Ah. Right. I missed the footnotes that point that out.
Reader: It doesn't need footnotes. It's obvious.
Me: Is it, though? Does the novice researcher reading these books think: Ah, they're obviously not talking about azaleas. They're talking about… well, what, exactly?
Reader: Significant matters. Research findings. People's experience.
Me: See, I think that does need footnotes. Something that explains where you're drawing the boundary between what's significant and what isn't. And why you're drawing it *there*.
Reader: It's the difference between objects and people. There are no objective, decontextualised truths about people's experience.
Me: But I've just been suggesting that objective, decontextualised truths aren't typical of the natural sciences, either. Felicitous falsehoods, and all that.

Reader: Scientific equations may include approximations, but they still generalise. And they're still deterministic in form. People interpret things
differently. You can't describe their experience with equations.

Me: I don't remember saying that you can. My point was that science
doesn't look for 'absolute', 'decontextualised', 'indisputable' *truth*
in the way many qualitative methodologists assume.

11.7   Situated truth

It remains to take a quick look at the other side of the P-truth/C-truth opposi-
tion. If it's difficult to make sense of ultimate, absolute, decontextualised,
'true' truth, is it any easier to make sense of local, partial, contingent, special,
situated, personal, community, subjective truth? One problem, of course, is
that these terms don't appear to be synonymous; and at least one of them,
'special', means anything or nothing. So I'll consider a brief selection, rather
than attempting a comprehensive analysis.

11.7.1   One general comment

As with P-truth expressions, these terms are mostly used without any explanation. It is just assumed (apparently) that the reader, even the research novice,
will understand them. There are few accounts of what 'contingent truth', 'subjective truth', and the rest, refer to; and, even when there is an extended discussion – Stajduhar *et al.* (2001) is one example – it usually focuses on abstract
debates between (in this case) the advocates of 'objective truth' and the
champions of 'subjective truth'. There is no analysis of what either expression
might mean.

11.7.2   Subjective truth

Stajduhar *et al.* (2001) might well object to this claim. But their paper is an
interesting one because it illustrates so many of the 'subjective truth' tropes.
For example (74):

Embracing subjective forms of truth acknowledges and values a multiplicity of experiences, supports the view that knowledge is contextual and
localised, celebrates the value of differing discourses, supports a diversity
of values, and honours ambiguity and uncertainty.[20]

In my terms, there is no attempt to say what 'subjective forms of truth' are, or
to give any examples. All we're told is that 'embracing' them *acknowledges*
something, *values* something, *celebrates* something, *honours* something, and
supports various things. There's nothing about *why*; and the ideas supported

and valued comprise an assortment of further concepts in need of explanation: the localisation of knowledge, a multiplicity of experiences.

Here is one point at which the Carnapian take on qualitative metaphysics becomes crystal clear. This is a manifesto for qualitative methods, not a philosophical argument. It calls for a bustling chaos of opinion without any attempt to judge, dissect, investigate, classify, analyse, order, adjudicate. The chaos is to be 'valued' rather than appraised, 'celebrated' rather than scrutinised. Lack of clarity and precision will be a virtue (honouring ambiguity), as will abstaining from logical inference (honouring uncertainty).

Now all of this is perfectly fine. You're welcome to make whatever proposals you like. What is *not* fine is the implication that there is a metaphysical account of truth – the 'subjective' account – which justifies this manifesto and which, on ontological and epistemological grounds, trumps 'objective truth'. To make the point again: you can make any recommendations about the conduct of qualitative research that take your fancy; what you *cannot* do is claim that there is a fundamental metaphysical fact about reality – the nature of truth – that somehow obliges the rest of us to adopt them.

11.7.3   Local truth

'In qualitative studies', says Postholm (2008: 146) '… often only one phenomenon or one setting is researched. This means that a contextual, local "truth" is developed that is difficult to transfer directly to other settings.' This is typical, but puzzling. Why does studying one setting mean that a 'local truth' is developed? Why doesn't it just mean that the researcher has some understanding of that setting? A different setting may well yield different results. Do we describe *that* as 'two local truths'? If so, why is this better than 'the truth about two different settings'? Or: 'an account of two different settings'? And note that Postholm uses inverted commas. What does this imply? An unease about the word 'truth'? If so, why use it? Why feel obliged to employ 'truth', but then qualify it with '….'? If 'local truths' are not *really* truths, why bother with the word at all?

We're back to the Carnapian take. What 'truth' does here is flag up the acknowledging, the valuing, the honouring and the supporting. Treat this setting, treat this locality, with respect. It has as much right to be taken seriously as any other. But you don't need 'truth', construed as a vague metaphysical postulate, to make this point. If your research shows that, in this setting, p, you don't need to worry about 'truth'. It will take care of itself. If you have found that p (in this setting), you have *ipso facto* found that 'p' is true (in this setting). You can recommend acknowledging, valuing, and honouring without having to appeal to a metaphysical version of 'truth'. Your proposals can't be justified with metaphysical conundrums, and don't need to be. And 'truth', not being a 'metaphysical' term, is ill-equipped to do the job anyway.

11.7.4 Embodied truth

Similar remarks apply here. Gomersall *et al.* (2012), discussing an interviewee who has type 2 diabetes and is a smoker:

> 'Lauren's statement "I'm enjoying those horrible things" portrays cigarettes as enjoyable with this perspective articulated by the "I": "I'm enjoying". This, for Lauren, is therefore a personal, embodied truth: a pleasurable experience of taking the smoke into her body'.
>
> *(388)*

What is the value-added of 'truth' here? Lauren finds smoking a pleasurable experience. So it's *true* that she does. Why is that transformed into 'a personal, embodied truth'? It feels like an intensifier: 'She *really does* enjoy it. I want you to *acknowledge* that, to fully *appreciate* her enjoyment of smoking. It's *important*.' But we don't need metaphysics to get the reader onside with this. It's not philosophy. It's a plea.

11.8   Concluding comments

Three possible responses to this chapter:

This is correspondence theory in disguise, isn't it? Nope. The correspondence theory is about ascribing properties to sentences or propositions. To say that '"p" is true' is to ascribe a property – correspondence with reality – to 'p'. On my view, truth isn't a property, and the predicate 'is true' does not ascribe any sort of property to anything. I haven't proposed a 'theory of truth', and I suspect many scientists don't have a theory of 'truth' either. They are much more interested in working out what X is, where it is, why it is, how it works, what it's made of – just as you're interested in working out where the coffee is. Or have you never been in that situation? If you have, did an aversion to the correspondence theory prevent you looking in the pot?

It's a form of realism, then, given that you're rejecting relativism, local truth, and all the rest. I'm not sure how you work that out – except on the basis of 'If you're not a relativist you must be a realist'. I've questioned 'subjective truth' (and its variations), and I've questioned 'absolute truth' (and its variations), on the grounds that sense can't be made of either of them (unless and until). I've cited writers who point out that science is riddled with fictions and falsehoods. And I've provided reasons for thinking that 'true' and 'truth' are just useful linguistic devices. How is any of that 'realist'? Why does it count as a realist theory of truth? I don't *have* a theory of truth.

You can't not have a theory of truth. Why not? I have assembled reminders about the uses of 'true', and I have sketched its function as a handy linguistic device. Why do I need to weld a theoretical abstraction on to that?

English has plenty of idioms, and they do all that's necessary. 'Corresponds with reality' is just a long-winded alternative to 'is true'. But it's been inflated into a metaphysical 'theory'. Redundant. A synonym posing as an 'explanation'. 'Theories of truth' are idioms with delusions of grandeur.

Notes

1 These quotes are all taken from qualitative research texts. In order: Merriam & Tisdell (2016: 73), Tracy (2020: 93), Patton (2015: 174), Holloway & Galvin (2017: 131), Brennen (2022: 39).
2 For Hacking (1999), 'truth' is another elevator word. He suggests that: 'we ought to attend to the commonplace ways in which we use the adjective, rather than the solemn ways in which we use the noun, "truth". There are also plenty of non-elevated ways in which to use the expression "the truth".' (229).
3 This applies to me – or did until I looked it up. I learned about Avogadro's hypothesis at school, but I had long since forgotten what it actually says. It can now be referred to as Avagadro's law.
4 The earlier sentences can also be classified using this scheme. Sentence (3) is an example of [A]. Sentences (1), (4), and (5) are examples of [D]. Sentence (2) is an example of [E].
5 There is no reason to think that 'true' and 'truth' are also learned through interjections. To imagine they are would be to indulge the craving for generality again.
6 See Price (2013) for some interesting takes on the expressivist theme, including those of Blackburn, Brandom, Horwich, and Williams. Wittgenstein is not the only impetus to exploring non-descriptivism or non-representationalism. There are several others, notably Sellars and Rorty.
7 Another instance where the 1963 translation is more memorable than Wittgenstein (2009), which reads: 'We don't notice the enormous variety…' (the section previously known as Part II, xi: §335).
8 For one account of how deflationism and expressivism fit together, see Brandom (2002), whose own deflationary theory of the use of the word 'true' takes an 'anaphoric' approach. 'So understood, "true" plays a crucial expressive role. Adding such a locution to a language substantially increases its overall expressive resources and capabilities' (103).
9 The two-headed arrow signifies reciprocal implication. For example, $p \leftrightarrow q$ means: if p is true, then q is true; and if q is true, then p is true. An alternative way of expressing the same relation: p if and only if q.
10 In addition to Horwich and Blackburn, I'd recommend (a classic) Strawson (1949).
11 The question about whether English-with-true is more useful than English-without is like the question as to whether a language with numbers is more useful than a language without numbers. If we decide that with-numbers is more useful, the question we then *cannot* ask, according to Carnap, is whether numbers *really*, *actually* exist (see Section 4.3). Similarly, if we decide that English-with-true is more useful than English-without-true, we cannot then ask whether there is something *'out there'* called 'objective truth'.
12 Of the various deflationary theories on offer – Horwich (2010) describes six – I incline towards the prosentential theory (Grover 1992, Brandom 2002). However, the differences aren't massive, and in any case are irrelevant to the very basic discussion here.
13 'Negative' adjectives are more common in this context than 'positive' ones. The same is true of the adjectives used with 'reality' ('stark reality', 'harsh reality', 'grim realities'). See Section 6.3.

14 Most of the qualitative writers who describe this view (e.g. Taylor & Francis 2013) don't actually endorse it. Rosenau herself attributes it to 'skeptical post-modernists', writers such as Derrida, Foucault and Baudrillard. In a similar vein, but from a different tradition: 'declarations of truth beyond tradition' are 'a step towards tyranny' (Mattes *et al*. 2004: 4). Gergen at his most hyperbolic.

15 'I have no use for those who put words like "true" and "truth" in ironical shudder quotes to indicate that the speaker has been liberated from such a discredited idea as truth'. It shows 'little respect for our shared means of communication, the English language' (Hacking 1999: 236).

16 Here's Croker's argument for this view: 'Since positivists believe that there is one universal reality, they also presume that any truths they discover about that reality are equally applicable to other groups or situations, regardless of the context' (Croker 2009: 6). The non-sequitur is a bit exasperating. Croker has not, apparently, considered the possibility that the 'one universal reality' might consist of different bits. *This* bit is X. One truth. *That* bit is not X. Another truth. Why does the X-ness of the first bit have to be generalised to the second bit? Croker's 'one universal reality' seems to be undifferentiated, uniform, blanket grey. Why can't the 'one universal reality' be variegated? Even highly variegated? Or 'dappled' (Cartwright 1999)?

17 Cartwright's title, *How the Laws of Physics Lie*, overeggs it. To lie is to promulgate a falsehood, to do it deliberately, with the intention to mislead. The laws of physics, in Cartwright's view, are deliberate falsehoods, but they are not intended to mislead. 'Deliberate falsehoods play a part in helping scientists to better understand the workings of the world' (Strevens 2017: 37).

18 As Wootton (2016: 568) reminds us: 'Astrophysicists still use Newton not Einstein to plot the orbits of space craft.'

19 This is a common situation: the sheer complexity of a physical process defeats attempts to represent it with complete accuracy. Another example: the equation $d = \frac{1}{2}gt^2$ calculates the distance, d, travelled by an object falling for time t. But you can't use it with pieces of paper, as the interactions between the air and the paper are very complex, and cannot be computed without approximations, abstractions, and simplifications (Tanabe & Kaneko 1994, Howison *et al*. 2019). See also Wilson (2017) on calculating the trajectory of Jack and Jill falling down the hill, 'bump by bump'. Doing this would require 'an accurate assessment of hillside topography, the elastic coefficients pertinent to children, etc., as well as a formidable computer' (xi).

I suspect many qualitative writers underestimate this complexity, assuming that the social world *must* be more complex than the physical world, which 'positivists' (these writers say) believe is deterministic, mechanistic, linear, immutable, context-free, and beyond space and time (Section 10.1). The examples in this section show why that assumption has to be revisited.

20 I must emphasise that this is not the position Stajduhar *et al*. (2001) themselves adopt. They attribute it to other writers.

References

Austin, J. L. (1975). *How To Do Things With Words. The William James Lectures Delivered at Harvard University in 1955*. Second Edition. Cambridge, MA: Harvard University Press.

Azzouni, J. (2017). *Ontology Without Borders*. New York: Oxford University Press.

Blackburn, S. (2017). *Truth*. London: Profile Books.

Brandom, R. B. (2002). Explanatory vs. expressivist deflationism about truth. In R. Schantz (Ed.), *Current Issues in Theoretical Philosophy: Vol 1: What is Truth?* Berlin: Walter de Gruyter.

Braun, V., & Clarke, V. (2021). The ebbs and flows of qualitative research: time, change, and the slow wheel of interpretation. In B. C. Clift, J. Gore, S. Gustafsson, S. Bekker, I. C. Batlle, & J. Hatchard (Eds.), *Temporality in Qualitative Inquiry: Theories, Methods and Practices* (pp. 22–38). New York: Routledge.

Brennen, B. S. (2022). *Qualitative Research Methods for Media Studies*. Third Edition. New York: Routledge.

Cartwright, N. (1983). *How The Laws of Physics Lie*. New York: Oxford University Press.

Cartwright, N. (1999). *The Dappled World: A Study of the Boundaries of Science*. Cambridge, UK: Cambridge University Press.

Croker, R. A. (2009). An introduction to qualitative research. In J. Heigham & R. A. Croker (Eds.), *Qualitative Research in Applied Linguistics: A Practical Introduction* (pp. 3–24). Basingstoke, UK: Palgrave Macmillan.

de Regt, H. W., & Gijsbers, V. (2017). How false theories can yield genuine understanding. In S. R. Grimm, C. Baumberger, & S. Ammon (Eds.), *Explaining Understanding: New Perspectives from Epistemology and Philosophy of Science* (pp. 50–75). Abingdon, UK: Routledge.

Elgin, C. Z. (2017). *True Enough*. Cambridge, MA: MIT Press.

Gomersall, T., Madill, A., & Summers, L. K. M. (2012). Getting one's thoughts straight: A dialogical analysis of women's accounts of poorly controlled type 2 diabetes. *Psychology and Health, 27*(3), 378–393.

Grover, D. (1992). *A Prosentential Theory of Truth*. Princeton, NJ: Princeton University Press.

Hacking, I. (1999). *The Social Construction of What?* Cambridge, MA: Harvard University Press.

Holloway, I., & Galvin, K. (2017). *Qualitative Research in Nursing and Healthcare*. Oxford: Wiley Blackwell.

Horwich, P. (2010). *Truth-Meaning-Reality*. Oxford: Clarendon Press.

Howison, T., Hughes, J., Giardina, F., & Lida, F. (2019). Physics driven behavioural clustering of free-falling paper shapes. *PLoS ONE, 14*(5), e0217997.

Lincoln, Y. S., & Guba, E. G. (2013). *The Constructivist Credo*. New York: Routledge.

Macarthur, D. (2010). Wittgenstein and expressivism. In D. Whiting (Ed.), *The Later Wittgenstein on Language* (pp. 81–95). London: Palgrave Macmillan.

Mattes, P., Schraube, E., & Gergen, K. (2004). Old-stream psychology will disappear with the dinosaurs! Kenneth Gergen in conversation with Peter Mattes and Ernst Schraube. *Forum: Qualitative Social Research, 5*(3), http://www.qualitative-research.net/fqs-texte/3-04/04-03-27-e.htm

Merriam, S. B., & Tisdell, E. J. (2016). *Qualitative Research: A Guide to Design and Implementation*. Fourth Edition. San Francisco: Jossey-Bass.

Morrison, M. (1999). Models as autonomous agents. In M. S. Morgan & M. Morrison (Eds.), *Models as Mediators* (pp. 38–65). Cambridge, UK: Cambridge University Press.

Papathomas, A. (2017). Narrative inquiry: from cardinal to marginal… and back? In B. Smith & A. C. Sparkes (Eds.), *Routledge Handbook of Qualitative Research in Sport and Exercise* (pp. 37–48). Abingdon, UK: Routledge.

Patton, M. Q. (2015). *Qualitative Research and Evaluation Methods: Integrating Theory and Practice*. Fourth Edition. Thousand Oaks, CA: Sage.

Postholm, M. B. (2008). Group work as a learning situation: A qualitative study in a university classroom. *Teachers and Teaching: Theory and Practice, 14*(2), 143–155.

Potochnik, A. (2017). *Idealization and the Aims of Science*. Chicago: University of Chicago Press.

Price, H. (2013). *Expressivism, Pragmatism and Representationalism*. Cambridge, UK: Cambridge University Press.

Rosenau, P. M. (1991). *Post-modernism and the Social Sciences: Insights, Inroads, and Intrusions*. Princeton, NJ: Princeton University Press.

Stajduhar, K. I., Balneaves, L., & Thorne, S. E. (2001). A case for the 'middle ground': Exploring the tensions of postmodern thought in nursing. *Nursing Philosophy, 2*, 72–82.

Strawson, P. F. (1949). Truth. *Analysis, 9*(6), 83–97.

Strevens, M. (2017). How idealizations provide understanding. In S. R. Grimm, C. Baumberger, & S. Ammon (Eds.), *Explaining Understanding: New Perspectives from Epistemology and Philosophy of Science* (pp. 37–49). Abingdon, UK: Routledge.

Tanabe, Y., & Kaneko, K. (1994). Behavior of a falling paper. *Physical Review Letters, 73*(10), 1372–1377.

Taylor, B., & Francis, K. (2013). *Qualitative Research in the Health Sciences: Methodologies, Methods and Processes*. Abingdon, UK: Routledge.

Tracy, S. (2020). *Qualitative Research Methods: Collecting Evidence, Crafting Analysis, Communicating Impact*. Second Edition. Hoboken, NJ: Wiley Blackwell.

Wilson, M. (2017). *Physics Avoidance: Essays in Conceptual Strategy*. Oxford: Oxford University Press.

Wittgenstein, L. (1963). *Philosophical Investigations*. Oxford: Basil Blackwell.

Wittgenstein, L. (1967). *Lectures and Conversations on Aesthetics, Psychology and Religious Belief*. Berkeley, LA: University of California Press.

Wittgenstein, L. (2009). *Philosophical Investigations: Revised 4th edition by P. M. S. Hacker and Joachim Schulte*. Malden, MA: Wiley-Blackwell.

Wootton, D. (2016). *The Invention of Science: A New History of the Scientific Revolution*. London: Penguin.

12

'EXPERIENCE'

'Experience is as real as rock' (Strawson 1994). 'The term "experience" is one of the most obscure we have' (Gadamer 1975). I read both quotes, coincidentally, on the same day. (I don't do autobiography, but this is a chapter on experience. I'm probably obliged.) I was already familiar with Galen Strawson's statement, but I had prised *Mental Reality* off the shelf to do some revision. *Truth and Method* I'd read before, but I didn't recall this bit. I sat there wondering. At first sight, and probably second, it's hard to see how both claims can be correct. So which do I accept?

As it happens, neither. Strawson: at one time I thought of 'real as rock' as a touchstone claim. Not just right but an important point of reference. Now I'm not even sure what he means. Gadamer: depends on who the 'we' refers to. If it refers to philosophers, he might be right. If it refers to speakers of ordinary English,[1] I think he's wrong. A bit complex, yes. Obscure, no.

A lot of this chapter is about ordinary uses of 'experience' (more reminders). There are several different ones, but none of them are obscure. Later, we'll look at what a selection of philosophers have said about 'experience', and what sense can be made of it in the context of qualitative research. Cards on the table. 'Experience' is a word whose functions are mainly, but not exclusively, syntactic. The problems begin if you assume that it's a *referential* expression and try to specify what it refers to. That's a metaphysical fumble. It misrepresents the word's pattern of use and risks a misunderstanding of what's going on in qualitative studies.

DOI: 10.4324/9781003306382-14

12.1   Uses of 'experience'

Qualitative research is often said – and not just by authors who self-identify as 'phenomenologists' – to be the study of experience, or the study of the way people make sense of their experience.[2] The word is not regarded as a 'meta-physical' term itself, and it doesn't usually appear in statements of ontological or epistemological 'belief'. It is taken to refer to what researchers set out to describe (or interpret). That's a pretty vague idea as it stands, but most authors make little or no attempt to get beyond it. Some writers do suggest that 'the concept of experience remains troubling and undertheorized' (Roth & Jornet 2014), but the task of rectifying the deficit is conceived as determining '*what* experience is' (106), and coming up with 'a *theory* of experience'.[3] My view is that this is a mistake. Asking what experience *is* assumes, from the outset, that 'experience' is a referring term. It's a noun, so it has to be the *name* of something.[4] Well, many nouns are. But to suppose that they *all* are is an example of the craving for generality. I do not think 'experience' names anything.

Anyway, here's a list of the main functions I think 'experience' has: place-holder noun, delexical verb, subject of a sentence, reifying term, philosophi-cal antonym word, operationally defined term.[5] Each of them will have a section to itself, but first a quick description.

12.1.1   Placeholder nouns

Are a recognised type of 'vague language' (Channell 1994), sometimes called 'dummy nouns' (Overstreet 1999). The most common in English include 'thing', 'stuff', 'whatsit', 'thingummy', and so on. The linguistics literature gen-erally confines itself to colloquialisms like these; but I'll argue that 'experience' is also used as a placeholder noun, just in a narrower range of contexts.

12.1.2   Delexical verbs

Are transitive verbs which have little semantic content themselves but which can be combined with a wide range of nouns. They include 'have', 'give', 'do', 'get', 'make', 'go' and 'take' (Wang 2016). They're interesting because the nouns they're paired with are unrelated. Having a baby is different from having a look, and both are different from having a dream, a birthday, a chance. I'll be suggesting that the verb 'experience' has a delexical function.

12.1.3   Sentence subject

Many words can be a mass noun or a count noun: 'medicine', 'burglary', 'coffee' (Pelletier 2012). Some of these 'dual-life' nouns are especially interesting when they appear as a mass noun (without a determiner) at the beginning of a sentence. 'Hope', for example, has a function in this position which is different from those it has when acting as a count noun (Paley 2021). 'Experience' is one of these 'dual-life' nouns. At the beginning of a sentence, it has a function which isn't characteristic of its count-noun uses.

12.1.4 Reifying term

A noun phrase which converts a non-referring expression into a referring one. 'Is red', for example, is not a noun phrase, so it can't function as the subject or object of a verb. However, the phrase 'the property of' can be used to transform it into a noun phrase, with the substitution of 'being' for 'is': 'The property of being red' (see Section 3.9). This *can* be used as the subject or object of a verb. 'The property of…' is a reifying term (Moltmann 2013). So are 'the fact that…' and 'the experience of…'.

12.1.5 Antonym word

To an extent, the sense of any word depends on what, in context, it is contrasted with. That is certainly true of 'experience'. As Jay (2005: 268) notes, its meaning 'can vary according to its preferred antonyms'. This applies especially to its uses in philosophy.

12.1.6 Operationally defined term

The expression 'operationally defined' is a reference to Bridgman (1954), whose concept of 'operational analysis' has been updated by Chang (2014). For this form of analysis, what researchers mean by 'experience' is not determined by the dictionary, or phenomenology, or James, or Dewey, but by what the researcher actually *does* – the operations she carries out – in order to delineate 'the experience of X'.

12.2 Placeholder noun

Linguists suggest three reasons for the use of placeholder words: (a) the speaker has forgotten the right word; (b) the speaker, for various reasons, does not want to use the right word; (c) English requires an adjective to be paired with a noun, even if there is no obvious 'correct word' to pair the adjective with (Fronek 1982). There are languages which don't have this requirement. For example, Italian can say 'L'importante è partecipare', but English has to insert a noun: 'The important *thing* is to participate.' No alternative to 'thing' really works here: 'point', 'issue', 'factor', 'consideration'. They all feel forced, and they're unnecessary. In this context, 'thing' is fully idiomatic, even in an academic publication. It doesn't count as 'colloquial'.

'Experience' can be used in a similar way. Consider a very common noun phrase in which 'experience' figures. It takes the following form:

< a(n) + ADJECTIVE + experience >

According to COCA, the range of adjectives in this construction is relatively limited. The top 20 can be classified under three headings:

Evaluative	great, good, bad, wonderful, positive, amazing, better, traumatic, pleasant, interesting (so mainly positive)
Comparative	similar, different, new, personal, unique, shared, common
Substantive	near-death, out-of-the-body, religious.

In most sentences featuring this construction, 'experience' functions as a placeholder word. Take a look at 'similar', for example:

(1) Given the lack of women's shots in ski films, she put together her own movie. 'I've seen what happened to my own footage, and I knew other girls had a similar experience.'

(2) I had a similar experience in an evolution course. The lecturer would bring in speakers from Bible colleges and play recordings of preachers.

(3) A friend reports a similar experience with his hearing aids, which 'so greatly magnified the noise of chewing that I couldn't eat and converse at the same time'.

To say that someone 'had a similar experience' is to say that 'a similar thing happened to' them, or that 'the same thing happened to them'. These are two alternative sentence structures: the use of different syntax to say the same thing. Suppose A says: 'When I visited x, I found a y.' In response, B can reply: 'Yes, the same thing happened to me.' Or: 'Yes, I had the same experience.' Does the latter really say anything more, or different, from the former?

If we transpose syntactically from 'the same thing happened to me' to 'I had the same…', it's not clear what other word would fit the gap. 'Thing' might work again (suggesting that 'experience' has the same function). Possibly 'situation', although that wouldn't really work if 'y' was an event. 'Event' definitely doesn't work. 'Problem' might, if the 'y' happening did in fact pose a problem. So various other words might do in certain contexts. However, 'experience' is a generic term that works in almost all cases, just as 'thing' does in 'the same thing happened to me'.

'Experience' when combined with many of the evaluative adjectives behaves in a comparable, though not identical, way. Consider 'positive', for example:

(4) For most women, sports participation is a positive experience, providing better health, wellbeing, and physical fitness.

(5) Have you used the Apple Maps app? Did you have a positive experience, or have you found some of these glitches?

(6) States that have a positive experience with medical cannabis, like in Colorado… that tends to lead to greater support of adult use.

The specific way in which the 'experience' was 'positive' varies with the context, and sometimes has to be inferred. In (4), the criteria for a 'positive' outcome are relatively explicit; in (5) and (6), the criteria have to be inferred, or can be derived from a familiarity with comparable apps, or from a knowledge of developments in Colorado following Amendment 20 in 2000. Example (6) is additionally interesting in that it ascribes the 'experience' to institutions (US states) rather than to an individual, or even a group of individuals. This is not at all uncommon, either for 'experience'-the-noun or for 'experience'-the-verb (as we'll see in Section 12.3).

In examples (4) to (6), there is no word that is more obviously 'correct' to fill the open slot in 'have a positive…' or 'is a positive…'; and all three examples are perfectly idiomatic. The same would be true of most, although not all, of the adjectives listed above: 'it was a new experience', it was an amazing experience'. One might argue, perhaps, that 'experience' paired with 'religious', 'near-death', or 'out-of-the-body' is not a placeholder, because each pairing refers to a 'subjective' episode. However, what's interesting about 'experience' is that it can be used to refer to 'anything that happens to us': an event, a situation, an activity, a problem, a psychological state. It can be a placeholder for any of them.[6]

Indirect evidence of the placeholder function of 'experience' is provided by Wierzbicka (2010). She lists example English sentences, together with their French translations.

(7) I had a pleasant experience.
Il m'est arrive une chose agréable.

(8) She went through some terrible experiences.
Elle est passée par de rudes épreuves.

(9) We had many unforgettable experiences there.
Nous y avons vécu bien de moments inoubliables.

(10) She swam in the nude, and it was an agreeable experience.
Elle a nagé toute nue et a trouvé cela agreeable.

(11) It wasn't an experience I'd care to repeat.
Ce n'est pas une aventure que je tiens à recommencer.

It's interesting that, in each of these examples, French deals with 'experience' in a different way, resorting to a series of different terms: 'chose', 'cela', 'épreuves', 'moments', 'aventure'. In English, 'experience' serves as the convenient pairing-noun if we employ the < *have a(n)* + ADJECTIVE + NOUN > construction to say that *something happened to us* (or that *we did something*) that was pleasant, terrible, unforgettable, new, interesting, scary, or whatever. Of course, we can always choose an alternative construction to convey this information; but if we adopt the < *have a(n)* + ADJECTIVE + NOUN > construction, then 'experience' is the go-to placeholder.

In this construction, 'experience' has little semantic content of its own, about as much as 'thing' has. It's more of a stand-in – a noun that can be paired with the relevant adjective. It does not refer to something about which one can enquire: 'What *kind* of thing is it? What is its ontological nature? And what is its relation to reality/realities?' If, instead of (10), it was stated that 'She swam in the nude and found that pleasant' (closer to the French version), one would not be inclined to ask: 'What *kind* of thing is finding-it-pleasant? What is its ontological nature? What is its relation to reality/realities?' So why do we feel motivated to ask these questions about 'experience' in an alternative construction, which is no more than a syntactic variant?

12.3 Delexical verb: 'experienced'

Delexical verbs are, in effect, the verbal equivalent of placeholder nouns. In a wide range of contexts, 'have', 'get', and 'do' have as much semantic content as 'thing' and 'stuff' – i.e. very little, and often none at all. A good way to approach them is to start with the word for a certain kind of *situation*, *event*, *state*, or *condition*. Meeting, idea, favour, drink, mistake, problem, flu, whatever. Suppose then that you want to refer to the fact that such a state obtains, or that the event in question is up and running. One way of doing this is to make the corresponding word the subject of a sentence: a meeting is taking place, an idea crossed her mind, a problem cropped up. But suppose now that you adopt an alternative syntax and make the event-noun the *object* of a verb whose subject is a person or group. This might sound a bit technical, but it's a construction that's perfectly routine.

(12) We're having a meeting.

(13) She had an idea.

(14) Can you do me a favour?

(15) She's got the flu.

(16) He's made a mistake.

In some instances, one delexical verb can be substituted for another. 'I've had an idea', or 'I've got an idea'. 'She's got the flu', or 'She has the flu'. However, while there are exceptions, delexicals are not, generally speaking, interchangeable. So not: 'We're getting a meeting', or 'He's done a mistake', or 'Can you make me a favour?'[7]

Delexicals, then, are extremely convenient. It's possible to use the construction

SUBJECT + DELEXICAL VERB + NOUN PHRASE

for a wide variety of circumstances without having to find a separate verb for each kind of event or situation that might be referred to. Birthday coming up? You're *having* a birthday. About to give birth? You're *having* a baby. Asleep on the sofa? You're *having* a nap. Bottom line success? You've *made* a profit. Got it all wrong? You've *made* a mistake. Upside down? You're *doing* a handstand. Contract with your supplier? You're *doing* business with them. The only problem is: idiomatically, it has to be the correct delexical verb. You're not *getting* a birthday, or *doing* a profit, or *making* a handstand.

Many uses of 'experience'-as-a-verb are comparable with the use of delexicals. For example, the 20 most common nouns following *experienced a(n)* (0, 2) can readily be sorted into four categories:

Amounts	lot, number, series, period, variety
Change	increase, loss, decline, change, surge, recurrence, decrease, drop, rise, fall, reduction
Sensory	moment, sense, kind
Substantive	miscarriage

Nouns in the *amounts* category refer to states or occurrences in groups: a lot of prejudice, a number of defeats, a series of reorganisations, a period of upheaval. Those in the *change* category refer to a shift in the value of a variable. The verb 'experience' can precede all of these:

(17) The country experienced a period of instability.

(18) Alberta experienced a change in the number of applicants.

(19) King's Cross station experienced a series of delays.

(20) *The Sun* newspaper experienced a fall in its readership.

(21) Anthony experienced a moment of uncertainty.

A possible alternative here is 'had'. This itself suggests that, in cases like these, 'experience' is delexical in the same way 'have' is. The difference between them can be fairly marginal. 'Experienced', I think, tends to imply a sequence of events, while 'had' is more staccato, a snapshot. But it's a delicate nuance.

Other points to note. First, the grammatical subject of 'experience' is frequently a group, a country, or an organisation (Anthony is the exception here). Second, the psychological states of individuals are not referred to, not even indirectly (again, the exception is Anthony).[8] It is not individual employees or the owners of *The Sun*, who 'experienced' the fall in readership. It's *The Sun* itself – the newspaper, the institution. Third, 'experience' can be paired, delexically, with features which characterise collectives: periods of instability, rail delays, falls in readership. So the < *SUBJECT* + *experienced* + *NOUN PHRASE* > construction does not have to refer to a person or imply 'subjective experience'. It can apply to a non-personal, institutional subject characterised by a rise or fall in a measurable property.

There are very few entries in the *substantive* category: miscarriage, miracle, hurricane, breakup, death. They are rare, compared to the other uses, and they usually cite the 'something that happened' without any direct reference to psychological reactions – although, given that these are all memorable events, there would certainly have been some.

I suggested at the beginning of this section that delexical verbs are the verbal equivalent of placeholder nouns, more or less; and I've shown that the verb 'experience' has a delexical function, just as the noun 'experience' acts as a placeholder. One way of thinking about the syntactic operations involved in both uses is to see them as providing constructions in which the grammatical subject is altered. So instead of saying, for example:

(22) Something odd happened to Lozen.

we can say:

(23) Lozen had an odd experience.

(24) Lozen experienced something odd.

This is a syntactic reversal. In (22), Lozen is, grammatically, an indirect object. In (23) and (24), she is the subject. Either way, there is no obvious change of meaning. These are just three alternative ways of saying more or less the same thing – though there will be contextual or pragmatic reasons for choosing one or the other. The relation between meaning and syntax, especially the use of grammatical resources such as singular/plural, negative/positive, and active/passive, is a central concern of systemic functional grammar. Unfortunately, a fuller examination would require a lot more space.[9]

12.4 Delexical verb: 'experiencing'

Other tenses behave in roughly the same way. For example, the present continuous, *is/are experiencing a(n)*, has a similar pattern to *experienced a(n)*. With three exceptions, the most common (0, 2) collocates can be sorted into the categories used in Section 12.3:

Amounts	lot, little, major, bit, high, severe, significant
Change	new, renaissance, resurgence, decline, loss, problem
Sensory	sense, kind
Substantive	drought, flood, crisis
Generic adjective	similar

The patterns associated with the first three categories correspond to those seen in the previous section.

(25) Many countries are experiencing a decline in population.

(26) The service centre is experiencing a high volume of calls.

(27) In this community we are experiencing a sense of belonging.

(28) Mars is experiencing a significant new decay in its orbit.

In most cases, the grammatical subject is a group of individuals or a collective; what is experienced is observable and often measurable; and (with the exception of 'sense') there is no reference to anything 'mental'. As for the *substantive* category, there are again very few entries – drought, flood, crisis – and they usually reference 'something that has happened' without any particular reference to psychological reactions.

The generic adjective, 'similar', behaves in a way parallel to 'a similar experience', discussed in Section 12.2, allowing for the change of syntax. The nouns paired with 'similar' are all from the list above.

(29) I've been experiencing a similar problem with my laptop.

(30) Parts of southern California are experiencing a similar renaissance.

(31) Young female college grads are experiencing a similar decline.

Turn to *experiencing the* (0, 2). the most common collocates here can be sorted roughly as before except that, for obvious reasons, *superlatives* replaces *amounts*.

Superlatives	most, worst, first, greatest, highest
Change	effects, consequences, loss, crisis, problem
Sensory	pain, joy, symptoms, trauma, moment
Substantive	power, presence, world
Generic adjectives	same, kind, real

By a distance, the most common collocate is 'same', which has more hits than the next seven entries put together. 'Experiencing the same...' is the definite article equivalent of 'experiencing a similar', only more common. It has a function comparable to 'had a similar experience' and 'had the same experience' (Section 12.2), with most of its collocates being generic references, without any mental component: things, problems, problem, thing, phenomenon, kind, issues, frustrations, challenges. The exception is 'emotions', but it is the only exception in the top ten collocates.

Finally in this section, 'experiencing...' followed by a mass noun, without a definite or an indefinite article. The most common (0, 1) noun collocates are life, pain, homelessness, problems, symptoms, difficulty, difficulties, music, things, anxiety, stress, shame, success, drought, feelings, growth, violence, abuse. Negatively inflected terms account for two-thirds of all occurrences. Some of these collocates do include reference to mental states, but the majority of uses refer to situations people find themselves in.

In summary, 'experience' as a verb has a delexical function, permitting it to be paired with a wide range of nouns, often where 'have' can be used as an alternative. While mental processes are sometimes referenced, the majority of uses don't extend beyond circumstances, events, and measurable phenomena. Surprisingly often, the subject of the verb is an organisation or a country, rather than an individual.

12.5   Subject of a sentence

'Experience' at the beginning of a sentence (when it is a mass noun) has a rather clear role. The ten most common verbs that follow it are: is, shows, suggests, tells, teaches, indicates, proves, confirms, means, makes. If we look at typical examples, we find a pronounced pattern:

(32) Experience suggests that a strong dose of caffeine makes me more alert.

(33) Experience proves that lying down makes you more stiff when you get up again.

(34) Experience has shown that they don't vote the same way in local elections.

(35) Experience had taught him to reveal as little of himself as possible.

(36) Experience is the best teacher.

'Experience' in this position is something that informs: it shows, tells, proves, teaches. It implies an accumulation of episodes that one has witnessed, or participated in, over a period of time; and it usually involves a generalisation over those episodes.[10] In some cases, the 'experience' in question refers to one person, as in (35). In others, at least by implication, it implicates a wider range of observers, with the speaker inferring a generalisation from other people's episodes as well as their own. Example (36) is a sort of meta-generalisation: you learn more from witnessing and participating than you do from, say, books.

This function of 'experience', in which it alludes to what has been learned from accumulated episodes of witnessing and participating, is echoed in other constructions:

(37) Our focus is on learning from experience.

(38) I know from experience that his eyes will glaze over.

(39) We're looking for someone with experience.

(40) I'm an experienced journalist/teacher/pilot.

(41) She has a lot of teaching experience.

All of these refer to the same idea, explicitly in (37) and (38), implicitly with the other three. Why are we looking for someone with experience? Why might we be interested in an experienced journalist, or someone with a lot of teaching experience? 'Experience', in this context, signals many episodes of observing/acting, and implies that these episodes have been varied enough for the person concerned to have learned how to deal with the likely contingencies. 'These things have happened to me, I have responded in such-and-such ways; and, over time, I have learned how to cope with what comes up. To that extent, you can be confident about my future performance.'

This sense of 'experience' is related to the German *Erfahrung* with its 'cumulative, knowledge-gained-over-time implications'. Wierzbicka (2010) summarises her semantic history of 'experience' by dividing its various senses, acquired over several centuries, into two groups:

A Past experience, accumulated knowledge

B A current experience, sensory or sensory-like

Roughly – *very* roughly – we can associate A with *Erfahrung* and B with *Erlebnis*. The A senses are older than the B senses, just as *Erfahrung* is older than *Erlebnis*.[11] Wierzbicka finds examples of A senses in Shakespeare. In contrast, the B senses have spread widely only since the 19th century. They have nothing to do with accumulation of knowledge over time. Indeed, these senses can refer to very short, one-off episodes; and, unlike 'experience' when it is the subject of a sentence, 'experience' in its B senses is always a count noun.

Wierzbicka argues that: 'by definition, as it were, *experience* in the B sense refers to an event seen from within… an *experience* in this new sense of the word cannot be gleaned from outside' (39). I think this is misleadingly Cartesian.[12] The B senses of the word *can* be used like this, but it is not 'by definition'. I'll return to this topic later. All I've done here is establish that one familiar function of 'experience' – paradigmatically when it is the subject of a sentence – is to refer to the accumulation of witnessing and participating in episodes over time, and to the knowledge, skills, and beliefs thereby acquired.

12.6 Reifying term

'The experience of…' is an expression which appears frequently in qualitative studies, often appearing in the title. An example is 'The experience of being a millennial nurse manager' (Saifman & Sherman 2019). According to Moltmann, phrases like this are 'reifying' expressions. They 'reify' terms which, in themselves, are not referential (Moltmann 2013: 202). A reifying term is composed of:

a definite determiner	'the'
a sortal noun	'experience'
a preposition	'of'
a denominative complement	'being a millennial nurse manager'

The effect is to create an 'entity' (in a grammatical sense, not ontologically) which can be referred to, even though the expression, 'being a nurse millennial manager', does not itself refer. Grammatically, then, the function of a reifying term is to convert a non-referring expression into referential one.

Other sortal nouns that can be used to introduce reifying terms include: 'property', 'possibility', 'fact', and 'concept'. Some are followed by 'of' ('the property of being red'); others are followed by 'that' ('the fact that Neptune is light blue'). In each case, the non-referring expression – 'is red', 'Neptune is light blue' – is converted into a referring expression through the use of the sortal noun plus 'of' or 'that'.

A reifying term can obviously be a useful linguistic device – anaphorically, syntactically, pragmatically – but the 'entity' it introduces has no ontological standing. Philosophical enquiries into the 'nature' of experience, facts, properties, possibilities, propositions, or concepts are unnecessary, and can never be resolved given that the corresponding words are just linguistic tools designed to convert non-referential expressions into referential ones. To that extent, the employment of a reifying term is a syntactic ruse. It has no ontological implications. This applies to 'the experience of…' as much as it does to, for example, 'the fact that…'. 'Experience', used in a reifying term, does not denote a kind of thing, a specific 'layer' of the world, any more than 'fact' does.

The various sortals used in reifying terms introduce the 'entity' in different ways. Or, more precisely: 'Sortals in their reifying function differ in the way they exploit different aspects of the presentation of the denominative complement' (Moltmann 2013: 205). For example, there are differences between 'the concept of learning a new language', 'the value of learning a new language', 'the process of learning a new language', and 'the experience of learning a new language'. What differentiates 'the experience of…' from the others is perspective. It necessarily implicates those who are actually engaged in language-learning. The others don't, or not directly. They implicate academic disciplines: linguistics, philosophy, psychology.[13]

The 'entity' introduced by the reifying term is singular. The very expression, '*the* experience of being a millennial nurse manager' implies that there is an experience *uniquely* associated with members of this demographic in this role. It's not as if the title of Saifman and Sherman's paper is: 'The various and diverse experiences of millennial nurse managers'. Rather, the implication is that, if you're a millennial nurse manager, you will *ipso facto* have *the* experience that millennial nurse managers have.[14]

This observation prompts an interesting question for qualitative studies which are designed to determine *the* experience of something. Given that the data collected in such studies is almost always drawn from several individuals, what is the relation between these individuals' *experiences*, plural, and the implicitly *singular experience* associated with the phenomenon concerned? One possible answer to this question is that the features which individual experiences have in common represent the core – or, for some writers, the essence – of the experience generically understood. This idea aligns with some familiar procedures of data analysis in qualitative research. Coded bits of data are sorted into 'themes' which appear to apply to all, or most, cases in the sample. *The* experience is then represented as the aggregate of themes, even if a great deal of the content of the *individuals'* experiences is lost along the way – inevitably, given that the formulation of themes necessitates the subtraction of specific contents that cannot be accommodated to the generic framework. But this answer only raises more questions – in particular, why it is assumed that there *is* a 'generic' experience of the phenomenon, rather than a collection of diverse experiences reported by people who have been in a similar situation. I'll return to these questions in Section 12.8.

12.7 Antonym word

Experience as opposed to what? In qualitative research, what is experience contrasted with? 'This is a study of the experience of X. It is not a study of...' Well, *what* is it not a study of? Something that's *not* experience, while still being relevant to X? This question is not typically answered in qualitative studies, so we have to look closely at how research on 'experience' is actually carried out. I will be doing this in Section 12.8. In the meantime, I'll consider more generally the *kinds* of contrast – between 'experience' and something else, or between a preferred concept of 'experience' and a pushed-aside one – that can be found in the philosophical literature. The word is 'rife with sedimented meanings that can be actualized for a variety of different purposes and juxtaposed to a range of putative antonyms' (Jay 2005: 12).

i A contrast between experience, on the one hand, and textual authority, pure reason, revelation, and dogma on the other, crystalised during the 17th and 18th centuries. This was the common thread in both empiricism and idealism, each of which took experience to be the foundation of knowledge.[15] It was an epistemological concept of experience, 'bracketing its other dimensions' (as Jay puts it), and coinciding with a gradual shift from knowledge-as-certainty to knowledge-as-the-probable.

> 'Knowledge was being restructured in a radically new way, '[e]merging as an essentially *probabilistic* process of discovery'. It was not measured by the standard of certainty, but aimed at 'the discovery of a limited understanding of the natural and human world'.
>
> *(Bates 2002: viii)*

In this sense, then, 'experience' involves observation of various kinds, measurement, experiments, interviews, whatever. It is the *non*-use of scripture, doctrine, intuition, armchair theorising, ancient wisdom, dreams, or Ouija boards.

ii As I observed in Section 12.5, there is a contrast between Wierzbicka's A and B senses, and what is arguably a comparable one between *Erfahrung* and *Erlebnis*. Though both these words are translated as 'experience', philosophers often take one as central, and reject (or distance themselves from) the other. It's a contrast, roughly, between experience-as-accumulated-learning and experience-as-significant-and-memorable-moments. Those who embrace *Erlebnis* prize vitality, immediacy, and (with some authors) the concept of something *prior* to subjective consciousness –'the immediate flux of life which furnishes the material to our later reflection with its conceptual categories' (James 1996: 23).[16] Those who adopt *Erfahrung*, on the other hand, are inclined to regard experience as 'what happens to us', and what the various consequences of those happenings are. Dewey, for example, sees it as 'a temporally extended sensorimotor process through which an agent interacts with an environment' (Levine 2019: 13), and as a result of which learning takes place. It is a process of 'undergoing', but it is necessarily active, not just passive. It is, in Dewey's words, 'a matter of *simultaneous* doings and sufferings' (Dewey 1980: 8).

iii A third contrast is between experience-as-what-it's-like and something more 'outer'. The modern *locus classicus* for this conception is Nagel's essay 'What is it like to be a bat?' (Nagel 1979). Each of us – humans as well as bats – has a sort of mental 'interior' which is beyond the reach of science, and which can only be known from 'inside'. This is experience as intrinsically subjective: 'it can in principle be fully understood only from *type* of point of view: that of a being like the one having the experience' (188). This line of thought has led naturally to the idea of *qualia*, which are 'experiential properties of sensations, feelings, perceptions... and thoughts and desires as well' (Block 1994: 514). They represent 'the subjective quality of experience... What it is like to think of a lion is subtly different from what it is like to think of the Eiffel Tower' (Chalmers 1996: 10). This notion of experience is not accountable to anything physical: events, behaviour, brain processes, or 'reality' in general. What it's like is what the person in question says it's like, and no third-person description can confound or disconfirm it.

iv It's possible to take 'experience' as the antonym of 'theory', 'ideology', 'interpretation', or some other discursive concept. The idea is that 'experience', in what is sometimes described as a 'thin' sense, is an encounter with the world prior to our attempts to make sense of it. This 'thin' contact with 'reality' is the result of sensory stimulation, and produces 'bare' observations – conceptually minimalist – which serve as the data for more elaborate theoretical or interpretive claims. In Janack's (2012: 44) terms, this represents the 'bifurcation of experience' into 'stimuli' and 'discourse'. This 'bifurcation', in analytic philosophy, is associated especially with Quine (1993), who treats experience as a purely psychological event, the 'input' on which more sophisticated scientific accounts of the world are based. It is, however, an idea that has been subject to repeated challenges, in various philosophical contexts. For example, the claim that observation is already theory-dependent (or language-, or discourse-, or ideology-dependent). In the philosophy of science, this challenge is associated with Hanson (1958) and Kuhn (1962). In the philosophy of perception, the claim that perceptual content is intrinsically conceptual is associated with McDowell (1996). The idea is that even (so-called) minimalist descriptions of experience are enmeshed in discourse, structured by concepts. What you 'observe', 'perceive', or 'experience' is a function of the resources provided by a language, a theory, concepts, discourse, culture, a paradigm. These debates – Is observation theory-free or theory-laden? Is experience conceptual or nonconceptual? – are played out in a number of variations, in both anglophone and continental contexts.[17]

v While paragraph (iii) refers to a contrast between the 'inner' and the 'outer', a further distinction between two ways of construing 'experience' remains within the 'inner'. On the one hand there is an intensity of feeling – heightened emotion, suffering, religious experience, aesthetic experience. Sort of *Erlebnis* squared. On the other, there is a cooler, more impersonal awareness involving perception, the intellect, imagination, and thought. Some authors assign 'experience', in its 'fullest' sense, to the first of these, regarding the second as involving a rational distancing from this intensity. Others regard cognitive processing as more fundamental, with heightened emotional intensity being relatively rare and atypical. The first is a radical form of experience-as-prelinguistic: not a 'thin' contact with reality, as in paragraph (iv), but a supremely intense one. As an example of the second, consider the work of Hurlburt (2011) on Descriptive Experience Sampling, given a philosophical gloss in Hurlburt and Schwitzgebel (2007).[18] The 'experience' described by this method is generally mundane, and (in the terminology of the participants) largely involves perception, imagination, and 'thinking', which do not appear to be prelinguistic.

vi Finally, qualitative research textbooks emphasise the contrast between the study of 'experience' and an approach to research based on so-called 'positivism', a 'belief system rooted in realism in which there is an undisputed physical reality governed by natural laws' (Ou *et al*. 2017: 2). I won't repeat the discussion of f-positivism from Chapter 2, but in the next section I'll look closely at what the 'study of experience' means in operational practice.

This section has been a greatly simplified account of some of the philosophical threads in discussions of experience. There are plenty more, and they all criss-cross each other, knotted in an almighty tangle. All I've tried to do is pull on some of the threads, and suggest that you can't undertake studies of experience without saying *something* about how you're using the word. The next section reinforces this conclusion.

12.8 Operationally defined term

The main point I want to make in this section is best explained by contrasting two different types of 'studies of experience'. One is interview-based qualitative research; the other is Descriptive Experience Sampling (DES), mentioned in Section 12.7. Although 'the study of experience' is a fair description of both of them, they adopt very different methods, and appear to mean completely different things by 'experience'. In order to make this clear, I will summarise the procedures of DES and QSE (qualitative studies of experience).

In DES, participants are given a beeper to carry about with them during everyday activities. At random intervals, the beeper sounds, at which point the participant makes a note of her 'inner experience' a split second before it occurred. Typically, this will happen six times during the day. Within 24 hours, she is interviewed, and invited to describe her 'experience' just before each beep as carefully as she can. The interviewer asks clarifying questions where it is not absolutely clear what the participant is referring to. This procedure is carried out over five to eight sampling days, starting with a 'practice/training' day' designed to help the participant improve her observational skills.[19] The DES aim is

> to "catch experience in flight", to describe lived experience as it actually naturally occurs, undisturbed by the means of its apprehension or by presuppositions about its appearance. Of course, DES falls short of that ideal; but the object of DES is to fall short in a way that remains as faithful to the pristine experience as possible.
>
> *(Hurlburt & Akhter 2008: 1373)*

In QSE, the researcher is interested in the experience of a certain type of situation or event. A sample of people who have been in this type of situation, or have witnessed/participated in this type of event, are interviewed and asked to describe it, along (usually) with their thoughts and feelings about it. The transcripts of these interviews are coded, and 'themes' are identified, with a view to generalising about 'the' experience of this type of event/situation. There are no protocols for how recent the experience should be (contrast the 24-hour condition in DES). In some kinds of phenomenology-inspired study, the researchers identify their own presuppositions, and either 'bracket' them, or present them to the reader.

I think it's clear, even from these brief accounts, that the practitioners of DES and QSE have completely different understandings of 'experience'. In some respects, they talk about it in similar ways – Hurlburt talks about 'lived experience', for example, and about identifying presuppositions – but in operational terms their methods are radically different, except insofar as both DES and QSE involve interviews. Let me review some of these differences.

12.8.1 Type of experience

QSE defines types of experience in terms of their objects: the criterion in each case is: *what* is it that is experienced? The experience of being a millennial nurse manager, the experience of mindfulness training among police officers. DES doesn't *have* to target types of experience in this sense of 'type'. It does not require that participants should all have experienced the same type of situation or event. What the participants are doing, or involved in, at the moment the beeper sounds is not always of concern. But it can be: Hurlburt (2011) reports on studies of experience among people with Tourette's Syndrome and bulimia nervosa, among others.

12.8.2   Experience in flight

DES aims to delineate 'experience in flight', interviews being undertaken within 24 hours of the beeps. This is not just about memories fading; it's also about a description that's as accurate as possible with respect to a brief moment in time. Hurlburt tries to understand exactly what was 'in the mind of' the participant at that *particular* moment. QSE is not typically interested in 'moments' but in sequences of events. There is no attempt to pin down a precisely defined 'snapshot' of experience, one that can be dated and timed (DES: 'The beep sounded at exactly 11:45 a.m. on the 25th. What was your experience *then*?'). Often, participants generalise about their experiences of the phenomenon concerned and make judgements about what caused what.[20] Researchers only rarely comment on this and do not usually assess the reliability of such judgements.

12.8.3   Pristine experience

The DES objective is to delineate 'pristine experience'. This is a careful, detailed, and hopefully accurate description of the 'snapshot' experience. What was the participant conscious of, feeling, thinking about at that precise moment? The description is intended to be an *accurate* rendition of what-the-participant-was-aware-of, just in that split second. This can range from sensory awareness (one's attention wholly absorbed by the act of pouring the milk from a jug), to a mix of thought and emotion that is difficult to disentangle. It is also intended to be a description shorn of the various assumptions – presuppositions – that participants typically have of what their experience must be like. Untrained participants characteristically 'report' what they *imagine* the experience must have been like, rather than what it actually *was* like. In contrast, while QSE researchers often try to bracket their own presuppositions, it is rare for them to train participants in bracketing theirs.

12.8.4   Presuppositions

Hurlburt's views on bracketing presuppositions: 'I think bracketing presuppositions is a high skill… Presuppositions are delusions, and their bracketing requires method, practice, repetition, instruction, feedback, instrument, and so on, applied consistently over time… presuppositions don't give up without a fight' (Caracciolo & Hurlburt 2016: 18/21).[21] This applies, in the first place, to researchers; but it also applies to participants. That is partly what 'practice runs' are about, but participants are not going to become *experts* in bracketing during such a short period of time. QSE authors don't equate presuppositions with delusions, and the methods canvassed do not have the same degree of difficulty as Hurlburt's comments imply. Tufford and Newman (2010), for example, suggest that bracketing is largely a matter of the researcher's self-awareness, honesty, and vigilance. They mention memoing, bracketing interviews with independent sources, and reflexive journals; but they see the problem as ultimately one of 'access' to one's motives, feelings, assumptions, role conflicts, and the power hierarchy. The details of precisely how this access is achieved are not gone into, and there is no equivalent of Hurlburt's claim that presuppositions 'don't give up without a fight'.

12.8.5   Participant training

While many QSE researchers are exercised about their own presuppositions, most of them don't seem too bothered about their participants'. This is slightly odd. The researcher invites the participant to describe her experiences of the phenomenon, but gives no thought to the question of how good she is likely to be at doing this. There is nothing at all problematic about being more interested in the participant's *experience* of what happened, as opposed to 'what really happened', but there is surely a question about how skilled the participant is describing this experience.[22] The participant might *think* she has described her experience accurately, even after a longish interval between the experience and the recounting. But how do we know that she has done so, given her own assumptions about the nature of the experience, and the accumulation of different experiences since? Does her account *now* of the sense she made of the experience at the time accurately reflect the sense she really *did* make of it at the time?[23] While most QSE authors seem to take little interest in this question, DES authors regard it as critical. Hurlburt argues that participants need to be trained in describing their pristine experience; otherwise, they will 'fill in' details that were *not* part of the experience, because of their presuppositions about what the experience *must* have been like.

12.8.6   The same experience

'The experience of X': being a millennial nurse manager; mindfulness training among police officers. It is ironic, for QSE researchers (who are usually suspicious of generalisation), that to use this expression is already to generalise. It is to assume that there is a *generic* 'experience' that can be identified in this way. This is why small samples in QSE are supposedly legitimate: all the participants have had the *same* experience – that is, 'the experience of X'. As I suggested in Section 12.6, and note 14, this is a kind of essentialising; and data analysis in QSE is designed to identify the common elements of 'the experience' which, by definition, *must* be there. DES authors take a different view.

> 'To say "the experience of Amsterdam" connotes misleadingly that there is something like an essence of Amsterdam that gets transmitted to the tourist... Furthermore, "experience of" connotes that this experiencing is a one-way affair, originating with Amsterdam and received by the experiencer'.
>
> *(Caracciolo & Hurlburt 2016: 56)*

On these grounds, Hurlburt rejects the expression 'the experience of' altogether. *There is no such thing as 'the experience of X'.* At least, one cannot simply assume there is. The question is: to what extent, or in what situations, or for which people, are our experiences similar? 'I think there are relatively huge unacknowledged differences' (Caracciolo & Hurlburt 2016: 108).

12.8.7   What is said

Inevitably, both DES and QSE rely on what participants say about their experience. But there are important differences between them with respect to how this 'what is said' is elicited. DES participants make notes immediately after the beeper sounds, restricting their attention to the moment immediately beforehand. They are interviewed within 24 hours by a researcher who, while remaining respectful, will be sceptical about the accuracy of the participant's account, and whose brief is to ask questions designed to probe it. QSE participants do not generally know that they will be interviewed on their 'experience of X', and there are no protocols about how recently this experience should have occurred. Interviewers in QSE, while equally respectful, do not treat their participants' accounts with scepticism (indeed, it is a QSE principle *not* to do so). They may seek clarification from time to time, invite further elaboration, or request a fuller description of the context; in some cases, they undertake 'member checks', in order to confirm that they have represented what the participant said accurately. But this is a question about the accuracy of the researcher's account of what the participant said. It is not a question about the accuracy of the participant's report.

My purpose in this section has not been to evaluate either DES or QSE. If I have spent rather more time on DES, that's because it is less well known. Rather, my point is that, while both forms of research are studies of 'experience', their respective uses of the term diverge hugely, given that they are radically different operationally. As a result, their findings are incommensurable. QSE generally finds that the participants' 'experience' has been broadly similar; DES generally finds that they are hugely diverse. I'm not asking who is right and who is wrong.[24] I am agreeing with Hurlburt:

'the fact that we use the same word "experience" does not imply that we always mean the same thing by experience, or that we know what we mean when we use that term, or that we recognize that our meaning of experience shifts on successive uses of the term'.

(Caracciolo & Hurlburt 2016: 79)

12.9   Incomplete conclusion

Here's a simple and incomplete take on the word 'experience'. Its basic function is to make possible talk about things that happen to people, things they witness, things they participate in. Call it a 'narrative' term, subject to the qualification that the narrative in question can be a description of situations as well as events. A further condition is that it is narrative from a specific perspective. This is not the narrative of the historian, the journalist, the scientist, the writer of encyclopaedias, the disinterested observer. It is that of the participant(s), the witness(es), the person(s) to whom things happened. Call this person the 'agent'. When the agent narrates the events, or when the events are narrated from their perspective, the narration is said to be a recounting of their 'experience'. Syntactically, as we've seen, it's a very useful term.

I think this gloss accounts for the vast majority of the ordinary uses of 'experience'; and I've presented evidence – again, incomplete – for that view in this chapter. But, of course, not all uses of the word can be counted as 'ordinary'. We have still to accommodate researchers who are drawn to justifying their methods in philosophical terms. Enter a troop of constructivists, interpretivists, phenomenologists, and hermeneuticists, stage left.

This troop applies various torques and tourniquets to the pattern of 'ordinary' use. But one of them is of particular significance. It is a reinterpretation of the idea of the agent's perspective. Instead of this being a reference to 'what something looks like *from-here*, as opposed to what it looks like *from-over-there*' – a line of sight, so to speak – it is taken as a reference to 'the inner', as opposed to 'the outer'. An 'inner' existence is conferred upon the person whose perspective it is, an invisible crucible of mental alchemy; and it is this inner something that the word 'experience' is now supposed to designate: something that's intrinsically subjective in a new, nongetattable-by-science sense.

There are numerous reasons why this particular torque is applied. Most importantly, western philosophy has been infatuated with the idea of the 'inner' since at least Descartes, despite 20th-century attempts to rein it in. ('Subjectivity thus constitutes the barrier to the unfolding of the question of being': Heidegger 2004: 70. '"Mental" is not for me a metaphysical but a logical epithet': Wittgenstein 1992: 63.) So the reinterpretation was inevitable. Note that I'm *not* saying it's wrong.[25] I'm observing that it adds a few more twists and turns to the semantics of 'experience', an extra tangle of senses that researchers can ricochet between.

In Carnapian vein, however, we can ask what expressive force the qualitative researcher's insistence on the 'study of experience' possesses. Operationally, it involves inviting participants to talk about what has happened to them (given a certain rubric), and identifying 'common themes' in what they say. So all the philosophy, all the -isms and -ologies, is about giving the word 'experience' a certain ideological spin. Asking people to talk about what's happened to them is nothing special, and their accounts are open to discussion, probing, questioning. Inviting them to talk about their *experience* is metaphysically – that is, expressively – significant. It stands for the decision to treat what they say as a report that must be 'trusted'. It takes precedence over other people's accounts. It gives the participant a 'voice'. It gives her a standing which can't be countermanded. No theorist, no science, no political body, can refute it.

This expressivist force is not illegitimate. It is a plea, a decision, a recommendation – and, indirectly, a joining, an enactment. Any researcher can adopt it. But it has no metaphysical ramifications. Ontology and epistemology, construed as accounts of how-things-are-fundamentally, are irrelevant. And this, of course, is the place in which we have found ourselves several times before. In the Epilogue, I'll give a quick sketch of what the implications of being in that place are.

Notes

1 Which, given that this is a translation from the German, it presumably doesn't. Gadamer's word in the original is *Erfahrung*. A different word, *Erlebnis*, can also be translated as 'experience'. I return to this point in Section 12.5.
2 There are several qualitative traditions that take no particular interest in 'experience', for example qualitative comparative analysis (QCA), ethnomethodology, grounded theory (in its original version). However, some textbooks get close to *identifying* qualitative methods with the study of experience. 'The basis of qualitative research lies in the interpretive approach to social reality and in the description of the lived experience of human beings' (Holloway & Wheeler 2010: 3–4).
3 In the case of Roth & Jornet, the theory provides an account of 'what it means for an experience to be transformative', an account 'consistent with the nondualist, nonteleological and antirepresentationalist stance that marks the philosophical traditions we bring together here' (121). A different view seems to be taken by Depraz *et al.* (2003), who define experience as: 'the lived, first-hand acquaintance with, and account of, the entire span of our minds and actions, with the emphasis not on the context of the action but on the immediate and embodied, and thus inextricably personal, nature of the content of the action. Experience is always that which a singular subject is subjected to at any given time and place, that to which s/he has access "in the first person".' Obviously, there's a lot in both cases that requires further explanation.
4 'A substantive makes us look for a thing that corresponds to it' (Wittgenstein 1964: 1).
5 In her foreword to the new edition of Strawson (2019), Allais observes that Strawson 'understands "experience" in something close to the way the word is used in ordinary thought and talk – to refer to conscious awareness of the world' (xi). I think that, in fact, this is a philosopher's use. Most ordinary uses, as Sections 12.2 to 12.6 illustrate, don't do this at all.
6 However, I don't want to indulge the 'craving for generality' here; so if anyone wants to dig their heels in over 'religious experience' or 'near-death-experience', that's fine. I won't go beyond suggesting that an important, possibly the primary, function of the noun 'experience' is that of placeholder.

7 You can see why people learning English as a second language have a problem with these verbs. This is the subject of a book on Chinese and Swedish learners' use of delexical verbs (Wang 2016), which has a chapter on errors and unidiomatic usage. Some of these involve incorrect verb choice: '*Having* experiments on animals is inhuman.' '... the community becomes unstable, which can *get* devastating consequences'. See Juknevičienė (2008) for similar problems encountered by Lithuanian learners.

8 But it is 'uncertainty' that is doing the referring. Compare: 'Euston experienced delays' and 'Anthony experienced uncertainty.' These are not two different senses of 'experience'. Any more than there are four different senses of 'have' in 'Namid had a look', 'Namid had a dream', 'Namid had a laptop', and 'Namid had a baby'.

9 Bloor & Bloor (2013) is an introduction to systemic functional grammar. The core text is Halliday & Matthiessen (2014).

10 These are not universal generalisations. Sentence (34), for example, does not imply that this happens *every* time. In linguistic terms, they are 'generics', and the tense used is, most commonly, the generic present. Of course, in some contexts, a single episode is sufficient: 'The experience taught her that...'. However, in this case, 'experience' is a count noun, and is preceded by a determiner referring to the single episode concerned.

11 Gadamer (1975: 55) observes: 'It is surprising to find that, unlike Erleben, the word Erlebnis became common only in the 1870s. In the eighteenth century it is not found at all, and even Schiller and Goethe do not know it... The word appears seldom in the fifties and sixties and appears suddenly with some frequency in the seventies. The word comes into general use at the same time as it begins to be used in biographical writing.'.

12 Wierzbicka's contrast between 'within' and 'outside' is reminiscent of the 'inner'/'outer' distinction that Wittgenstein was trying to dismantle. There is certainly a difference between the A and B uses, but I would not myself describe it in this way.

13 The 'of' in 'the experience of...' is not the 'of' of possession. 'Of' is comfortably the most common preposition in English, and has several different functions (Dixon 2021). The possessive is only one. In Dixon's terms (111), its function in 'the experience of...' is one of expansion: it is used in cases where the denominative complement expands the sortal noun by specifying the *kind* of experience in question. 'I've had an unfortunate experience.' 'What experience was that?' 'The experience of falling off a bike.' This is worth mentioning because the syntax changes when 'experience' is plural. The (0, 1) collocates of 'the *experience* of...' in COCA are usually participles: being, having, living, seeing, working. However, the top collocates of 'the *experiences* of...' are groups of people: women, people, students, others, those, children, men, American, African, individuals. These are already sortals, and the 'of' *is* possessive. The construction does not specify the *type* of experience concerned; it specifies *whose* experiences they are. It's another example of a minor adjustment to the morphology giving rise to a significant change in function.

14 This is a kind of essentialising, and it is related to questions of identity. The assumption is that 'subjects have such experiences *because* they are members of a particular identity category' (Janack 2012: 94; my italics). Janack is particularly interested in the categories of gender, race, class, and sexuality, but this idea could apply much more widely. 'Woman' and 'millennial nurse manager' are both categories. If essentialising one of them is problematic, why isn't it also problematic to essentialise the other? For a useful discussion, see Scott (1991). I return to the essentialising typical of qualitative research in Section 12.8.

15 Authors in both traditions disagreed about the details: whether experience is the passive reception of sense impressions, or whether it is in some sense 'active';

whether there is a viable distinction between primary and secondary qualities; what the relation is between sensory experience and 'external' objects (and whether the latter exist at all); whether there is a 'self' which is a conscious 'subject' of experience; whether that 'subject' is transcendent or immanent; whether it is immortal; and so on. However, this was a debate about the conditions and implications of experience as foundational. It was not a debate about whether it really *is* foundational.

16 This thread in James' thought is influenced by Bergson and, especially, Dilthey (Kloppenberg 1986, Chapter 2). However, James' accounts of experience aren't entirely consistent. 'For James, individual attentiveness to the fringes, transitions, pulses of one's own particular "pure experience" was never effectively reconciled with "experience" as immersion in the tangled density of a shared, mutually inhabited world' (Crary 1999: 352).

17 See Janack's (2012) discussion in her Chapter 4.

18 See also the discussion between a literary theorist (Caracciolo) and a psychologist (Hurlburt) in Caracciolo & Hurlburt (2016).

19 Crucial to this introductory phase is encouraging the participant to identify the *actual* experience, as opposed to her assumptions about what it *must* have been. The researcher tries to 'foster the notion that getting their experience right… is more interesting than getting it in line with their (or with their perceptions of my) presuppositions' (Caracciolo & Hurlburt 2016: 14). Hurlburt constantly emphasises that getting past one's presuppositions is difficult, time-consuming work, which requires a great deal of practice. I think that's exactly right. You can't just 'set them aside'.

20 This is true of both the examples mentioned earlier: millennial nurse managers (Saifman & Sherman 2019) and police officers receiving mindfulness training (Eddy *et al*. 2021).

21 Or again: 'Presuppositions (aka delusions) are blindnesses. If Marco has presuppositions, he will not, in fact cannot possibly, recognize them and must energetically deny their existence – that's the nature of delusion' (Caracciolo & Hurlburt 2016: 7).

22 This is not a question that crops up often in discussions of qualitative methods. Interesting exceptions include Allen & Cloyes (2005), and Atkinson & Delamont (2008), though in both cases the approach is different from the one adopted here.

23 In principle, there are three key questions: (a) What actually happened? (b) What was the participant's understanding-*at-the-time* of what happened? (c) What's her understanding-*now* of what happened? You can defend being more interested in (b) than (a), or thinking that (a) is, for one reason or another, not a valid question. But if you *are* interested in (b), then presumably you will also be interested to know if (b) is accurately reflected in (c), which is all you've got to go on, after all. Unless you discount both (a) and (b), and think that (c) is where the only action is. In which case, fine, but your reasons had better not be metaphysical.

24 It may seem that I favour the DES account, but I don't. In fact, I agree with many of Schwitzgebel's sceptical comments about DES in Hurlburt & Schwitzgebel (2007). My main point is that DES and QSE represent distinct understandings of the word 'experience', which the comparative operational analysis makes clear.

25 Actually, I do think it's a mistake. I'm with Heidegger and Wittgenstein on that one. But I'm not *saying* so. It's not part of the argument in this chapter.

References

Allen, D., & Cloyes, K. (2005). The language of 'experience' in nursing research. *Nursing Inquiry*, *12*, 98–105.

Atkinson, P., & Delamont, S. (2008). Rescuing narrative from qualitative research. In B. Harrison (Ed.), *Life Story Research. Volume I* (pp. 309–318). London: Sage.

Bates, D. W. (2002). *Enlightenment Aberrations: Error and Revolution in France*. Ithaca, NY: Cornell University Press.

Block, N. (1994). Qualia. In S. Guttenplan (Ed.), *Blackwell Companion to the Philosophy of Mind* (pp. 514–519). Oxford: Blackwell.

Bloor, T., & Bloor, M. (2013). *The Functional Analysis of English: A Hallidayan Approach: Third Edition*. Abingdon, UK: Routledge.

Bridgman, P. W. (1954). *The Logic of Modern Physics*. New York: Macmillan.

Caracciolo, M., & Hurlburt, R. T. (2016). *A Passion for Specificity: Confronting Inner Experience in Literature and Science*. Columbus, OH: The Ohio State University Press.

Chalmers, D. J. (1996). *The Conscious Mind: In Search of a Fundamental Theory*. New York: Oxford University Press.

Chang, H. (2014). Epistemic activities and systems of practice: units of analysis in the philosophy of science after the practice turn. In L. Soler, S. Zwart, M. Lynch, & V. Israel-Jost (Eds.), *Science After the Practice Turn in the Philosophy, History and Social Studies of Science*. New York: Routledge.

Channell, J. (1994). *Vague Language*. Oxford: Oxford University Press.

Crary, J. (1999). *Suspensions of Perception: Attention, Spectacle, and Modern Culture*. Cambridge, MA: The MIT Press.

Depraz, N., Verla, F. J., & Vermersch, P. (2003). *On Becoming Aware: A Pragmatics of Experiencing*. Amsterdam: John Benjamins.

Dewey, J. (1980). *John Dewey. The Middle Works, 1899–1924. Volume 10: 1916–1917*. Carbondale, IL: Southern Illinois University Press.

Dixon, R. M. W. (2021). *English Prepositions: Their Meanings and Uses*. Oxford: Oxford University Press.

Eddy, A., Bergman, A. L., Kaplan, J., Goerling, R. J., & Christopher, M. S. (2021). A qualitative investigation of the experience of mindfulness training among police officers. *Journal of Police and Criminal Psychology, 36*(1), 63–71.

Fronek, J. (1982). *Thing* as a function word. *Linguistics, 20*, 633–654.

Gadamer, H.-G. (1975). *Truth and Method*. New York: Sheed & Ward.

Halliday, M. A. K., & Matthiessen, C. M. I. M. (2014). *Halliday's Introduction to Functional Grammar*. Fourth Edition. Abingdon, UK: Routledge.

Hanson, N. R. (1958). *Patterns of Discovery: An Inquiry into the Conceptual Foundations of Science*. New York: Cambridge University Press.

Heidegger, M. (2004). *Four Seminars*. Bloomington, IN: Indiana University Press.

Holloway, I., & Wheeler, S. (2010). *Qualitative Research in Nursing and Healthcare*. Third Edition. Chichester, UK: Wiley-Blackwell.

Hurlburt, R. T. (2011). *Investigating Pristine Inner Experience: Moments of Truth*. New York: Cambridge University Press.

Hurlburt, R. T., & Akhter, S. A. (2008). Unsymbolized thinking. *Consciousness and Cognition, 17*, 1364–1374.

Hurlburt, R. T., & Schwitzgebel, E. (2007). *Describing Inner Experience? Proponent Meets Sceptic*. Cambridge, MA: The MIT Press.

James, W. (1996). *Essays in Radical Empiricism*. Lincoln, NE: University of Nebraska Press.

Janack, M. (2012). *What We Mean by Experience*. Stanford, CA: Stanford University Press.

Jay, M. (2005). *Songs of Experience: Modern American and European Variations on a Universal Theme*. Berkeley, CA: University of California Press.

Juknevičienė, R. (2008). Collocations with high-frequency verbs in learner English: Lithuanian learners vs native speakers. *Kalbotyra, 59*(3), 119–127.

Kloppenberg, J. T. (1986). *Uncertain Victory: Social Democracy and Progressivism in European and American Thought 1870–1920*. New York: Oxford University Press.

Kuhn, T. S. (1962). *The Structure of Scientific Revolutions*. Chicago: University of Chicago Press.

Levine, S. (2019). *Pragmatism, Objectivity, and Experience*. New York: Cambridge University Press.

McDowell, J. (1996). *Mind and World: With a New Introduction by the Author*. Cambridge, MA: Harvard University Press.

Moltmann, F. (2013). *Abstract Objects and the Semantics of Natural Language*. Oxford: Oxford University Press.

Nagel, T. (1979). *Mortal Questions*. New York: Cambridge University Press.

Ou, C. H. K., Hall, W. A., & Thorne, S. (2017). Can nursing epistemology embrace p-values? *Nursing Philosophy, 18*, e12173.

Overstreet, M. (1999). *Whales, Candlelight, and Stuff Like That: General Extenders in English Discourse*. New York: Oxford University Press.

Paley, J. (2021). *Concept Analysis in Nursing: A New Approach*. Abingdon, UK: Routledge.

Pelletier, F. J. (2012). Lexical nouns are both +MASS and +COUNT, but they are neither +MASS nor +COUNT. In D. Massam (Ed.), *Count and Mass Across Languages* (pp. 9–27). Oxford: Oxford University Press.

Quine, W. V. O. (1993). In praise of observation sentences. *Journal of Philosophy, 90*(3), 107–116.

Roth, W.-M., & Jornet, A. (2014). Toward a theory of experience. *Science Education, 98*, 106–126.

Saifman, H., & Sherman, R. O. (2019). The experience of being a millennial nurse manager. *The Journal of Nursing Administration, 49*(7/8), 366–371.

Scott, J. (1991). The evidence of experience. *Critical Inquiry, 17*(4), 773–797.

Strawson, G. (1994). *Mental Reality*. Cambridge, MA: MIT Press.

Strawson, P. F. (2019). *The Bounds of Sense: An Essay on Kant's Critique of Pure Reason*. Abingdon, UK: Routledge Classics.

Tufford, L., & Newman, P. (2010). Bracketing in qualitative research. *Qualitative Social Work, 11*(1), 80–96.

Wang, Y. (2016). *The Idiom Principle and L1 Influence: A Contrastive Learner-Corpus Study of Delexical Verb + Noun Collocations*. Amsterdam: John Benjamins.

Wierzbicka, A. (2010). *Experience, Evidence, and Sense: The Hidden Cultural Legacy of English*. Oxford: Oxford University Press.

Wittgenstein, L. (1964). *Preliminary Studies for the "Philosophical Investigations". Generally known as The Blue And Brown Books*. Oxford: Basil Blackwell.

Wittgenstein, L. (1992). *Last Writings on the Philosophy of Psychology. Volume II: The Inner and the Outer 1949–1951* (C. G. Luckhardt & M. A. E. Aue, Trans. G. H. von Wright & H. Nyman, Eds.). Malden, MA: Blackwell.

EPILOGUE

The take-home message of the book consisted of two theses.

THESIS 1 It is generally assumed that a necessary preliminary to qualitative research is the formulation of ontological and epistemological beliefs. However, the sentences which supposedly express these beliefs are referentially unsuccessful. They appear to make information-providing statements but fail to do so. The constituent words are meaningful, but the sentences themselves don't *say* anything. So they cannot be used to justify, or ground, or align with, methodological decisions.

THESIS 2 The metaphysical sentences can still be construed as having a function, but it is not to describe reality (or realities) at any 'fundamental' level. Instead, their role is one of resolving and recommending; they are optings and joinings. For the qualitative researcher, they *enact* the joining of a research culture, they do not *justify* it. They are essentially performative.

If these are accepted, metaphysical claims are redundant in qualitative research, unless they're construed as proposals, joinings, enactings. This Epilogue briefly indicates the implications of that conclusion.

Aside from deciding to ignore the whole thing, there are three basic options. (A) Continue to regard the metaphysical sentences as making information-providing claims, but explain clearly how they can be interpreted in such a way that they actually manage to say something. This is the 'unless and until' option that I've referred to throughout the book. (B) Continue to use the metaphysical sentences, but accept the neo-Carnapian, expressivist

DOI: 10.4324/9781003306382-15

interpretation of them. Their function is to make proposals and recommendations, and to perform enactings and joinings. (C) Cease to use metaphysical sentences, and give up the doctrine that qualitative research must be 'underpinned by', 'grounded in', or 'aligned with', metaphysical 'beliefs'.

[A] *Unless and until.* At various points in the book, I have emphasised that the claim 'this metaphysical sentence makes no sense' is subject to an 'unless and until' clause. In Carnap's terms, 'Unless and until they supply a clear cognitive interpretation' (Section 4.4); in my terms, 'unless and until you supply a clear explanation of how you are using the key words'. For example, an explanation of what the words 'absolute', 'unchanging', 'subjective', 'embodied', and so on, mean when they are paired with the word 'truth' (Section 11.5). Or an explanation of how Burr is using the word 'refer' when she says: 'All that language can do is to refer to itself' (Section 7.8). Or an account of the relation between 'the knower' and 'the known', which explains what kind of 'separateness' or 'inseparability' is at issue (Section 8.4); or which, instead, introduces an alternative term that explains more clearly what kind of dealings 'the knower' and 'the known' are supposed to have (or not to have). If these explanations can be provided, and if they're intelligible, well and good. Then we'll know what reality-describing statements are being made when the metaphysical sentences are uttered.

But I'm not optimistic. Too many of the metaphysical claims made in textbooks seem rather glib, a mere rehearsal of the standard tropes, cycled and recycled without much analysis. And I suspect that the line of thought pursued in Part II will sometimes be dismissed as word-play and pedantry. 'Everyone knows what these words mean. "Reality", "single", "multiple", "universal"… You're trying to create problems where there aren't any.' However, there are instances in which 'an entire domain of discourse must be rejected as nonsense and can't be made sense of' (Cappelen 2013: 25); and, in any particular instance, to establish that a suspect domain can (or can't) be rejected 'requires detailed knowledge about a linguistic practice' (40). This detailed knowledge is not something that can just be dispensed with.

[B] *Expressivism.* Carnap's metametaphysics provides researchers with the option of continuing to use metaphysical sentences, but *without* assuming that they make reality-describing statements. There is a spectrum of possibilities, but they are of two broad types. One is to construe the metaphysical sentence as a resolution, proposal, or recommendation. Instead of 'this is how things are', we understand: 'this is the language I propose to adopt'. In such cases, the proposal will be to extend the uses of an expression or to place restrictions on when it can legitimately be applied. For example, 'The knower and the known are interactive, inseparable' can be construed as restricting the occasions on which the word 'know' can be used in the context of research. These occasions will be limited to studies in which there has been a close and continuing relationship between the researcher and the participants (Section 8.6).

The relevant restrictions will have to be defined exactly. A 'close and continuing relationship with participants' is fine as an opening gambit, but greater precision will be required if the new definition is to be workable. How close must 'close' be, if the relationship is to count as 'interactive'? For how long must a 'continuing' relationship continue for it to count as 'inseparable'? What kind of 'relationship' does it have to be? Who, apart from the researcher, counts as the 'knower' (Section 8.1)? Who counts as a participant? This is what Carnap means by 'stating his methods clearly', and 'giving syntactic rules, rather than philosophical arguments'. No-one objects to you introducing a non-standard use of 'know', but the 'introduction' requires a comprehensive set of rules for the proposed usage (Section 4.5).

The second type of expressivist understanding of metaphysical sentences construes them as joinings and enactings: not so much specific resolutions and recommendations, but something more performative. To express the belief that there are multiple realities, for example, is akin to making a vow, reciting a creed, saluting the flag. It is to enact a ritual, like a wedding, confirmation, or initiation ceremony, and thereby become a member of a particular group: a married couple, a church, or the masons. But, in this case, the qualitative research community. Metaphysical sentences, on this reading, are part of a creed: things said to confirm membership of the tribe. Credentials, articles of faith, the masonic handshake, the possession of a research licence (Section 4.7).

None of this, in itself, is unreasonable. What *is* unreasonable, Carnap says, is to adopt this expressivist reading, to recite the creed – and then to say: 'But there really *are* multiple realities! The knower and the known really *are* inseparable!' Nor can you justify your proposals and recommendations by referring to metaphysical 'truths'. Can you justify them in any other way? Well, you can appeal to moral, political, and aesthetic arguments. But none of these has the kind of compelling force that metaphysical truths about reality are supposed to have. My politics may well be different to yours, and you can't point to 'how things fundamentally *are*' in your attempt to override my objections. The best justification – the one Carnap suggests – is that your language is, in practice, more *useful* than mine. It gets better results. Call that pragmatism if you like, but it's ultimately an empirical claim about what we can achieve with *this* language, compared to what we can achieve with *that* one.

[C] *Without metaphysics*. To the sceptical outsider, the function of metaphysical sentences is to place restrictions on the use of particular expressions, or on what counts as legitimate research practice. For example, constructivists place restrictions on words such as 'reality', 'single', 'multiple', 'know', and 'truth', at the same time prohibiting generalisation, causes, and explanation. If qualitative metaphysics is quietly binned, these prohibitions and restrictions will no longer remain in force; so the range of things qualitative research might aim to achieve, and the methods it might adopt, can be greatly extended (see Chafe 2023 for a parallel argument).

For example, there is no longer any reason to identify qualitative research with the study of 'experience' and 'meanings' in the way that constructivists (and others) do. The aim of 'describing', 'understanding', 'interpreting', or 'capturing' experiences 'in all their contingency' remains viable, but it's now just part of a smorgasbord of options – none of which are forced on us by metaphysics, and all of which already have an established place in the history of qualitative social studies. It's possible to describe things other than experience: behaviour, interaction, language use, conversation, documents; and the characteristics of these items, sequences, encounters, and engagements can be *explained* rather than merely 'captured' or 'understood'. Instead of being confined to individually 'attached' meanings, qualitative researchers can generalise (subject to certain qualifications), study causation, and devise their own categories and concepts instead of being locked into those of participants.

Constructivists assume that action is not caused; 'rather it is constructed through an ongoing process of meaning making' (Donmoyer 2012). Donmoyer makes a very awkward-looking case for supposing that causation is, after all, consistent with constructivism. But here we're being a bit more radical, dropping metaphysics altogether. We can therefore get on and *do* causation in qualitative research without any 'metaphysical' worries about social action 'not being caused'. It's not as if there aren't any qualitative methodologists talking about causation already (see, for example, George & Bennett 2005, Cooper *et al.* 2012, Goertz & Mahoney 2012, Maxwell 2012, King *et al.* 2021, Ragin 2023).

'Mixed methods' is a no-brainer, obviously, but mixed methods without all the head-scratching about 'paradigms' (old ones, new ones, loved ones, neglected ones). But mixed methods, or merged methods (Gobo *et al.* 2022), isn't just about *combining* qualitative and quantitative. It's about refusing to see the distinction between qualitative and quantitative as a sort of 'watershed'. In that sense, there's nothing to be 'mixed' or 'merged'. At most, there is a continuum – or, perhaps better, a multi-dimensional array of methodological possibilities, any one of which (or any permutation of which) might be selected, on a particular occasion, because it's the best way of getting the job done. A way which, in the absence of metaphysical flakiness, doesn't require any epistemological contortions.

Once past the qualitative/quantitative divide, it's possible to be more relaxed about what qualitative research can draw from physics, biology, or cognitive science. Metaphysics says that the methods of 'hard' science can't be applied to the social sciences because 'causation', because 'complexity', because 'uniqueness', because 'meaning', because 'laws', because 'constructed realities', because 'objectivity'. If metaphysics fades to black, these reasons take one step backwards. They don't exit altogether, as it might be possible to turn them into empirical claims. For example: Human beings are more complex than falling pieces of paper. Not because it's "obvious", but because it's been empirically confirmed that tracking the behaviour of a person is more difficult than tracking the trajectory of a piece of paper. It would be difficult to establish this, of course, for several reasons, one of which is that it would require an understanding of the physics of falling paper (Chapter 11, note 19), and another of which is that it's unlikely to be true.

One reason why it's unlikely to be true is that the purpose of mind-shaping (Zawidzki 2013) is to ensure that individuals are as alike as possible.

> We succeed in our social endeavors *not* primarily because we are good at projecting self-perceived mental states onto others, *nor* because we are good at inferring others' mental states from observed behavior, but, rather, because we are good at shaping each other to think and act in predictable ways in shared contexts.
>
> *(Zawidzki 2017: 479)*

This – socialising, training, educating, acculturating – is not something we can do with bits of paper. But it's something we do with other people routinely, as part of the project of 'making human minds and behavior more homogeneous and hence easier to predict and interpret' (Zawidzki 2013: 29). There are several ironies here. One of them is that the attaching of 'meaning', and the capacity for understanding, are both dependent on the mechanisms of conformity required to ensure socially functional levels of prediction.

One consequence of mindshaping is that the behaviour of people, as individuals or as groups, can be explained by various mechanisms: psychological, social, linguistic, ecological. Things such as habit, imitation, dissonance reduction, implicit bias, framing, confabulation, cultural selection, boundary activation, diffusion, subliminal transmission

(Hedström & Swedberg 1998, McAdam *et al.* 2001, Wheatley 2009, Elster 2015, Glennan & Illari 2018, Caruana & Testa 2021). Similarly, metaphor models can be applied to social encounters, identifying forms of 'interaction order'. Examples include dramaturgy (Goffman 1959), scripts (Schank & Abelson 1977), game theory (Colman 2003). None of these are 'universal', 'deterministic', 'law governed', even 'mechanistic' (at least as qualitative writers use the expression). Elster calls them 'nuts and bolts', an assortment of explanatory tools which can be useful in different circumstances, and which can increase our understanding of 'how this works' or 'why that happened'.

In Section 11.6, I discussed scientific models and the idealisations they often incorporate. Idealisation, too, is something qualitative research – or, rather, research that has finessed the Q/Q divide – can make use of. Indeed, this happens already. Take, for example, Glaser and Strauss (1964), who conclude that the greater the degree of social loss represented by the death of the patient (as assessed by the nurse), the higher the quality of nursing care afforded to that patient. This is basically a mathematical function (though Glaser and Strauss do not represent it like that), which says: the more of one thing (social loss), the more of another thing (high-quality care). More formally: q (the quality of care) is proportional to s (the degree of social loss). Or:

$$q = Cs$$

The quality of care is equal to the degree of social loss multiplied by a constant. Compare the equation:

$$v = Gt$$

This calculates v (the velocity of a falling object) as the product of t (the length of time it has fallen), multiplied by G (a constant, gravity). Structurally, the two equations are identical. In both, one thing is proportional to something else (though, of course, Glaser and Straus make no attempt to attach values to any of the terms). Moreover, both equations incorporate idealisations. The gravity equation ignores air resistance, wind speed, and what the object is made of (a bowling ball is different from a bit of paper). The quality-of-care equation ignores individual differences between nurses, patients, and hospitals. Both are generalisations whose point is *not* to predict the outcome precisely in any single case but to assess relationships between variables. Both can add to our understanding of 'how it works' (Potochnik 2017). Neither aims at 'absolute truth', or 'multiple realities', or 'lived experience'.

Importantly, different models can be used to explain different aspects of the same phenomenon/system. Sometimes these models are complementary, but sometimes they are inconsistent with each other. For example, the atomic nucleus is modelled in different ways, depending on what is being explained, ways which make incompatible assumptions about its structure and dynamics. 'There is no way to determine which of the models can be said to even approximate the true nature of the nucleus' (Morrison 2015: 8). Equally, there is no reason why models used to explain in the human sciences – and specifically those used in qualitative studies – should necessarily be consistent, or why they should have to 'capture' the 'true' nature of the 'phenomenon', the 'lived experience', or the 'meaning'.

Of course, no-one in qualitative research is obliged to do any of this: track causal relations, construct models, identify mechanisms, adopt felicitous falsehoods, correlate variables, employ formalisms. If that's your preference, you are obviously at liberty to continue as you did before, steady as she goes. I'm *not* arguing for an alternative 'metaphysics' which somehow compels you. It's not, as I keep insisting, a matter of smuggling positivism back in. But, equally, what *you* can't do is give 'metaphysical' reasons to justify your preference, or to argue that others should follow suit.

Reader: Several times you've said you're not smuggling positivism back in, but that's exactly what you're doing. Causation, quantification, mechanism … What's that but positivism?

Me: Causal language and arithmetic are ubiquitous. They only count as 'positivist' if they're derived from 'positivist' metaphysics. 'There exists a single objective reality'. 'The knower and the known are independent, a dualism.' All that.

Reader: Oh, right. So you're changing the meaning of 'positivism'. Nothing to do with causation, quantification and mechanism. Of course not.

Me: Look, if I don't believe in a 'single objective reality' or 'the dualism of knower and known', on what basis can you say I'm a 'positivist'?

Reader: The thing is, though, you *do* believe in a single reality. If you reject multiple realities – which you obviously do – then you *must* think there is a single reality. Where else is there to go? It's either one or the other, single or multiple.

Me: You're assuming that I reject 'There are multiple realities' because I think it's untrue. I don't. I reject it because I don't know what it means.

Reader: Okay, let me help you with that. Here's what it means. It means there are multiple realities.

Me: But that's like saying there are multiple Xs. What is this 'reality', this 'X', that there are lots of? Or, if you're a 'positivist', just one of? That's what you haven't explained.

Reader: This is mad. How can you not understand what reality is?

Me: Well, I know how *I* use 'reality', but I don't know how you're using it. So let's see. 'Multiple realities'. Is that the same as 'multiple universes'?

Reader: Of course not. This isn't about cosmology and black holes.

Me: So is it the same as Schutz's 'multiple worlds'?

Reader: No, those are just different walks of life, different social domains.

Me: So are multiple realities like multiple Narnias? Existing on the other side of wardrobes?

Reader: No. Obviously. You're just being facetious.

Me: So if not multiple universes, multiple worlds, multiple Narnias … then multiple whats?

Reader: You *know* the answer to that. Multiple constructions. Multiple meanings.

Me: Right, so now we're switching out of ontology mode, and going back to anthropological truisms. If you really do want to stick with that, then *of course* there are multiple realities. People don't always see eye to eye. They disagree about stuff. Obvious. Boring. What's that got to do with ontology?

Reader: A new meaning constructs a new reality. *That's* what it's got to do with ontology.

Me: So 'multiple realities' is the same as 'multiple meanings'.

Reader: No, I said that meanings *construct* realities. I didn't say they were the same.

Me: Okay, so multiple realities aren't the same as multiple meanings. But they aren't the same as multiple universes, or multiple worlds, or multiple Narnias either. So what *are* they the same as?

Reader: See, I'm right. It's multiple realities you object to. It's always multiple realities that get the 'What does it mean?' treatment. You don't have a problem with a single reality. That's why you're really a positivist, whatever you say.

Me: But if I don't know what the 'X' is when you tell me there are lots of them, then I also don't know what it is when a 'positivist' says there's only one. Your logic is: if I reject 'multiple realities', I must believe in a single reality. If I'm not a constructivist, I must be a 'positivist'. The truth is, I don't understand either of them. This isn't me trying to smuggle 'positivism' back in. It's you trying to cling on to the metaphysics.

Wittgenstein helped me to stop clinging. 'What *we* do is to bring words back from their metaphysical to their everyday use' (Wittgenstein 2009: §116). Rejecting qualitative metaphysics altogether, so-called 'positivism' as well as constructivism, isn't preferring one to the other. It's not thinking 'single reality' makes sense and 'multiple realities' doesn't. It's equal opportunities metaphysical scepticism. As I might possibly have said before.

References

Cappelen, H. (2013). Nonsense and illusions of thought. *Philosophical Perspectives*, *27*, 22–50.

Caruana, F., & Testa, I. (Eds.). (2021). *Habits: Pragmatist Approaches from Cognitive Neuroscience to Social Science*. Cambridge, UK: Cambridge University Press.

Chafe, R. (2023). Rejecting choices: the problematic origins of researcher-defined paradigms within qualitative research. *International Journal of Qualitative Methods*, *22*, https://doi.org/10.1177/16094069231165951

Colman, A. M. (2003). *Game Theory and its Applications in the Social and Biological Sciences*. Second Edition. New York: Routledge.

Cooper, B., Glaesser, J., Gomm, R., & Hammersely, M. (2012). *Challenging the Qualitative-Quantitative Divide: Explorations in Case-focused Causal Analysis*. London: Continuum.

Donmoyer, R. (2012). Can qualitative researchers answer policymakers' what-works question? *Qualitative Inquiry*, *18*(8), 662–673.

Elster, J. (2015). *Explaining Social Behavior: More Nuts and Bolts for the Social Sciences*. Revised Edition. New York: Cambridge University Press.

George, A. L., & Bennett, A. (2005). *Case Studies and Theory Development in the Social Sciences*. Cambridge, MA: MIT Press.

Glaser, B. G., & Strauss, A. L. (1964). The social loss of dying patients. *American Journal of Nursing*, *64*(6), 119–121.

Glennan, S., & Illari, P. (Eds.). (2018). *The Routledge Handbook of Mechanisms and Mechanical Philosophy*. Abingdon, UK: Routledge.

Gobo, G., Fielding, N. G., La Rocca, G., & van der Vaart, W. (2022). *Merged Methods: A Rationale for Full Integration*. Thousand Oaks, CA: Sage.

Goertz, G., & Mahoney, J. (2012). *A Tale of Two Cultures: Qualitative and Quantitative Research in the Social Sciences*. Princeton, NJ: Princeton University Press.

Goffman, E. (1959). *The Presentation of Self in Everyday Life*. Second Edition. Harmondsworth, UK: Penguin.

Hedström, P., & Swedberg, R. (Eds.). (1998). *Social Mechanisms: An Analytical Approach to Social Theory*. Cambridge, UK: Cambridge University Press.

King, G., Keohane, R. O., & Verba, S. (2021). *Designing Social Inquiry: Scientific Inference in Qualitative Research*. New Edition. Princeton, NJ: Princeton University Press.

Maxwell, J. A. (2012). *A Realist Approach for Qualitative Research*. Thousand Oaks, CA: Sage.

McAdam, D., Tarrow, S., & Tilly, C. (2001). *Dynamics of Contention*. New York: Cambridge University Press.

Morrison, M. (2015). *Reconstructing Reality: Models, Mathematics, and Simulations*. New York: Oxford University Press.

Potochnik, A. (2017). *Idealization and the Aims of Science*. Chicago: University of Chicago Press.

Ragin, C. (2023). *Analytic Induction for Social Research*. Oakland, CA: University of California Press.

Schank, R. C., & Abelson, R. P. (1977). *Scripts, Plans, Goals and Understanding: An Inquiry into Human Knowledge Structures*. Hillsdale, NJ: Lawrence Erlbaum

Wheatley, T. (2009). Everyday confabulation. In W. Hirstein (Ed.), *Confabulation: Views from Neuroscience, Psychiatry, Psychology, and Philosophy* (pp. 205–223). Oxford: Oxford University Press.

Wittgenstein, L. (2009). *Philosophical Investigations: Revised 4th edition by P. M. S. Hacker and Joachim Schulte*. Malden, MA: Wiley-Blackwell.

Zawidzki, T. W. (2013). *Mindshaping: A New Framework for Understanding Human Social Cognition*. Cambridge, MA: MIT Press.

Zawidzki, T. W. (2017). Mindshaping and self-interpretation. In J. Kiverstein (Ed.), *The Routledge Handbook of Philosophy of the Social Mind* (pp. 479–497). Abingdon, UK: Routledge.

LINGUISTICS GLOSSARY

Many readers will not be familiar with some of the terms I've taken from linguistics. This glossary provides a brief explanation but doesn't include expressions that are discussed in the main text (e.g. 'subject-predicate' and 'feature-placing' in Chapter 5). A linguist would no doubt find these explanations cursory at best, but I doubt that readers will want anything too technical or involved. I avoid definitions, preferring examples.

Anaphora The use of a word which refers back to a word already used in the text, avoiding repetition of the original word. 'When Lisa arrived, she was eating a muffin.' Here, the pronoun 'she' refers back to Lisa. 'This argument has been criticised.' In this sentence, 'this argument' refers back to an argument which has been elaborated previously in the text.

COCA The Corpus of Contemporary American English, containing over 1 billion words from eight genres: spoken, fiction, popular magazines, newspapers, academic texts, TV and movie subtitles, blogs, and other web pages. It is freely available online.

Collocate A corpus can be searched to identify words which occur close to a target word: for example, 'experience'. Such words are called 'collocates', since they are 'co-located' with the target word. If the search expression is 'experience (2, 2)', the corpus will return words which are found either one or two words before 'experience' (whenever it appears in the corpus texts), or one or two words after it, placing them in frequency order. If the search expression is 'experience (0, 4)', the corpus will return *only* words which, in various corpus texts, occur as one of the four words immediately following 'experience'.

Construction   In construction grammar, a construction is a syntactic string which has a recognisable pattern across variations. For example, the COM-PARATIVE CORRELATIVE construction is instantiated by 'the more, the merrier'; 'the bigger they come, the harder they fall'; 'the less he knows, the better'; 'the older she gets, the more confident she becomes'; and so on. Some constructions can be analysed as an indispensable core, plus one or more additional 'slots'. The O'CLOCK construction has up to three slots available: a number-between-1-and-12 slot, a morning-or-afternoon slot, and a where-in-the-world slot. 'It's *five* o'clock in the *afternoon* in *Lisbon*.' It's only mandatory to fill the first slot. 'It's five o'clock', on its own, will be interpreted relative to context, and will normally be taken to mean 'here'.

Corpus   A database of machine-readable texts, which permits (among other options) searches for the collocates of a target word. In this way, the various linguistic contexts in which the target word appears can be identified. Probably the most widely used corpus in English is the Corpus of Contemporary American English (COCA).

Count noun, mass noun   A count noun denotes something which is capable of being counted, and which can form a plural. 'Book', 'three books', 'several books'. A mass noun denotes something that cannot be counted, and cannot (in general) form a plural. 'Mud', 'muds'? 'Advice', 'advices'? Many nouns can be either. 'Coffee', 'medicine', 'burglary'.

Deictic there   The use of 'There' to draw attention to the presence of something. 'There's the dog.' 'There are the children. On the beach.' It's the linguistic equivalent of (and may be accompanied by) pointing.

Denominative complement   The expression 'denominative complement' is not in widespread use in linguistics, but it is an expression used by Moltmann to refer to the non-referential part of what she calls a reifying term (Section 12.6). The reifying term itself consists of the definite article, a sortal noun, and a non-referring phrase, with a linking word ('of', 'that'). 'The property of being wise.' (Determiner: 'the'; sortal noun: 'property'; denominative complement: 'being wise'.) 'The possibility that it might thunder.' (Determiner: 'the'; sortal noun: 'possibility'; denominative complement: 'it might thunder'.)

Determiner   There are four types of determiner: articles ('the', 'a'); possessives ('our', 'her', 'their'); demonstratives ('that', 'these'); quantifiers ('some', 'all', 'many'). In all cases, the determiner serves to restrict, or determine, the reference of the noun it is combined with. *These* cats, as opposed to others. *My* book, as opposed to anyone else's. *Some* writers, as opposed to writers in general.

Expletive   In linguistics, an expletive is not a swear word. It is a term that does not contribute any meaning to the sentence but instead fills a syntactic hole. An example is 'It' in the sentence 'It is raining'. English requires a nominal subject at the beginning of a sentence. We can't say 'Is raining'. So 'It' takes the grammatical subject role. But it's not a subject in the usual sense. There's no answer to the question 'What is raining?'

Finite and non-finite verbs   A finite verb has a subject, tense, and number (singular or plural). 'The child cries', 'the children cried.' A non-finite verb has none of these. It is a participle or an infinitive. 'It's fun supporting your team', 'It's fun to support your team.'

Head   The head of a phrase is the word that governs the syntactic category into which the phrase falls. For example, the head of the phrase 'the cat in the garden' is 'cat', a noun. ('In the garden' describes the cat, not the other way round.) So the phrase as a whole is a noun phrase, with 'cat' as its head.

Morphology   The branch of linguistics that deals with the modification of individual words to achieve certain grammatical effects – for example, the way English creates plurals (cat/cats, child/children) or past tenses (walk/walked, drink/drank).

Nominal   Generally applied to an expression which does not contain a noun, yet functions as a noun phrase. 'The poor', 'the known'.

Noun phrase   This is a phrase consisting of a noun and some other term(s) that modify it. 'The cat in the garden' is a noun phrase in which 'in the garden' modifies 'cat'. The noun phrase can be used in the same way a noun on its own would be. '*The cat* climbed a tree.' '*The cat in the garden* climbed a tree.'

Periphrastic causative construction   A construction containing two verbs, the first of which denotes a causing event or action, while the second denotes the caused event or action. 'My mother made me write a thank-you note.' The first verb is finite ('made'), while the second is non-finite ('write').

Prepositional phrase   A phrase beginning with a preposition, and followed by a noun phrase. 'Under the table', 'up the narrow staircase', 'through the park at the end of the road'.

Sortal   Sortals are concepts which apply to things that can be individuated, reidentified, classified, and counted. In philosophy, sortals are possible answers to the question 'What is it?'. They are sometimes identified with universals, essences, or kinds. In linguistics, a sortal noun is, in effect, a count noun.

Transformation rules   These were originally associated with early forms of transformational grammar, although accounts of their significance have changed over time. The basic idea is that transformation rules can be applied to a 'starter' – or 'kernel' – sentence to create a sentence with a different syntax, and usually a different sense or emphasis. There are four main types of transformation rule: deletion, insertion, substitution, and movement. The 'there-insertion' rule discussed in Section 5.2 combines a 'movement' rule (slide the preverbal NP, 'A unicorn', to the right of the verb, 'is') and an 'insertion' rule (insert 'There' at the beginning of the sentence). An even simpler example of a movement rule is the shift from 'I understood that' to 'That I understood'. The latter places greater emphasis on 'that'.

INDEX

Bott, O. 214, 225
Bradley, D. 13
Brandom, R. B. 250n6, 250n8, 250n12
Braun, V. 243, 246
Brennen, B. S. 34–35, 243, 250n1
Bretz, S. L. 173
Bricker, P. 84n15
Bridgman, P. W. 256
Broughton, G. L. 13
Burr, V. 150–153, 156n27, 281

Campbell, J. 209, 214, 229n33
Campbell, J. K. 185
Canfield, J. V. 61n1
Capaldi, E. J. 35
Cappelen, H. 12, 54, 62n18, 81–83,
   85n32, 85n33, 113, 130, 281
Caracciolo, M. 271–273, 277n18,
   277n19, 277n21
Carnap, R. 66–85; attitude towards
   metaphysics 69–70; cognitive content
   72–73; expressivism 9, 76–78,
   281–282; internal and external
   questions 70–72; language
   frameworks 70–72, 75, 106,
   123–124; logical positivism 31–33;
   non-factualism 74–76; nonsense 69,
   72–73, 82; Principle of Tolerance 69,
   75; recent interest in 13, 69; 'unless
   and until' challenge 72–74, 78, 281
Carpenter, D. R. 185
Cartwright, N. 110n34, 213, 244–245,
   251n17
Caruana, F. 285
Castañeda, C. 121–122
causation 208–229; 'cause' and corpus
   218–220; causal language 214–218;
   laws 35, 60, 174, 208–212; pluralism
   211–212, 228n12; and reasons 209,
   217, 221–224; singular causal
   statements 211, 213–216; straitjacket
   assumption 212, 228n10; theories of
   causation 210–214
Chafe, R. 38n21, 283
Chalmers, D. J. 33, 70, 130n5, 268
Chang, H. 179n8, 256
Channell, J. 255
Checkerboard illusion 188, 193
checking 188–190, 193–199, 201–203;
   see also science
Chen, M. K. 179n10
Chierchia, G. 110n32
Chomsky, N. 3, 96, 108n9
Clarke, V. 243, 246
Cloyes, K. 277n22

cognitive bias 190, 194–197, 205n10
Cohen, W. A. 13
Collin, F. 139
Collins, H. 140
Collins, J. 62, 155n17
Colman, A. M. 285
'constructed' 135–156; act of construction
   136–137, 148; shared constructions
   137, 139–140, 148–149; 'socially
   constructed' 8, 136, 139–140, 154n9;
   see also Guba; Lincoln
constructionism 35, 140, 150, 154n1;
   The Social Construction of Reality
   138–139
constructivism 35–36, 140–141,
   179n14, 283
Cooper, B. 283
copredication 143, 155n17
Corpus of Contemporary American
   English (COCA) 160, 219, 241–242,
   257, 276n13
Crary, A. 12
Crary, J. 277
Crasnow, S. 228n12
Creath, R. 13, 69, 83n6
Creswell, J. W. 22
Croker, R. A. 244, 251n16
culture 9, 24, 79, 117, 130, 136,
   146–147, 155n23

Danziger, K. 154n1
Daston, L. 204
Davidson, D. 221, 227n9
DeCanio, S. J. 132n18
deflationism 8–9, 63n28, 69–70,
   239–242, 250n8
DEICTIC THERE 92, 108n6
Delamont, S. 277n22
De Lara, J. 12
Dennett, D. C. 63n25
de-ontologizing 38n21
Depraz, N. 275n3
De Regt, H. W. 244
descriptive experience sampling (DES)
   269–273, 277n24
descriptivist fallacy 76, 237
determinism 31–32, 35, 60, 127,
   174–176, 180n30, 208–209,
   211–212, 227n1, 251n19
de Vreese, L. 212
Dewey, J. 256, 268
Dilman, L. 131n8
Dixon, R. M. W. 276n13
Donmoyer, R. 37n5, 283
Dowe, P. 211

Milton Keynes UK
Ingram Content Group UK Ltd.
UKHW022137100924
448171UK00016B/92